# South Africa

# INVENTING THE NATION

**Series Editor:** Professor Keith Robbins, Former Vice-Chancellor of the University of Wales, Lampeter

'Nationalist' writers and politicians have been apt to take the 'nation' as a 'given' entity, perhaps, indeed, a providential one. But the histories in this series explore the extent to which 'nations' are made, not born, whether through conscious manipulation of the elite, guided by more 'popular' imperatives, or a combination of the two. Each volume in the series explains how and when the modern nation-state of its title came about, and at the same time demonstrates that the process was complex, contingent and anything but pre-ordained.

**Published:**

*India and Pakistan*, Ian Talbot (2000)
*Russia*, Vera Tolz (2001)
*Italy*, Nicholas Doumanis (2001)
*China*, Henrietta Harrison (2001)
*Ireland*, R. V. Comerford (2003)
*Germany*, Stefan Berger (2004)
*France*, Timothy Baycroft (2008)

**Forthcoming:**

*Spain*, Carsten Humlebæk (2014)
*Poland*, Rafal Pankowski (2014)

# South Africa

## Inventing the Nation

**ALEXANDER JOHNSTON**

Bloomsbury Academic
An imprint of Bloomsbury Publishing Plc

B L O O M S B U R Y
LONDON · NEW DELHI · NEW YORK · SYDNEY

**Bloomsbury Academic**
An imprint of Bloomsbury Publishing Plc

| 50 Bedford Square | 1385 Broadway |
| London | New York |
| WC1B 3DP | NY 10018 |
| UK | USA |

www.bloomsbury.com

**BLOOMSBURY and the Diana logo are trademarks of Bloomsbury Publishing Plc**

First published in 2014
Reprinted 2014

© Alexander Johnston, 2014

Alexander Johnston has asserted his right under the Copyright, Designs and Patents Act, 1988, to be identified as Author of this work.

All rights reserved. No part of this publication may be reproduced or transmitted in any form or by any means, electronic or mechanical, including photocopying, recording, or any information storage or retrieval system, without prior permission in writing from the publishers.

No responsibility for loss caused to any individual or organization acting on or refraining from action as a result of the material in this publication can be accepted by Bloomsbury or the author.

**British Library Cataloguing-in-Publication Data**
A catalogue record for this book is available from the British Library.

ISBN: HB:   978-1-7809-3270-5
PB:   978-1-7809-3192-0
ePDF:   978-1-7809-3193-7
ePub:   978-1-7809-3195-1

**Library of Congress Cataloging-in-Publication Data**
Johnston, Alexander, author.
South Africa : inventing the nation / Alexander Johnston.
pages cm
Includes bibliographical references and index.
ISBN 978-1-78093-270-5 (pbk.) – ISBN 978-1-78093-192-0 (pbk.) –
ISBN 978-1-78093-195-1 (epub) – ISBN 978-1-78093-193-7 (epdf) 1. South Africa–Politics and government – 1989–1994. 2. South Africa – Politics and government – 1994–
3. Nation-building – South Africa. 4. Nationalism – South Africa. I. Title.
DT1945.J64 2014
320.968–dc23
2013048258

Series: Inventing the Nation, 17545943

Typeset by Newgen Knowledge Works (P) Ltd., Chennai, India
Printed and bound in Great Britain

# CONTENTS

*Acknowledgements* vii
*List of abbreviations* viii

Introduction: The problem of nationalism in post-apartheid South Africa   1

**PART ONE**   The raw material of nation-building   13
1   Who are South Africans?   15

**PART TWO**   Nationalism and the end of apartheid   49
2   Legacies   51
3   Improvising the nation: 1990–6   99

**PART THREE**   Beyond the improvised nation   135
4   Over the rainbow: From the Mandela moment to the Mbeki project   137
5   From reconciliation to social cohesion   183

**PART FOUR**   South Africans today: Coming together or pulling apart?   203
6   Do South Africans have a shared life?   205
7   The spectre of anomie: Deviance and national citizenship   265

**PART FIVE** The problem of nationalism in South Africa today 287

8  Nation-building 20 years on   289

Conclusion: A minimum nation and an identity of convenience   319

*Notes*   327
*Bibliography*   333
*Index*   345

# ACKNOWLEDGEMENTS

I acknowledge research funding received from the University of KwaZulu-Natal which enabled me to complete this manuscript. Keith Robbins has been a congenial and efficient general editor. The staffs of the British Library and the libraries of King's College, London, and the University of KwaZulu-Natal were helpful during the research phase of this project. I am especially grateful for all the help that I have received from Professor J. E. (Jack) Spence throughout my career. He has been an inspiration and professional exemplar. My greatest source of support and encouragement in this and in every other enterprise has been my wife, Anthea, to whom this book is dedicated.

# LIST OF ABBREVIATIONS

| | |
|---|---|
| ACDP | African Christian Democratic Party |
| AIC | African Independent Churches |
| AIDS | Acquired Immune Deficiency Syndrome |
| AMCU | Association of Miners and Construction Union |
| AMPS | All Media Products Survey |
| ANC | African National Congress |
| AV | Afrikaner Volksfront |
| AWB | Afrikaner Weerstandsbeweging |
| BAC | Business Against Crime |
| BBBEE | Broad-based Black Economic Empowerment |
| BCM | Black Consciousness Movement |
| BEE | Black Economic Empowerment |
| BIG | Basic Income Grant |
| BLA | Black Lawyers Association |
| BMF | Black Management Forum |
| BPC | Black People's Convention |
| BUSA | Business Unity South Africa |
| CASAC | Council for the Advancement of the South African Constitution |
| CDE | Centre for Development and Enterprise |
| CODESA | Convention for a Democratic South Africa |
| Cogta | Department of Cooperative Governance and Traditional Affairs |
| Contralesa | Congress of Traditional Leaders of South Africa |
| COSAG | Concerned South Africans Group |
| Cosatu | Congress of South African Trade Unions |
| CP | Conservative Party |
| CSA | Cricket South Africa |
| CST | Colonialism of a Special Type |
| DA | Democratic Alliance |
| DAC | Department of Arts & Culture |
| DLTC | Driver Licence Testing Centre |
| DoJ | Department of Justice |
| DP | Democratic Party |
| DRCA | Dutch Reformed Church in Africa |
| DRMC | Dutch Reformed Mission Church |

# LIST OF ABBREVIATIONS

| | |
|---|---|
| DWCPD | Department of Women, Children and People with Disabilities |
| FCO | Foreign and Commonwealth Office |
| FF | Freedom Front |
| FFC | Financial and Fiscal Commission |
| FIFA | Federation of International Football Associations |
| FRELIMO | Front for the Liberation of Mozambique |
| GAA | Gaelic Athletic Association |
| GEAR | Growth Employment and Reconstruction |
| HIV | Human Immunodeficiency Virus |
| HRC | Human Rights Commission |
| HSRC | Human Sciences Research Council |
| ICD | Independent Claims Directorate |
| IDASA | Institute for a Democratic South Africa |
| IEC | Independent Electoral Commission |
| IFP | Inkatha Freedom Party |
| IJR | Institute for Justice and Reconciliation |
| IPL | Indian Premier League (Cricket) |
| MDDA | Media Development and Diversity Agency |
| MDG | Millennium Development Goals |
| MK | Umkhonto we Sizwe |
| MNC | Multinational Corporation |
| MRC | Medical Research Council |
| MRM | Moral Regeneration Movement |
| NDP | National Development Plan |
| NDR | National Democratic Revolution |
| NEC | National Executive Committee |
| NGK | Nederduitse Gereformeerde Kerk |
| NGO | Non-governmental Organization |
| NLM | National Liberation Movement |
| NPC | National Planning Commission |
| NUM | National Union of Mineworkers |
| NUSAS | National Union of South African Students |
| OAU | Organization of African Unity |
| OECD | Organisation for Economic Co-operation and Development |
| PAC | Pan Africanist Congress |
| PanSALB | Pan South African Language Board |
| PMG | Parliamentary Monitoring Group |
| PSC | Public Service Commission |
| PSL | Premier Soccer League |
| RDP | Reconstruction and Development Programme |
| RWC | Rugby World Cup |
| SAARF | South African Audience Research Foundation |
| SABC | South African Broadcasting Corporation |
| SACC | South African Council of Churches |

| | |
|---|---|
| SACP | South African Communist Party |
| SADF | South African Defence Force |
| SAIRR | South African Institute of Race Relations |
| SAMP | Southern African Migration Project |
| SAPA | South African Press Association |
| SAPS | South African Police Service |
| SARS | South African Revenue Service |
| SARU | South African Rugby Union |
| SASAS | South African Social Attitudes Survey |
| SASO | South African Students Organization |
| SIU | Special Investigating Unit |
| StatsSA | Statistics South Africa |
| TEC | Transitional Executive Committee |
| TI | Transparency International |
| TRC | Truth and Reconciliation Commission |
| TUC | Trades Union Council |
| UCM | University Christian Movement |
| UDF | United Democratic Front |
| UN | United Nations |
| URCSA | Uniting Reformed Church of South Africa |
| USSR | Union of Soviet Socialist Republics |
| VAP | Voting Age Population |
| VAT | Value Added Tax |
| WAN-IFRA | World Association of Newspapers and News Publishers |
| WHO | World Health Organization |
| ZCC | Zion Christian Church |

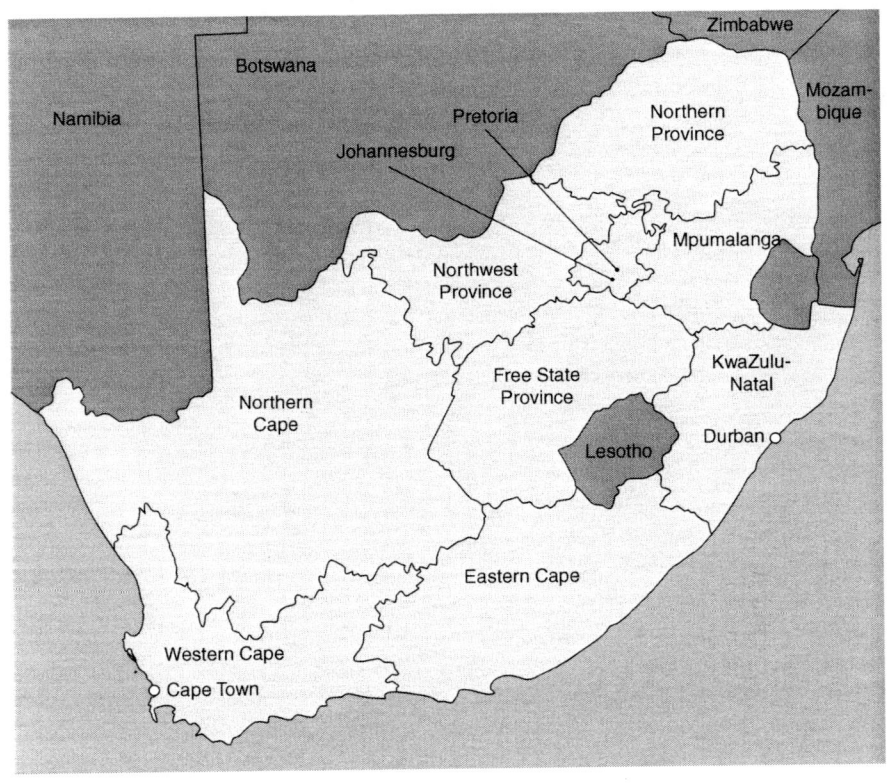

# Introduction: The problem of nationalism in post-apartheid South Africa

## Introduction

This volume is in some respects a departure from others in this series. The nations and nationalisms that have been the subjects of the previous titles have lent themselves to treatment by narrative overview of individual national consciousnesses and identities as they developed and changed, usually over several centuries. It is true of course that there were sharp discontinuities in some of them, revolutions in France, Russia and China being obvious cases in point. However, continuities tended to reassert themselves: it did not take France long after the revolution to resume its status as an imperial nation-state; 24 years after the Russian revolution the Soviet government was cultivating suppressed national symbols from the pre-revolutionary past in what for reasons of survival was dubbed the 'Great Patriotic War' against German invaders; the Chinese revolution was in many respects a national revolution against Western and Japanese imperialism. With such substantial continuity and lengthy perspective, much can be said with confidence about the mature nations and nationalisms that have been the subject of previous volumes in this series and there are historical and comparative debates about them to evaluate.

These things are not true of South Africa where the nation is the recent product of late and accelerated democratization and is very much a work in progress. South Africa could not have the luxury of separating the national and the democratic components of the revolution that has changed the country so profoundly. In particular it could not postpone the democratic question until after the national question was solved. South Africa could not become a nation unless it was democratic and it could not democratize unless it was (or could at least pretend to be) a nation. That is by contrast with many other nations and nationalisms, nation-building in South Africa in its current form has taken place in a much more compressed time frame, is more diffused in focus and more uncertain in outcome. Insofar as grand narratives and long-term structures exist – legacies of colonialism and apartheid – they tend to complicate and compromise current efforts at nation-building rather than support them. Instead of being able to draw on the resources of a national *longue durée*, contemporary nation-building efforts in South Africa can appear to be event driven and shallow.

As a result, there are more questions than answers about the state of nation-building in South Africa today. This is reflected in the present text which considers three forms of nation: an Afrikaner nation, which had to die in order that a democratic South African nation could be born; a civic nation, hastily improvised to provide a platform of legitimacy for constitutional democracy during the negotiations which brought apartheid to an end; and an African nation which is glimpsed but not fully articulated in the ideology of African nationalism, and which has struggled to find expression in post-apartheid South Africa. The subject matter of this book is the juxtaposition of these differing conceptualizations of the nation in such a short period and within such a limited political space. The problems of coexistence between these various expressions of identity have taxed South Africa's nation-builders and the conditions under which nations appear and disappear set interesting explanatory challenges for theorists of nationalism. These issues are also addressed in the pages that follow.

In South Africa what were literally life-or-death questions of democratization and national identity were addressed in a brutally short and intense period of negotiation between 1990 and 1993.[1] For the negotiations to succeed, this also had to be a time of high-speed introspection, quick learning and rapid improvisation for all concerned. This was especially true for the main protagonists: the African National Congress (ANC) under the leadership of Nelson Mandela and the National Party (NP) under the leadership of F. W. de Klerk. All of this had to be managed among emotional highs of mutual recognition between hitherto sworn enemies and lows of mistrust, violence and vertiginous brinkmanship.

This does not mean that there was no history of nationalism in South Africa prior to 1990. Primordialists and constructivists may differ on dating the origins of Afrikaner nationalism, but it is clear that the momentum of national consciousness among Afrikaners was well underway by the mid-nineteenth century at the latest. Founded in 1912, the ANC is the oldest national liberation movement in Africa, although it was the last on the continent to achieve power as the successor to colonial and/or white minority rule. However, neither Afrikaner nor African nationalism was a convincing vehicle of democratic national consciousness for all who lived within the external borders of South African territory. Indeed Afrikaner nationalism brutally dismissed the possibility of any such nation coming into being. For its part, during the years of struggle, African nationalism never managed a definitive synthesis between national liberation for a putative African nation and the realization of a non-racial nation that embraced all South Africans.

The legacies of these historical pedigrees have been ambiguous at best and toxic at worst. While it was clear to all but dogged reactionaries, even before 1990, that Afrikaner nationalism had had its day, this did not automatically mean the triumph of African nationalism in South Africa. African nationalism was and remains far too valuable for the ANC to abandon, but it has had to be cautious in explicitly cultivating and exploiting this asset for the purposes of legitimacy, while simultaneously promoting the values of the civic nation. Such have been the ANC's inconsistencies of practice and silences of theory in this regard that inevitably views differ on the place and role of African nationalism in post-apartheid nation-building. There are liberal critics who think that the ANC single-mindedly practises an unreconstructed and anachronistic form of African nationalism which in itself is an obstacle to constructing a civic nation: they believe that African nationalism, like Afrikaner nationalism will have to die if the civic nation is to mature fully. On the other hand there are African nationalists who think their nationalist birthright has been betrayed and marginalized in favour of the cosmopolitan, alien and spurious politics of syncretic identity.

The account which follows, then, while it acknowledges the historical pedigrees of Afrikaner and African nationalism, concentrates largely on the past 25 years or so. This period begins in the mid-1980s when apartheid was in crisis, the liberation struggle was at its height and clandestine negotiations to find a way out of the violent impasse were hesitantly underway. It continues to the present day when much has been achieved to embed democracy but much remains unresolved in terms of nation-building. These open questions and imponderables cluster around three themes: the death of Afrikaner nationalism; the continuing ambiguities of African nationalism and, especially, the uncertain progress of the improvised civic nation towards the goal of well-rooted permanence.

This introduction continues with a series of questions about the relationship between the democratic settlement and nation-building, as well as issues for theorists of nationalism which arise in post-apartheid South Africa, of understanding and analysing the nation and nationalism. Part One of the book surveys the raw material of nation-building by addressing the question, 'Who are South Africans today?' Data from censuses in 2001 and 2011, along with material from other sources, are used to draw up a demographic, linguistic, socio-economic and ethnic profile of the people from and for whom the South African nation is being constructed. Part Two steps back to consider the legacies of Afrikaner and African nationalism, in particular how they affected the negotiated settlement of 1990–6 and the improvised nation which underpinned it. One inescapable result was that ambiguities were built into the settlement: these threatened to compromise the future trajectory of the improvised nation. The progress of nation-building after the first democratic election in 1994 is discussed in Part Three. This part notes discontinuities between Mandela's lived exemplar of humanistic reconciliation and Thabo Mbeki's wholesale reworking not only of what reconciliation could and should mean but also his wholesale reconceptualization of the South African nation. Part Three also notes that well before Mbeki was forced out of the presidency in 2008, government perspectives on nation-building shifted from emphasis on black–white reconciliation to a concern for social cohesion in the whole population. This shift was forced by worrying signs of fragmentation and incoherence. Part Four considers whether, after 25 years of nation-building, South Africa is coming together or pulling apart. The contributions to a shared life for South Africans of civil society, media and the public sphere, sport, religion and values, as well as citizenship and the polity are discussed. The special case of African traditional culture and authorities is also treated in this section. Another chapter weighs the effects of crime, corruption and other deviant behaviours on the development of shared national citizenship. In Part Five the progress of nation-building after 20 years of democracy is assessed and, in conclusion, the questions that began the study are revisited.

## The problem of nationalism in post-apartheid South Africa

As South Africa approaches the twentieth anniversary of its first democratic election, the country's record of building on the negotiated constitutional settlement which paved the way for it will be examined from various standpoints, with the intention of assessing future democratic prospects. The integrity of the Constitution in areas such as the rule of law, the protection of property and in the realization of the promise of economic and social rights will be one point of examination. Another will be the sustainability of democracy where the ruling party has never lost power in an election, and where there appears to be no immediate prospect of this happening. As a result, the prospect of genuine electoral competition developing and the likely political fallout if it does will be a focus of speculation. This in turn leads to another key issue for democratic prospects: the single-minded pursuit of fusion between party and state apparatus which has been sought by the ANC ever since it became the ruling party in 1994. All of these strands will be intertwined with concerns about the sustainability of democracy in a country which is generally acknowledged to be one of the most unequal in the world. These concerns are sharpened by the fact that inequality is largely, though not exclusively, linked to historical injustices derived from racial classification, discrimination and stratification.

One frame of reference will, to the extent that it features at all, provide only a minor theme for analysis and reflection. This frame of reference is the nation, nationalism and nation-building. This is surprising for two reasons: first, because a good case can be made that whether they are openly acknowledged or not, questions of nationhood and identity underlie all the other aspects of South Africa's democratic progress and prospects which are listed earlier; secondly, because, especially in the early post-apartheid years, nation-building was a constant preoccupation of South Africa's elites. For a short period the label 'Rainbow Nation' attached itself to South Africa and globally it became one of the most potent political tropes of the late twentieth century. However, the speed with which it fell into disfavour in South Africa itself is an indication of the problematic nature of nationalism in the post-apartheid era.

The first problem was the toxic legacy of Afrikaner nationalism: 'The manipulations of race and ethnicity, backed up by a massive repressive apparatus, and the use of notions of culture, self-determination and national homelands in the service of reprehensible policies of dispossession and human rights violation gave credibility to the case against identity as a positive focus of analysis' (Greenstein 1998: 4). It could be added to this verdict that it was bad enough that nationalists did this in furtherance of their own selfish conception of identity needs, but they also tried to gloss over the offence by claiming that what they were doing was also serving the identity needs of the oppressed. Attempts to spawn progeny in the form of 'self-governing Bantu nations' led only to a series of forlorn miscarriages in the veld. Only in KwaZulu where Chief Mangosuthu Buthelezi grafted what the Pretoria government had to offer onto the robust stock of Zulu identity was there anything like vigorous progeny. However, during the period of negotiation and transition the unabashed militarism and separatist brinkmanship of Buthelezi and the movement he created did nothing to establish the legitimacy of identity politics – at least in ethnic form – in the wider population. The effect was quite the reverse.

The second problem was that the well-merited discredit that Afrikaner nationalism visited on identity politics generally helped to confirm widespread scepticism about its principal antagonist, African nationalism. Concerns about replacing one form of ethno-racial domination with another were not confined to whites, or even to the combination of whites, Coloureds and Indians that accounted for more than 20 per cent of the population in the early post-apartheid days. Tricky questions such as who qualified to be called 'African', what values, customs and bonds of kinship made up 'African' culture and how they could be translated into forms compatible with a stable, inclusive democratic polity in a diverse, heavily modernized and urbanized economy and society, would have to be resolved quickly if African nationalism were to be the basis of the new state. However, even if it were to be remodelled, the adoption of African nationalism as the overt governing ideology would be a statement of victory rather than compromise and would court at best withdrawal and at worst open rebellion from whites. In any case, by the 1990s, African nationalism all over the continent was looking sclerotic and decayed, and the 'new tribalism' that stalked the immediate post-Cold War world in the Balkans, the former Soviet Union and Africa, sent powerful messages about the potentially pathological nature of ethno-national identity politics. Negative stereotypes of this sort were confirmed closer to home. If Buthelezi and Inkatha, the movement he led, represented what African nationalism in an atavistic ethno-nationalist form would turn out to be, then the message to South Africa's nation-building elites was clear enough; this particular genie had to be kept in the bottle. It would not only be racial minorities that would have something to fear if this kind of African nationalism were to take off on a national scale, but also communists, trade unionists, feminists, constitutional democrats and many others in the loose coalition of members and fellow travellers which the ANC acquired as its momentum built in the 1980s.

In short, by the time the prospect of South Africa achieving a negotiated settlement to its conflicts became a reality, nationalism had acquired many unsavoury associations. These included conflict, separatism, absolutist versions of sovereignty and authority, pre-modernity in the form of corrupted and manipulated traditions, as well as (confusingly enough) some of the less appealing sides of modernity, in which Afrikaner nationalism applied exclusive notions of kinship to help shape exploitative, economic relationships which were thoroughly modern. These negative associations coincided in any case with the practical limitations of the situation South Africans found themselves in as apartheid approached its endgame. The first was that the balance of power simply did not lend itself to African nationalism declaring itself the victor, even if the ANC as its principal torchbearer had wanted to. Secondly, there was the incorrigible fluidity of South African identity. As one account puts it: 'In South Africa the political transition from apartheid to democracy keeps running up against the substance of "the people". In the absence of any unifying principles (of language, culture, religion, race and so on) the identity of South Africans is elusive' (Chipkin 2007: 190). To which might be added, even the crudest building blocks, 'black', 'white', 'African' could not be relied upon to give a solid foundation since each of these categories imperfectly conceals a variety of historical experience and linguistic and cultural markers.

At the same time there was unprecedented intellectual encouragement for alternatives to discredited versions of nationalism, which nonetheless preserved the idea of the nation. Ideas of civic nationhood and citizenship, constitutional patriotism, post-nationalism and cosmopolitanism were gaining wide currency in global academia and in wider debate as South Africa's negotiated transition progressed. There were local variants. One much-cited version (Degenaar 1991 and 1993) not only ruled out an ethnic basis for nationhood, but discarded the whole idea of vesting sovereignty in the nation – 'the mistake of the French Revolution' and advocated replacing it with a vision of the 'sovereignty of justice' that was, frankly, utopian.

Less disinterested but better-rooted versions of alternative bases for national cohesion came from ANC legal academics and ideologues. The result of all this was a part-principled, part-pragmatic, widely shared agreement to differentiate between good nationalism and bad nationalism. Bad nationalism is exclusive, based on ethnic and racial criteria and leads to conflict. The government's 2011 National Development Plan (NDP) sums up the view of bad nationalism which has officially informed nation-building since 1994, when it advises:

> We must constantly guard against narrow nationalism, dislike of 'others' or the development of a superiority complex in relation to people from other countries or continents. Nationalism, taken to an extreme, engenders new forms of racism, discrimination and chauvinism. (NPC November 2011: 466)[2]

Good nationalism is inclusive, generous in its recognition of cultural diversity, rejects the 'melting pot'[3] model of identity and relies for binding force on the values of the Constitution, which is the supreme law (NPC June 2011: 14). According to the NDP, the principal binding values are those of 'human dignity, non-racialism, non-sexism and the rule of law' (ibid. 464). These values: 'Set out a vision for how South Africa can overcome its history and build a society based on equality, freedom and dignity: enable South Africans to have a common bond and provide normative principles that ensure ease of life, lived side by side: afford broad standards by which particular actions are judged to be desirable and right' (ibid.). The Constitution goes further than this by setting the goal of 'transforming South Africa into a more equitable, integrated and just society' (ibid.). In this sense, in terms of official nation-building discourse, the Constitution is not about what the South African nation is, it is about what it will become.

This version of the nation and national citizenship, based on the idea of constitutional patriotism, was certainly an elegant solution to the problems of nationalism as they presented themselves to the negotiators who were responsible for all the procedural and substantive issues of South Africa's transition to democracy between 1990 and 1996. It would be a mistake, however, to assume that constitutional patriotism was a wholly organic, principled outgrowth of struggle and negotiation in which the negotiators were working from scripts, shaped for them by their respective constituencies, which just happened to coincide. Constitutional patriotism had two pragmatic, political purposes which were, first, to express compromise and recognize that no other basis for nationalism could deliver peace and stability; and secondly, to keep the genie of populist ethno-racial nationalism in the bottle. It is very hard to imagine a better outcome to these various problems and South Africa was very fortunate that the negotiators, with crucial support from non-partisan experts and facilitators, could find their way to it. However, even 'good' nationalism in its constitutional form brought a new generation of problems with it. Four in particular stand out, several of them related to the chronic lack of trust in South African society.

The first problem was that the Constitution and the citizen nation on which it was based represented a fresh start but not a clean slate. To agree on a fresh start was uncontroversial. However, a clean slate is not the same thing, and there was ample scope for differences over whether or not one was possible or desirable. What constituted an accounting for the past was far from clear. As to the future, there could be no argument about the need for measures of redress for past injustices: the Constitution plainly stated this agreement. However the scope, limits, pace and modes of redress were not and could not be stated in a document of this sort. This area of policy uncertainty offered fertile ground for narratives of betrayal which could undermine civic nationalism. One was the accusation from the Left that the ANC government had sold out redistribution to global neo-liberalism. What might merely be a disagreement over macroeconomic policy in a more mature democracy, with a more settled nationhood, has in South Africa been a much deeper rift. Even more so, the racial/national narrative of betrayal, especially over the accusation that shortcomings in government delivery of land reform targets have been attributable to constitutional limitations on expropriation, remains a direct challenge to property rights and other premises of civic nationalism. Furthermore, the choice of modes of redress, especially the crude yardstick of race rather than any more nuanced criteria of disadvantage, has led to accusations that the principles of the Constitution have been betrayed.

The second problem was the question of ownership of the settlement, the Constitution and the civic nation. There was an unmistakable air of elite bonding and social distance from constituencies about the whole process of negotiation and constitution-making. The unconscious tendency to appropriation, exemplified by many of the politico-legal elite which oversaw the transition, is well caught by Constitutional Court Judge Edwin Cameron speaking in 2013: 'To many, the culture of high-minded civic aspiration that characterised *our* struggle for racial justice and *our* transition to democracy seems distinctly frayed, if not in tatters' (Cameron 2013: 1, emphasis added). Doubtless Cameron was indeed inspired by high-minded civic aspiration; it is not only admirable but fortunate for South Africa that he and his colleagues were. However *his* struggle was not everybody's, not even that of the majority. Most of those who took part on both sides of the struggle, which preceded the negotiations, were motivated by things that were a lot more raw and earthy than high-minded, civic aspiration.

The third problem with the civic nation was linked to this problem of ownership. Nation-building in the South African context has had to strike a difficult balance between civic nationalism based on universal human rights and the need for legitimacy rooted in some kind of Africa-specific context. On the positive side, universal values served better than parochialism the purposes of a transition to democracy, one of whose main themes was 'rejoining the world' after decades of varying degrees of isolation. A constitution that was lauded as 'the most advanced in the world' and a nation to support it were useful sources of soft power for the country's diplomats, official and unofficial. Indeed for a time cosmopolitan high-mindedness became the principal means with which South Africans of all persuasions made an impression on (and sometimes irritated) the rest of the world. At the same time, however, there were several sources of pressure to ground the civic nation in something more indigenous. First, there was the need to broaden and authenticate the base of identification with the civic nation; secondly, there were the imperatives of cultural retrieval and rebuilding respect for Africa and Africans after centuries of denigration; thirdly, the ANC and its supporters were and remain sensitive about 'foreign' values, especially any that could be suspected of being 'Western' and worst of all, 'liberal' in provenance. In short, a 'pure' civic nation would not be enough, if indeed it is possible to bring such a concept to life anywhere other than the dreams of philosophers. However, indigenizing the civic nation would not be easy. The whole point of choosing shared, civic values for nation-building in South Africa was because kinship across the whole population was not an option and there were not enough shared indigenous political and cultural experiences on which to base the nation. Such shared experiences as existed had been entered into and maintained by force and had shockingly unequal outcomes. Shared experiences could always be manufactured, of course; after all, cultural manipulation is a recognized part of inventing nations all over the world. However, in the South African case this would require barefaced trickery on a formidable scale. The only other possibility would be to pick and choose from the historical and cultural repertoire of the demographic majority of Black Africans and invite all South Africans to identify with the choices. However, the legacy of Black African tradition is in itself contested and unstable, and would in addition risk setting up an ethno-national rival to the civic nation.

Fourthly and lastly, the future orientation of the civic nation – the idea that South Africa was not a nation yet but would one day be one – was problematic. In effect South Africans had already to *be* a nation in order to contemplate the joint task of *becoming* one. South Africans were constantly being exhorted to display nation-like qualities – assuming responsibilities of citizenship, accepting sacrifices for the greater good, showing solidarity with one another, affirming common and binding values – and at the same time being reminded that they would not be a nation until other conditions, notably a dramatic reduction in poverty and inequality, had been achieved. These conflicting states of consciousness were different for black and white people, but they were dissonant for both. Poverty and inequality were the key problems because they turned nation-building into a race against time; not only were these reminders of the legacy of the past morally offensive in both scale and racial provenance, and thus an obstacle to the horizontal attachments which are essential for nation-building, but they were also linked to all manner of social pathologies which had to be cured before things fell apart altogether. Above all, race-linked poverty and inequality posed quite different problems from the familiar configurations of the developed West. It has not been a question of relatively equal and affluent majorities accommodating poor minorities: in South Africa the demographic and moral balances were turned around. No wonder that South Africa's favourite post-apartheid political metaphors have been the pressure cooker and the powder keg.

One nation-building challenge in particular encapsulated these problems. The post-colonial period in Africa seemed to indicate that African nationalism, especially where wrapped in a liberation movement ethos, was at best sceptical of and at worst hostile to pluralism. There was a powerful example close to home: the sclerotic decline of African nationalism in Zimbabwe was under way as South Africa made the transition to democracy and the toxic outcomes of the inability of liberation movement legitimacy and political pluralism to coexist unfolded dramatically in 2000, six years after South Africa's first democratic election. The challenge for South Africa was to do better, and for African nationalism to adapt, via non-racialism, to accommodate pluralism.

## From goldmine to graveyard: South Africa and the study of nationalism

Post-apartheid South Africa posed some awkward problems and challenges for South Africa's nation-builders, but what of students of nationalism? For decades, South Africa provided a wealth of material for social scientists and historians with an interest in the politics of identity. Race, ethnicity and nationalism were salient organizing features of South African politics on both sides of the liberation struggle. Scholars in these fields had a living, and from the mid-1970s, a fast-evolving social laboratory to work in. What is more, urgency, topicality, high moral drama and uncertainty of outcome brought their work to life in ways that few other situations could match. Under these conditions it was not surprising that South Africa and South Africans attracted more than their fair share of scholarly attention. If we add popular accounts, Afrikaners probably had more books written per head of population about their national identity and aspirations than any other ethnic group in the world. This is no longer the case. The caravan has moved on. It is true that Afrikaners still retain a hold on the scholarly imagination and a few books are still produced. The emphasis is mainly on the past (Giliomee 2003; Van der Westhuizen 2008), but the present also receives some attention (Davies 2009). However, the interest tends to be turned inwards these days. No-one is very interested in Afrikaners now except those who, sometimes reluctantly, identify themselves with the designation. At times this comes with a measure of anguished self-interrogation (e.g. Krog 1998).

Less predictably, the question of 'South African nationalism', the potential of a form of nationalism to evolve which could embrace the whole country has attracted comparatively little systematic attention. One full-length monograph addresses the subject of the post-apartheid South African nation in terms of a theoretically grounded case study of a subset of African nationalism. Its rather austere and provocative title: 'Do South Africans exist?' (Chipkin 2007) suggests the same line of enquiry that prompted this work, though readers of both will quickly see differences of approach. Otherwise people have tended to deal with the subject in passing or to steer clear of it altogether. This is a pity because post-apartheid South Africa poses a number of interesting questions for students of nationalism.

One of them is, 'Where do nations go when they die?' The extraordinary journey of Afrikaners prompts speculation about what the demise of a nation – more or less going into voluntary liquidation and certainly not because it has been suppressed – tells us about the nature of nationalism. It could mean that a new nationalism can be voluntarily chosen in exchange for an old one because it better suits a recalibration of material needs. It could mean that identity needs are eternal, but have to be disguised in new forms – such as that of a 'minority' – in the face of unfavourable political power balances. It could also mean that identity needs simply relax into an agreeable menu of choices when a certain level of material security is achieved. All of these possibilities contain the intriguing question of whether Afrikaner nationalism succeeded or failed.

A second question is 'How viable is a civic nation without the backing of pre-existing kinship bonds?' Or to put it in the terms of debates about the nature of nationalism, can we have a *demos* without an *ethnie*? Certainly a tougher stress test for the idea of the civic nation could scarcely have been devised than South Africa, with its historic divisions and present-day inequalities. It is tempting to say that if civic nationhood can survive in South Africa it can survive anywhere. The argument can of course be turned around: perhaps it is only in a country like South Africa that such a pure form of the civic nation has to be essayed as the last, best and only hope of any kind of nation at all. The situation of South Africa also prompts speculation as to whether a people – or a nation-building elite which chooses to call a people into existence – can simply choose from a repertoire of nationalisms the one which best fits the needs, as well as the limits of political possibility of a given time and place.

A third and final question is whether post-apartheid democracy has sealed a lasting contract or whether nation-building since 1990 has been just another turn in the wheel. Since the beginning of the twentieth century,

South Africa has seen attempts by the British to create a settler imperial nation, by Afrikaner and English-speaking politicians of the interwar years to create an indigenous settler nation, by Afrikaner nationalists to dominate and balkanize the country on a power base of kinship and cultural exclusivity. A sort of 'resistance nation' of which African nationalism was a part, but crucially not the whole, brought these vain attempts to an end in the 1980s. Writing in 1998, historian Charles van Onselen noted that:

> Each turn of the wheel has brought forth ambiguous and often contradictory responses from members of regionally ensconced ethnic minorities and majorities, as they cast about for new identities in their family, communal and national settings. Exhausted, South Africans now choose to see themselves as constituting a 'rainbow nation'. It is an exercise that remains fraught with tension and pain. (Van Onselen 1998)

Whether the wheel has turned yet again is one theme of this book as it tries to illuminate the questions and challenges posed by post-apartheid South Africa for the country's nation-builders and for students of nationalism. Much will depend on a characterization that will appear often in the pages to come, the 'improvised nation', which saw South Africa through the transition to democracy. It is a label which conveys the quality of these fractious, anxious and euphoric years rather better than the popular 'rainbow' image. Whether this improvised nation has been sustained and built on since is the principal subject of this book.

**PART ONE**

# The raw material of nation-building

# CHAPTER ONE

# Who are South Africans?

Nation-builders, no matter how committed and ingenious, have to work with the materials at hand in inventing the nation. Even – perhaps especially – where the nation is conceived in civic terms the provenance and material conditions of the people who are its citizens shape the prospects of its realization. Accordingly, this chapter considers the demographic, spatial, socio-economic, linguistic and ethnic features which contribute to a profile of the South African people.

Of all the adjectives used to describe South Africans, 'diverse' and 'divided' are two of the most common. Diversity usually signals a source of strength and an asset. In ways that are rarely interrogated, or even fully articulated, the belief is propagated that South Africa is united because, or in spite of being diverse, or even sometimes both at the same time. The South African Constitution itself cautiously endorses this position, as well as the principle that diversity should not only be recognized but encouraged. This is on the grounds, implied rather than stated directly, that diversity is not only good in itself, but because it is prudent in the interests of social cohesion, political stability and sustaining democracy to treat diversity with indulgence, at least up to a point.

Diversity has also had a role to play in what might be labelled the external dimension of nation-building. Countries are branded and marketed for the purposes of soft-power diplomacy, investment and tourism. South Africa has enthusiastically promoted its diversity – and experience in dealing with the problems of diversity – in the interests of helping other countries deal with their own problems and at the same time creating a favourable image by comparison with more monochrome and less exciting destinations. In these positive connotations a diverse society is one that is at ease with itself and enriched by difference. However, South Africans also frequently describe themselves as a divided society and this is the dark side of diversity.

For about two decades – the 1970s and 1980s – analyses of the South African conflict were substantially shaped by (or in opposition to) the two complementary discourses of rival nationalisms and divided society. The rival nationalisms template was effectively dead by the time the negotiation process began in earnest but the divided society frame of reference has retained political leverage for much longer, though its durability owes much more to rhetorical effect than to analytical rigour. The idea of a divided society purports to be more than a handy label to signal the commonsense understanding that, in most democratic societies, identities are multiple, and resources are unevenly distributed. In academic usage it is a quasi-scientific diagnosis of pathological social and political conditions that calls for special prescriptions to manage. This usually involves some form of constitutional engineering to guarantee meaningful political and economic participation across ethnic and racial lines. This is because divided societies are generally defined in terms of the presence of hardened ethnic, religious or racial identities, often described as 'vertical' lines of division, which are not ameliorated by cross-cutting ('horizontal') allegiances and cleavages like those of class, for instance. These identities shape political power relations, which in turn define conditions of political and economic inclusion or exclusion. Divided societies can coexist with formal democracy which allows majorities to exclude minorities as long as ethnic, racial or religious identities and affiliations are converted into electoral choice. For minorities to exclude majorities it normally requires undemocratic methods of simple coercion or of coercive partitions to create 'artificial' majorities. The key feature of divided societies, however, whether they are formally democratic or undemocratic, is rigid barriers to mobility and fluidity of identity, allegiance and participation.

In the course of the transition to democracy, South Africa shed all of the formal, legislated, attributes of a divided society, and officially adopted the goal of eroding the informal ones. However, a 'divided society' remains a potent rhetorical reminder of lack of progress, and provides metaphorical leverage to justify pressures for increased, state-led redistribution. Effectively there has been a tactical reversal. During the last two decades of apartheid the concept 'divided society' was the preserve of those whites whose prescription for South Africa's conflicts was constitutional engineering along the lines of consociationalism. The ANC and its allies insisted on the unity of the people in order to achieve majoritarian democracy in a single polity. That achieved, it then appropriated the rhetoric of divided society to highlight racial inequality and to justify state-led redistribution and race-based measures of redress.

The problems of nation-building in post-apartheid South Africa have to be seen in the coexistence of a unified and open polity along with an officially celebrated single South African identity, with what many define as a still-divided society. A significant number of South Africans, whether government representatives, opinion-makers or ordinary citizens, are capable of going from celebrating the diversity of their people and culture to lauding their unified and open polity to lamenting their divided society without pausing for breath, never mind for reflection on connections between these three things. What needs to be acknowledged, and rarely is, is that celebrating and promoting diversity, sustaining non-racial, constitutional democracy and eradicating the remaining features of a divided society, may require different emphases in the nation-building process, if not different approaches altogether. One of the most significant weaknesses of nation-building in post-apartheid South Africa has been failure to acknowledge that this is not one seamless task, but several tasks which are essentially interdependent and complementary but, confusingly enough, potentially contradictory at the same time. The failure to communicate this clearly and honestly and, at the same time, to admit how difficult it is to harmonize the various dimensions of nation-building has been a serious inadequacy.

Much depends of course on the definition of a divided society, especially when the markers of formally legislated difference fall away. This in turn depends to an important extent on the essentially subjective conception of which markers of difference fall under the (acceptable) label of 'diversity' and the (unacceptable) label of 'division' and, even more importantly, how and to what extent the two intersect. An apparently simple, though in reality, highly complex version of this question is what level of inequality can any given democracy tolerate and still sustain itself? In South Africa, the problem is especially complex because not only is the level of inequality very high, but the provenance of inequality is rooted to an unusually blatant degree in historical injustice. That is, in any democratic society it matters not only how unequal people are but also how they came to be unequal. In South Africa this matters more than in most.

In short, it quickly became apparent after 1994 that the improvised nation which saw South Africa through the difficult process of creating a democratic and integrated polity was superimposed on a confusing mixture of diversity and division. If it was to be the task of this unified polity to invent a more enduring nation out of this raw material, then it would matter a great deal how people understood and reacted to the relationships between diversity and division.

## Demography: Race, generation and geography

There have been three census reports in South Africa since democratization: in 1996, 2001 and 2011. These are the main sources for constructing any profile of the South African people and for clues about any resources and challenges for nation-building. The tone is immediately set for perceptions of diversity and division in the population when it becomes clear that the first aspect of South Africa's human face which each census enumerates is the racial make-up of the population in terms of the old apartheid classifications: Black African; White; Coloured (mixed race) and Indian or Asian. It is true of course that today's classifications lack the element of fetishistic policing that was characteristic of apartheid, exemplified, for instance, in this extract from classification guidelines:

> Coloured means any person who is not a white person, Asiatic, Bantu or Cape Malay as defined, and shall include Bushmen, Griqua, Hottentot or Koranna; and a white person means a person both of whose parents are or were members of a race whose national to [sic] ethnical home is Europe, and shall include any Jew, Syrian or other person who is in appearance obviously a white person unless and until contrary is proven. (James 2012: 30)

In its democratic form, official racial classification invites citizens to assign race to themselves rather than forcing it on them administratively. It is also true that Black Africans are not subdivided, as they were in the past, into 'Bantu' tribes or nations. There is also an additional category, 'other', presumably for people who are unsure of their racial status, believe they belong to a race other than those alternatives offered by the state, or who as a matter of principle do not wish to classify themselves at all. In the 2011 census, 280,454 people (or 0.54% of the population) availed themselves of this option.

The virtual uniformity with which South Africans fall in with the state's desire to classify them racially may be attributable to a number of things: habits of conformity, indifference or resignation, all might play a part; so might an underlying and possibly implicit belief that racial differences are in fact part of the natural order of things and it is only practical to enumerate the population on that basis. Probably many African people simply identify with the reason offered by the state for perpetuating classification: 'Statistics South Africa continues to classify people by population group, in order to monitor progress in moving away from the apartheid-based discrimination of the past. However membership of a population group is now based on self-perception and self-classification, not on legal definition' (Statistics South Africa 2003: vii). The mildly Orwellian logic – a recurrent quality in South African official discourse – with which race classification is justified, is heightened by the characteristic South African euphemisms with which the state habitually refers to racial groups – 'previously disadvantaged' and 'previously advantaged'. However, constitutional backing can be claimed for this approach. The equality provisions of the Bill of Rights include the stipulation that: 'To promote the achievement of equality, legislative and other measures designed to protect or advance persons or categories of persons disadvantaged by unfair discrimination may be taken' (Constitution of the Republic of South Africa, Chapter 2 (9) subsection 2). And the principle is also established (subsection 5) that there are categories of 'fair' and 'unfair' discrimination, and discrimination on the part of the state against anyone on various specified grounds (subsection 3), including race, may be fair. The Constitution does put the onus on the state to prove that discrimination of this sort is fair; what it does not do is specify that the redress measures it allows for must or should be on the basis of racial classification alone. That is a policy choice, not a constitutional stipulation.

No matter what efforts are made to rob it of unhealthy associations (redress rationale, voluntary self-designation, extensive use of euphemism), and although the overwhelming majority of the population cooperates, the ANC's determination to continue classifying South Africa's racial demography is bound to be controversial. Certainly, it contains a number of complications for any conceivable nation-building project. In the first place, there is virtually universal agreement that 'race' has no biological foundation and that apartheid classifications were a matter of, 'political logic devoid of any scientific coherence' (Butler 2004: 35). Arguably, to believe this about race and yet to persist in classifying people on this basis, for whatever purpose, is at worst sophistry or at best merely absurd. Despite this, the vigour and speed with which race is ejected from the ontological front door is matched only by the alacrity with which it is readmitted via the pragmatic rear entrance labelled, 'redress'. A second objection is that insofar as race is a social construct, it is deemed to have had irredeemably destructive and divisive effects, especially in South Africa. Inviting people to perpetuate in their own minds this tainted form of social consciousness which in terms of its lack of scientific validity is, strictly speaking, false consciousness, does not encourage confidence in the nation-building project. To set against this there is only the official ANC and government line which protests that continuing to monitor the racial make-up of the population does not perpetuate racial consciousness and that such classification can be quarantined for worthy purposes.

The task of reconciling the legacies of racism with the ideals of non-racialism and the ambitions of African nationalism calls for ideological hard labour, as it has done for generations of political activists. The task is made even more onerous by the need to harmonize these contradictions with nation-building under a constitution based on the rule of law and individual rights. For the moment, however, the first answer to the question, 'who are South Africans?' has, perforce, to be answered in terms of racial groups.

One of the main forces undermining the self-confidence of South Africa's white minority rulers and one of the main drivers of political change was the declining share of whites in the make-up of the population. Writing in 1987, Giliomee noted that: 'Between 1910 and 1960, whites constituted 20 per cent of the total population, but from that year the white demographic base began to shrink. By 1985 the proportion of whites to the total population had fallen to 15 per cent and it is projected to shrink to 11 per cent by 2020' (1987: 372). In fact the shrinkage occurred far more quickly than predicted. By the time of the 2001 census the white percentage was 9.6 and by 2011 the share of whites had fallen again to 8.9 per cent. To some extent this drop has been the result of emigration. For instance, the government statistics body, Statistics South Africa (StatsSA), in its mid-year population estimates for 2010, 'assumes an outmigration of 447,000 whites' since 1996 (StatsSA 2010: 5). StatsSA gives neither source nor methodology for this assumption and in general emigration statistics are hard to compile with authority. Emigration rates are very important in any discussion of nation-building and they will be discussed more fully in a later assessment of white reactions to nation-building after 1994. For the moment it will be enough to note StatsSA's estimate and the general point that whites have, to a significant extent, voted with their feet in (or from) the New South Africa. However, their absolute numbers are not declining.

The 2011 census counted nearly 300,000 more whites than in 2001, but in the 10 years between the 2 censuses the whole population grew by close to 7 million, from nearly 45 million to the more than 51 million in Table 1.1. In general then, the white population is declining in percentage terms, but not dramatically; it is not plummeting as the white population of Zimbabwe did after independence. In any case it is difficult to compare the comparative shares of population groups between the 2001 and 2011 censuses, since the former did not include a category 'other' and this accounted for 0.5 per cent in 2011, while the decline in the white population was 0.7 per cent, leaving room for speculation as to exactly who classified themselves as 'other'.

While the absence of precipitate decline in the number of whites is worth noting in the context of nation-building, raw numbers do not tell a great deal on their own. However, racial headcounting can be

**TABLE 1.1** The make-up of South Africa's population (2011)

| Population group | Number (2011 Census) | Percentage |
|---|---|---|
| Black African | 41,000,938 | 79.2 |
| Coloured | 4,615,401 | 8.9 |
| Indian or Asian | 1,286,930 | 2.5 |
| White | 4,586,838 | 8.9 |
| Other | 280,454 | 0.5 |
| Total | 51,770,560 | 100.0 |

Source: Statistics South Africa: Census 2011: Census in brief, tables 2.3 and 2.4.

informative when combined with other statistics. Among the most important of these are measures of wealth distribution, education and skills and rates of participation in the economy. These will be discussed below under 'inequality'. Other important correlates of racial headcount are generational and geographic distributions of racial demography. These are important for drawing up a profile of who South Africans are. South Africa's population is indeed diverse, but diversity is concentrated in a few provinces; the distribution of racial groups is far from even. The sheer demographic weight of nearly 80 per cent of Black Africans means that they are the dominant presence almost everywhere; however, the minorities are highly concentrated. Coloureds constitute 8.9 per cent of South Africa's people, but 61.5 per cent of them live in the Western Cape where they make up nearly half (48.8%) of the population. Another 10 per cent of them are in the sparsely populated Northern Cape, where they are 40.3 per cent of the population. The next highest proportion of Coloureds is 3.5 per cent in Gauteng. Indians account for a mere 2.5 per cent of South Africa's population, but in KwaZulu-Natal, where 59 per cent of them live, Indians are 7.5 per cent of the population. Only 2.9 per cent of Gauteng's people are Indian and 1 per cent of the Western Cape's. In each of the other six provinces the percentage of Indians is less than 1 per cent. As far as whites are concerned, their proportions of the wealthiest and most urbanized Gauteng and Western Cape populations are almost identical: 15.6 per cent and 15.7 per cent respectively. In the other seven provinces whites range from a high of 8.7 per cent (Free State) to a low of 2.6 per cent (Limpopo). Black Africans account for over 86 per cent in six of the nine provinces with highs of 96.7 per cent in Limpopo and 90.7 per cent in Mpumalanga. They are in a lesser majority in Gauteng (77.4%), a bare majority in Northern Cape (50.4%) and only in the Western Cape are they in a minority (32.8%).

This distribution is to a large extent a function of historical urbanization patterns. In 2001, 56.3 per cent of South Africa's population was classified as urban, but the population groups varied in the extent to which they were urbanized (Table 1.2) and there was substantial variation between the provinces (Table 1.3).

The 2011 census does not deal with urbanization as directly but it is clear that since 2001 the move to the cities has continued briskly. The 2011 survey noted that the largest increases in population came in the provinces (Gauteng and Western Cape) with the largest cities. The National Planning Commission (NPC) reported estimates of 'close to 60 per cent in 2007' (NPC June 2011: 1) and the South African Institute of Race Relations in its Annual Survey of Race Relations (2013) quoted a figure (based on World Bank data) of 62 per cent, up from 52 per cent in 1990. However, urbanization in South Africa is not easy to assess. Apartheid spatial planning, including forced removals, 'homelands' consolidation and failed attempts at industrial decentralization, created areas of high population density which are neither rural nor urban in any strict definition of the terms. During the negotiations which drew up local government boundaries, the ANC largely prevailed in demarcating the largest metropolitan agglomerations to add townships and peri-urban, informal settlements to old 'core' cities (with their heavy concentrations of minorities). This was an ANC priority to ensure that the core cities could not avoid the responsibility of cross-subsidizing areas which had little prospect of revenue generation and to engineer ANC electoral majorities. Nevertheless, we can generalize by saying that population, minorities and especially economic activity are highly concentrated in the largest metropolitan areas ('metros' as they are called) as Tables 1.2–1.4 illustrate. South Africa's largest metros account for 25 per cent of the overall population but over 50 per cent of GDP.

The addition of the other four, smaller metros brings the metro share of population to 38 per cent and of GDP to 56 per cent (also 2010 figures). It is also worth noting the concentration and dispersal of South Africa's metropolitan areas and the way they contribute to the profile of South Africa's provinces. Johannesburg, Tshwane and Ekurhuleni all border each other; between them they form a sizeable agglomeration which ensures that Gauteng, the smallest province by area, is the largest in population and on its own contributes more than one-third to South Africa's GDP. It is also South Africa's melting pot, since only 56 per cent of its inhabitants were born there, by contrast with KwaZulu-Natal, where, despite having the country's third largest metropolitan area, eThekwini/Durban, 92 per cent of its people were born in the province. If the Gauteng metros represent concentration, the distance between them and the others draws attention to dispersal. Johannesburg is 1,400 kilometres from the next largest metro (Cape Town) and 568 from the third, eThekwini/Durban, which in turn is 1,646 kilometres from Cape Town. Apart from kilometres, there is not a great deal between them – certainly not in the way of development and economic activity.

**TABLE 1.2** Urbanization levels by population group (2001)

| Population group | Urbanization level (%) |
|---|---|
| Black African | 47.5 |
| Coloured | 86.8 |
| Indian/Asian | 97.5 |
| White | 89.9 |
| All South Africa | 56.3 |

Source: Roux 2009: 11, table 2.

**TABLE 1.3** Urbanization levels by province (2001)

| Province | Urbanization level (%) |
|---|---|
| Gauteng | 96 |
| Western Cape | 90 |
| Northern Cape | 80 |
| Free State | 75 |
| KwaZulu-Natal | 45 |
| North West | 41 |
| Mpumalanga | 39 |
| Eastern Cape | 38 |
| Limpopo | 11 |
| All South Africa | 56 |

*Source*: Roux 2009: 11.

**TABLE 1.4** South Africa's five main metropolitan areas

| Metropolitan area | Population (2010) (in million) | GDP (2010) (in billion) |
|---|---|---|
| Johannesburg (Gauteng) | 3.775 | R408 |
| Cape Town (W. Cape) | 3.499 | R269 |
| eThekwini (Durban: KwaZulu-Natal) | 3.409 | R266 |
| Tshwane (Pretoria: Gauteng) | 2.365 | R233 |
| Ekurhuleni (East Rand: Gauteng) | 3.409 | R163 |
| Total | 13.048 | R1,339 |
| Total as percentage of South Africa (2011 census) | 25 | 50.3 (SA GDP 2010: R2,664) |

*Sources*: South African Cities Network: www.sacities.net: National Treasury: Medium Term Budget Policy Statement 2011: 6.

**TABLE 1.5** Age distribution of Black African and white population groups

| Age band | Black African (%) | White (%) | All South Africa (%) |
|---|---|---|---|
| Below 30 years | 62 | 37 | 59 |
| 30 to 59 years | 31 | 42 | 33 |
| 60 years and over | 7 | 21 | 8 |
| Total | 100 | 100 | 100 |

*Source*: Compiled from StatsSA: Census 2011: Census in Brief: Figures 2.4, 2.5 and 2.8

Combining generational distribution with the racial make-up of the South African population draws attention to another dimension of diversity and concentration. In particular the age distribution of the white population differs markedly from that of Black Africans (Table 1.5).

In age group 0–4 years, there are 18 Black Africans for every white person; in age group 20–25, there are more than 14 Black Africans for every white person; over the age of 60, there are 3.3 Black Africans for every white person. These generational disparities are situated in a wider demographic picture: 29 per cent of the total population is aged between 15 and 29. This is just below the 30 per cent 'youth bulge' which is internationally recognized as a danger in developing countries (NPC November 2011: 98). The disparities also exist within as well as between racial groups: 72 per cent of Africans are under 35 years of age; there are 3.6 Africans between the ages of 15 and 29 for every one between the ages of 50 and 64; African males of 15–29 outnumber their counterparts of 50–64 (the age group from which, on average, political leadership comes) by more than four to one. None of these figures is necessarily threatening. However, when demographic preponderance is combined with extreme vulnerability, then the implications for the social cohesion on which nation-building depends could be serious. Of South Africa's unemployed, almost three quarters (72%) are younger than 34 years. In the age group 15–19 the rate is 65 per cent: for 20–24 it is 49 per cent and 25–29 it is 34 per cent. Vulnerability extends also to health. HIV prevalence for females is highest between 25 and 29 years and for males between 30 and 34 years. The race/age group most affected by violent assault is black men between the ages of 20 and 34.

# Inequality

There is virtually universal agreement that South Africa is one of the most unequal countries in the world, and that the origins of this situation lie in a history of racial domination, oppression and exclusion. A recent discussion paper on inequality in South Africa summarizes the point:

> [F]or most of the past century, national policy discriminated vigorously against the majority of the country's population. Among other iniquities, people were denied access to decent education, the right to own property and accumulate assets, the right to move freely, and the right of equal access to the labour market. Add to this the labour market protections enjoyed by white South Africans, the heavy spending on white education and training and the associated adoption of a capital-intensive economic growth path and it becomes clear that high levels of inequality were inevitable. (CDE 2010: 3)

Several assumptions are commonly made on the basis of this widely accepted understanding of South Africa's historical legacy: inequality is very highly correlated with race; the racial dimension of inequality is persistent; and it is the main stumbling block to nation-building. There are still strong grounds for each of these assumptions, but after nearly 20 years of state-led, redistributive efforts, they present an oversimplified picture of inequality. Oversimplified or not, the brute facts of inequality are still arresting. The most frequently cited evidence for the scale of South Africa's inequality is the fact that its Gini coefficient has been the highest or one of the highest in the world for many years. Although the Gini measure is a standard way of comparing inequality across countries, it is a rather blunt instrument and is not much more than a shorthand way to dramatize inequality. Depending on whether data such as social transfers are included, South Africa's might be as low as 0.58 or as high as 0.83[1] (Van der Berg 2010). Even the lower figure would be at the high end for comparable countries. The Gini can give a false impression of evenness given the extremely high level of geographic disparity in economic activity and participation levels; if South Africa's former bantustan areas are excluded, its Gini is much more like other middle-income countries. Separate calculations can be made for all South Africa's racial groups; the Gini for each one of them has increased since 1994, that for whites the most sharply; the Gini for Black Africans is the highest (ibid.).

## Health

Measures of health inequality are generally more directly informative than overall measures of inequality and because of their, literal, life-or-death quality they are politically very sensitive. Despite difficulties in getting up-to-date information and some variance at any one time in competing versions of quite basic indicators (such as life expectancy), a compelling picture of inequality in health outcomes is available. In theory the constitutional right to healthcare is secured through free (or very low-cost), comprehensive medical treatment, available universally through a public health system of hospitals and clinics funded by general taxation. In practice, as a result of underfunding and gross mismanagement, this service is of generally poor quality. Disastrous policy errors in dealing with the HIV/AIDS pandemic under the Mbeki presidency greatly exacerbated dysfunction in the system. At the same time there is a high-cost, high-quality, private healthcare system. In 2009, life expectancy for South Africans who had private medical insurance was in the mid-70s; the South African average was in the low 50s (if the deaths attributable to HIV/AIDS were stripped out, the average was in the low 60s); for the non-insured population life expectancy was in the high 40s (CDE 2011: 26). In 2013, the privately insured population comprised close to 8.7 million beneficiaries or nearly 16.8 per cent of the population (Council for Medical Schemes 2013: 228). Despite growth in the black middle class, there has been only marginal increase in the privately insured population in recent years. In 2007, close to 70 per cent of whites, just over 30 per cent of Indians and just under 20 per cent of Coloureds had private medical insurance. Fewer than 10 per cent of Africans had such cover (Van Eeden 2009). Of course, racial disparities in rates of mortality and disease are not attributable solely to differences in access to quality healthcare in the form of curative and preventive services, important as these are. In addition, they 'reflect racial differences in the access to basic household living conditions and other determinants of health' (Coovadia et al. 2009: 824). Among the differences noted by this source are the variation in infant mortality rates of 7 per 1,000 in the white population and 67 per 1,000 in the black population.[2]

## Education

South Africa spends 6 per cent of GDP on education and its teachers are, in purchase parity terms, among the highest paid in the world (NPC June 2011: 14). Despite this, South African pupils are routinely graded close to the bottom in international studies of achievement in literacy, mathematics and science. There is a pronounced racial element in this record of underachievement. A small minority of African pupils attend publicly funded schools that under apartheid (when educational expenditure was heavily skewed towards whites and to a lesser extent Indians and Coloureds) were reserved for whites or other minorities and are now open. In some of them today they are the majority of pupils. In such schools they benefit from greater parental involvement, including the payment of voluntary supplementary fees to boost resources, as well as better management and better teaching. There they are likely to perform within the normal range of achievement. A small number of publicly funded African schools perform in the same way, perhaps through a historical tradition of achievement and/or inspiring leadership from principals, teachers and parents. However, these are exceptions and overall the quality of education for black children is very low. The NPC's Diagnostic Report cites lack of early childhood education for low-income children, inadequate school infrastructure in poor areas, low levels of literacy among parents, poor nutrition, violence and social fragmentation as factors in poor educational outcomes. However, echoing a consensus in and out of government, backed by authoritative research, the report places a large share of the burden of responsibility on a poorly managed, public education system whose close-to 400,000 highly unionized and comparatively highly paid teachers are often poorly qualified, unproductive and ill-disciplined. Results bear out this gloomy analysis: 'While there have been some improvements as measured by the pass rate of those who sat the 2010 matriculation exam which was 67.8 percent, this hides the fact that only 15 percent achieved an average mark of 40 percent or more. This means that roughly seven percent of the cohort of children born between 1990 and 1994 achieved this standard' (ibid.). Inevitably these results are carried forward into higher education as Table 1.6 makes clear.

It is true that considerable progress has been made in opening access to higher education to Africans. Fifty one per cent (31,453) of the graduates completing a bachelor's degree in 2010 were black, compared to 43 per cent (21,052) just five years earlier. For the moment whites (at just under 500,000) make up the single largest number of graduates in the labour market, but they will be soon overtaken by African graduates (who now number 432,000) (CDE 2013). In terms of higher education more broadly defined, in 2011, 54 per cent (2,019,228) of those aged 20 or over whose highest level of education was 'higher' were Black Africans: 34 per cent (1,280,846) were white (StatsSA Census 2011 table 2.23). This still meant that whites with 11 per cent of the population over 20 years old had more than one-third of those with higher education. Despite these strides, Africans receive a lower return from tertiary qualifications than whites,

**TABLE 1.6** Participation in post-school education, age 20 and over by race and sex (2011)

|  | Black African (%) | Coloured (%) | Indian/Asian (%) | White (%) |
| --- | --- | --- | --- | --- |
| Male | 7.9 | 7.3 | 22.1 | 38.1 |
| Female | 8.75 | 7.5 | 21.2 | 35 |
| Total | 8.3 | 7.4 | 21.6 | 36.5 |

Source: Institute for Justice and Reconciliation 2012: 16, based on Census 2011.

are more likely to drop out, take longer than the minimum time to qualify and are more likely to be unemployed as graduates.

## Unemployment

One of the most striking features of the South African labour market is an unusually high premium for skills by international standards, both in securing employment in the first place and in remuneration levels. It follows then that disproportionate educational outcomes will be reflected in unemployment figures.

The census data (Table 1.7) clearly show strong racial and gender bias in producing unfavourable labour-market outcomes. Unsurprisingly, given the age structure of the population and the poor quality of education, there also is a strong youth element in unemployment. According to StatsSA's Quarterly Labour Force Survey (QLFS) in the third quarter of 2012: 'Approximately a third of young people aged 15–24 were not in education, employment and training (NEET)' (StatsSA 2012c: xv). Given the large demographic preponderance of Black Africans in this age group and the various other disadvantages listed earlier, the assumption is that a very large majority of this 'NEET' group is black. The QLFS also demonstrates the clear connection between education and employment. In the third quarter of 2012, 61 per cent of the unemployed had less than a school leaving certificate ('matric'), 32.8 per cent had matric and 5.9 per cent had tertiary education. The interesting and disquieting figure here is that nearly a third of the unemployed had a school leaving certificate. This is despite employers regarding matric as a baseline: 'As the number of matric

**TABLE 1.7** Official and expanded[a] unemployment rates by sex and population group

|  | Black African (%) | Coloured (%) | Indian/Asian (%) | White (%) | Total (%) |
|---|---|---|---|---|---|
| Men: official | 30.5 | 21 | 9.7 | 5.0 | 25.6 |
| Men: expanded | 39.8 | 28.6 | 14.0 | 8.1 | 34.2 |
| Women: official | 41.2 | 23.8 | 14.5 | 6.9 | 34.6 |
| Women: expanded | 52.9 | 34.4 | 23 | 12.5 | 46 |

[a]The 'expanded' definition includes 'discouraged' work seekers, those not actively looking for work at the time of the survey.

Source: StatsSA: Census 2011, Statistical Release P0301.4 (adapted from figures 3.37 and 3.38, p. 48).

graduates expands, employers increasingly require this qualification at a minimum, when less than a matric previously would have been sufficient. This is "credential inflation" without a concomitant rise in earnings or skills requirement' (NPC June 2011: 12). Youth, race and lack of education also combine to make those who are employed especially vulnerable to job loss. According to the NPC 'almost all' the close to a million job losses which occurred in 2008–10, in the global economic downturn, were experienced by those under the age of 30 and with less than a grade 12 education (i.e. high school final year).

## Income and poverty

Inequalities in health, education and labour-market outcomes interact with each other and with poverty levels and income inequalities in a toxic cycle of reproduction. Statistics for poverty and for income distribution when taken in conjunction with the measurements reported starkly illustrate this. The poorest 20 per cent of the population earns about 2.3 per cent of national income while the richest 20 per cent earns about 70 per cent of the income (NPC 2011: 9). Tying race to income inequality, the 2011 census reports that the average household headed by a white person earns six times as much (R365,134) per annum as the R60,613 per annum earned by one headed by a Black African person (StatsSA 2012: 39). Assessing the extent of poverty in South Africa, indeed even discussing the nature of poverty in the country at all, is chronically hampered by the absence of a single official benchmark for poverty conditions. Using the figure of R524 a month per person ($2 per day), the NPC calculates that nearly half of South Africa's families (48%) live in poverty (NPC 2011: 9). Using StatsSA data, the Institute for Justice and Reconciliation (IJR) reports that in 2010, 57 per cent of young people aged 15–24 and 43 per cent aged 25 to 34 lived in households with a per capita income of less than R570 per month. Taking race and gender into account: '66 per cent of black females between the ages of 15 and 24 lived in poor households with this low per capita income compared to only three per cent of their white counterparts' (IJR 2012: 16).

Given how deep and persistent inequality in South Africa is, and how obviously it is rooted in historical injustice, it is scarcely surprising that it is also a given of both official and societal discourse that inequality is a major obstacle to nation-building. Perhaps because so much about inequality in South Africa appears seductively obvious, there is surprisingly little debate on how inequality works to frustrate nation-building. Some degree of complexity is increasingly implied, as for instance in this passage from the NPC's Diagnostic Overview: 'The continued social and economic exclusion of millions of South Africans, reflected in high levels of poverty and inequality, is our biggest challenge. In our view, these high levels of poverty and inequality have a historical basis in apartheid and are driven principally by the fact that too few people work and that the quality of education for many black people remains poor' (NPC June 2011: 6). This implies that the 'historical basis' of inequality has been exacerbated by policy failure over the 17 years of democracy between 1994 and the publication of the NPC's report. It is not only the brute facts of inequality themselves, but the partisan and opportunistic politics of explaining continuing inequality that frustrate nation-building.

## Inequality and nation-building

South African inequality may indeed be deep, persistent and rooted in historical injustice, but in the past 18 years it has not been unaddressed and has not been static. The levels of inequality, as well as its shapes and perceptions of the factors which sustain it have all been in a state of change for the 20 years of democracy since 1994. Before discussing the relationship between inequality and nation-building in South Africa, it is worth considering some contextual factors.

## Redistribution

Redistribution has been addressed since 1994 through redirecting public expenditure and through race-based programmes of redress. One of the great tasks of post-apartheid governments was to address racially skewed patterns of public expenditure, which had their most destructive effects on education for black people: 'At the height of apartheid the state spent about nine times as much on each white person than on each black. This ratio has been reversed to the point where the state now spends about twice as much per capita on blacks than on whites' (Van der Berg 2010: 12). South Africa has a very progressive system of public healthcare financing:

> The richest quintile – which receives 68.7 per cent of total income – contributes 82 per cent of total healthcare funding. . . . Of this amount, about 45 per cent is retained as direct benefit from private healthcare (32 per cent) and public health services (13 per cent). Fifty-five per cent of total contribution by the richest quintile is redistributed to other quintiles. All other quintiles derive a greater share of benefit than the financial contributions they make. (Harrison 2010: 25)

In education, public spending has been drastically redirected away from schools previously reserved for minorities. Better-off people, black and white, retain an advantage less through opting out of public provision altogether: only about 5 per cent of South Africa's 13 million pupils attend private schools, though the number is growing. Advantage is gained more by augmenting publicly funded resources with private supplements. According to the National Treasury, by 2012, 57 per cent of government expenditure was social spending, 'targeted at low-income households', up from 49 per cent in 2002–3 (National Treasury 2012a: 78). In 2012, 15.3 million people received non-contributory social grants, up from 2.5 million in 1995 and expenditure on these grants now amounts to 3.4 per cent of GDP (ibid. 87).

## The changing face of inequality

The changing focus of public expenditure and the expansion of opportunities for black people to participate more fully in the economy by virtue of the abolition of statutory discrimination, as well as the effects of affirmative action and Black Economic Empowerment (BEE) programmes, plus steady (though disappointing) economic growth, have had salutary effects on poverty and inequality. Using the $2 per-day benchmark, the percentage of South Africans living in poverty fell from 53 per cent in 1995 to 48 per cent in 2008 (NPC June 2011: 9). However, positive this may be, it represents a relatively limited return for a revolution in public policy, which has been achieved largely through palliative, rather than participative, means. This is because as poverty levels have been lowered, the composition of the household income of the poorest 40 per cent of the population has been 'dramatically' altered as social grants have increased and wage income and remittances have fallen (ibid.).

There are also positive things to say about interracial inequality, but potentially discordant messages can be taken from even relatively good news. The proportion of Africans in the top 20 per cent of income earners increased from 39 per cent in 1995 to 48 per cent in 2009 (ibid.). Calculations of African contribution to membership of the middle class (Table 1.8) are also encouraging, but can be interpreted to indicate merely that one type of inequality has been substituted for another.

What is more significant? That the share of Black Africans in the higher middle class increased by four times after 1995 and in 2008 stood at more than one-third? Or that this share represented only 5.5 per cent of blacks? By 2008, 17.1 per cent of the African population could be defined as middle class (higher and lower), compared to only 5 per cent in 1995. Is this enough for a racial group that by 2011 comprised 79.2 per cent of the population? Cases can clearly be made for saying that the glass is either half full or half empty when it comes to interracial inequality. However, increasing attention is being paid to the spectre of rising intraracial inequality,

**TABLE 1.8** Black percentage share of the higher working/lower and higher working class (1994–2008)

| Higher middle class (above R40,000 per capita per annum in 2000 terms) | 1994 | 2004 | 2008 |
|---|---|---|---|
| % of whole population | 8.1 | 10.4 | 11.7 |
| % of Blacks | 1.3 | 3.3 | 5.5 |
| Black share of higher middle class | 12.3 | 24.7 | 36.4 |
| **Working and lower middle class (above R25,000 per capita per annum in 2000 terms)** | **1994** | **2004** | **2008** |
| % whole population | 13.5 | 16.5 | 20.6 |
| % Blacks | 3.7 | 7 | 11.6 |
| Black share of lower middle class | 21.1 | 33.3 | 44.0 |

Source: Van der Berg 2010: 11 (abbreviated).

particularly of course among Black Africans, whose share of the overall population continues to rise:

> South Africa's high aggregate inequality has not fallen. Indeed going into the future, South Africa's socio-economic dynamics still contain considerable inequality generating momentum despite a post-Apartheid policy milieu that has explicitly taken on the task of addressing this legacy. A demographic trend that will have a bearing on these dynamics going into the future is that the African group accounts for 80 per cent of the population now and this share is rising. Thus intra-African inequality and poverty trends are already and will increasingly dominate aggregate inequality and poverty trends. This is not to say that the country's racial footprint has gone. Indeed . . . the between-race component of income inequality remains remarkably high by international standards and its decline has slowed since the mid 1990s. Moreover the bottom deciles of the income distribution and poverty profile are still dominated by Africans and racial income shares are far from proportionate with population shares. Nonetheless, South Africa's changing population shares imply that a policy focus on race-based redistribution will become increasingly limited in the future as the foundation for further broad-based social development. (Leibbrandt et al. 2010: 21)

## Language diversity

There is no greater testament to the diversity of South Africans, as well as to the new South Africa's commitment to diversity in nation-building, than multilingualism. The synergy of unity and diversity, which is the key theme in the official doctrine of nation-building, receives its most insistent official affirmation in this context. For instance, launching a multilingual initiative in 2010, the then Minister of Arts and Culture said: 'It has sometimes mistakenly been believed that diversity is an obstacle to the development of any country. Today we see that the opposite is true. It is actually the bond of our nation. Without respect for diversity, unity is impossible. The different races cannot join together in a common project in which they do not acknowledge each other' (Xingwana 2010).

The 1996 Constitution (Chapter 1, Section 6) established eleven official languages, all to enjoy 'parity of esteem'. Positive measures are required of the state to 'elevate the status and advance the use' of 'the indigenous languages of our people', as a result of their historically diminished status and use. Fifteen languages other than the eleven official tongues are mentioned in the Constitution as deserving not only respect but promotion, including sign language and several languages attached to religions which may be 'major' in global terms but have only tiny numbers of adherents in South Africa. A Pan South African Language Board (PanSALB) is mandated to serve these purposes.

South Africa's indigenous languages fall into three main clusters:

- Nguni: in this group are isiZulu, isiXhosa, isiNdebele and siSwati. With 22.7 per cent of the population nominating it as their home language in the 2011 census, isiZulu is the most widely spoken; between them isiZulu and isiXhosa account for 38.7 per cent of the population and with the two smaller languages, the Nguni group accounts for 43.4 per cent of the population.

- Sotho, Sepedi, Setswana and Sesotho share 24.7 per cent of the population in similar proportions, with Sepedi the largest (9.1%).

- Two other minority African languages do not constitute a group but are individual outliers: Tshivenda (2.4%) and Xitsonga (4.5%) are concentrated in the north east of the country and have strong cross-border affinities: Tshivenda with the Shona people and language of Zimbabwe, and Xitsonga with the Shangaan people and language of Mozambique.

The relationship of Afrikaans to Africa – and hence its claim to indigeneity – is a matter of perception and politics. Its roots are in Europe, but it developed in South Africa. Confusingly enough it has served the contradictory political purposes of being both a badge of affinity with Africa and a mark of attachment to whiteness and being European. Many Afrikaners fiercely defend its claim to indigenous status, more so following the end of apartheid, since when there has been a much more obvious premium for being indigenous. Africans tend to accord this claim a mixed reception: strategic acceptance, outright rejection or indifference, according to political predispositions or needs. Afrikaans has the third largest share (13.5%) of home language choice in the 2011 census, after isiZulu and isiXhosa. It is the choice of 75.8 per cent of Coloureds and 60.8 per cent of whites, which means that a substantial majority of Afrikaans first language speakers are not white. Only 1.5 per cent of Black Africans describe Afrikaans as their home language.

English is the lingua franca of government and business to the extent that Anglophone foreigners tend to assume that South Africa is 'an English-speaking country'. South Africa's membership of the Commonwealth probably reinforces this major misconception, which has the effect of seriously distorting expectations and perceptions of South Africa, especially in the eyes of the United Kingdom and possibly the US media. South Africa is English-speaking only in a very narrow sense: just 9.6 per cent of the population claim English as their home language, a fraction more than Sepedi and considerably less than half of isiZulu's share. English is the first language of 35.9 per cent of whites, 86.1 per cent of Indians/Asians and 2.9 per cent of Black Africans. Yet, at the same time proficiency in English is a major asset in the labour market.

Comparison of the choices of home language in the 2001 and 2011 censuses in the Table 1.9 suggests that there has not been dramatic change in first (or 'home') language usage during ten years of urbanization, social mobility and change in the workplace and wider society.

First use of isiZulu and isiXhosa has dropped by 1.1 per cent and 1.6 per cent respectively; Afrikaans first usage has been static and use of English has increased by 1.4 per cent. In 2001, when whites comprised 9.6 per cent of the population, 21.5 per cent of the people chose Afrikaans or English as first language. By 2011 the percentage of whites had dropped to 8.9, but the combined share of Afrikaans and English had grown to 23.9 per cent. These are not insignificant changes, but they do not appear as yet to bear out apocalyptic prognoses of the inexorable hegemony of English which are common to Afrikaans and African language activists. This kind of scenario sees 'neo-liberalism' and the market working on the newly dominant African middle class who send their children to English-medium schools, read English-language newspapers and neglect African languages in any high-status context. The late Neville Alexander, liberation movement activist and key advocate of an assertive multilingual programme to 'intellectualize' African languages, warned against this kind of English hegemony:

> One of the most debilitating effects of hegemony is to make speakers of languages other than English – in this case – begin losing faith in

**TABLE 1.9** Official languages as spoken by South Africans as 'first' languages: 2001 and 2011

| Language | 2001 (%) | 2011 (%) |
| --- | --- | --- |
| Afrikaans | 13.3 | 13.5 |
| English | 8.2 | 9.6 |
| IsiNdebele | 1.6 | 2.1 |
| IsiXhosa | 17.6 | 16.0 |
| IsiZulu | 23.8 | 22.7 |
| Sepedi | 9.4 | 9.1 |
| Sesotho | 7.9 | 7.6 |
| Setswana | 8.2 | 8.0 |
| SiSwati | 2.7 | 2.6 |
| Tshivenda | 2.3 | 2.4 |
| Other and sign | 0.5 | 2.1 |
| Total | 100 | 100 |

*Source*: StatsSA: Census in Brief 2001 (figure 6, p. 14) and Census in Brief 2011 (figure 2.3, p. 24). Census 2001 refers to 'the language most often spoken at home'. Census 2011 refers to 'first language spoken'.

the value of their home languages. . . . If English stands at the top of the global linguistic pyramid, the indigenous languages of the African continent are to be found as close to the base as possible. In Africa, the disempowering effect of the hegemony of English has gone so far that we can be forgiven for seeing it as a kind of social pathology. (Alexander and Bloch 2004: 2)

Despite the rapid increase in size of the African middle class, however, only small changes in the proportions of households using African languages, English or Afrikaans are apparent. This is the case even in Gauteng and Western Province, which are the most heavily urbanized and racially mixed of the main centres of economic activity. The share of Afrikaans as a home language actually fell in the Western Cape between 2001 and 2011 and English rose by less than 1 per cent. In Gauteng, the centre of growth in the African middle class, the share of Afrikaans fell by 2 per cent and English rose by just over 1 per cent. The shares of African languages in the main economic centres were stable over the ten years, registering only small increases and some decreases. In Gauteng it was, if anything, the minority African languages that gained share, doubtless following internal migration from other provinces.

However, it is possible that by categorizing languages as 'home' or 'first' languages, the censuses fail to reveal important attributes of, and trends in, language use in South Africa. It is well known to anyone with knowledge and experience of living conditions in South Africa that many Black Africans – and most in urban areas – can communicate with varying, but often high, degrees of fluency in several of the official languages. But this is not easy to quantify, never mind to assess the degree of fluency. However, based on interpretations of a PanSALB survey of language use, Heugh calculated that in 2000 about 36 per cent of South Africans could understand English, 30 per cent of the population could understand isiZulu, 29 per cent Afrikaans and 21 per cent isiXhosa. On this basis she argues that these four should all be regarded (and encouraged) as emerging linguae francae. Since isiZulu and isiXhosa overlap to a considerable degree, about 50 per cent of South Africans probably understand isiZulu/isiXhosa (Heugh 2000: 25). By confining choice to first or home languages, the censuses may be concealing important trends in multiple language use which could contribute to effects of the kind that concerned Alexander and other African and Afrikaans activists. Another influence to be considered is generation. A key factor could be the person who filled in the census form, since households might differ between younger and older members in language use and levels of literacy.

Effectively, South Africa's diversity in language is important for nation-building in three ways. First, language policy may be directly used as an instrument of state-led nation-building. Secondly, possible links between language and ethnic identity need to be explored. Thirdly, language as a factor in the acquisition of skills and for entry to the workplace may be a determinant of inequality and a factor in shaping people as 'insiders' or 'outsiders' in the economy and society.

## Language policy in nation-building

As we have already noted, the South African Constitution includes an emphatic statement of the value of language diversity and a requirement that all official languages should enjoy 'parity of esteem'. This in return invokes the statutory requirement of monitoring and regulating their use at all levels of government, as well as redressing the historical wrongs visited on the indigenous African languages. The new government that took office after the April 1994 election was quick to set initiatives in train to meet the Constitution's requirements. However, a brief summary of the progress of these initiatives gives an indication of the low priority which was in reality accorded to nation-building through the constitutional requirements for official linguistic diversity and parity of esteem. It is worth following this issue in some detail since the lack of progress in making good the promises of the Constitution in this context usefully exemplifies the gap between the stated goals of official nation-building and the actual devotion of resources to bring them about in a context of weak state capacity.

PanSALB was set up in 1995, under the Department of Arts and Culture (DAC), as provided for in the Constitution and a language task group began work under its aegis.

In 2002, a national language policy framework was published by the DAC in order to give effect to the requirements of the Constitution. It included a South African Languages Bill (drafts of which had been made public as early as 2000), a bill to regulate translators and other 'language practitioners' and an Implementation Plan which envisaged the passing into law of the South African Languages Act in September 2003.

The Languages Bill was introduced in 2003: by the end of 2004 it had been rejected by the Cabinet and it was withdrawn from the legislative process in 2007.

In 2009, an application was made by a private individual to the North Gauteng (Pretoria) High Court to force the government to promulgate the Languages Bill. The court ruled that 'the adoption of a National Language Act was not a constitutional obligation, but nevertheless ordered the national government to regulate and monitor the use of the official languages by means of legislative and other measures' (Du Preez 2011). A new bill, the Use of Official Languages Bill, was passed by parliament in September 2012; that is, 17 years after the first steps had been taken to fulfil the government's obligations under the Constitution. The Act is a relatively simple piece of legislation, requiring government departments and public bodies to have language policies, to choose three official languages for departmental use and to set up language units to monitor and regulate compliance with the Constitution.

At the meeting of the Parliamentary Portfolio Committee on Arts and Culture which passed the Use of Official Languages Bill (June 2012), the minister briefed the committee on a report on PanSALB which he had commissioned at the committee's urging. Seventeen years after it was set up as the body mandated to deliver the constitutional requirements on language policy and nation-building: 'PanSALB had materially failed to meet its mandate and was unable to translate its mandate into a meaningful and aligned set of strategic objectives and performance activities. The board was dysfunctional and should be disbanded' (Parliamentary Monitoring Group 6 June 2012).

It is not clear from publicly available sources why the Cabinet rejected the original bill and quite why progress in complying with the Constitution has been so painful, so limited and so slow, although in some respects it is a familiar story of weak government capacity and institutional malaise, which can be replicated over many legislative areas in the same period. However, criticism of the Use of Languages Bill in its public discussion phase by multilingual advocates and civil society groups (Alexander 2012) suggests that the government's foot-dragging is also the result of conflict between two different conceptions of language in the nation. In one conception the African languages should be developed to fit 'high-status' functions in government and the economy, which in the eyes of advocates is essential for democracy to be meaningfully accessible to the majority and hence to be sustainable. In a more pragmatic conception, minimum compliance with the Constitution on 'parity of esteem' goes along with covert acquiescence in the inevitable (and in fact desirable) hegemony of English. In the eyes of critics it is this policy of minimum compliance which has prevailed in the current legislation, a policy which Alexander bemoans as: 'a middle class policy that benefits those who are more or less proficient in English or who are aspiring to become so and have the means to do so' (ibid.). In this view, language policy is reinforcing the 'insider/outsider problem, rather than fulfilling its role as an instrument of nation-building.

## Language and ethnicity

One of the most striking features of the 2011 census findings on first languages is the degree of concentration of the main languages. Afrikaans is the only one which combines high concentrations with quite wide, geographical dispersion: in the Western Cape, the percentage of people choosing Afrikaans as their first language (49.7%) was more than twice that of the nearest rival which was isiXhosa, with 24.7 per cent. In the Northern Cape, which has the smallest population of all the provinces, the share of Afrikaans was more than half (53.8%). In three other provinces, Eastern Cape, Free State and Gauteng, Afrikaans was chosen by more than 10 per cent of the people. By contrast, English had no high concentrations; its largest share was in the Western Cape (20.2%) and of the other provinces, only in Gauteng and KwaZulu-Natal (just above 13 per cent in each) did it get more than 10 per cent. The two main African languages have similar profiles to each other, that is, approaching 80 per cent in each 'home' province, either one or two other concentrations and negligible everywhere else. In this way, isiXhosa has 78.8 per cent in the Eastern Cape and one other concentration, 24.7 per cent, in the Western Cape. IsiZulu has 77.8 per cent in KwaZulu-Natal, 19.8 per cent in Gauteng and 24.2 per cent in Mpumalanga. IsiXhosa in the Western Cape and isiZulu in Gauteng are driven by migration to the main centres of economic activity; Mpumalanga alone of the provinces is a historical patchwork of languages; none receives more than 27.7 per cent share (siSwati), while three more get more than 10 per cent and another gets over 9 per cent. Only Gauteng qualifies as a melting pot of recent, economically driven migration. IsiZulu leads with a 19.8 per cent share there, while Afrikaans, English, Sepedi and Sesotho all get more than 10 per cent and Setswana gets over 9 per cent.

Given the close historic links between language and ethnicity, such patterns of high concentration and relatively low dispersal help to put ethnicity on the agenda for nation-building in post-apartheid South Africa. However, it remains an uncertain, confused and largely submerged agenda.

Ethnicity is a subject almost as sensitive as race in South Africa. There is a strong historical current in the ANC which would define it out of South Africa altogether: at another extreme there is a tendency to rebrand it as cultural diversity.[3] Part of the problem has been the incorrigible association of ethnicity with 'tribalism', not only in South Africa itself but also in Africa as a whole. Tribalism has the ability to convey powerful images and messages, but its usage is diffuse, imprecise, frequently pejorative and often coded. It has long been taken beyond the bounds of reasonably precise anthropological or ethnographic usage. In terms of political metaphor it can be met as a synonym for ethno-nationalism – used in this way either because people do not know any better or as a piece of evocative journalese, or as part of a calculated effort to discredit some or other claims to political identity. More accurately, it is used to describe subnational fragments without structured, political identities or aspirations to nationhood and self-determination, but with the capacity to undermine or even destroy broader efforts at nation-building. Afrikaners will sometimes proudly take up the self-serving, political metaphor of the 'white tribe of Africa' to appropriate an identity more indigenous than that of settler. In doing this they are probably the only people in South Africa happy to be referred to as a tribe.

Adding to this confusion, and linked to tribalism's reputation for nation destroying, is the question of pejorative usage. For Leroy Vail, the issue is simple: 'If one disapproves of the phenomenon, it is "tribalism"; if one is less judgmental "it" is "ethnicity"' (1991: 1). Others might want to frame the distinction as being between ethno-nationalism as rational, modern, state-building, driven by democratic principles like self-determination, and tribalism as irrational, atavistic and obstructive or even destructive of modern state forms. Yet another pejorative association of tribalism is with identities created or elaborated, or perpetuated from above by colonial authorities for the purposes of indirect rule. Whichever set of criteria is used, analytical and normative distinctions between ethnicity and tribalism are difficult to sustain consistently, and the political and academic usage of 'tribalism' in Africa (and elsewhere for that matter) is condemned in large part to the vagaries of subjective dislike and vulgarized categories whose boundaries are difficult to police.

Despite all this potential for confusion and abuse, the term tribalism remains in everyday currency in South Africa. There are two main reasons for this. The first is the powerful and durable attraction exerted by tribalism on the minds of journalists and other opinion-makers in the developed world, as the key to understanding the politics of Africa, and within it, South Africa. A degree of determinism about the allegedly poor prospects of sustaining democracy against the pull of subnational gravity often goes with the kind of interpretation which tribalism invites. To a large extent this is a matter of popular and journalistic stereotype, originating and circulating outside South Africa, crude but effective nonetheless in shaping investor perceptions to some extent. South Africans in general and the ANC in particular react angrily in denial of this version of Afro-pessimism. Paradoxically however, at the same time, it suits the ANC to keep the idea of tribalism alive. It should not be forgotten that if the ANC's main reason for existing was to replace white minority rule with majority rule, in whatever form this notoriously ambiguous concept might be realized, a powerful and complementary theme was the mission to prevent South Africa breaking up completely. As long as the ANC views itself as a national liberation movement, there will be a need for it to justify itself in these terms. Subnational loyalties and associations will be invoked as an ever-present danger against which the ANC is an enduring shield and revolutionary sword, and as one possible answer to the blunt question, 'what is the ANC *for*?'

The association of ethnicity with tribalism is not the only source of confusion over the place and role of ethnicity in the politics of post-apartheid South Africa. In the first place, the politics of racial and ethnic identities has been conceptually and linguistically mixed for decades. As biological determinism was discredited and became untenable in the second half of the twentieth century, white minority rule was increasingly justified in the eyes of its practitioners in terms of cultural essentialism; ethnicity became a proxy for race in the eyes of whites (Glaser 2001: 143). Secondly, ethnicity has also become entangled with the politics of African leaders and communal life and values generally. 'Tradition' has a mixed provenance in the South African context, including reference points like pre-colonial African societies, indirect colonial and white minority rule, and a material base in rural areas where particular African languages predominate. As a result, the institutions of tradition are sometimes regarded with suspicion in terms of subnational identity and specific ethnicities but, confusingly enough, sometimes to be celebrated as pan-South African features of African life. The picture is further complicated by the increasing recognition that where African demotic life is concerned, the discontinuities between urban, rural, traditional and modern are by no means absolute, and there are strong linkages between all of them. The truth probably is that the champions of tradition in post-apartheid society are able to move between all these registers according to the perceived political needs of the moment.

The labour market is not immune to ethnic influences either. The informal survival of the migrant labour system, especially in the mining industry, has prolonged the synergy and sometimes the conflict between ethnic and worker identity which several historians have documented in the past. In what remains to a degree a segmented labour market, mining companies often recruit for particular job categories in particular geographic areas of the former bantustans. An uncomfortable reminder of the durability of ethnic effects in labour relations was provided by the events which culminated in the violent encounters at the Marikana mine in September 2012, which left over 40 dead, most at the hands of the police, the rest killed by striking miners. The militant determination of the Marikana rock drillers to break with the established National Union of Mineworkers (NUM) and from the legal framework of wage bargaining was likely encouraged by solidarity that some would call ethnic, derived from most of them sharing the same roots in Pondoland in the Eastern Cape. The clearest overt expression of this was the practice of carrying – and using – 'traditional' weapons.

Lastly, the anxieties of the period of negotiation and transition cast a long shadow into the first years of democratic politics, offering incentives to look in the wrong places and learn the wrong lessons about ethnicity and politics in post-apartheid South Africa. The ambiguous ethno-nationalism represented by Buthelezi and the IFP seemed to confirm the expectation of outsiders that African politics are necessarily cast in an ethnic mould, and that the integrity of African states will inevitably be challenged on this basis. This seemed to be regularly confirmed by evidence of the fissiparous nature of African states in the post-Cold War 1990s, a pattern which probably did much to raise the fears of Buthelezi's opponents and the hopes of his overseas, right-wing supporters. The ANC took many of their cues in dealing politically with Buthelezi from elsewhere in Africa; while the top leaders engaged him diplomatically, at all levels below these courtly African exchanges, the ANC routinely compared him to Jonas Savimbi, the Angolan leader, whose insurgent civil war against the MPLA leadership in Angola the apartheid government exploited to great effect in the 1980s. Doubtless there was an element of opportunistic denigration in this, but probably also real fear. As it turned out the political space that opened up in the tense and febrile interregnum between 1990 and 1994 was not conducive to an ethno-nationalist coup, whether at the negotiating table, the ballot box, in the street or the barracks. However, this anxious time did have an effect on the way people thought about and debated ethnicity. The dangers of the period offered an invitation to interpret ethnicity in politics solely in terms of ethno-nationalist separatism and to confidently dismiss the relevance of ethnicity anywhere but in the IFP.

The subsequent history of post-apartheid South Africa suggests that the forms and the locations of ethnicity turned out to be more varied than bargained for by those who accepted that invitation. Not everybody did of course, and sharp exchanges on the role of ethnicity in the IFP–ANC wars of KwaZulu-Natal and the Witwatersrand (now Gauteng), as well as using ethnicity to interpret the internal dynamics of the ANC itself, were a prominent part of the ongoing war of political public relations that characterized the period.

Such disagreements were essentially between those who followed Buthelezi in designating the ANC as 'Xhosa-dominated' and those who upheld the ANC's self-image as being purely pan-tribal and non-racial, some of whom denied outright all meaning and validity to subnational categorization of African people in South Africa. Undue emphasis on designating the ANC as a 'Xhosa organization' and insisting that the conflict between the ANC and the IFP was a tribal war probably hindered proper evaluation of ethnicity as a political force in the late-apartheid and transition years. There were a number of serious stumbling-blocks to this interpretation. Although the fighting spread to the urban areas of the Witwatersrand after 1991, the violence had its origins, lasted the longest and caused more casualties in KwaZulu and Natal. If the war deserved any kind of ethnic designation, it was as a Zulu civil war. It is true that 'Zulu' was a meaningful political identity as well as a linguistic and cultural one, in the sense that through Buthelezi and the IFP, claims made in the language of self-determination were built round it. The same is simply not true of 'Xhosa', and people who used the language and (like Mandela) revered the traditions associated with the name, sought political expression exclusively through the ANC. Despite the ambiguities and vagaries of the ANC's versions of non-racialism and African nationalism, there is no evidence to suggest that they were smokescreens to obscure a 'Xhosa agenda' driving the ANC. It is hard to believe that the many non-Xhosas, including significant numbers of whites and Indians in leadership positions, calculated on rising to power on the back of a Xhosa revolution or were simply its dupes. Even harder to fit into this template would be those Zulu-speakers born and bred in Natal and Zululand who fought against the IFP.

Against this background it is not easy to assess with confidence the place and role of ethnic factors in the politics of post-apartheid South Africa. If the official struggle ideology of the ANC were to be believed, the end of formal white political power should have been the end of ethnicity, since it was the divide-and-rule machinations of colonialism and apartheid that were behind the demon of tribalism. Instead there is a widespread, though somewhat inchoate, popular consciousness of ethnicity, and at least tacit acceptance (including in the ANC) that, 'Whites did not invent African ethnicity out of thin air, and nor indeed did late twentieth-century mobilizers like Mangosuthu Buthelezi' (Glaser 2001: 143). Survey data around the mid-1990s seemed to confirm the strength of ethnic identity, leading to some pessimism about nation-building (Mattes 1999: 273). However, the potential ambiguity of survey findings was demonstrated in Mattes' review of several studies, and he was able to extract a much more optimistic reading for the late 1990s from them: 'over 90 per cent of the legal citizens of South

Africa: (1) accept the appropriateness of the demarcated territory known as South Africa; (2) see themselves as members of that community; and (3) are proud of that membership'. On this basis he was prepared to make a claim for 'widespread patriotism' in South Africa, despite its diverse communal identities, vastly different historic experiences and wide geographic dispersion, and to go further in postulating 'a widespread degree of "state nationalism"' (ibid.). In the face of such inconclusive (and obligingly flexible) evidence, both optimism and pessimism about ethnicity coexisted for the first dozen years or so of South African democracy. Writing in 2001, Glaser takes as his starting point the view that sub-African ethnicity has been 'relatively mute . . . though not entirely silent' in post-apartheid South Africa and in fact, 'It is the relative weakness of sub-African ethnic politics in South Africa, rather than its strength, which needs explaining.' In doing so he points to moderating factors acting on ethnic identities including the long-run effects of modernization and urbanization, the inertial pull of 'large ethnicities' that is, racial identities, and the lack of economic heartlands to consolidate linguistic bases (Glaser 2001: 153–4). Until about 2007 it was the optimistic view that predominated in the upper reaches of analysis (though not in popular consciousness), especially among those inclined to take the ANC at its word: 'A disciplined political movement, the ANC has been historically intolerant of ethnic politicking at provincial or local level' (Butler 2004: 37); or alternatively to believe that what the ANC leadership says actually determines what happens in the regions.

From about 2007 a sea change in the way ethnicity was discussed in public forums took place. A landmark in this transformation was the ANC's national conference in December 2007, not only fixing the change in time, but also marking a change in focus. Up to this point, ethnic identity had been regarded for the most part as an incompatible alternative to the ANC. Whatever identification with the ANC meant to any given individuals – pan-tribalism, non-racialism, black consciousness, pan-Africanism and all the other influences the ANC had absorbed over the decades – it was not supposed to be ethnicity. From this point on, however, it became increasingly acceptable – even fashionable – to recognize that ethnic identity was an integral part of the way the ANC now worked. For a small minority of those who studied and commented on the ANC this was nothing new; it had always been thus. Since 2007 the number of those who are prepared to include ethnicity in interpretations of the ANC's internal dynamics has grown. This new respectability has been licensed by the ANC itself, some of whose leading figures denounce the intrusion of ethnic factors from the organization's pulpit.

According to some accounts which use this new interpretative template, the revolt against Mbeki at and after Polokwane was motivated in part by resentment against the old bugbear – 'Xhosa domination' of the ANC leadership; similarly the breakaway party Congress of the People (COPE), formed by disgruntled Mbeki supporters, was denounced by the ANC itself as an attempt to form a Xhosa party. In this vein, the rise of Jacob Zuma to the ANC leadership was seen as fuelled by a wave of Zulu chauvinism. Subsequently he consolidated his power by high-level appointments of individuals from KwaZulu-Natal in key security and police positions, and secured his second term as ANC president in 2012 by cultivating his home base in KwaZulu-Natal, where ANC votes and membership have increased enormously since 2007. Former ANC Youth League (ANCYL) leader Julius Malema's political and business power base in his home province of Limpopo has been seen by some in similar ethnic terms.

This tendency to look now for ethnic patterns and motivations can be attributed to three separately identifiable factors which nonetheless interact closely with each other. These are the incorrigible regionalism of South African politics; the evolving internal dynamics of the ANC, especially the rise of populism and 'factionalism'; and the emergence of a demotic African voice in popular politics.

Whether under white minority rule or open democracy, regional forces in South African politics have been very strong. This has been the result of the sheer size of the country, patterns of settlement and dispersion of population, variations in sources and rates of economic growth, accentuated by the legacies of pre-Union colonies, republics, kingdoms and other African polities. Regional rivalries in white politics were strong, with Natal a reluctant and sometimes restless partner in Union; the balance of power between the Cape and the Transvaal was always important in the politics of Afrikaner nationalism. The constitutional settlement of 1990–6 recognized this mixed legacy in the interests of democracy and peaceful transition and, by incorporating federal elements which fell short of federalism, perpetuated and underlined that historical legacy. This quasi-federal structure provides that the big-spending budgets (notably health and education) are delivered through provincial and not national government departments, which makes provincial government an important and semi-independent source of patronage and corruption (not to mention dysfunction).

This inherited, regional cast to South African politics interacts with the developing organizational practices of the ANC. The market place of interparty electoral competition has been dominated by the ANC's narrative of struggle against racial injustice in the past, race-based inequality in the present and revolutionary struggle into an indefinite future. On this basis the ANC has achieved close to a two-thirds majority in every national election since 1994. In the shadow of this domination an alternative political market place has developed within the ANC itself, in which contestants compete for strategic positions which will allow them to profit from the party's guaranteed access to governing power. Affirmative action, cadre deployment and BEE provide excellent cover for patronage, especially in those provinces and local government areas where there are few opportunities for self-generated economic advancement. The result has been extensive factional competition to be on lists for electoral office under the country's proportional representation party list system and for leadership positions. This shadow market place used to be denied by the ANC and references to it were largely ascribed to mischief-making by a hostile media and conspiracies by 'reactionary forces' out to destabilize the ANC. Now the phenomenon of factional competition has been documented in successive ANC Secretaries-General' reports, and is reluctantly acknowledged and deplored. This shadow market place has come to dominate public understanding and media discussion of politics in South Africa, as the months preceding the leadership elections at the Mangaung conference in December 2012 made clear.

The dynamics of this shadow political market-place are poorly understood and there is a dearth of hard, factual information. References to allegiances and membership of factions are often vague and obscure and patterns of activity are hard to discern. It is in this context of uncertain affiliation and sparse information that the growing tendency to attribute motivation and tactical choice to ethnicity has taken place.

Several factors have encouraged this. When the ANC came to power in 1994 it subscribed to a mythology that discipline would be maintained by a self-sustaining ethos of self-sacrifice and commitment to common values and ideas. This did not last long. Mbeki tried to substitute strong, central leadership and organizational discipline. This effort to modernize the party was one of the reasons which led to his downfall. There is now a widespread sense, inside the organization as well as in the eyes of outside observers and critics, that the ANC has come adrift both organizationally and ideologically. Ethnic affiliation is one candidate to fill the resulting vacuum of organization and discipline, encouraged by one organizational principle that remains central to the ANC's functioning: the delivery of blocs of provincial votes for elections to the National Executive Committee (NEC) and leadership positions.

In short, in the way the business of both the ANC and of government are organized, central authority is weak, ensuring that provinces are power bases, sources of patronage and sites of struggle for control of resources. As we have seen, provinces correspond to some extent with linguistic and cultural concentrations. This is especially true of the Eastern Cape (isiXhosa), the historic heartland of the ANC and KwaZulu-Natal (isiZulu), formerly the home of Zulu ethno-nationalism and more recently the fastest growing, and by now, biggest concentration of ANC members in the country.

It is a short step from being seen to build a provincial power base to being seen to build an ethnic one, and the strong, gravitational pull to the provinces in the government and ANC has encouraged a blurring of the lines between the two. The temptation to accuse political and factional rivals of playing the ethnic or tribal card is strong.

Another essential contribution to the loosening of restraint on ethnic expressiveness in the ANC has been Zuma's crafting of an exuberant and populist African vernacular style. The ANC has never satisfactorily resolved the different emphases of Articles 3.4 and 3.5 of its own constitution. The former prohibits 'any form of racial, tribalistic or ethnic exclusivism and chauvinism', while the latter promises to respect, 'the linguistic, cultural and religious diversity of its members'. Under Mbeki the ANC's style was bloodless, technocratic and politically correct. Zuma changed all that and offered a populist Africanness, which had the (probably unintended) effect of encouraging awareness of and loosening restraint on the expression of particular ethnicities. It is important to note, however, that Zuma's African vernacular style may be based on his own pride in Zulu language and culture, but it is sufficiently syncretic and general in its appeal – for instance, in its freely expressed masculinity – to be embraced throughout South Africa.

If there has been an 'ethnic turn' in the ANC it has been facilitated by the failure of organizational discipline and the growing tolerance of populism. It has also been encouraged by the gravitational pull of the provinces as building blocks of political mobilization, conduits of government expenditure and sources of patronage. It is important to note, however, that this has been completely unconnected to any separatist ambitions, desire to control natural resources (as elsewhere in Africa) or any systematic programme, overt or covert, to favour an ethnic group or region. It is possible now to observe with the benefit of longer historical perspective that, if there ever was a Xhosa agenda in the leadership of the ANC, then they made a thoroughly bad job of pursuing it. After nearly 20 years of ANC government, Eastern Cape Province, the heartland of the Xhosa people, is a byword for poverty, incompetent government and low development indicators, to the extent that throughout the post-apartheid period it has had, by a considerable margin, the highest outmigration rate of all the provinces (StatsSA 2012: 23).

In summary, it is becoming more important to acknowledge the ethnic factor in the politics of the ANC, but equally important not to exaggerate it. The fact that Zuma hails from KwaZulu-Natal and identifies closely with the language and culture of the African people of that region was central to his successful bid to be re-elected as president of the ANC in December 2012. This is because KwaZulu-Natal is the second largest province by population and the only one in which the ANC has gained substantial numbers of voters and members in recent years. However, while ethnicity may be one factor which helps predict who will rise in the ANC hierarchy, it is of no use in predicting what his or her policies will be, and there is no sign that it is becoming a destabilizing factor either in the ANC or in the country as a whole.

## Division and diversity

This profile of South Africans today suggests that the most stringent stress tests facing South Africa's improvised nation arise from socio-economic disparities and sharp differentials in life chances among its citizens, rather than from the classic nationalist preoccupations with culture, language and kinship, whether ethnic or racial. In this sense it is division rather than diversity that is the problem. In some respects there is nothing particularly revelatory about this. It has been a given of 'normal' democracy that politics is in large measure about organizing to defend and promote interests based on socio-economic divisions and where these are so great or so morally offensive as to be a threat to stability, to work rationally to ameliorate them. To a large extent this last point captures what the official government view of nation-building in South Africa has become.

It is not as simple as this, however. In the South African context it is not feasible to avoid the entanglement of socio-economic disparities with race and to treat them as pure problems of economic policy making. Although this seems to many, if not most people – and certainly to most black people – as obvious in a commonsensical way, it greatly complicates the task of secular, civic nation-building and leads all concerned into varieties of unhelpful doublethink. These expedient habits of mind are partly the legacies of nationalist thought and practice as they developed under apartheid and the struggle against it. It is to these legacies that we now turn.

# PART TWO
# Nationalism and the end of apartheid

# CHAPTER TWO

# Legacies

## From nation to minority: The growth, maturity and decay of Afrikaner nationalism

Most recent analyses of Afrikaner nationalism treat it as a phenomenon created since the mid-nineteenth century in response to assertive British imperialism, along with economic changes brought by the discovery of gold and diamonds and the subsequent strains of urbanization and industrialization in the wake of their exploitation. The forms of political and cultural expression taken by Afrikaner nationalism and its modes of mobilization and organization were subject to change as South Africa and the world around it changed. This account is in marked contrast to the tendency of nationalists everywhere to claim that their nations existed before they became fully conscious of themselves and to stress more or less seamless continuity of development from conveniently distant and obscure origins to an open-ended future. So well defined is Afrikaner nationalism's life cycle of growth, maturity, decay and disappearance, and so accelerated has its trajectory been within a time span of not much more than one hundred years, that its history provides a particularly stiff challenge to the notion that nations are eternal.

The most authoritative chronicler of Afrikaner nationalism describes the slow, gradual and often tentative growth of a 'distinct Afrikaner ethnic consciousness which could be mobilized for political purposes' (Giliomee 1991: 21–3). The group which began to develop this consciousness after about 1870 and became known as 'Afrikaners' was formed from settler stock, particularly from people of Dutch, German and French backgrounds in the seventeenth and eighteenth centuries. Genealogists also calculate a 6 or 7 per cent contribution from non-Europeans. In this version there was also a 'secondary' phase of full-blown Afrikaner consciousness in the twentieth century, intensifying from the 1930s, which culminated in the general election victory in 1948 of the Herenigde ('Reunited') Nasionale Party and the establishment of apartheid. However, the same account cautions against seeing too much organic continuity between these phases and the role of contingency – notably in the election victory of 1948 – is well ventilated in many other historical treatments.

Overcoming constitutional and political obstacles to the development of the apartheid state – notably the suppression of black resistance – took from 1948 until after recovery from the Sharpeville massacre (1960) and the flight of skills and capital that followed it. With the benefit of hindsight it is remarkable how short a period of stability Afrikaner nationalism enjoyed, despite its quite undeserved, contemporary reputation for immovability and permanence. However, between the post-Sharpeville recovery in the early 1960s and the onset of political and economic crisis in the mid-1970s, Afrikaner nationalism and the state it created briefly achieved maturity and deceptive stability. The vehicle for this was a movement which claimed to embody the interests and aspirations of a people defined in ethnic terms irrespective of region, class, religious denomination (although Calvinism of one kind or another provided a binding force) or other difference. It was led by a political party and rested on a base of educational, cultural and social organizations, which functioned to encourage kinship and conformity, partly by assertively discouraging deviance. Despite these forces for unity, the movement was not monolithic, but a coalition of economic, social and cultural interests. It had an organizing ideology which contained many strains and attempted to serve varied ends and interests. Among these were: Afrikaner nationalist claims to self-determination; white fears of being swamped in a black state; the control and direction of African labour; community organization along the lines of communal segregation and discrimination, and securing a disproportionate share of public spending for whites. Despite this eclectic and not always harmonious nature, apartheid ideology served as a focal point, giving justification, direction and interpretation. The people (*volk*) in question was defined in terms of ethnic kinship and common historical experience, as separate from British imperialism in both its metropolitan and local settler forms, and from the black majority population. Relatively few in number and lacking geographical concentration, Afrikaner nationalists were forced to stress unity at all costs. They set out to concoct a system, through partition and repression, in which they would be in a majority. This 'White South Africa', under Afrikaner leadership and dominance over other white groups, would satisfy them (if no-one else) in terms of self-determination, upward social and economic mobility and democracy in the form of racial oligarchy under ethnic leadership.

Probably more was written about Afrikaner nationalism in the last third of the twentieth century, in both academic and popular accounts, than about any other nationalist movement. This was true even before the South

African liberation struggle became one of the defining conflicts of the late twentieth century. To some extent this reflected a fascination with how long such an apparently anachronistic movement could survive. Afrikaner nationalism's enticing mixture of ancient and modern was irresistible to Western metropolitan audiences, offering something to everybody. To conservatives and reactionaries (not to mention racists) it offered a case study in swimming against the tides of the late twentieth century and thus was the subject of sympathy and envy, sometimes open, often covert. Liberals, progressives, Third World nationalists and Marxists were appalled and baffled at the nationalists' effrontery: Afrikaner nationalism threw down all sorts of theoretical and political gauntlets to them all. Each tendency in its own way took up the challenge of liberating the understanding of Afrikaner nationalism from the nationalists' own idealist terms of reference.

The cross-fertilization between popular and academic accounts of Afrikaner nationalism and the nationalists' own self-understanding produced some vivid characterizations. There was the 'granite monolith', usefully evoked by the official Afrikaner taste for megalithic monuments and the forbidding aspect of late-apartheid architecture. This characterization emphasized primordial attachments and tablet-like verities on subjects such as the inevitability of conflict as a result of racial contact. There was the 'white tribe' image which usefully reflected the nationalists' own claims to be indigenous to Africa yet unique in it. It also appeared to confirm the inevitably tribal nature of all identities and affiliations in Africa, another plank in the case of official Afrikaner self-justification. More academically arcane and less part of popular discourse was the image of a 'fragment society' (in South Africa's case two societies, Dutch and English) in which European values and concepts in settler societies are warped and refracted by arid isolation and the African sun. Unsurprisingly, given the centrality of the Dutch Reformed Church to Afrikaner nationalism, theology has provided a rich vein of interpretation and imagery. 'Puritans in Africa' and 'peoples of the Covenant' (other examples of which are Israel and Ulster Protestants) are cases in point. A classic statement of the Covenant interpretation rather baldly puts the idealist case, which the other images share to a greater or lesser extent. Afrikaner nationalists belong to one of the societies which are much more determined by belief than economics: 'In these parts of the world, mind literally overcomes matter' (Akenson 1992: 146).

What these and other similar accounts had in common, apart from their idealism, was an image of fixity, if not immovability. However, as early as the beginning of the 1970s, alternative approaches to understanding Afrikaner nationalism were being developed. The publication in 1971 of German–Canadian sociologist Heribert Adams's *Modernizing Racial Domination* was a seminal moment. From this point, through the 1970s and 1980s a number of works were published whose principal quality was to stress the pragmatic and *adaptive* nature of Afrikaner nationalism.

Central to this change of emphasis was the work of Afrikaner historian and political scientist Hermann Giliomee, who often wrote in collaboration with Heribert Adam and South African sociologist Lawrence Schlemmer. These writers acknowledged the legitimacy of identity concerns, especially that of language, as a focus for political value, for political mobilization and as interests to pursue and defend. They saw them as real, not products of some glib formula such as 'false consciousness', to which attempts at Marxist deconstruction of nationalism were prone to resort to in some degree or another. However, they saw these concerns in instrumental rather than in transcendent terms, and they were determined not to be seduced either into taking nationalists at their own estimation, or by the pleasures of easy moralizing at their expense.

In this version, Afrikaner nationalism provided a template for nation-building. If ever a nation was invented, this was it. Language, race, ethnicity, political mythology, economic mobilization and, latterly, ruthless exercise of the prerogatives of state power, were all deployed in this epic of pragmatism. However, the central message was that all this was done in the service of a project of transformation by bringers of modernization, and even where self-conscious use was made of theology and political mythology, the roots of the project were not in isolation, backwardness and transcendental idealism but in self-conscious striving for political and economic development. The purpose behind the drive for modernization and the nation- and state-building it required was cultural and economic survival in the face, first of the various challenges of British imperialism and later the perception of a looming threat from the political aspirations of an African majority.

It was not difficult to read into this interpretation a message for the politics of the 1970s and 1980s. It pointed to a possible way forward; South African conflicts can legitimately be understood in communal terms (indeed they must be); Afrikaners have legitimate communal and identity concerns, however, they are not sacramental but of this world and should be treated with realism; Afrikaner nationalism is adaptive and transformative, so faced with an impasse and under crisis conditions it can be expected to and encouraged to change, if these legitimate concerns are addressed with respect, rather than moral condemnation and revolutionary rhetoric. The message was delivered with due acknowledgement of the appalling damage wrought by apartheid on the lives of black people; it contained many caveats, and gave due weight to contingency, but it was clear enough. The combination of motives which inspired it may have included objective scholarship and/or desire to make an intervention in an increasingly fraught and dangerous situation: this mattered little, then as now. The message was there to be read and heard.

Certainly by the mid-1970s, the need for new thinking and new approaches was alarmingly apparent. The economic and political crisis which was signalled by strikes in the major port and manufacturing centre of Durban in 1973, and confirmed by the Soweto uprising in 1976, showed Afrikaner nationalists a number of things: the economic costs of imposing apartheid; the limits to their freedom of action imposed by economic interdependence (albeit an unequal one) with that part of the black majority that now had a foothold in urban areas and in the industrial economy; the deterioration of the demographic position of whites; the resilience of black resistance and its ability to challenge repression through a combination of old forms in new circumstances (mass protests, boycotts, armed action) and new forms of organization (trade unions and black consciousness groups); the failure of 'independent' homelands to gain any but tiny, opportunistic acceptance either inside or outside the country, as was demonstrated by the case of Transkei in 1976; the ominous widening of the frontline of struggle though the intensification of guerrilla war in Rhodesia and the independence of Portugal's African colonies. Under these circumstances it was clear to enough supporters of the government that would make a difference, that the costs of repression would inevitably escalate and that resources were finite.

The various elements of this crisis were objectively difficult enough to manage, but to make matters worse the base from which the government had to deal with it – Afrikaner nationalism and the nation it had invented – was a lot less stable than it looked. Indeed, successful as the project had been, it was still riddled with contradictions and ambiguities. In a movement that set such store by its Christian character, there was the glaring problem of squaring the universality of Christianity with the racial exclusiveness of apartheid. Afrikaners' communal identity depended so much on a mythology of victimhood and struggle for self-determination against British imperialism, that it was difficult to reconcile this with oppressing other peoples and denying genuine self-determination to them. The nationalists' self-image depended so much on being a people indigenous to Africa yet they insistently emphasized being 'Europeans' in the language of discrimination and in the self-appointed role – just like the imperialists – of being the bearers and defenders of 'civilization' on the continent. The status of being 'white' threatened to confuse the basis of identity claims. Clearly there were times when being white trumped the ethnic designation for reasons of strategic convenience and others when being Afrikaner trumped the racial designation in the interests of a purer form of nationalism. Underlying most if not all of these conundrums was a moral question: what value is survival if it can be gained only through the denial of justice to others? Much theological, philosophical, ideological and jurisprudential hard labour went into trying to reconcile these contradictions because the inventors of the Afrikaner nation were, if nothing else, people who valued and pursued justification for their actions in the eyes of men, God and themselves, in ascending order of probability of success.

However, important these contradictions were in the Afrikaners' sense of self, they were not the most important. Greater concerns centring on the geopolitics of who occupied what territory were crucial. Afrikaner nationalism lacked only one thing to be the most successfully crafted nation of modern times. Unfortunately it was the most important element of all – a territorial base in which the nation that claimed self-determination constituted an unambiguous demographic majority.

The political conflicts of apartheid South Africa were often interpreted in 'communal' terms and as symptoms of a 'divided society'. Understandably these terms were not universally acceptable, some arguing that they conceded too much to the Afrikaner nationalists' terms of reference. However, the conflicts were indeed about competing senses of nationhood and rival claims to self-determination, both based on conflicting claims to territory, reflecting on the one hand a primal sense of dispossession, and on the other a tenacious sense of long-held assets under siege-like conditions. In these respects the 'communal' and 'divided' labels make sense. Self-determination has probably caused more trouble (and possibly more deaths) than any other abstract democratic concept in the past hundred years or so. Deceptively simple, it is in fact based on a riddle. 'On the surface self-determination seemed reasonable: let the people decide. It was in fact ridiculous because the people cannot decide until someone decides who are the people' (Jennings 1956: 56). A particularly intractable form of self-determination dispute revolves around the status of settler-descended populations in colonial or post-colonial situations. Do they form part of inclusive nations with indigenous majorities? Do they have a claim to separate political existence in a form of state which reflects and secures their choice?

Afrikaner nationalism's answers were characteristically robust, but equally characteristically they were constructed with gravity-defying logic. According to this logic, there was no greater South African nation; South Africa was not even a nation of minorities, the territory and peoples were divided into a constellation of nations. The only solution to the questions of coexistence thrown up by this diagnosis – which also included a crude theory of conflict under which all forms of interracial contact inevitably led to friction – was partition. Partition was the most important element in apartheid; failure to conclude partition satisfactorily would mean the failure of the whole project because partition provided the basis for whatever claims apartheid could make to validity in terms other than naked racial self-interest. This fiction rested on the erroneous assumption, indeed the fantasy, that the division of South Africa into a white state and independent states for the black 'nations' would be expressions of the same democratic principle of self-determination for all of them and should be regarded as being within internationally accepted norms. In addition, if wholesale population transfers of black people could be carried out from 'white South Africa' to the homelands, then white claims to political supremacy would not appear so unjust or repressive.

'Grand apartheid' or 'separate development', as apartheid-as-partition was variously known, was undermined by several fatal flaws of self-defeating logic. In the first place, in its creators' eyes grand apartheid had to be buttressed by the remorseless application of 'petty apartheid' in white South Africa. Building on the basis of colonial colour bars of various kinds, petty apartheid was needed to reinforce the alien status of blacks and their lack of rights in white South Africa. Without petty apartheid there would be no logic for directing blacks to the homelands to enjoy their rights. In any case the 'friction' theory that racial contact always and inevitably leads to conflict demanded petty apartheid. The problem was that petty apartheid completely undermined any hope of rationalizing apartheid as a just solution to conflicting claims of self-determination.

In the second place, partition was to be carried out under colonial or quasi-colonial terms; that is, in a completely one-sided way. However, even if the white government had been inclined to negotiate a division of territory and population instead of imposing it by force, any substantial black negotiating partner would have rejected it outright. The third example of self-defeating logic was the fact that partition was based on the 1936 Land Act which meant that the homelands only received 13 per cent of greater South Africa's surface area. This therefore meant that they could never compete with the major centres of population and already-developed economy in 'white' South Africa; they would remain pitifully dependent on subventions from the white government. However, if the government unilaterally or by negotiation granted the kind of resources that would make the homelands viable, it would be helping to create states with which it might find certain areas of coexistence difficult, such as the treatment of blacks in South Africa and irredentist claims. Far from reducing conflict, partition on this basis would institutionalize it. If on the other hand the homelands were kept so that they could be manipulated at will, then their puppet status would be obvious and there would always be a black majority population in white South Africa, which meant petty apartheid, imposed by repression in perpetuity.

As if these three things were not enough, there was another fatal source of self-deception. Generally it proved impossible to manufacture plausible national identities out of the ethnic materials at hand. Even where the materials were most promising, as they were in the Zulu homeland of KwaZulu, the Nationalist government could not forge an unequivocal commitment to partition on the part of their interlocutor. In Chief Buthelezi, they found a leader who would play the ethnic game, but he had his own ideas on the rules, and the ethnic materials at his disposal were substantial enough to give him a strong hand which later he could play to advantage with the ANC too. Lastly, and perhaps most telling in all issues of identity and partition, no plausible scheme could be found which could bestow national aspirations on the Coloured (mixed race) or Indian populations and fit them into a scheme of territorial division.

It is not possible to fix with authority the point at which apartheid-as-partition officially ceased to be the vehicle for expressing Afrikaner aspirations to self-determination. Indeed the point is obscured by the split which saw the breakaway of the Conservative Party (CP) from the National Party (NP). This breaking point came over the introduction of power-sharing institutions to accommodate Indian and Coloured political rights with whites. However, radical neo-partition, to create a more viable white South Africa, became the policy which defined the CP and the paramilitary Afrikaner Weerstandsbeweging (AWB) which supported it. Perhaps F. W. de Klerk's epitaph for grand apartheid will suffice to fix the point in time when, summarizing the homelands' lack of viability, their rejection by the vast majority of black South Africans and noting the rejection of independence by six of the ten homelands, he cites a 'hardly noticed announcement' in P. W. Botha's 'Rubicon' speech of 15 August 1985 as 'the death knell for separate development'. In Botha's words, 'Should any of the black National States therefore prefer not to accept independence, such states or communities will remain part of the South African nation, are South African citizens and should be accommodated within the political institutions within the boundaries of South Africa' (De Klerk 1997). This, according to De Klerk, 'set the government on the road that ultimately led to the transformation of our society' and as a result, a substitute for partition had to be found. The answer was accommodation through constitutional engineering.

By the time P. W. Botha spoke in 1985, power-sharing schemes had been exhaustively aired and debated for several years. Dutch political scientist Arend Lijphart's ideas on consociational schemes of constitutional engineering were commonplace reference points in academic debate from the late 1970s onwards, and became absorbed in political and policy-making circles shortly thereafter (see, for example, Lijphart 1977). Elite pacting, mutual veto, segmental autonomy and grand coalition all became familiar concepts. However, all too often the rather demanding contextual conditions for success, which Lijphart and others painstakingly elaborated, were marginalized in the discussions, and the schemes concocted by the Nationalist government to represent accommodation bore no great fidelity to consociation theory. As the then opposition leader Frederick van Zyl Slabbert put it: 'The underlying philosophy of the President's Council recommendations, as well as the Government's constitutional guidelines, represent, the crudest bastardisation imaginable of the logic of consociational democracy. It is academically too embarrassing to take seriously' (1983: 43). It may have been based on smoke and mirrors, but arguably even in this form accommodation was an advance on partition as a basis for further progress towards the substance and not merely the appearance of democracy.

However, in two respects accommodation displayed a disturbing degree of continuity with apartheid. In the first place, the process of 'reform' was almost as one-sided as partition. The initiatives, the executive actions and the tests of approval took place almost exclusively within the white polity. The development of policies of accommodation went hand in hand with, indeed was made possible by the violent suppression of all black resistance to reform. In the second place, accommodation represented only a partial retreat from racial separation. The tricameral constitution of 1983 represented the incorporation Coloureds and Indians (viewed as minorities vis-à-vis both whites and Africans) into the white polity. This guaranteed them limited power-sharing, at the expense of entrenching the principle of apartheid in the concept of reserving groups' rights to administer generously defined 'own affairs'. This entrenched white domination. No coherent or meaningful alternative was found for Africans. The useful coinage 'constitutionalized apartheid' (Giliomee and Schlemmer 1989: 140) captures the essence of the phenomenon.

To make matters worse, the lack of clarity and coherence of the power-sharing schemes became legendary. Prior to 1990 the NP had reached a low point in this respect by decreeing that while all South Africans would be enfranchised by virtue of their membership of a particular racial group, anyone who rejected this racial basis could choose to enjoy political rights as part of a 'non-group group'. The 'non-group group' concept usefully marks how far these constitutional 'reforms' departed from any conceivable political reality. In the parlance of the day, while the Mafia would make you an offer you cannot refuse, the NP would make you an offer you cannot understand.

By the time De Klerk became president in September 1989 the Afrikaner constituencies he and his party represented were already far down the road towards a group identity quite different from that with which he and they had grown up. Apartheid-as-partition had been abandoned as unworkable and ceded to the neo-partitionist Afrikaner right-wing, along with the goal of territorial self-determination as the highest expression of national identity. The form of identity on offer was shifting in its base and ambiguous in its expression. Whiteness had always been part of Afrikaner nation-building, albeit an ambiguous and contested element as regards English speakers, but now it became ever-more important in the face of the split in Afrikanerdom. Ever since the introduction of the tricameral constitution as the centrepiece of reform apartheid, Coloureds and Indians had an acknowledged part, though ambiguous and contested one, in identity politics. However, at the bottom of all this shape-shifting and remoulding of plastic identities, core Afrikaner concerns remained and the state was still an overwhelmingly Afrikaner-dominated set of organs. The power to determine the boundaries of these identities and the means by which they would be expressed politically remained largely with the state. Both these things were lost as a result of De Klerk's 1990 reforms and the negotiation process that followed, the next and final stage in the divorce of Afrikaner and white claims to group identity from overtly national forms.

De Klerk's achievement is generally understood along the following lines. By lifting the bans on the ANC and other liberation movements, he created the conditions for a negotiated settlement to the South African conflict by freeing his opponents from repressive restrictions on their political activities. He took the community he represented beyond privilege by abolishing the formal inequalities which protected 'his own' people and disadvantaged others. He took Afrikaners beyond the politics of ethnic and racial identity into a situation of shared and formally equal citizenship and mutual cultural recognition with other 'groups' who were previously defined as irredeemably 'other'. In doing so he recognized that neither Afrikaners nor whites generally constitute a self-determining nation, but a minority, or minorities, within a greater South African nation. He came to accept, however reluctantly, the impracticality of elaborate constitutional mechanisms based on ethnic or racial affiliation ('group rights'). He achieved this in the face of vehement political opposition from something like one-third of white voters and a majority of Afrikaners many of whom resorted to paramilitary mobilization to express their resistance.

Not everybody would agree with this summary of De Klerk's leadership. There is ample scope for debate as to how much these developments owed to his personal initiative and direction and how much to political, economic and social changes which long preceded his emergence as the custodian of Afrikaner and white interests, a point which he frequently noted himself. There is also plenty of room for discussion on how far he intended the results and the extent to which he, like Mikhail Gorbachev in a frequently cited comparison, was overtaken by events and outmanoeuvred by determined opponents. In the last analysis the crude demographic balance of power forced him to accept much he did not want. Despite these caveats, there are grounds for the claim that De Klerk was responsible for leading whites and Afrikaners out of narrow identity politics and into a post-nationalist discourse of secular citizenship and constitutional rights where, if there was to be any nation at all, it would not be based on race or ethnicity.

Although De Klerk has been praised for bold and visionary leadership, the project with which he has been identified – divorcing white and Afrikaner identity politics from explicit nationalist claims – was fraught with ambiguities of meaning and agency. These were obscured in the urgency and high stakes of the interregnum during which negotiation and transition took place, and by the relief and euphoria which surrounded the first years of democracy and majority rule. The core ambiguity concerned the status and meaning of white and Afrikaner identities. One message was that the 'white' and 'Afrikaner' retained their meaning as identities which were the bearers of rights and group interests, but that it was no longer strategically possible to express the identities and pursue the interests through overt nationalist mobilization and claims to territorial self-determination. The De Klerk project began on this basis and with the promise to express these identities and interests through negotiating special statuses within an overall context of equal rights and uniform citizenship. When this failed, De Klerk was in the awkward position of persuading those he represented that their identities were still meaningful, but that in the overall interests of stability and democracy they would now be protected only by uniform citizenship and equal rights.

How did such a compromised and ambiguous project meet with such success? The Afrikaner nationalist coalition, which dominated white politics and suppressed black political aspirations so forcefully from 1948, was such a highly elaborated movement of ethnic mobilization and wielded state power with such determination and at times ferocity, that its progressive denationalization and demobilization seem to confirm the mythology of the so-called South African Miracle.

In fact, as we have seen, the Afrikaner nationalist coalition had a number of attributes which made this transformation possible. In the first place, despite its image as a granite monolith, Afrikaner nationalism was quite flexible and pragmatic. It is true that for nearly all of its history in power, Afrikaner nationalism was inflexible on the issue of sharing political rights in common with Africans, and that in the service of this grand apartheid, the application of detailed racial ideology (petty apartheid) could be inflexible and dogmatic. However, from the beginning it had to be flexible enough to accommodate elements that were not always internally coherent. Disparate class and ideological interests when combined with regional peculiarities meant that nationalism and apartheid were throughout their lifetime works in progress – contested at that – rather than revealed truths on which the final word had been said.

This quality was greatly heightened by the nature of the Afrikaner nationalist project. It was a task of transformation rather than preservation. The survival of the nation which Afrikaner nationalism invented and elaborated depended on its transformation from a people of labourers and farmers to one of managers, administrators and professionals in both public and private sectors of an advanced, industrial economy, presided over by an increasingly powerful state. Inevitably this project yielded far-reaching change in the class structure of Afrikaner nationalism and when, in the early 1980s, Botha began to talk of the need to 'adapt or die', he was merely transferring to the new challenge of coming to terms with black political aspirations what had always been the working principle of his predecessors. The one thing Afrikaner nationalism could never afford to do was stand still. Its most enduring myth was one of an epic journey, the Great Trek. Despite the best efforts of English-speaking historians, Afrikaner nationalists never quite accepted that the frontier had closed. And for those that did grasp that the frontier had closed in South Africa, there was always the continental frontier. When Botha threw down this challenge, there were enough people in his core constituency for whom change and movement had some experiential resonance, to make his slogan ideologically plausible. And when De Klerk took the process of change much further than his predecessor, enough of *his* constituency (in influence if not in numbers) felt sufficiently secure in the skills and assets they had acquired to contemplate doing without, not only the formal protection of discriminatory legislation, but also the aspiration to be a self-determining national community.

The denationalization of Afrikaner politics was also facilitated by the high degree of integration of the Afrikaner nationalist coalition. Although it broke up when the CP broke away, there was little danger of the reformers being overwhelmed by revolt from below. The CP confined itself to constitutional opposition and achieved only limited electoral success. Whatever the political strains in the coalition, its constituents – workers, farmers, capitalists, churchmen, intellectuals, cultural entrepreneurs and latterly soldiers and bureaucrats – were tightly bound together, often by family ties and there was little room for traditions of popular initiative or independent action by any one class- or interest-based group. The realities of demography were well-enough understood to make the dangers of destabilization apparent. In any case the dividends of social mobility gave most whites much to lose. These things meant that any radical core of discontent could be labelled as outsiders, losers and fanatics.

Another critical factor was that from the late 1970s the state apparatus rather than the party, far less the *volk*, had become the focus of Afrikaner nationalism. The state was effectively insulated from capture (or recapture) from below, and as long as the modernizers and reformers kept a critical mass of support in the upper reaches of the bureaucracy and the military, their strategies were secure from opposition.

Lastly, the division of the Afrikaner nationalist coalition was sealed by the breakaway to form the CP and the growth of the paramilitary AWB. Debilitating though this may have been in some respects for the prospects and progress of reform during the 1980s, it performed a crucial function in consolidating and pushing forward the reform project in the De Klerk era. The neo-nationalism of the CP and the AWB looked to radical repartition to save the concept of Afrikaner (and white) self-determination from the equivocation and betrayal of reform. But so unpromising was this alternative as a basis for peace and international acceptance that it could be portrayed by reformers as a kind of 'dark other' which, even if only by default, gave meaning to an otherwise somewhat incoherent project. De Klerk and his supporters played this card for all it was worth, especially during the whites-only referendum (17 March 1992) in which a 'yes' vote was a mandate for De Klerk to continue down the road of negotiation with the ANC. Nothing strengthened De Klerk's hand in delivering a majority of whites for the new order more than the all-too-plausible doomsday scenarios which could be attached to radical, white neo-nationalism. One of De Klerk's most effective posters was 'If you want majority rule vote "no".' As it turned out of course, a 'yes' vote had the same result.

Although the endogenous factors discussed so far were central to delivering enough support from the Afrikaner nationalist coalition (and crucially from the upper reaches of the Afrikaner state apparatus) to make denationalization viable, some external factors also worked in De Klerk's favour. Prominent among these was the fact that the ANC's prosecution of its armed struggle scarcely touched the white population directly. How to distribute credit for this has yet to be resolved by historians. The repressive capabilities of the white state (and its bantustan allies), strategic and perhaps ethical choice of ANC politico-military commanders and limited operational capacity of the ANC's armed wing, Umkhonto we Sizwe (MK) all played a part. Whatever the case, if whites (and especially Afrikaners) had felt that they were the target of an ethnically or racially motivated communal assault, then they would have been much more difficult to deliver for a project of reform and ultimately denationalization.

The international context in which De Klerk embarked on the final journey of Afrikaner and white identity politics was certainly helpful in some respects. Gorbachev's reforms in the Soviet Union deprived the ANC of its staunchest supporter; the subsequent fall of communism in Eastern Europe and the breakup of the Soviet Union caused confusion in the ANC Alliance, and greatly increased the credibility both of Western liberal constitutional forms and values and of Western capitalism. All of these things strengthened De Klerk's hand. However, his position was undercut by the extraordinary international prestige bestowed on Nelson Mandela, which was to a large extent transferred to the ANC. It helped to soften the liberation movement's image, to conceal how shallow its resources of capacity and leadership were, and at the same time to camouflage the many fissures and contradictions in the movement.

Another external factor concerns the nature of African nationalism. At its simplest it is easier to redefine your own political aspirations in post-nationalist terms if you are not confronted by an aggressive 'other' nationalism to which you have to submit. South Africa's conflicts were often characterized in terms of a clash between Afrikaner and African nationalism. To some extent this is true, but in its final phases the conflict was between an increasingly fragmented and demobilized Afrikaner nationalism and an inchoate and ambiguous African nationalism. As we shall see in the next section, African nationalism was a powerful emotional force in the last stages of the struggle. However, the ANC's strategic political choices, the diversity of the anti-apartheid coalition and the anomalous position of some important African political forces – notably Chief Buthelezi and the Inkatha movement – kept official expressions of African nationalism comfortably vague and relatively unthreatening to anyone who might fall outside them. As with the case of the armed struggle, it is debatable how much the underplaying of African nationalism was a deliberate, confidence-building strategy in a conflict that was heading for negotiation rather than violence, or was more to do with factors internal to the ANC and its constellation of allies, or whether in general terms the conditions for a hegemonic African nationalism simply did not exist. Whatever the case, however, the relatively low profile which African nationalism had in the final stages of the struggle certainly helped in dissolving the national aspirations of white and Afrikaner politics.

This had the additional benefit of helping portray the final act as a bargaining contest over the shape of secular citizenship rights and institutions that would manage them, rather than a confrontation between competing and antagonistic expressions of identity needs. This quality was not completely absent of course. It lurked beneath the surface on both sides of the negotiation table, and it openly inspired the radical neo-nationalism of the CP, the AWB and the Afrikaner Volksfront (AV), as well as the Zulu, ethno-national concerns of Buthelezi and Inkatha. However, the operating principle of 'sufficient consensus' between the ANC and the NP, which emerged to drive the negotiations forward, was able to marginalize the identity dimension of the negotiation process. With the focus on rights and institutions rather than identity there was substantial inertial pressure for continuity, another quality that was crucial in taking whites beyond identity politics. Of course, the accumulated *detritus* of apartheid institution-building – tricameral parliaments and bantustans – would be swept away and the administration would be drastically rationalized. However, the political and military institutions of state that mattered to whites were not swept away. They were extensively reworked to operate in a constitutional democracy and to better reflect South Africa's demography, but they remained quite recognizable, and whites did not have to accommodate themselves to new and alien structures and practices of government. Indeed, the spectacle of the liberation movement struggling to accommodate itself to the very institutions (including significantly the security forces), which it had dedicated itself to overthrow, was a comforting one for whites and it helped Afrikaners in particular see themselves as something other than a nation.

These things also helped smooth the progress of the final acts of reform and negotiation, even though the outcome was not what De Klerk had argued for and not what many whites who voted 'yes' in March 1992 had expected. The ANC was unimpressed by arguments about deeply divided societies and constitutionally engineered special rights for self-described minorities within them. As far as the liberation movement was concerned these were nothing more than new bottles to contain the old wine of racial privilege, and they would have none of them. Their hand was strengthened by four critical facts: their knowledge that the Western powers would not support De Klerk's conception of power-sharing; the sheer demographic weight of their support which was now free to express itself; their capacity to destabilize government if they felt they needed to and by the knowledge that the white reformers could not make common cause with the rejectionists in defence of something as nebulous as power-sharing.

## Out of the past: Into the future

All that is solid melts into air, all that is holy is profaned and man is compelled to face with sober senses his real condition of life and his relations with his kind.

Marx and Engels 2012: 38

The words of the Communist Manifesto provide an unlikely text for true believers in Afrikaner nationalism, but if they had read them in the mid-1990s they would have found in them powerful echoes of their own experience and their own condition. What had 'melted into air' in the decade or so before South Africa's first democratic election (1994) and constitution (1996) was a symbiotic trinity: Afrikaner nationalism; apartheid as a set of laws and practices and the Afrikaner state which coordinated and managed the mutual dependence between the other two. This trinity was solid enough, especially to those who felt the burdens of its exclusions and its oppressive intolerance to those who opposed it. To true believers it had indeed been holy. To those who subscribed to it, who depended on it and served it, the purpose of this trinity was precisely to save them from having to 'face with sober senses their real condition of life and their relations with their kind'. The elaborate ideological façade that made this evasion possible was penetrated by the *verligtes* (the 'enlightened ones') who drove the reform project that turned, with what degree of intention on their part it is difficult to say, to one of denationalization. However, they were motivated by the understanding that this façade merely concealed a conflicted hinterland that urgently needed to be engaged with. For this, despite all their hesitations, qualifications and obfuscations, they deserve credit. If this is true of the intellectual (and moral) leaders, the mass of Afrikaners who saw the disappearance of much of what had structured their world and given it meaning were faced with the choice of what to take forward from the past to help them face their 'real condition of life' and their relations 'with their kind'. After the demise of their pretensions to be a nation, they had to decide how much of this legacy would continue to demand distinctive recognition and how much might be selectively incorporated into the mixture of a new South African sense of identity.

In the first place they could face the future from an impressive material base. By 1994, Afrikaners had narrowed the once-formidable income gap between themselves and English speakers to a negligible distance. By measures like ownership of listed companies, Afrikaners were also well placed. Heavy investment in mother-tongue schools and universities meant access to skills and social capital on favourable linguistic terms. Provided there was not a direct assault of expropriation – the property rights provisions of the new Constitution offered protection against that – and although Afrikaners were stratified economically and socially like any comparable community, generally they could face the future with some confidence.

There were, however, non-material dimensions to the challenge of finding a place in the new order while recasting or jettisoning altogether those identity needs that once seemed so secure. It is as well to be cautious about attributing essential qualities about a group or a people and in doing so reduce its members to bearers of a few collective characteristics. On the other hand, it would be foolish to ignore vernacular beliefs about self and other that pervade discourse among and about South Africa's various historically constructed peoples. Nations are invented and dissolved not only in the theories of cultural entrepreneurs, but also in the everyday market-place of vernacular self-belief and image in the eyes of others. Several themes emerge from the past and have a bearing on how Afrikaners faced a future without a nation.

The first is an attachment to Africa, a resolution to have no other home and to celebrate Africa's qualities with a devotion that borders on the mystical. This is combined with a sense of challenge and threat that did much to shape the concerns of cultural and even physical survival which loomed large in the invention of the Afrikaner nation. Harshness of climate, both literal and figurative, is central to this motif. Terrain, weather, contact with alien forms of human society all played their part in constructing it. Evocation of a pioneer spirit usually accompanies this, albeit latterly in somewhat *ersatz* terms. Even those Afrikaners whose lives are irredeemably suburban (which is to say nearly all of them) will happily opine for the foreign visitor: 'Afrika is nie n' plek vir sissies nie' ('Africa is not for the faint-hearted'). Such is the enduring power of frontier mythology in the nationalist or even post-nationalist imagination.

The attachment to Africa overlaps with a second element of self-portraiture, that of openness to the numinous in both public and private life. This was most visible in the central part played by formal religion in the construction of Afrikaner nationalism and Afrikaans collective life generally. However, it has taken other forms, notably the felt experience of the landscape in literature, especially poetry. Susceptibility to such romantic and spiritual sentiments is perhaps more widely diffused in Afrikaner society than in other comparable populations – probably by design as much as by natural affiliation. Certainly such evocation of the numinous was influential in bestowing a transcendent quality on the Afrikaner's sense of nationhood.

To these things might be added a sense of kinship in which the upward mobility of the collective was inseparable from individual advance. This was a community whose weakest members would be supported – though usually at heavy cost to those considered outside the nation.

A fourth element that was crucial in binding Afrikaners together was one that Afrikaner nationalism had in common with many other nationalisms; that is a sense of historical wrong, principally at the hands of British imperialism. By the 1970s and 1980s most of the Afrikaners' self-composed agenda of redress had been accomplished. The achievements included in the polity are separation from the British crown and Commonwealth in an independent republic; reinvented national symbols and reshaped institutions; ethnic capture of the public service; equality of language with English. Much had been achieved in the economy too: substantial ownership of listed companies; ethnic preference in what was often sheltered public employment; support for ethnic entrepreneurs and a central role in economic development for parastatal companies, which were as ethnically dominated as the public service.

Impressive as all of this was for a demographically challenged and somewhat isolated people, these achievements had a number of paradoxical effects. Equality of respect for culture and language was not gracefully achieved and there was a strong element of overreach in both goals and means. The classic, but by no means, sole example of this was the imposition of Afrikaans as a language of instruction on African school children. This triggered the 1976 Soweto uprising, an event recognized as the key turning point in the development of the last phases of the liberation struggle. To a significant degree, respect for the Afrikaners' culture and language was extorted rather than freely given and many Afrikaners knew it.

Another paradoxical effect of righting the historical wrong by achieving prosperity and esteem was that these developments were helped to an extent by isolation that was both self- and externally imposed. Prosperity promised take-off into an increasingly globalized, secular and materialist world, and at the same time threatened to remove the shelter behind which the cultural and linguistic achievements had been fostered. Lastly, each item that was ticked off on the agenda of historical redress loosened the ties which bound the ethnic coalition together, accentuating the difference between those for whom explicit and narrow ethnic mobilization was becoming an encumbrance and those who clung to it either through ideological zealotry or feelings of individual and collective insecurity. The combined effect of these paradoxes was to set challenges of preservation in the short and long term. This in turn called for recalculation of threats and prioritizing what could and must be preserved from the achievements of the past.

The fifth component of Afrikaners' sense of self and the final one for our purposes was a need for collective self-justification; a preoccupation with rule-bound behaviour, with legalism if not always with justice. To have the right and to be in the right were important components of self-image, although justification for the provenance and status of the binding rules and the legitimacy of applying them to others received little official attention.

Naturally not all these tendencies were present in all Afrikaner nationalists all of the time, nor did they always necessarily pull in the same direction; they could be a source of contradiction as well as integration. Indeed some of them – notably the last – helped motivate those few Afrikaners who opposed the invention and expansion of the Afrikaner nation on grounds of conscience. Be that as it may, these ingredients of individual and collective self-image and self-promotion were important shaping influences, not least in how others saw Afrikaners as potential partners in or disrupters of the new South Africa. What influence might they have as the Afrikaners made the transition from nation to minority?

Probably the most fertile source of comfort and leverage in the new South Africa was the attachment to Africa. The vanity image of being a white tribe in Africa could be reworked for a new set of circumstances. Hitherto the idea of a tribe, of African soil but with access to Western skills, technology and forms of socio-political organization, underpinned the Afrikaners' claims to lead and rule. Reworked to emphasize being at the service of the new order rather than dominating it, this somewhat hackneyed motif still had some life in it. There was an ancillary ingredient that could be invoked. Afrikaners habitually promoted themselves as being more honest in their dealings with Africans than the English (both metropolitan and local); hard perhaps, but plain speaking and not deceitful. To a degree that has always baffled English speakers, Africans often appear to concede this point, though this might at times be for reasons of politeness or strategic duplicity on their own part. Much of this has conveniently fitted with the ANC's own ideological needs. In the dimension of ideology as high theory, apartheid may have been the highest form of white supremacy, but it was neither the first, nor the last, nor to be seen in isolation from the imperialism and metropolitan settler colonialism that spawned it. Liberals have tended, for their own reasons, to emphasize the singularity of Afrikaner nationalism; the ANC tends to insist on its family connections. Imperialism in its various historical avatars bears the brunt of the ANC's ideological analysis. This has come of an understandable desire for the ANC to position itself, according to the needs of the day, in terms appropriate to its Cold War benefactors, *dependencia* theory, Third Worldism and, today in opposition to 'global neo-liberalism'. This ideological positioning also has the useful spin-off of undercutting (in the ANC's own eyes if no-one else's) any claims of South African liberals – with their Western and pro-capitalist leanings – to progressive credentials. In general terms, Afrikaner nationalism holds nothing like the fascination for ANC ideologues that it has done for generations of Western academics and journalists for whom it provided an inexhaustible source of copy. It is different at the rougher end of ANC populism where 'the Boer' is the principal target of hate songs. However, the overall ideological positioning of the ANC held out the promise of at least some traction for reworked Afrikaner vernacular traits in the new society.

The sense of the numinous and the presence of the spiritual in collective life had largely gone by the time Afrikaners were called upon to re-evaluate themselves; a casualty of secularization, opening to the world and perhaps in the case of younger generations, disillusion and rejection of the values that led their parents and grandparents to oppress others. Appreciation remained from unpredictable directions: Vice-president Thabo Mbeki's 'I am an African' speech to parliament in May 1996 on the occasion of the adoption of the new Constitution nodded generously in the direction of Afrikaner spirituality, and hinted at a new spiritual home for them. It is also possible that this quality, as well as the need for justification, may have contributed to the decisions of those individuals who showed contrition for acts they committed in defence of apartheid or at least were prepared to go through the rituals of contrition, but they were too few to make a general case. De Klerk's much underrated apology for apartheid was widely criticized for being more justification than apology. Whether or not these criticisms were fair, De Klerk's speech was a textbook demonstration of the traits and qualities which both invented and then dissolved the Afrikaner nation, hinting that something had endured.

Fraternity was another casualty of modernization and differentiation in the context of social mobility and the division of labour. From the perspective of the democratic dawn in the mid-1990s it appeared that however Afrikaner needs and identities would be defined and satisfied in the future, fraternity of the sort that invented the nation would not play a part. Perhaps because it was confined safely to the past, however, it was one of the traits which those who were trying to redefine African nationalism in post-liberation terms would sometimes refer to with approval. Such African voices (which can still be heard) would, with somewhat selective memory, retrospectively praise the fraternal dimension of ethnic solidarity in Afrikaner nationalism and bemoan its perceived absence in contemporary African nationalism.

## The legacies of Afrikaner nationalism

There is a deceptive conceptual neatness in the verdict that Afrikaners in the transition from apartheid to democracy themselves made the transition from nation to minority. This is a handy enough thumbnail analysis, but the larger picture is inevitably more complex and uncertain. Engaging with this complexity is important for two aspects of the legacy of Afrikaner nationalism, both of which present themselves as questions: how would Afrikaners conduct themselves in the new South Africa? How should students of nationalism understand the Afrikaner transformation? Both these questions will be addressed later in this work, but it is important to sketch some points now.

The NP reformers did not intend to take their metamorphosis as far as it reached in 1994. What began as an opportunistic extension of legitimacy in the interests of continued ethnic survival turned, through the momentum of contingent and collateral effects, into what was effectively a defence of an entrenched, class position. This was achieved partly through negotiated constitutional rights which were individually based rather than on the preferred but unacceptable group basis and partly through strategic domination of the economy. Also important were limitations (some self-imposed, some imposed from outside) on the ANC's capacity to carry out revolutionary transformation. What had begun as a planned and limited withdrawal became, if not a rout, then at least a hasty forced march to the rear, latterly with diminishing semblance of good order. However, although it was a bit of a scramble, the post-nationalist haven that they reached was a surprisingly congenial one. What Afrikaners needed, and indeed what everybody needed, was some kind of organizing principle of conduct to guide them in this new situation. Although group rights had been denied, the claim to minority status was one possibility. But numerous problems attached themselves to this superficially attractive status.

The first problem was the ANC's disinclination to recognize as valid anything that hinted at a dilution of its commitment to treating South Africa as a unity in population and territory. The second was a host of confusions as to who might or might not be included in any definition of minority. De Klerk and the NP might claim to speak for Afrikaners in particular and whites in a general sort of way, but it was not clear which was the minority. Equally unclear was where the Afrikaner neo-nationalists fitted in. The AV, a front organization cobbled together out of political and paramilitary organizations under General Constand Viljoen, claimed to speak for most of the 50 per cent or so of Afrikaners who voted 'no' in De Klerk's referendum. This was a substantial minority in its own right, but one that the majority of whites wanted no part of. As an incentive to take part in the first democratic election, which it was threatening to boycott, the AV was even granted the promise of consideration of its claim to territorial self-determination for Afrikaners after the poll. Through political naivety or a lack of credible alternatives, Viljoen accepted this (as it turned out) worthless bribe which uncannily paralleled a similar undertaking to Buthelezi over the future of the Zulu monarchy, for which the ANC had other plans. To anyone paying attention, these two strategically cynical (or simply bad faith) agreements clearly signalled the ANC's complete confidence that they would be able to dismiss any formal claims to ethnic minority status after the elections.

There were other confusions. Among those whose status would be ambivalent if minorities were to be defined in ethnic, linguistic or racial terms were English speakers who had voted in large numbers for the white, liberal opposition and Afrikaans-speaking Coloureds who identified with the ANC. Even if some sort of settled criteria could be found for national-type minorities, it is hard to see how they could be applied in anything but the loosest way.

Two further problems remained. The first was that international law and diplomatic practice have made little provision for minorities that had formerly been politically dominant, were comparatively rich, skilled, mobile and still almost completely dominated the economy. The second involved a dilemma of political conduct. Afrikaners and whites would have to calculate how enthusiastically to act on the status of being a minority. Appearing to spurn any nation-building initiatives on behalf of the new order would probably be self-defeating. Nothing is more likely to bring on threats to a minority than aggressively behaving like one. On the other hand overly passive behaviour could end in being boiled like a lobster. The terms of coexistence between being part of a minority and a citizen of a new nation – especially one furnished with extensive provisions for individual human rights – promised to be very difficult.

The alternatives facing Afrikaners in the transition to democracy – especially the starkest one which asked in what sense, if at all, they *remained* Afrikaners – draw attention to the question of how students of nationalism should see the life cycle of Afrikaner nationalism. For something that seemed a fixed part of the political and diplomatic firmament for nearly all of the second half of the twentieth century, it had a remarkably short effective life. Recapping and summarizing its periodization we can distinguish the following phases: from about the mid-nineteenth century onwards until the capture of power in 1948 a period of consciously directed nation-building during which there was no guarantee of the final form the nation would take and in which contingency played as much part as agency; from 1948 to the mid-1960s, a phase in which the settled form of an ethnic coalition took shape (though as we have seen never without internal contradictions) accompanied by intensive state-building; from the mid-1960s to the mid-1970s, a short period of maturity in which management of the ethnic coalition, state-building and economic development went for the most part in harmony, and external pressures were managed relatively easily through domestic repression and a relatively unthreatening diplomatic environment; from the mid-1970s to the mid-1990s, a period of crisis management which saw the dissolution of the nationalist coalition and of the state with which it lived in mutual support. By the standards of national movements and states, this is a somewhat compressed, though intensely active life cycle. In any kind of long-range perspective, Afrikaner nationalism had lived hard and died young.

## The ambiguities of African nationalism

During the liberation struggle the contradictions of Afrikaner nationalism were repeatedly exposed, and its ideologues' gravity-defying attempts to reconcile them were dissected. By comparison, African nationalism in South Africa largely escaped outside scrutiny. There were several reasons for this. The cruelties, large and small, of exclusion and oppression which apartheid visited on all 'non-whites', but especially Africans, were applied with unrepentant arrogance. Moral repugnance at this discouraged too many hard questions being asked of those struggling against what came to be defined as a crime against humanity. Those who did ask tough questions risked being branded apartheid apologists and in some cases they actually were. African nationalism in South Africa in any case fitted well into an era of decolonization and development of a culture – or at least rhetoric – of human rights, as well as Cold War conflicts that pitted Third World solidarity against 'imperialism'. As a result, a sense of teleological entitlement attached itself to the South African version of African nationalism, as colonies all over the continent achieved their independence on the basis of claims to national self-determination. This also discouraged sharp questioning. There were in any case handy capsule versions of the presumed content of African nationalism in South Africa which on the whole sufficed for global consumption. These were provided by Nelson Mandela's address to the court in the Rivonia trial (1964):

> I have fought against white domination, and I have fought against black domination. I have cherished the ideal of a democratic and free society in which all persons will live together in harmony with equal opportunities.

and by the Freedom Charter (1955):

> We, the People of South Africa, declare for all our country and the world to know: that South Africa belongs to all who live in it, black and white, and that no government can justly claim authority unless it is based on the will of all the people.

It would have been churlish to subject the noble words of a resistance hero on trial by his oppressors to undue interrogation. The Freedom Charter might have been a different matter, but it was not until the ANC was on the verge of taking power that it received much in the way of critical analysis on its provenance and content. This, despite the fact that anyone reading beyond the first couple of lines would have found:

> All National Groups Shall have Equal Rights! . . . All national groups shall be protected by law against insults to their race and national pride.

The reader might wonder that if South Africa was one people, why race and 'national groups' were being invoked and what was 'national' about racial groups and their 'national pride'. However, these and related questions were not a matter of great urgency in the heat of the liberation struggle.

Until the very last stages of the conflict it looked to most outsiders that although liberation would not be denied, it would certainly be delayed long enough to comfortably postpone consideration of what form of nation would accompany and crown it.

None of this means that African nationalism in South Africa went completely unexamined before the era of public negotiation and transition began in 1990. On the contrary, within the ANC and its constellation of supporting organizations and movements, issues of nations and nationalism were subjected to much debate and theoretical fine-tuning. There were pressing reasons for this. In the first place, the 'demon of tribalism' haunted the ANC ever since its foundation in 1913. The words of one of its founders, Pixley ka Izaka Seme, have echoed over the century since he wrote them in 1911: 'The demon of racialism, the aberrations of the Xhosa-Fingo feud, the animosity that exists between Zulus and Tsongas, between the Basuto and every other Native must be buried and forgotten. . . . We are one people. These divisions, these jealousies, are the cause of all our woes and all our backwardness and ignorance today' (Walshe 1987: 33). All ANC thinking and practice had been conditioned by the unshakeable belief that the African people of South Africa *were* one people and *must be* one people in order to realize their liberation from white domination. All contrary possibilities have to be ignored or extirpated. However, another equally unshakeable belief runs counter to this. That is, South Africa's African people are at all times beset by fissiparous temptations from their own weakness, as well as pressures from white divide-and-rule tactics, to which they will succumb without the ANC to hold them together. Apartheid's determined efforts to balkanize South Africa into primordial, pre-ordained black 'nations' provided ample confirmation of this concern. In short, the ANC throughout its history has been shaped by the tensions surrounding Seme's 'We are one people.' What he was expressing was an aspiration and an imperative, not an established fact. As a result, questions of identity and nationhood were squarely on the agenda.

A second source of concern was competition to define African nationalism (indeed to define 'African') from rival movements: first the 'Africanist' breakaway from the ANC itself, the Pan Africanist Congress (PAC) and later, in the 1970s, the Black Consciousness Movement (BCM). This forced consideration of a whole range of issues, including who should be the legitimate interpreter of African nationalism and its custodian. Another task was to harness, but at the same time discipline Africanism into modernizing, rather than primordial forms, and towards redress, rather than revenge when its time came.

A third incentive for reflection and self-analysis was the powerful influence of left-wing ideologies through the South African Communist Party (SACP) and later the Congress of South African Trade Unions (Cosatu). The SACP learned the lesson early from other colonial and anti-imperial liberation struggles, that the prospects of socialism in developing countries, even in relatively developed and industrialized ones like South Africa, were dim unless socialist parties came to terms with nationalism. That is, they had to learn to ride the nationalist tiger without being devoured by it. Cosatu was and probably remains more sceptical of nationalism than the SACP, but the imperatives of the struggle in the 1980s and 1990s, as well as the balance of forces in society, economy and politics thereafter, meant that it too had to make its accommodation with nationalism. Partly because so many of South Africa's communists and early trade union activists and intellectuals were white, the need to find ways for nationalism and socialism to come to terms with each other dramatized and lent immediacy to another imperative for reflection on the subject of where whites fit into a liberation movement and a nation which are defined as African. Implacably rooted in South Africa and until late in the twentieth century demographically imposing, whites could not be wished away like settlers in other colonies. What to do about this economically vital but apparently indigestible oppressor bloc was the subject of long-term theoretical disputation, most of which was jettisoned as soon as it became a practical, rather than an ideological challenge.

All of these pressures forced the ANC into ideological contortions which bore a distant, but unmistakable cousinly resemblance to the labours of their Afrikaner counterparts. Both sets of ideologues strove hard to craft theoretically coherent and sustainable blueprints for their nations in the face of South Africa's intractable and in some respects exceptional conditions. Thus it came about that Colonialism of a Special Type (CST), the National Democratic Revolution (NDR) and non-racialism – the only one of these to gain currency outside the ANC itself – came to define the ANC's understanding of the nation and nationalism. It did not do so with complete coherence and authority, leaving many inconsistencies and unresolved contradictions; the most basic was 'who is an African?' and what this status meant. In any case CST and NDR were conceptualized in documents that were not widely read and even less widely understood. They were constructed for purposes of mobilization and discipline in the internal dynamics of the liberation movement, rather than mobilization in competitive, popular politics, from which of course the ANC was barred by apartheid's repressive legislation. For the purposes of mobilization from its disadvantageous underground status, what was much more to popular taste and to the ANC's advantage was casual reification of 'the people' and its elision with 'African'. As far as communicating with the wider world of diplomacy and global political public relations, the non-racialism of the Freedom Charter and Mandela's speech from the dock were well suited. This became the ANC's global calling-card, especially when Mandela became an international human rights icon. However, beyond the essential minimum promise that in a liberated South Africa no-one would be oppressed by virtue of their race, the actual content of non-racialism was not well defined. The principle was more important as stirring rhetoric to help lever the ANC into power, rather than as a detailed guide to the contours of a post-liberation society that no-one on either side of the struggle divide could envisage with any degree of authority in an extremely uncertain situation.

In its incarnation as an exiled and underground liberation movement, the ANC was much more than a political party. Writing in the mid-1980s, Tom Lodge made the point that although exile can be a hazardous condition for political movements, the ANC flourished as 'a state-in-exile': 'It has been able to offer to its partisans a hermetic world which has taken its moral and physical authority to heights that vastly exceed those of a political party' (1986: 27). One of the ways it was able to do this was in the development of a number of ideological positions that achieved the status of sacred texts in the hands of a priesthood of keepers and interpreters. The question that remained was how effectively these ideologies would prepare the ANC for the world of open, legitimate popular politics and the exercise of governing powers. A subsidiary question was in what combination they would be retained, modified or discarded under these new circumstances. These questions applied across the board in all areas of political organization, management and policy making, and among them were issues of what African nationalism could and should mean under conditions of formal democracy. In order to answer these questions it is necessary to address the meaning of African nationalism in the years of struggle and consider some of the sacred texts.

The ANC's narrative of evolution is familiar. It was founded in 1912 by a group of African notables several hundred strong, in order to make claim to rights within a white-dominated polity and society. Its methods matched this moderate and evolutionary approach. From about 1940, it began to broaden its membership, its appeal and the horizons of its claims. It became more ambitious and assertive in its methods. The pressures of heightened segregation legislated in the mid-1930s, the increasing incorporation of Africans into the economy during the Second World War and the example of the Atlantic Charter (1943) were influential in these developments. Central to them was the ANCYL, founded in 1944. Among the ANCYL's notable contributions to the ANC was the call to focus on 'Africanism'. As the League's founding manifesto put it (ANCYL 1944):

> Africanism must be promoted i.e. Africans must struggle for development, progress and national liberation so as to occupy their rightful and honourable place among nations of the world.
>
> The formation of this League is an attempt on the part of Youth to impart to Congress a truly national character.
>
> The Congress Youth League must be the brains-trust and power station of the spirit of African nationalism; the spirit of African self-determination.

Central to the Africanism proposed by the ANCYL was the rejection of 'trusteeship'. In the words of the manifesto, far from 'helping the African on the road to civilised life', this confidence trick through which white minority rule attempted to justify itself, 'has meant, as it still means, the consolidation by the White man of his position at the expense of the African people, so that by the time national awakening opens the eyes of the African people to the bluff they live under, White domination should be secure and unassailable' (ibid.).

Under the changing social, economic and political conditions of the time, the development of a more explicit and assertive articulation of African nationalism was a logical one. However, it gave rise to two sorts of tension. The first was between those who, according to Walshe, saw the need for African political assertion, but were constantly aware of the dangers of: 'an extremist and inward-looking black racialism'; while others, 'were less inclined to worry about the dangers of engendering anti-white (or anti-Indian) attitudes as long as an ideology could be developed that was dynamic enough to rouse the African masses to awareness and action' (1987: 355–6). In the space of only a couple of years, 'Africanism' went from being a general invocation of African pride and self-determination to a somewhat pejorative term. It became associated with the kind of narrow racialism that inspired the attempt (which was rejected) to introduce a motion at the ANC conference in Bloemfontein in 1945, 'Africa for the Africans and the White Man for the sea!' (ibid. 363). The broader understanding of the ANCYL's recommendation of Africanism – that which embraced non-racialism, albeit with varying degrees of recognizing African predominance – became more generally termed 'African nationalism'. The tension between non-racialism and African predominance remains to this day.

The second source of tension was over the role of communists in the ANC and in the struggle against unjust and discriminatory laws generally. The two tensions were of course linked, since many communists were white or Indian. However, added to the racial edge of tension and resentment of communism's 'alien' provenance was a measure of straightforward, ideological disagreement.

Both these tensions were pushed into the background through the pressures generated by the election of the NP government in 1948, and the intensified repression which came in its train. In practice if not in theory, the 'liberal' or non-racial interpretation of African nationalism held sway, through landmarks like the Defiance Campaign (1952) and the Congress Alliance (1953), culminating in the Freedom Charter (1955). However, the breakaway of disgruntled Africanists to form the PAC (1959), on the grounds the Freedom Charter was a communist document and that as all whites were beneficiaries of segregation and repression, white liberals and radicals could not be trusted as struggle partners, showed that the tensions were not resolved. Furthermore, it would be a mistake to think that the PAC breakaway removed from the ANC all those who held these views of communists and whites. As a result, in order to assert primacy in the now-divided liberation movement and leadership in its own house, the ANC would have to resolve the tensions in theory as well as in practice. It is against this background that we have to consider CST and Non-racialism.

## Colonialism of a Special Type

CST was first articulated in the SACP document, *The Road to South African Freedom* (1962). It is worth noting that CST is, if anything, a default exposition of African nationalism. It is not a systematic treatment of the subject; it is neither enquiring, nor discursive, nor does it hold up different possible models for analysis. However, in the absence of any treatment of the subject that *is* systematic in these senses, in its own indirect ways it has been adopted as the defining text of the ANC on the subject of African nationalism. It appeared in spirit, if not in language, in the ANC's Strategy and Tactics document at the Morogoro Consultative Conference in 1969, and by the time of the Kabwe Consultative Conference (1985) was acknowledged by name as central to the ANC's ideology. It forms the backbone of all the ANC's Strategy and Tactics documents up to the present day.

The essential insight of CST can be quite succinctly stated:

> South Africa is not a colony but an independent state. Yet masses of our people enjoy neither independence nor freedom. The conceding of independence to South Africa by Britain, in 1910, was not a victory over the forces of colonialism and imperialism. It was designed in the interests of imperialism. Power was transferred not into the hands of the masses of people of South Africa, but into the hands of the White minority alone. The evils of colonialism, insofar as the non-White majority was concerned, were perpetuated and reinforced. A new type of colonialism was developed, in which the oppressing White nation occupied the same territory as the oppressed people themselves and lived side by side with them. (SACP 1962: 20)

This is not merely a situation in which a dominant class subjects the classes subordinate to it to exploitation and repression. Class divisions are replicated within both the 'white nation' and the 'oppressed people', although class antagonisms are masked among whites by the benefits of racial status and among blacks by the universality of imposed racial inferiority. In this sense the disabilities of Africans are *national* in character, underlined by the fact that the oppressor group does everything it can to emphasize its alien 'European' character.

In the face of this national oppression, the African people, subject to no antagonistic class divisions 'are moving inevitably and consciously to the formation of a single, modern nation' (ibid. 24). The understanding is that it is only the national liberation of this African nation that will undo the damage of CST and fulfil the mission of the NDR. However, there are clear signposts in the document to the fulfilment of an inclusive non-racial nation. The interest of all 'non-whites' as well as 'the bulk' of whites (workers, middle classes and professional groups) lies in the national liberation of Africans. Replicating the confusions of the Freedom Charter, CST sees South Africa as being composed of, 'national groups', whose 'rights, dignity, culture and self-respect' (ibid. 23) all have to be upheld.

The peculiarity of CST then is that the oppression of Africans is 'national oppression', but this conception of Africans is made to coexist with the idea of an inclusive nation. According to CST, Africans may be any or all of the following things: an already-existing nation subject to 'national oppression' and aspiring to national liberation; a nation-in-the-making and a 'national group' which is a part of an inclusive nation and by implication, on demographic and moral grounds, the most important part of it. The primary inconsistency or contradiction in CST is, according to the theory, that the African people or the African majority both is and is not a national community. It *is* a national community in the sense that it is subject to national oppression and is striving for national liberation from this condition. In all senses but one it is in the same position as the contemporaneous, national liberation movements elsewhere in the Third World which in 1962 were struggling against colonial powers. The one sense is that the oppressor state is an indigenous one, already severed in all formal, political ways though not economic ties from the metropole. On the other hand, in CST's scheme of things, the African people do *not* constitute a national community in the sense that they are part of an inclusive nation which, given the indigenous nature of the national oppression, cannot easily be denied without the danger of reverse racial chauvinism.

What accounts for this duality in CST, and how influential has it been to questions of nation-building before and after the end of apartheid? In order to address these questions we have to consider the provenance and context of the original document and try to interpret what purposes it served and for whom it served them.

It may seem ironic that the SACP gave the ANC its main text on African nationalism, given that one of the principal sources of tension in defining African nationalism in South Africa was the role of communists in the liberation movement. However, the irony is only superficial. The departure of the main Africanist bloc to form the PAC in 1959 left a gap and an urgent imperative to resolve questions of nation and nationalism conclusively, in order to keep in line however many of the Africanist persuasion did not choose the exit option. It was a gap that it was very much in the SACP's interest to fill and, in any case, what better way to demonstrate the reality of the Congress Alliance and build on the Freedom Charter, than to have the SACP draw up the theoretical definition of national liberation and the manifesto of a movement that would be its principal bearer?

The Road to South African Freedom made its appearance three years after the PAC breakaway and two years after the post-Sharpeville security crackdown which reduced the ANC to a tenuous existence underground and in exile. This was also two years after seventeen African colonies achieved national liberation, considerably swelling the ranks of Third World organizations and anti-colonial caucuses in the UN system and elsewhere. The road to South African Freedom, then, made its debut at the time when the ANC's fortunes were at their lowest and the momentum of the international anti-colonial movement was at its highest. Under these circumstances, CST made a strongly assertive bid to frame South Africa's struggle against apartheid in terms of the international movement for colonial freedom. It mattered – for reasons of solidarity, resources, legitimacy and the progressive isolation of the oppressor state – that apartheid was not merely an oppressive, unjust system that cruelly denied human rights, but that it was a *colonial* system that did all these things. From this point on the ANC hammered home, not just an analogy with colonialism, but a full-blown identification with it. 'Juridical formalities' of independence from any metropolitan country and possession of sovereign independence 'should not be allowed to cloud the colonial content of the white supremacist state' (ANC: 1987). The message was plain: South Africa was not just a repressive state which denied democracy to its people (of which in 1962 there were numerous examples in many other parts of the world, not all of them colonies). The racist state was 'essentially colonial', and 'the South African struggle is an anti-colonialist, national liberation struggle. It may differ in form from the struggles waged in other countries, but in its content it has the same aspirations. . . . The struggle of the South African people has therefore centred on the abolition of the colonial white state and the creation in its stead of a democratic state based on the principle of majority rule' (ibid.). The conception of 'majority' invoked here is clearly not one of a fortuitous majority of people exercising democratic rights at the same time in an election, but one carrying with it inescapable overtones of national destiny.

It was not only in the theatre of international relations, crucial as it was that CST sought leverage. Although a degree of teleological legitimacy has been conferred on the ANC's (and SACP's) version of the struggle, four alternative conceptualizations posed dangers for the ANC. Since, given the nature of apartheid repression, they could not be confronted in a market-place of popular politics and open political organization, they had to be banished in theoretical documents that kept the faithful in line and presented a united front.

The first danger was that of racial populism. 'Africanism' combined anger, racial solidarity, a sense of primal possession that had been violated by colonial theft and a hunger for repossession of land and resources. None of this was alien to the ANC, but the danger was that Africanism would be dissipated in inchoate protest and spasmodic violence, easily quelled by the better-organized and equipped forces of the white state. Even if successful however, racial populism would threaten transmutation into revanchism and reverse racial chauvinism, not to mention the resurrection of regressive social practices under the guise of 'tradition'. None of this would fit with the ANC's (not to mention the SACP's) self-image as a modernizing force that alone could bring rational and humane organization and evolution to the only industrial society in Africa. By personifying Africans as a nationally oppressed people on the road to national liberation, CST sought to exploit their anger and sense of dispossession, but at the same time to harness and discipline them in a rational and modernizing context. This included situating the African nation in a wider context of a South Africa of peoples, national groups and racial designations, which corresponded for the most part with apartheid classifications. There is no record of anyone in the ANC or SACP being embarrassed by this coincidence.

The second danger was the demon of tribalism. By casting the South African situation as a colonial one and juxtaposing the entire white community with the assumed wholeness and integrity of the African people, the blandishments of 'ethnic entrepreneurs' and the divide-and-rule tactics of the apartheid state could be fought off.

The third danger was the siren call of liberal individualism. By casting the struggle as one for national self-determination – albeit clouded by ambiguities over the constitution of the self – CST headed off the possibility that the struggle could be conceptualized as one for individual rights. In the same way the fourth danger – reformism – could also be dealt with. As a later SACP (1989) document, 'The Path to Power', put it: 'Our struggle is not, and cannot be, merely for civil rights within the framework of the existing system. This system is rooted in the special colonial subjugation of the majority of the South African people and the denial of their basic rights.' CST's characterization of South Africa as a colonial state led the analysis to the conclusion that the state had to be 'smashed' (a favourite ANC word). This was a misreading of decolonization, perhaps wilful, perhaps the result of wishful thinking, since elsewhere in Africa there was almost invariably a substantial measure of continuity between the colonial state and its liberated successor, down to details like security legislation.

Although it was cast in a form that addressed potentially thorny issues for the ANC, CST also performed several useful ideological purposes for the SACP itself. It short-circuited potentially inconvenient debates about internationalism and the appropriateness of communists struggling to install a nationalist government in power. By quarantining white workers in the colonial, oppressor nation which had its own class structure – physically present in South Africa perhaps, but ideologically inhabiting a metaphysical metropole of privilege – the SACP also took a short cut past the theoretical maze of false consciousness. Even in this respect, however,

CST was flexible. Although all white people were stigmatized as profiting from African people's exploitation and misery, the principal focus for blame was housed in a convenient abstraction. Since 'monopoly capital' is sufficiently unlike any white person anyone has actually met, the prospects of including white people in non-racialism were not choked off altogether.

By defining Africans as a nation bound together by their oppression and not by conventional measures like language, race, ethnicity, common history and culture, CST made sure that the struggle against apartheid was firmly situated in the anti-colonial *zeitgeist* of the era, positioned the ANC advantageously against populist, liberal and ethnic competitors and tidied up some loose ends of communist ideology. In doing so it created a doctrine that was both durable and supple enough to serve the purposes of discipline, organization and management in the 'hermetic' world of exile and underground activity that Lodge described. This was not the only discipline it provided. At least since the 1940s, the ANC had been preoccupied with the problem of how to exploit Africanism constructively – anger, frustration and outrage at injustice – without being swept away by erratic populism and destructive racial chauvinism. CST tried to confine the genie of Africanism to a bottle labelled 'African nationalism'. However, there was another label on the reverse side, which said 'non-racialism'.

## Non-racialism in theory and practice: From the Freedom Charter to the United Democratic Front (UDF)

Non-racialism is the quality that came to define the ANC in the great global awakening to South Africa's liberation struggle between the Soweto uprising in 1976 and the unbanning of the liberation movements in 1990. The ANC's association with non-racialism was of inestimable value in establishing its credentials among those who were merely ignorant about apartheid, and even among some that had hitherto insisted on associating South Africa's liberation struggle with chauvinistic African nationalism and terrorism. The ANC's assiduous cultivation of an image of non-racialism also went some way to defusing white South African concerns about the directions the liberation movement would take if it were ever able to operate freely. The ANC's professions of non-racialism worked their magic on the bridge-builders and pilgrims who in the late 1980s, as townships burned, went in a blaze of publicity to visit the ANC in Lusaka and Dakar, as well as on those who more discreetly held meetings in England and reported back to the government in Pretoria. Their changing perceptions were gradually diffused among the white population. Relief and in some instances euphoria at the prospect of South Africa finding a painless way out of its deepening and increasingly violent crises was, on the whole, enough to obscure the fact that neither in theory nor in practice was the ANC's conception of non-racialism consistently, fully or finely articulated. It was never clear whether non-racialism was what had always been there, what was at hand, or what was to come.

Unsurprisingly, verdicts vary on the place of non-racialism in the ideology and practice of the ANC. In 1990, the year the ANC was unbanned, activist-journalist Julie Frederikse published an account of the ANC's non-racialism, based on interviews with its members, under the title, *The Unbroken Thread*. The overall verdict of academic reviewers was that by eschewing an inquiring, never mind a critical, approach to the material provided by her subjects, Frederikse had produced what amounted to a corporate hagiography. This approach, whatever its faults, was at least in tune with the times. Nevertheless, there was clearly something about the metaphor in the title of Frederikse's book that struck a chord. Colin Bundy concluded that: 'A skein of complementary and competing threads might better describe the history of national liberation' because, among other things, 'non-racialism has meant different things to different people within the same organizational and ideological traditions at different times' (2000: 61). Shula Marks stayed with the metaphor but (writing in 1994) hedged her bets. Looking back at a history of non-racialism marked not only by idealism but also a stiff dose of pragmatism (not to mention opportunism) she saw non-racialism as 'the ANC's "habit of mind"'. Despite this optimistic if unspecific verdict she added, 'if we look back on this complex history of non-racialism in South Africa . . . the threads remain eminently breakable. Indeed some are beginning to fray' (Marks 1994: 22).

An indication of the way in which African nationalism and non-racialism jostled for pre-eminence in ANC thought and practice is provided by one of Frederikse's interviewees, ANC grandee Max Sisulu (interviewed in 1987):

> The point is that we're not simply fighting for non-racialism, because if you fight for non-racialism it becomes simply a civil rights struggle. Ours is a struggle for the seizure of power and its transference to the majority of the people. Non-racialism is a form that the struggle takes, but it is not the content of the struggle, it is not the objective. We're not simply fighting for non-racialism for non-racialism's sake – no we are fighting to put an end to a situation which prevails where we are foreigners in our own land, where we have no votes and no say, no nothing, and we are simply beasts of burden for the benefit of the minority and the multi-national corporations. (Frederikse 1990: 267)

By stressing the instrumental nature of non-racialism and declining to define it in terms of enduring or essential value, Sisulu hints that it is a handy and flexible tool which can be redefined or possibly discarded according to the demands of the struggle, before or after liberation. Effectively, non-racialism is whatever the ANC needs and does. Stirring but content-free formulations like 'You actively fight against racism: that is the essence of non-racialism' (ibid. 78) help confirm the image of flexibility.

David Everatt, whose researches on the history of non-racialism in the liberation struggle (Everatt 2009b) are to date the most exhaustive and authoritative traces the history of how it came to be:

> since democracy was ushered in, in 1994, that a critical weakness was the failure to *define* non-racialism, to give it content beyond that of a slogan or a self-evident 'good thing'. It made intuitive sense uniting races where apartheid divided them, but beyond that, what was the meaning of non-racialism? How should it be implemented? What was it, in practice? (Everatt 2009a: 1)

Everatt concluded that non-racialism was no more than a slogan, despite being central to the canon of all anti-apartheid organizations, from the Freedom Charter in 1955 to the making of the 1996 South African Constitution. He based this on three main arguments. In the first place, non-racialism was permanently in the shadow of African nationalism in all its various and competing incarnations and no-one was ever able to draw up a rigorous account of the relationship between them, either before or after the end of apartheid. Secondly, beneath non-racialism 'lay a contradictory and bitterly fought-out set of ideologies within the Congress Alliance'. The third factor – more germane to the post-apartheid period – was a wider failure, responsibility for which stretched beyond the ANC and its allies: 'As a nation we have failed to imagine a different future beyond the border of race' (ibid.).

The first and second of these factors overlapped to a considerable degree, centring on the ANC's interpretation of the practice of non-racialism, to mean *multiracialism*. We have already noted how the Freedom Charter invoked a South Africa composed of 'national groups', and how the ANC-led Congress Alliance committed the struggle for freedom to the organizational form of separate, race-based congresses. It was only at the Morogoro conference in 1969 that whites were permitted to join the ANC, and at the Kabwe conference in 1985 they were permitted to join the National Executive Committee (NEC). However, multiracialism was not the only way to configure the struggle. The SACP, both in its pre- and post-banning (1950) incarnations, had a non-racial structure. So too did the Liberal Party (1953–68). So the ANC's interpretation of non-racialism to mean multiracialism in practice requires explanation. According to Everatt, multiracialism was the organizational form: 'that would allow Africans to lead the struggle of all races for equality for all'. The key factor was sensitivity to nationalism, 'to the anti-white (and anti-Indian) hostilities that lay fairly close to the surface, and to the need for full African leadership in the face of energetic support from other race groups with better access to resources'. Added to this was the argument that political organization was more efficiently done on a racial basis, 'each race group had a better entrée to its own areas, languages and cultures' (Everatt 2009a: 5–8), an explanation confirmed by Sisulu's blunt verdict, 'You can't as an African go and mobilize the whites – it's impossible' (Frederikse 1990: 78).

In Everatt's account, far from being an 'unbroken thread', non-racialism was a maelstrom of ideological contestation within the Congress movement. For instance, many members of the white component, the Congress of Democrats, were unhappy and even humiliated at being confined to the thankless task of converting their fellow whites. The wrangling raged even more fiercely in the wider progressive movement. Liberals, Trotskyists and African nationalists all had their bones to pick with multiracialism, often from a vehemently anti-communist (or at least anti-Stalinist) perspective. Indeed, it is surprising that the apartheid government did not make more of the Congress Movement's commitment to multiracialism for propaganda purposes, given that its premises mirrored apartheid's racial classifications so closely – a point that Congresses' progressive critics were not slow to make. Fortunately for Congress, however, most of the ideological wrestling took place far from the public eye, in obscure journals and meetings whose records Everatt has heroically excavated, but which left so little trace on public awareness that when the ANC was reborn at the end of the unbroken thread in the 1980s, there was no collective memory to question it – at least not where it mattered.

Everatt's account provides a compelling and authoritative guide to the vagaries of the relationship between African nationalism and non-racialism, with multiracialism as a queasy go-between. However, some additional factors can still be added. One of them is the ability of the South African progressive political class to tie itself in knots on the subject of race. Prominent among the entanglements is the 'ontological status of race'. Writing today, but in terms that are applicable to the whole history of ANC non-racialism in South Africa, ANC activist and intellectual Raymond Suttner says:

> At an ontological level we can say that race does not exist. But it does and does not exist. While it has no ontological status, it does exist continually in history and a range of social relations in various states both now and in the past. (2011b:18)

The pressing need to simultaneously deny the existence of race and to deal with it in political practice is a form of political schizophrenia that runs – like an unbroken thread – through the history of the ANC's non-racialism. No matter how earnest the plea that complex ideas and practices are required to deal with the unbearably complex social relations spawned by South Africa's history of colonialism and white minority rule, this sort of formulation is a vulnerable one. It opens its holders to accusations that race exists when it suits them, and does an ontological disappearing act when it does not.

Arguably, however, it helps to put multiracialism in perspective. In a sense, multiracialism could be seen as no more than a way of coping with the world of actually existing race relations; a world which the racist 'other' had cast with ferocious single-mindedness. From this angle the multiracialism of the Freedom Charter can be seen as making the best of a bad job; admitting the division of the country into 'national groups', celebrating their diversity and acknowledging that they all deserve respect for their languages, cultures, and so on. However, celebrating diversity had its limits. Diversity had to take second place to the overriding need for the oppressed African people to achieve self-determination for itself, and to lead the other groups to self-determination in a putative South African nation. What could not be accepted, in the ANC's view, was that any other 'group' could define itself in any way that might constitute a claim to self-determination. The ANC would (in its own self-estimation) go quite far to celebrate diversity, but at the same time had to reserve the right to limit and if necessary cut off expressions of diversity it would not tolerate. What this self-assigned right was based on was never very clear. Arguably, the ANC did have a case as long as apartheid existed, that the only valid claims to self-determination were those of the African majority, whose numbers and experience of oppression gave it both demographic and moral pre-eminence, plus the putative, unified, non-racial South African people. In the absence of free expression of political preferences, how could any other claims be valid? On the one hand, any white claim would be based on force and denial of self-determination to others (albeit the basis for much successful, state-making practice across the world and across history). On the other hand, any claims from any subgroup of Africans – 'tribalism' – would of necessity in the absence of political freedom be distorted, the result of coercion, bribery and other divide-and-rule tactics, not least suppression of 'genuine' liberation aspirations. To bolster its case against alternative claims to self-determination, at the time when such things mattered, the ANC had the additional imprimatur of the OAU's insistence of the sanctity of colonial borders. These were real difficulties of principle and practical politics, but whether or not they conferred on the ANC the right to determine the forms and limits of self-determination for everybody else may have been another matter. These issues in any case existed only in the abstract as long as apartheid was extant and it was not surprising that little if any theoretical consideration was given to the hypothetical question of what to do if some identifiable portion of the South African population (especially if it were African) chose self-determination under conditions of democracy. This comfortable situation would not outlast apartheid.

Before the end of apartheid, however, the opportunity arose to reopen the question of non-racialism and advance, or at least clarify, its theory and practice, especially in terms of its relationship to African nationalism. The opportunity was presented by the emergence of the UDF in 1983. The UDF was a popular front, umbrella body of more than 400 organizations, involving around 3 million people drawn from all four of the 'national groups' recognized in the Freedom Charter. The provocation that sparked the formation of the UDF was not so much heightened oppression of Africans, but the promise of limited reform for Coloureds and Indians, thus confirming the age-old political truism that oppressive regimes are most vulnerable when they try to evolve through reform. It was the campaigns against Coloured and Indian referenda – and rejection of the principle that reform could be viable on a racially segmented basis – that solidified the UDF. However, it soon exploded into a country-wide constellation of localized protest on a wide variety of community, workplace and classroom issues. In this way all grievances were credibly linked to the central injustices of white minority rule and, thanks to the UDF's recognition of ANC inspiration and leadership, awareness of the ANC's history, values, policies and iconography was successfully disseminated on a mass basis.

According to one account of the peak years of the struggle in the 1980s, the UDF represented 'a conscious return to the principle of non-racialism' (Marx 1992: 203). In one practical respect this was true. By frustrating the reforms which offered Coloureds and Indians a junior position of privilege in a tricameral system of government with whites, the UDF denied reform apartheid any hope of providing a solution to South Africa's crises. This sent a very powerful message of minority solidarity with Africans, who had been excluded from the tricameral system and offered a separate and inevitably inferior deal. This message could be interpreted, according to taste, as one of racial solidarity (black unity), or non-racial solidarity (common South Africanness). The non-racial interpretation was the majority view both of the constituents of the UDF (at least those who were its public face and voice) and of outside observers, in Western countries especially, to whom it also meant a strong message of hope for the future. Whether or not it was the view of the less well-connected majority of African components of the UDF may be another matter. None of this meant in any case that the ambiguities and confusions of the relationship between non-racialism and African nationalism had been miraculously cleared up in a coup d'état of practice at the grass roots over theory as dictated from exile. As another account of these years puts it, the UDF brought Coloureds, Indians and even some whites into popular protest as, 'part of a protest nation that couldn't fit neatly into African nationalist templates' (Seekings 2000: 288). The relationship between the UDF and the ANC was complex and involved: given the distances between the ANC in exile and the UDF, as well as the conditions of extreme repression that they worked under, much had to be improvised. In some respects the UDF subordinated itself to the ANC in almost slavish deference to the perceived historical authority of the older organization. In other respects, 'while not self-consciously challenging the perspectives of the ANC and SACP – in practice the UDF implied something different from them' (Suttner 2004: 696). The principal, implicit challenge was in the working concept of popular democracy that was improvised locally in forms of struggle – including, significantly, negotiation with local white administrations and businesses over boycotts and other tactics of confrontation – rather than in a 'big bang' theory of national liberation through the seizure of state power.

The UDF's mass mobilization and exploitation of specific grass-roots grievances gave the ANC a reach and symbolic presence that was as great if not greater than its peak in the 1950s, and the ANC's blessing gave the UDF legitimacy based on historic continuity which exponentially increased its own reach. However, the UDF's influence on issues of nation-building should not be exaggerated. In particular, the idea that the UDF returned the ANC to its non-racial roots or decisively shunted it onto a non-racial track for the future should be treated with caution. The UDF left no theoretical legacy to clarify, never mind challenge CST. UDF activists were too preoccupied with mass organization and tactical issues, including staying out of detention or surviving in it, and too much in awe of the ANC and SACP to do any such thing. Or perhaps it was the moral and demographic weight of the oppressed African majority that shaped the UDF's' ultimate acceptance of the ANC's version of African nationalism. Even in practice the UDF was forced into the kind of multiracialism that characterized the Congress Alliance, that of organizing within national groups rather than across them. However, although the UDF officially toed the Congress line on the importance of the primacy of African leadership, 'the roles played by Coloured, Indian and even white activists were disproportionate to the racial composition of even the metropolitan population' (Seekings 2000: 312). Unsurprisingly, this helped to foster an ominous reminder of the durability of tensions between non-racialism and Africanism. This came in the form of long-running accusations within the liberation movement that the UDF (especially in Natal) was being controlled and manipulated by a 'cabal' which monopolized resources and decision making. Nationally, but especially in Natal and the Western Cape, 'criticism of the 'cabal' took on a racial dimension with activists in African areas critical of the disproportionate influence wielded by Indian and Coloured activists in the UDF leadership' (ibid. 20).

In the final analysis, the UDF raised the profile of non-racialism in several ways. The prominence of Coloured and Indian activists in its ranks was a reminder of the extent of the country's diversity and a useful corrective to the tendency to see the struggle for South Africa as being exclusively between Afrikaner and African nationalism. It must have been a rude shock to the constitutional engineers who were constructing reform apartheid institutions to learn that their 'natural' allies – other minorities – were opting for a future under African nationalism rather than one under the protection and tutelage of continued white rule. This was a notable victory for non-racialism, broadly conceived. Of course, this was not entirely a matter of how these minorities conceived their preference for affiliation in terms of abstract nation-building. Probably a calculation of the odds on alternative patterns of future power relations, given South Africa's demography, had something to do with it too. African nationalism was risky but a better bet.

The UDF also performed the feat of associating non-racialism with democratic practices. The simmering tensions over the cabal and well-publicized abuses and cruelties like intimidation, kangaroo courts, the notorious practice of 'necklacing', and witch hunts against alleged collaborators and informers all testify that the UDF's claims to be democratic were not unproblematic. However, real people of all South Africa's races emerged in great numbers, visible to insulated whites and world opinion alike, as subjects, players and stakeholders. This put a human face on non-racialism that could not be ignored, and recovered for the ANC some of the ground it had lost in exile and underground. Perhaps only relatively few whites were involved as activists, but the point of non-racialism was made even in situations of adversarial negotiation. White businesspeople negotiated with the representatives of boycotting communities, and employers negotiated with a burgeoning trade union movement which operated in harness with the UDF. The point being made was that non-racialism meant interdependence and interdependence meant non-racialism. All of this had important constructive effects. However, it did not resolve the issues of how Africanism could be married with non-racialism in a unifying version of African nationalism, and whether African nationalism was the same thing as *South* African nationalism. According to Anthony Marx, the UDF had successfully offered a version of non-racialism to counter-reform apartheid's bogus incorporation, but its alternative vision was not too far distant from, 'the mobilizing potential of racial assertiveness'. As a result, 'ideological vagueness allowed the UDF to incorporate diverse interests and motivations, much as the ANC had benefited from a vague inclusiveness to attract a wide alliance' (Marx 1992: 203). Despite this, the UDF had populated non-racialism – which ever since the post-Sharpeville repression had been for the most part a country of the imagination – with real and visible people. This was crucial for opening up space in which to address those questions of nation-building for which the UDF, in its close and dependent relationship with the ANC, had neither the inclination nor the aptitude and resources to tackle on its own.

## Africanism, the PAC and Black Consciousness

We have already seen how conflicting understandings of African nationalism led Africanists to break away from the ANC to form the PAC.

This division of the forces of African nationalism never really troubled the ANC's confidence in its self-designation as the leading force in liberation politics. Such diplomatic support as the PAC was able to acquire was as a result of other rivalries, such as the Sino-Soviet split. It was this which induced the People's Republic of China (PRC) to back the PAC because it was the rival to the Soviet Union's protégé, the ANC. Such considerations of power politics had nothing to do with the respective claims of the ANC and PAC either to represent African people or to possess organizational and ideological merits. The PAC was quite unable to produce a coherent and strategically credible account of how liberation might be achieved and what it might look like when it was. The ANC, whatever its own shortcomings on these scores, could only shine by comparison in the eyes of anyone with an interest in the future of South Africa and who, unlike the PRC had no geopolitical axe to grind. As far as support within South Africa went, the ANC's problem was not rivalry with the PAC, but the post-Sharpeville wave of repression which laid waste its organizational capacity and scattered its leaders both in jail and far beyond South Africa's borders. Even if the PAC had been a more credible organizational and ideological rival it faced the same unforgiving conditions of repression.

Both inside South Africa and internationally, the PAC was a convenient 'other' against which the ANC could set itself off. Organizationally chaotic and ideologically incoherent, the PAC did not fit easily into any of the Cold War categories and characterizations that its rival became adept at navigating. The ANC was equally capable, on the one hand, of telling US congressmen that it was on a mission to realize the goals of the American constitution and, on the other, assure the Soviet Politburo that it was at the forefront of world revolution. And of course there was no way that the PAC, with its narrow chauvinism and anti-white rhetoric, could charm audiences of rock stars and other celebrities. If anything, as the struggle intensified in the 1980s and the possibilities of prosecuting it multiplied, the oblivion to which the PAC was confined hardened the ANC's own sense of mission and entitlement.

The Black Consciousness (BC) movement, although it had substantially the same roots in Africanism and many of the same preoccupations as the PAC, presented quite a different prospect to both the ANC and the white government. At first it was not at all clear exactly what challenge the movement posed to the government and what opportunity it represented for the ANC although it is likely that some far-sighted individuals in the ANC grasped the possibilities quite early on. Above all, it would have been very difficult for anyone on either side of the struggle divide to predict in the early 1970s that the inspiration of BC, if not its organizational expression, would prove the single greatest and most enduring catalyst of African resistance and struggle when its ideas sparked the Soweto uprising in 1976.

In what is a not-unfamiliar kind of political irony, the BC movement had its origins in two spectacular if short-term successes of the white minority government. The first was the suppression of all substantial African dissent in the 1960s. The second was a sustained period of economic growth in the same years. However in the case of the first, politics, like nature, abhors a vacuum, especially where, as in the case of African-South Africans, there were such manifold causes for discontent and a burning need to express them. As for the question of economic growth, whether you took a demand- or a supply-side view, there was an unmistakable need for more blacks as consumers and skilled workers if the momentum of growth was to be sustained. Sustained it had to be, to cope with a growing population whose proportions, as classified in apartheid categories, were changing. The 1970 census was quite a shock to white South Africa. In the 40 years from the 1911 census to the 1951 census, the population of South Africa more than doubled, but the proportion of whites declined by less than half a per cent. In the 19 years between the 1951 and the 1970 censuses, the population nearly doubled again from 8.6 million to 15 million and the percentage of whites dropped by 3.35 per cent, from 20.8 per cent to 17.5 per cent. In economic and political terms, if not in day-to-day, segregated perceptions, whites were becoming a noticeably smaller proportion of a noticeably more populous country.

The issues of population and economic growth on the one hand and black political expression on the other were unintentionally brought together by the Extension of University Education Act (June 1959). White liberals were quick to point out the Orwellian overtones of the Act's name, given that one of its principal purposes was to eliminate the freedom of hitherto 'open' universities to admit 'non-white' students, and to require ministerial permission for any future registrations of this sort. However, one of its other purposes was to establish new, segregated universities for Indians, Coloureds and several of the 'Bantu nations' designated in apartheid legislation. The legislation was prompted by a combination of far-sighted concern for the future economic development of 'white South Africa' and grand apartheid dreams of taking the development of the 'homelands' to its logical conclusion though in what proportion these considerations were influential it is difficult to say. What is clear is that the new educational institutions provided space in which new forms of dissent could develop, and from which they could be disseminated. To call these 'liberated spaces' would be going too far, given their segregation, their predominantly Afrikaner staff and the isolated locations that made surveillance and control easier. However, they offered some kind of freedom and could bring together critical masses of critical young black people. This context gave rise to a black consciousness which, over just short of a decade from the late 1960s to the late 1970s, gave new life to dissidence and a voice and profile to black resistance in South Africa. BC provided a language, a philosophy and a psychological disposition to a new generation of Africans. Above all it brought forward a charismatic, iconic and all-too-soon martyred leader in Steve Biko.

Influences on BC are variously described as being American Black Power (racial pride and community organization), theorists like Frantz Fanon (liberating and remaking the psychology of the colonized), and liberation theology (spiritual inspiration and a basis in Christian ethics for confronting racism). However, in basic outlook, BC is better seen in continuity with South African Africanism. The principal tenets of BC were relatively few and relatively simple and they did not need exotic influences for their impact, useful though they may have been for situating South African issues in a wider context. Among them were a sense of primal possession of the country, a rejection of victimhood in favour of outraged pride, the imperatives of self-reliance and rejection of white involvement in black struggles for liberation and, binding them all together, the need for psychological liberation. All of these had antecedents in earlier African nationalist discourse, from Anton Lembede, the inspiration of the ANCYL in the 1940s, through to the PAC. BC was also firmly embedded in African nationalist tradition and mythology in its emphasis on generational renewal. The idea that it is the mission of young people to purify and renew African nationalism periodically has been around since the 1940s, and is still relevant today, if in the somewhat debased form of Julius Malema. This idea of generational mission was a key source of energy for BC.

Although it was rooted in South African theory and practice, BC did strike out in new directions. It challenged the ANC's non-racialism from a much more informed and strategically sophisticated standpoint than the PAC. However, the movement confirmed the status of Coloureds and Indians as 'black' so long as they identified with Africans. There might even be a place for whites, since the position on the 'white question' was not always consistent or unambiguous over time and between BC adherents. For some, being 'African' was a matter of consciousness rather than race, a creative and in its way generous construct, if wholly impractical. BC challenged both the ANC and the PAC in terms of the timing and phasing of the struggle; confrontation was premature until the self-management and self-consciousness that come from psychological rehabilitation were well advanced. It challenged the PAC's naïve belief that unified African national consciousness was already a latent, revolutionary force which required only the spark of bold leadership to ignite, by emphasizing the need for hard consciousness-raising labour. Much of this, of course, was strategy and tactics (which could be challenged by the ANC in turn); the key things – self-reliance, pride, outrage at dispossession – could selectively be put to use by anyone.

BC's organizational life was brief and not extensive. The South African Students Organization (SASO 1968) grew out of Biko's rejection of white domination of the non-racial National Union of South African Students (NUSAS), at that time the most radical voice of dissent that could operate legally. The Black People's Convention (BPC 1972) combined cultural, community, health and education work. The University Christian Movement (UCM 1967) used the relative freedom of religious organization to explore the potential of liberation theology for African dissent. BC was never a mass movement and had no apparent strategy to become one. Consistent with its priorities it had no strategy for immediate confrontation with the white state. For this reason, BC had a surprising amount of room to manoeuvre in its early days. Probably the more sophisticated of the security police greatly relished the movement's vehement rejection of white liberals and, such was the capacity of apartheid ideologues for fantasy, some of them may have briefly believed that BC could be compatible with apartheid's ends. However, even if BC as a philosophy was not dedicated to immediate and broad-front confrontation of racism, Biko was committed to it as an individual, especially if provoked by insult or injury, and he was banned as early as 1973. BC's greatest achievement was as a raiser of consciousness. It is ironic that although BC doctrine preached the long game of psychological preparation for liberation, its impact on South Africa's liberation struggle should have been to provide a sudden and cataclysmic acceleration of conflict. History shows that BC's legacy was to provide the inspiration for the Soweto protests in June 1976 against the imposition of Afrikaans as a medium of instruction in schools. In the face of brutal and murderous repression of the initially peaceful gatherings, protest became uprising, at the eventual cost, in the disputed official count, of 176 lives. For once a much overused verdict is appropriate – nothing would ever be the same again.

It would not be the organizations of BC that would profit though. Even before Soweto they were on a collision course with the apartheid state over celebrations of the coming to power of liberation movement FRELIMO in Mozambique as a result of the Portuguese revolution in 1974. Some BC members were imprisoned, others banned. After Soweto the repression widened, the organizations themselves were banned and there was a massive outflow of young refugees. The ANC's diplomatic legitimacy, contacts and resources meant that the overwhelming majority joined, to be re-educated in CST, non-racialism, Marxist economics and the necessity for the armed struggle, which the ANC had adopted in 1961 and BC had rejected as an option. However, the continuing appeal of Africanism had been amply demonstrated and the need for the ANC to absorb its energy in ways that did not compromise non-racialism while demonstrating its own sensitivity to the special needs of African national aspirations was emphatically reconfirmed. Neither the PAC nor BC represented a serious challenge to the ANC's leadership of resistance to apartheid. The conditions of white minority rule simply could not allow any African political movement to reach maturity, and both were cut down while still full of formative contradictions and ambiguities. In any case it is likely that most Africans who harboured doubts about the ANC thought these uncertainties less important than the need for unity in the face of uniform persecution. However, if the ANC's position as leader of African nationalism was not too difficult to achieve and maintain, it did come at the expense of tolerating many ambiguities and contradictions in the ANC itself. Some of them were, as we have seen, part of the ANC's own heritage and some were the result of absorbing other traditions like BC. This latter point raises the question of the ambiguous Zulu factor in the development of African nationalism in South Africa. Did Buthelezi and the movement he led make a genuine contribution to African nationalism or were they only the latest and most dangerous version of the demon of tribalism?

## The ambiguous Zulu factor: The demon of tribalism or popular ethnic politics?

Chief (or alternatively, Prince) Mangosuthu Buthelezi and the movement he led presented the ANC with the most complex problems of all in coming to terms with alternative or rival conceptions of the meaning of African nationalism. As part of a far from flattering portrait of Buthelezi, Mark Gevisser, Thabo Mbeki's biographer, describes him as: 'At times a far-sighted and courageous visionary and at times a dangerous spoiler, Buthelezi has been the tempest of South African politics, its ungovernable storm' (Gevisser 2007: 328). Despite a measure of figurative overkill, this verdict captures the centrality of Buthelezi and the force of his presence in all questions of nation-building – at least up until the late 1990s. What needs to be added to this sketch is the ambiguity which attached itself to Buthelezi's career. Some of this ambiguity was, as it was for the ANC, forced on him by the constrictions of apartheid and the limits on strategic and tactical choices thus produced. Some was forced by the looming presence of the ANC itself. African nationalists who did not from the beginning subordinate themselves to the ANC or who broke away from it, not only had to navigate in the restricted space allowed to them by apartheid, but they also had to find terms of coexistence with the ANC itself.

Born in 1928 of aristocratic and royal Zulu lineage, Buthelezi straddled the old and new generations of the ANC of his time. Like the founding notables he was of rank, but he was educated in two of the forcing grounds of nationalist politics: Adams College in Amanzimtoti (South of Durban) and Fort Hare University (in the Eastern Cape), where he joined the ANCYL, struck up a lifelong friendship with Oliver Tambo and knew as colleagues Robert Sobukwe (founder of the PAC) and Robert Mugabe. He assumed the chiefship of the powerful Buthelezi clan in 1953, a position that traditionally carried with it the office of senior adviser to the Zulu monarch (although Buthelezi's antagonists in the ANC challenged this claim). In 1970 he became leader of the KwaZulu Territorial Authority, the governing body for the KwaZulu homeland set up by the apartheid government, and subsequently, as the homeland developed more powers under the white government's plans for its 'independence', he became its Chief Minister. In this position he made the most of any chance to frustrate the apartheid authorities and display whatever independence he could. Ironically Buthelezi's main exercise of independence was to refuse to exercise apartheid's bogus self-determination and take 'independence' for KwaZulu. According to Gevisser, 'he ran rings round the dull-witted conspirators of apartheid whose interest he supposedly served' (ibid.). Attracted by Buthelezi's ability to oppose apartheid from an official position within it and by his ANC credentials, the ANC saw in him the potential to lead a mass opposition to apartheid in South Africa, and negotiated with him to do so under the aegis of, or at least in association with, the ANC. This was an ill-founded and unstable relationship. Quite apart from the entirely asymmetrical terms of their existence – the ANC banned and exiled, Buthelezi in the heart of the apartheid system – which posed very severe restrictions on outward recognition of the association, from the start Buthelezi made it clear that he was totally opposed to armed struggle, that only non-violent means were acceptable to him, and he rejected the communist influence on the ANC. One thing at least seems agreed, that the ANC favoured the creation of a movement to give Buthelezi a mass base with which to oppose apartheid. Thus it was that Inkatha was created (or more accurately, 'revived', since there had been an earlier organization of that name) in 1975 as a 'cultural organization'. Gevisser says that the intention was that it should be a 'crypto-ANC organization' (ibid. 329–40). This may have been the ANC's view, but it is unlikely to have been that of Buthelezi and the corps of traditional leaders (chiefs and headmen) on whom he depended. If the ANC indeed saw Inkatha and its leader as no more than a pawn – and such an interpretation fits with the general ethos of the ANC – then it is no wonder the relationship foundered openly by 1979. The breakup was so acrimonious, and the documentary evidence of its existence and substance is so scanty, that it is very hard to know exactly what either side hoped to get out of the relationship, how each side hoped to use the other, how sincere they were in cooperating and for that matter what the cooperation consisted of.

Buthelezi's short-lived and enigmatic period in the role of stalking horse for the ANC coincided with his effort to build a genuinely national African nationalist constituency. He treated the PAC and its leaders with respect, drawing on his long-standing relationship with Sobukwe who, despite his marginalization through both his personal banning and the ineffectiveness of the organization he founded, remained revered across the range of African nationalist opinion. He also made overtures to the BCM but was excoriated for his 'collaboration'. The end of these overtures came at Sobukwe's funeral in 1978 when, such was the animosity shown to

Buthelezi by some of the mourners, that Archbishop Desmond Tutu advised him to leave for his own safety and so that the dignity of the occasion could be restored. Despite these setbacks, Buthelezi entered the 1980s with footholds in the apartheid state system, in the bases of traditional authority in KwaZulu and in tentatively emerging prospects of negotiation between African nationalism and representatives of white interests (principally in Natal) other than the apartheid state itself. In this way, Buthelezi was able to claim that Inkatha was a genuine contender for a different conception of African nationalism to that of the ANC. He could do this by claiming, first, to represent authentic African traditions and historical continuity with pre-colonial polities which resisted imperialism, and in contemporary terms to represent principled, non-violent struggle against racism and white minority rule. Secondly, he could claim that Inkatha held out the hope of genuine reconciliation through negotiation and through moderation and acceptance of the role of business and enterprise as the only hope of development and prosperity, rather than the centralized, authoritarian, communist-shaped vision of the future promised by the ANC. Unsurprisingly the ANC contested these claims in every detail; tradition had been corrupted and continuity ruptured by colonial subjugation; armed struggle was the true legacy of pre-colonial resistance; deals with white capitalists were the stock in trade of sell-outs. Despite the ANC's protestations, four things strengthened Buthelezi's position. In the first place, Inkatha had an open and legal presence on the ground and limited, but real space to exploit it; it mobilized for elections and administered its own territory. Secondly, the potential for ethnic mobilization in African politics was greater in KwaZulu – and 'white' Natal – than in other parts of the country. The nineteenth-century Zulu kingdom offered a mythological resource to political entrepreneurs that was unmatched elsewhere in South Africa. The sheer vigour of its projects of state- and nation-building and the extent to which these shaped South African history ensured that pre-colonial social formations and resistance to colonialism obtruded further there into contemporary political conflict than anywhere else. Thirdly, the geopolitics of KwaZulu and Natal differed in one important respect from those of other regions. KwaZulu was the only homeland whose territory impinged significantly on the borders of white cities and their satellite (African) townships. Indeed Natal's principal cities, Durban and Pietermaritzburg, were surrounded by territory administered by KwaZulu. As a result, the major *casus belli* between the UDF and Inkatha, in the violent conflict which developed between them in the 1980s, was the threatened incorporation of some townships outside Durban and Pietermaritzburg into KwaZulu; a crucial power struggle which would help decide the outcome of the competition for African popular support. In addition, this geopolitical factor ensured that Inkatha figured in the consciousness and calculations of Natal's white business and political elites in a way that no other black political movement did before the unbanning of the liberation movements in 1990. The fourth factor was the configuration of white politics in Natal, which, without a sizeable Afrikaner population, had no natural constituency for the NP. In 1910, Natal was ambivalent about the Union; in 1960 it rejected the Republic and continued to identify with its own colonial origins and English ethos. Thus the mutually reinforcing alienation between Natal and the central government disposed white elites to consider separate negotiations with black political forces. They found a receptive partner in Buthelezi, who saw that such negotiations would give him useful political space in which to resist the government's pressure to take independence, and in which to prosecute Inkatha's rivalry with the ANC. Such initiatives of this sort that did take place, notably the Buthelezi Commission (1982) and the KwaZulu-Natal Indaba (1986), were inconclusive. However, they served to accustom all concerned to the idea of negotiations between black and white interests. They also warned the nationalist government and the ANC that excessive immobilism on their parts would open the way to initiatives that they could not control.

The interaction of all these factors allowed Inkatha to transcend the stereotype of homeland patronage politics, to create a political movement which shared concerns with white business and political elites as well as conservative Africans, and still had a foothold in the urban, African politics of 'white' South Africa. This did not mean that patronage was an insignificant part of Inkatha's mobilization capacities. On the contrary, the KwaZulu government's role as a conduit for central state expenditure and as a major employer offered considerable resources of patronage to whoever controlled it and Inkatha exploited this ruthlessly. Patronage offered a material return for the ethnic identities propagated by Inkatha, and ethnicity cloaked patronage in the mantle of popular politics. This self-reinforcing relationship grounded Buthelezi's claims to be a popular leader and Inkatha's to be a mass movement – albeit now in a regional rather than a national context. These claims led in logical sequence to another; one in which Buthelezi and his movement could play the role of broker between black and white interests. Buthelezi appeared to channel black aspirations within limits compatible with white vested interests. On the other hand, for conservative blacks he appeared to hold out the prospect of liberation from apartheid without the traumas of armed struggle and sanctions, or indeed the self-mutilating strategies of strikes and educational boycotts favoured by the UDF and behind it, the ANC. What is more, his conception of liberation did not threaten to sweep away the established practices, prerogatives and relationships of African tradition in a general upheaval of revolutionary modernization. In this way it was his claim to be a popular leader which validated his leverage in white circles, and this supposed leverage then validated his claim to rival the ANC with an alternative liberation strategy.

## The balance sheet of inheritance

Understandably the principal legacy of Afrikaner nationalism to the new South Africa has been as an example of the dark side of ethno-nationalism. Driven on to extravagant ambitions of state-building by elemental fears, it resorted to unchecked, often brutal power in the face of impossible odds. Yet as befits such a contradictory and ambiguous phenomenon, this is not the only lesson that can be learned from it. We can also reflect on how something which was designed to create and defend an elemental identity became so mutable, to the point that the claim can be seriously made on behalf of the people who bore it, that they chose to 'exit with some grace' (Giliomee 2003: 634) from the history they made for themselves. Perhaps the lesson is that invented nations can be temporary instruments of prosaic goals such as economic security and social mobility, rather than vessels of destiny.

By the time it had arrived at the threshold of negotiations, the ANC had developed an institutional reflex for accommodation that placed it at the head of an assorted liberation movement. Already those who were committed to principled non-racialism as well as doctrinaire communists and black racial nationalists could see what they wanted (or at least a path to achieving it) in the ANC's lightly sketched iterations of the nation and nationalism. It remained to be seen whether this reflex — which optimists saw as inclusivity and sceptics feared was co-option — could be extended to broader questions of nationhood and nationalism. The ANC had got to this point by being inventively adaptable and not losing too much sleep over the contradictions that inevitably accompany adaptation. The question was however, if all went well, whether this institutional reflex to accommodate all comers would suit the questions that power would ask of it, as well as it had undoubtedly suited the liberation struggle. First would come confrontation not only with the various legatees of white minority rule, but also those who, in the shape of Buthelezi and Inkatha claimed to represent a force with which the ANC had scarcely engaged — that of traditional African society and values.

# CHAPTER THREE

# Improvising the nation: 1990–6

## The nation and the settlement

By 1990 the struggle for South Africa's future, conceived as a stand-off between Afrikaner and African nationalism, appeared to have run its course. That is one among numerous reasons – the others included stalemate on the ground between rebellion and repression, economic crisis and a changing international context – that made the unbanning of the ANC and other liberation movements not only possible but essential. By 1989, Afrikaner nationalism was no longer a coherent and credible vehicle for the majority of Afrikaner aspirations and fears, never mind broader white concerns. The ANC was under insistent pressure to formulate a credible position on negotiations, not only from Western governments and bodies such as the Commonwealth, but also from the leaders of the Frontline states in Southern Africa and now even its erstwhile sponsors in the rapidly dissolving Soviet bloc. The ANC did this, in the form of preconditions contained in the OAU-sponsored Harare Declaration (1989). With this document, more than two decades of convoluted and ambiguous ideological baggage appeared to have been set aside in favour of a statement of principle that was startlingly eloquent in its clarity and simplicity of purpose. Although the declaration contained preconditions for negotiation, its true significance lay in the fact that it went much further than that by specifying the principles that the *outcome* of the negotiations should embody. These included that South Africa should become a united, democratic and non-racial state, with common and equal citizenship and nationality, as well as universal suffrage in a multi-party system. All the citizens of this new state should 'enjoy universally recognized human rights and civil liberties under an entrenched bill of rights'. At a stroke the Harare Declaration appeared to accept the removal of all questions of identity and nation from the conflict, to define liberation exclusively in terms of the realization of rights and to resolve the ambiguities and contradictions between Africanism and non-racialism in favour of the latter. It was immediately clear that this was a bold challenge to the white government to respond in the same terms. What was less clear, except to those who had taken the trouble to follow ANC discourse in its strategic documents and pronouncements over the previous decade was the extent of the challenge it presented to its own supporters.

Given the mobilizing role played on both sides, both officially and unofficially, by ethnic and racial nationalism, the possibility that South Africa's conflicts could be resolved by negotiation, without further reference to questions of identity and nationhood beyond common and equal citizenship, appeared to be a radical development. However, it was a possibility that had some historical grounding. South Africa had been a self-governing state since 1910. Its boundaries had not been in dispute, especially given the degree of integration of what was clearly a national economy. The recognition of this economic interdependence was one of the key motivations for the abandonment of apartheid by its architects. Throughout its history, up to the point when negotiations began, South Africa had never been subject to ethnic separatism. The only fissiparous threat was apartheid's coercive devolution of 'sovereignty' to the homelands. One of the legacies of Afrikaner nationalism had been to discredit the idea of nationalism in the eyes of many people. Nationalism was by now indelibly associated with racism, denial of rights and economic exploitation, rendering it difficult for believers in alternative, positive forms of nationalism to make a case. Ethno-national or racial, or any other non-voluntary form of exclusive national association, appeared in any case to be a non-starter given South Africa's diverse population; unless it were to be a majoritarian, African ethno-nationalism. This possibility would be fraught with many problems, not least the fact that no such nation yet existed. Colonialism and apartheid did not impose themselves on a unified African polity across the territory that became the Union of South Africa, an absence which was a major ingredient in imperial and settler success. The various nineteenth-century African societies that were forced into submission were keenly aware of their distinctiveness even when not actively in conflict with each other. Any contemporary expression of the aspiration to African nationalism had to use the past tactfully and selectively. There was some material that could be reconstituted and reclaimed, such as warrior resistance to colonial armies, although even this had to be used sensitively to avoid hints of tribal chauvinism. However, for the most part, a mythology of African nationalism had to be created in the struggle by exemplary heroism and sacrifice, as well as patient education. The ANC espoused these nation-building ideals in theory, but under extremely difficult conditions could only deliver with patchy cover.

Despite all this, it was still remarkable how quickly the basis of negotiations solidified around the working principle that questions of national identity had been resolved – at least for the main protagonists: the

ANC and the NP. Given their histories, these two were unlikely standard-bearers for secular, civic conceptions of democracy. The conversion was swift and somewhat opaque on both sides: 'Yet the common ground between these unlikely partners in democracy turned out to be the classic discourse of liberal constitutionalism' (Johnson and Schlemmer 1996: 8). Given the sheer weight of both the NP's base in the state apparatus and the ANC's in the population, it was not surprising that this agenda was recognized by all 19 participants in the Convention for a Democratic South Africa (CODESA), in a Declaration of Intent of December 1991. However, none of the various statements and declarations made an overt statement of what would bind all the parties and their supporters together in any long-term resolution of their differences. In this respect it is hard to say when or even if civic nationalism – loyalty to constitutional arrangements rather than some combination of culture, ethnicity, race and religion – came to be the mainstream position on national identity. The whole process of negotiation from beginning to end was based on the tacit assumption that such a sense of identity was already there or would emerge. However, it was silent on where such confidence came from, not to mention how it would be expressed in practice and then sustained.

In the light of all these things, there seemed little to negotiate other than the form and content of rights and constitutional engineering to give effect to them. Nation and nationalism appeared no longer to matter to the main protagonists once negotiations began in earnest. However, they did to some of the junior partners negotiating South Africa's future, despite their signing the CODESA Declaration of Intent, which appeared to rule them out. The most obvious residual influence was in ethnic separatism which for the first time revealed itself as a threat. One manifestation of this was the neo-partitionist stance of the Afrikaner nationalist rump, the CP and the paramilitary AWB, which were in sometimes uneasy alliance. The second was the Inkatha Freedom Party (IFP), into which Inkatha had transformed itself when free and open national political activity became possible after February 1990. Any lingering illusions held by Buthelezi that he and his movements could be the principal African negotiating partners of the white government on a national basis did not long survive Mandela's release from prison. Any ambitions the IFP had to compete for the African popular vote would have to be on a regional basis. Fortunately for Buthelezi, at this time Natal and KwaZulu (they were not formally joined together as the province of KwaZulu-Natal until 1994) constituted the most populous segment of the country and represented a considerable electoral prize.

Even before 1990, Inkatha projected a confusing and enigmatic menu of possibilities. Two of these stood out. The first was as the militant defender of indigenous traditional values, ways of life and structures of power. What threatened them in the eyes of Buthelezi and his supporters was the ANC's uncompromisingly modernizing and alien agenda, driven by cosmopolitan and communist influences acquired and honed in exile. The second was as the moderate interlocutor of white fears and partner in the shared interest of preserving South Africa's core economic capacities from precipitate, coercive redistribution by expropriation and nationalization. As the negotiation process developed, the ANC drastically modified its positions on economic policy, jettisoning nationalization and predicting a strong role for private enterprise in a mixed economy. A by-product of this was the devaluation of Buthelezi's currency as the moderate face of African nationalism. It also became clear that the ANC and the NP believed that there was a real threat of anarchy unless they developed a meaningful partnership – albeit an adversarial one – to take control as the chief arbiters of the negotiations, and thereby bringing them to a successful conclusion. In parallel to this, the IFP's agendas became expressed in ever-more confused terms which combined ethno-nationalism, federalism, confederalism and outright secession, the emphasis shifting between them on a virtually day-by-day basis. It was never very clear whether the IFP wished to be understood as a secular, moderate, right-of-centre political party or a separatist liberation movement of ethno-nationalists. While the principal parties quite soon lost patience with this, neither of them and in particular the ANC, could afford to ignore the various challenges posed by the IFP.

However, it was not only through the destabilizing potential of separatism that issues of identity and nation continued to make themselves felt. The extent to which they had ceased to influence the main protagonists was more apparent than real. What had happened was not that they had abandoned their national concerns in favour of confidence in a new democratic, national unified state, but that they had adapted or postponed their strategies for dealing with them in the new circumstances. For the NP, ethno-nationalism had long since ceased to be a viable means of organizing and securing Afrikaner interests and territorial separation through bogus self-determination, and as a viable way of containing African nationalism. By midway through the negotiations, the NP could claim support for continuation of negotiations from around half of Afrikaners and overall from more than two-thirds of whites who voted in the whites-only referendum of March 1992. They could also hope optimistically for the support of some Coloureds and Indians and even some conservative Africans. By no stretch of imagination could this be called a nation and it had no organizing and legitimizing ideology. Even the whites-only referendum was only an imperfect guide, since it wisely did not allow voters to say anything about their preferred outcomes for the negotiations, merely whether they wanted them to continue or not. What the NP claimed to stand for were the interests of all who felt they had something to lose from the triumphal accession to power of a combination of Marxist populism and African nationalism, bound together by the insurrectionary rhetoric that had propelled the ANC and its surrogates through the 1980s. The onset of negotiations and the ANC's changes of course on constitutional principle and economic policy had made this prospect more remote, but did not banish it altogether. Certainly there were many who were sceptical about the sincerity of the conversion. The NP had to walk a fine line between hinting at these fears and not being swamped by them, thereby pushing its supporters in the direction of the white right. Accordingly throughout the process, its negotiating positions conflated and confused common and plural conceptions of society and proposed various constitutional forms to express them. These began with a kind of neo-consociationalism and ended with federalism as a kind of 'partition-without-tears'. What the various points along the route had in common with each other (and with reform apartheid before them) was that they were rearguard efforts to ward off 'simple majoritarianism' or what Mandela took to calling 'ordinary democracy'. The subtext to this of course was the fear that majoritarianism would mean racial domination through the vehicle of African nationalism, propelled by elections that would be racial censuses, and conceivably helped along by the kind of tricks of incumbency that a dominant party can use to create a de facto one-party state (tricks in which, historically, the NP was itself well versed). In short, the subtext was that to believe that the triumph of non-racialism was enshrined in the Harare Declaration was a short-sighted view. In the longer view non-racialism was probably a Trojan horse, out of which the shock troops of African nationalism would pour once the democratic niceties were concluded, and power was painlessly and legitimately transferred.

Naturally enough, this conception of what was at stake challenged the ANC's own conception of a single state run as an 'ordinary democracy', in which it would have every legitimate reason to expect to take and retain power for the foreseeable future, subject only to whatever limitations would be negotiated in the Bill of Rights envisaged by the Harare Declaration. This was not all however. National issues retained significance and threatened repercussions on the ANC's own side of the table in the aftermath of its apparently unqualified and somewhat insouciant endorsement of non-racialism in the Harare Declaration. In reality, such a confident manifesto could not simply sweep away all the ambivalences about the status of settlers and the 'nature of the ruling class', which made the relationship between CST and non-racialism such a queasy one. Indeed, with the revival of the ANC's fortunes in the 1970s and the intensification of the struggle in the 1980s, the relationship seemed even more unstable. As early as 1966 the General Assembly of the United Nations had labelled apartheid a 'crime against humanity'. The convention which defined the nature of the crime, those criminally responsible and the steps to be taken by member states to prosecute them, came into force in 1976 and the determination of apartheid's criminality was endorsed by the Security Council in 1984. Doubtless there was a good deal of diplomatic posturing in all of this, and in any case the ANC was always more concerned with fashioning instruments to intensify the struggle than to give thought to their future once the struggle was successfully concluded. However, given the generosity with which the scope of the crime and the identity of those responsible were drawn, to anyone in the least literally minded, all whites were guilty at a minimum of having profited from a crime against humanity and many thousands were perpetrators of it. Leaving aside the jurisprudential merits of the Convention and the prospects of finding a practical application for it, it was nevertheless an unpromising basis for non-racial nation-building.

The ANC (and the SACP) did intermittently try to address this kind of issue by considering theoretically the make-up of the white population. As the parties geared up for negotiation, the most recent effort had been a discussion paper, *The Nature of the South African Ruling Class*, presented at the ANC's Second Consultative Conference at Kabwe in 1985 (ANC 1985). The paper began with unusual frankness by admitting that the vague terms customarily employed in ANC documents, such as 'white group', 'white minority', 'racist minority', were 'not much assistance in clarifying who exactly the ruling class in South Africa are'. Despite this promising beginning, *The Nature of the South African Ruling Class* proved to be no more than a reiteration of conventional pieties from CST and previous 'Strategy and Tactics' documents. The key element was the confirmation that majority rule meant rule by the *African* majority: 'In neither the revolutionary programme nor the alliance for national liberation can there be any ambiguity about the primary role of the African majority. This is equally applicable to the organs of self-determination and people's power that will assume the reins of power in the post-revolutionary society' (ibid.). This requirement, by adding a national qualification to a democratic concept, was likely to set up all manner of expectations in those who were members of this putative 'majority' as well as stoking the fears of those who were not. As for whites, the paper recycled the dogma that only a tiny number of them had an interest in preserving capitalism. In this version, enacting the Freedom Charter would entail, 'the seizure of economic assets presently owned by either South African capitalist firms or transnational corporations'. These measures would, 'place political power in the hands of the black masses and transform South Africa from a country belonging to and exploited by a small class of white capitalists and their imperialist allies into a country belonging to all who live in it, black and white'. The conceptualization of South African capitalism and the whites' relationship to it was crude and naïve, glossing over, for instance, how pension funds and managerial interests broadened and deepened the roots of South African capitalism in the white (and even to a limited but growing extent the black) community. The idea that only a 'small class of capitalists' would be inconvenienced by wholesale expropriation was not credible, but for those prepared to suspend disbelief, it stretched a fig leaf of absolution over the 'crimes' of the vast majority of whites by casting capitalism rather than apartheid as the principal villain. Sustained, critical self-reflection on the ANC's economic ideas – which they had never received – was now urgently needed from the perspective of a government-in-waiting. Perhaps, it was their very crudity that allowed them to be jettisoned early in the negotiation process in favour of intensive work, which began behind the scenes, on more nuanced policies for redistribution that were more in tune with economic reality.

Smoothing the path for negotiation with the white government and white capitalists was a pressing imperative; so too, however, was keeping its own base intact. During the 1970s and 1980s a new generation of activists was recruited who, whether or not they formally belonged to the ANC's military wing MK, regarded themselves as soldiers. The ANC publicly prided itself on how well it had received new generations from different backgrounds like BC or no political backgrounds at all, integrating and re-educating them in ANC doctrines, especially non-racialism. An integral part of this was to extend and intensify the militarization of the liberation movement. This was not only to satisfy the desire of the new recruits for action against the brutal regime, but also to extend military discipline to them whether or not they bore arms and in doing so take the opportunity to impose political uniformity. Inevitably the success of this process was greater when it took place in the closed conditions of exile camps. The fluid and dynamic conditions of township uprising were a different matter, especially since the 1976 uprising and its aftermath in the townships had been such a forceful statement of generational self-assertion by the young – something never to be underestimated in ANC internal politics. This generation had been inspired by the vision of African national liberation in which a majority is defined racially and not in a civic, race-blind, ahistoric, shifting way, expressed by rational voter choice on the part of a non-racial, rights-bearing population. After all, this was what (among other contradictory things) their leaders told them to expect. They were also inspired and led by ANC (and SACP) documents with a vision, not of compromise but victory achieved by insurrection, seizure of power and the destruction of the enemy state. It might be an overstatement to claim with such certitude, as Martin Legassick does, that: 'Certainly the overwhelming viewpoint in the factories, townships, schools and countryside in South Africa in the 1980s was that the struggle for democracy would culminate in a revolutionary, armed seizure of power by the masses' (2002: 8). Equally however, it was unlikely that the many people who fought and made innumerable, painful sacrifices, including the supreme one, did so solely because they were inspired by the embryonic spirit of an as-yet-unnamed civic, non-racial Rainbow Nation. It is little wonder that as the prospects for negotiation improved, commentators and observers were preoccupied with the problems of ANC leadership.

Writing in the immediate aftermath of the Kabwe conference in 1985, Tom Lodge predicted that, 'It would need formidable organization and very great qualities of leadership to call the children's army off the street. It would require even greater gifts to hold their allegiance during the complicated compromises and give and take of a negotiating process'

(1986: 13). As it turned out, the success of the security forces in repressing the insurrection between 1986 and the unbannings in February 1990 went far to make the first half of the leadership's task easier. After 1990 the momentum created by De Klerk's *coup de théâtre* and the aura created by the new-found proximity and freedom of the leaders, not to mention the prospect of imminent access to political power, did much to help.

Nevertheless, in mid-1991, Heribert Adam could write:

> Even the acclaimed ANC leadership is increasingly viewed with suspicion and scepticism. The more it presses on with negotiations and confidential understandings, the louder the whispers about sell-outs and shouts of autocratic behaviour. At best the activists see negotiations as war by other means, designed to culminate in a 'transfer of power'. The ANC leadership and returning exiles make heroic efforts to coax the grassroots into line, but even the credibility of the SACP is strained by its advocacy of 'guarantees for the bourgeoisie'. When Mandela courageously met with Buthelezi in January 1991, he did so at great risk and will have to pay the price in the months to come. Every encounter with de Klerk reinforces Mandela's image as the saviour of the whites but diminishes his standing within his own radical ranks. (1991: 8)

In short, the ANC leadership was faced across the negotiating table by adversaries who feared that non-racialism was a Trojan horse, while behind them were the ranks of its own supporters, some of whom feared that non-racialism was a conjuring trick, designed to deliver a white rabbit safely from the confines of a black hat.

So despite the tacit assumption that civic nationalism or something like it could underpin a negotiated democracy, and although national identity was not officially on the negotiating table, national issues swirled around the negotiations like ghosts at the feast. Although they were the concern of all the parties involved in the negotiations, the questions they raised were more numerous and serious on the ANC side of the table. Indeed they went to the heart of the ANC's most serious concerns – the integrity of the South African state and the wholeness of the African people. In addition, the ANC was the recognized heir apparent to whatever configuration of state power emerged from the negotiations, so that whatever residual problems of nation and nationalism remained would be for it to address.

Essentially the legacy of Afrikaner nationalism left two problems and the legacy of African nationalism another two. To different degrees but similar in principle, the claims of the neo-partitionist right and the NP's pluralist visions threatened the balkanization to which the ANC was acutely sensitive. The legacy of African nationalism determined that a decision had to be made on whether the IFP's Zulu ethno-nationalism should be treated as the demon of tribalism or an authentic, alternative expression of African popular politics. Finally, a way had to be found to accommodate the sense of national oppression and dispossession, which the ANC had elaborated over so long a time, with the liberal constitutionalism that it now espoused, and in doing so to marry national liberation with civic nationalism. These were formidable enough problems but circumstances were helpful to the ANC. The negotiations were grounded in fear of anarchy which affected the ANC and the NP most, but at crucial moments such anxieties affected even those who themselves threatened destabilization as part of their negotiation repertoire. The NP and the ANC also grasped early and conclusively that neither of them was able to impose its first-choice solutions on the other. The IFP and other spoilers came later to this recognition, but they got there too.

This, according to the somewhat downbeat conclusion of Johnson and Schlemmer, 'helps explain the paradox that the three main parties hammered out an essentially liberal democratic constitution, though none of them much believed in it' (1996: 8). The ANC was also able to count on a substantial measure of help from the imposing state apparatus which the NP still controlled in the eventuality that they had to enforce 'sufficient consensus' agreements made between them on dissidents of whatever persuasion. In the wider context, as the negotiations progressed both the main parties knew that they could count on support for any reasonable settlement from the majority of a population that was war weary, and after a couple of years of on–off negotiation and violence had had enough of glimpses of the abyss and too much of a permanent diet of uncertainty and hope. Both the ANC and the NP could also count on an impressive degree of moral and technical support from smaller players like the white liberal opposition, and from business, the media and non-aligned (but often at this stage pro-ANC) groups in civil society. This is a factor in improvising the nation that should not be underestimated.

The greatest threat to the improvised, civic nation which ANC and NP elites were conjuring into existence came from the neo-partitionist right. De Klerk's mandate for the continuation of negotiation in the whites-only referendum of March 1992 put the electoral strength of the white right in perspective, and made it clear that inclusive democracy could not be blocked using the resources of the old, racially exclusive polity. Nonetheless a constituency sufficiently large to be potentially troublesome remained among workers, public servants, farmers and individual members (though crucially not whole units) of the security forces. In the aftermath of the referendum this support was mobilized into political, cultural and paramilitary movements that at best were difficult to coordinate and at worst were factious and chaotic.

The main elements of the right were the CP and the AWB. The CP was overtly and proudly reactionary, clinging to the pieties of Afrikaner nationalism abandoned by the NP, and which by now were visible only in the rear view mirror of the rest of the country, as it accelerated into the future. The AWB was a *lumpen*, racist rabble. Such was the frustration, especially among farmers, with this ill-assorted coalition, that a new leadership emerged. In May 1993 General Constand Viljoen, a 'soldiers' general', who had been head of the army and of the defence force, answered the call from retirement on his farm, briefly lending a Shakespearean or even biblical dignity to the anachronistic and rather amateur, though undeniably threatening forces of the right. The Volksfront, which coalesced behind Viljoen, looked fleetingly as if it might become a force capable of landing a decisive blow for the right's principal goals: ethno-national mobilization, partition, territorial control and self-determination. That it did not was due to several factors. The CP remained too inhibited to throw itself wholeheartedly into sedition. The AWB was too undisciplined and volatile to fit into any coordinated strategy. However, there was more to it than organizational weakness.

The fundamental fact which shaped all others was the weakness of the case for partition – for the creation of a *volkstaat* as it came to be called – in both principle and practice. The ANC came to accept the Volksfront's claims under the respectable label of 'self-determination', instead of, as it might easily have done, the continuation of racism by other means. However, this only made matters worse. To be viable, a claim to self-determination starts with a pre-existing relationship between a people and a territory. The more consolidated the territory and the bigger the majority which the people constitutes on it, the better. The Volksfront's claims, to give them as full credit as is possible, began with an aspiration to self-rule and then had to continue with a search to find an artificially contrived territory to match the aspiration. This would have been a highly unusual, if not unprecedented, application of the principle of self-determination. In this eventuality two kinds of problem would interact; economic viability would require as wide borders and control over resources as possible, which in turn would mean either population transfers or a mixed population. A mixed population would invoke the 'minority within a minority' problem which bedevils most conflicts of self-determination (the Northern Ireland problem, for instance). The interaction of these factors would make coexistence between the white enclave state and greater South Africa very difficult indeed.

These facts were not unknown on both sides of the table when complex negotiations took place in late 1993 directly between the Volksfront and the ANC, led by Mbeki (see Gevisser 2007: 614–22 for an account of the negotiations). The Volksfront was by now allied with the Concerned South Africans Group (COSAG), a coalition of the disaffected led by Buthelezi, which had left the negotiations in June 1993 in protest against the ANC/NP condominium, which was directing the negotiations towards jointly agreed conclusions. Mbeki, who by then had been superseded at the head of the ANC negotiating team by Cyril Ramaphosa, was tasked with bringing first the Volksfront and then Buthelezi back, both into the negotiations and into the first democratic elections scheduled for April 1994. The negotiations were made complex by the fact that any agreement made by Mbeki was subject to the approval of Ramaphosa and Roelf Meyer, the chief NP/government negotiator, who were members of the Transitional Executive Council (TEC), the body effectively overseeing the final stages of transition, with the authority of Mandela and De Klerk behind it.

Because no-one knew where the *volkstaat* was, all the Volksfront's options were weak. It could not do what other claimants to self-determination could; simply declare independence on a consolidated territory it demographically dominated and invite anyone who disagreed to dispute the independence by force. Its only alternatives were to petition to be granted a territory peacefully, or go to war in order to define a territory in terms of wherever and whatever it could hold. The only possible middle road would be to continue the boycott and refuse to participate in the election. However, a passive boycott of the poll would probably be ineffective and an active boycott – dissuasion and disruption – would probably slide into anarchy and war anyway, especially given the indiscipline of some of the right's supporters. That the Volksfront took the pacific option is conventionally credited to the quality of Mbeki's diplomacy. This fits in with a general narrative of the transitional negotiations which ascribes near mystical powers of persuasion to the ANC in general and Mbeki in particular. Certainly Mbeki seemed to be gifted at stringing an adversary along until the impracticalities and weaknesses of his position become too obvious for him to ignore. Probably the Volksfront negotiations are a case in point, helped along by the fact that Viljoen and his colleagues' dislike for and distrust of the NP were deep and bitter enough to make the ANC appear straight dealers by comparison. Mbeki and Viljoen reached an agreement on a mechanism to move forward on consideration of a *volkstaat*. It is probable that each party saw different things in this agreement, but in any case it was much diluted over Mbeki's head by the upper reaches of the ANC/NP axis. Even so, the white right was back on the threshold of participation.

Contingency and another structural weakness of the right combined in one last twist to secure the Volksfront for democratic participation in at least the first South African democratic election. Under the new circumstances of open politics, even the most blinkered enthusiast for Afrikaner or white self-determination could not remain unaware of the need for allies from within the 75 per cent or so of the population that were African. Since Buthelezi was forced to scale down his ambitions to regional self-determination, he made an attractive ally with genuine assets. However, the bantustan leaders who made up the other components of COSAG were always likely to be a source of weakness to their white allies and opportunity to the ANC. So it proved in the case of Lucas Mangope, leader of Bophuthatswana. Contingency played its part when Mangope refused to cooperate with the transitional authorities in preparing for elections in the territory. A popular uprising against him, orchestrated by ANC activists to bring about reincorporation, prompted him to call for help. Viljoen arrived to organize Mangope's army, but the AWB also intervened, with fatal results. Its brief inglorious incursion combined farce and tragedy, culminating in the summary execution in front of TV cameras of three, already-wounded AWB men by a Bophuthatswana policeman in retaliation for the injury and killing of some local people in indiscriminate shooting by the AWB. Viljoen drew the lesson that with forces like the AWB behind him any military option would be disastrous, and without a military option in the background he had to participate in the election or accept total marginalization. He registered his party, the Freedom Front (FF) for the election the next day. Self-determination might live to fight another day, but it would be a democratic and peaceful day. The tide was now running strongly for the ANC/NP axis, especially in favour of the liberation movement, and the TEC seized the opportunity to depose Mangope.

Thus it was in a combination of patient coaxing, a remarkable facility for speaking with more than one voice and in more than one register, allied to speed of thought and action to take advantage of a dramatic and fast-moving situation that the ANC managed to defuse the secessionist threat of the white right. It was able to rely on the NP to back it up, not least in the gamble of relying on the loyalty of the South African Defence Force (SADF).

It remained to deal with the other dimension of the white problem, the NP's threat to the ANC's vision of a unitary state based on majoritarian democracy, which remained undiluted by special constitutional arrangements or strong federal powers. On this front the ANC was rather less engaging and accommodating than it had been in tactically indulging the fantasies of self-determination of the white right. However, it did not opt for full-on confrontation fuelled by the rhetoric of national liberation. Instead it remained consistent with and faithful to the liberal–democratic agenda sketched in the Harare Declaration and signed up to by all the other parties in the CODESA Declaration. In doing so it treated the NP to a remorseless lesson in the logic of the path that the negotiations had taken, and it signalled that it expected others to remain faithful to this logic too.

An early example of this position was outlined in 1990 by Albie Sachs, constitutional lawyer, former political prisoner, victim of state terror and later to be a Constitutional Court judge (Sachs 1990: 149–73). As he put it, the white problem was reflected in claims for special constitutional treatment on spurious grounds of minority rights and the allegedly superior democratic quality of federalism. These claims and proposals threatened to dilute the democratic quality of the eventual constitution by giving 'every consideration' to race and colour. Minority rights and federalism were ways of insulating privilege from change: building a new nation would require establishing the means by which whites became ordinary citizens: 'their true interests as citizens, no better or worse than anyone else's can be protected and this includes their interests both as individuals and as members of cultural, religious and other groups'. As for federalism, South Africa had been a union for 80 years, and 'Only now that the prospect of universal suffrage is on the near horizon does unity suddenly become weakness.' The issue was simply one of dressing up self-interest as principle. Federalism in South Africa would draw boundaries around race and ethnicity: 'This would prevent the emergence of a national government, keep the black population divided, prevent any restructuring of the country and free the economically prosperous areas of the country from helping develop the vast poverty-stricken areas.' In contrast to the various spurious claims that were no more than disguised bids to maintain privilege beyond their statutory abolition, Sachs posed an ideal future of nation-building: 'not as a country of majorities and minorities, each seeking selfish advantages against each other, but as a kind of diverse people sharing a common humanity and embarking on the difficult road of establishing a common loyalty and patriotism'. What would secure a stable democracy and a nation of citizens, however, would be more than just 'common humanity', but the tangible features of the new polity and society, including equal rights, accountable government, political pluralism, a mixed economy and separation of powers. Insofar as it makes sense to talk of a 'liberal wing' of the ANC, Sachs probably represented its outer edge. However, nothing in this exposition deviated much from the ANC's negotiating line in the development of the new constitution.

Admirable in its clarity, unsparing in its conclusions, it is a remarkable example of the resources available to the ANC to express itself according to tactical need with formidable command of a wide range of vocabularies – a heady mixture of classic liberal and social democratic in this instance – irrespective of whether what is being said in them is in harmony with other voices in the movement and its allies. Only Sach's tiny reference to 'keeping the black population divided' hinted at another concept of the nation. Whether this ethno-racial hint represented a conception of the nation that was to be superseded by civic nationhood or whether it was merely under wraps for the duration of negotiations was not clear. As usual, audiences both inside and outside the ANC had to make up their own minds which of the movement's voices they ought to take seriously.

African nationalism had concerned itself much over many years with the question of who should be left out, or the conditions under which they might be admitted – the white problem. A less well publicized, though just as pressing concern, was those who should not be allowed to defect. That is both inside and outside the ANC's version of African nationalism there has normally been an element of policing what is considered the 'proper' identity for Africans to assume. As we have seen, the history of African nationalism has been punctuated by this concern, beginning with Pixley ka Seme's warnings against intertribal 'racialism', and it will recur again in discussions of nation-building after 1994. However, the most dramatic example of the dilemmas raised by the question, 'What are the acceptable expressions of African identity?' was raised by the ANC-IFP conflict in the last stages of the liberation struggle and in the transition period.

In what is certainly not an overstatement, Suttner notes that, 'The overall understanding of the ANC as bearer of the national vision does not envisage much space for independent identities . . . profound awareness of distinct identities was neither possible nor necessary for the tasks at hand' (2011a: 16). That is, it was not enough for the ANC to claim leadership in questions of strategy and tactics in the liberation struggle, but it also claimed the right to be arbiter of what were acceptable expressions of African identity. Not everyone shared this vision of course. Chief among those who did not was Buthelezi. His resistance to ANC hegemony fuelled his ethno-nationalism, which in turn hardened the ANC's conviction that challenges to its hegemony represented illegitimate deviations from African nationalism and could not be tolerated. This was the principal dynamic for the war between the Inkatha/IFP and the ANC/UDF which escalated after 1983, was centred on the urban townships bordering Durban and Pietermaritzburg in Natal and, after 1990, increasingly spread to the Johannesburg area (the Witwatersrand). It would be a mistake to think that ethnic or tribal tension was the only dynamic in this complex and ill-defined civil war. Ethnicity became the form into which several sources of tension flowed and which became a means of simplifying the terms of conflict and mobilization to pursue them, not to mention a signifier of targets. Many of these contributory tensions were associated with urbanization, first under the constrained terms of apartheid legislation, then in the release of pent-up demand after the repeal of influx control legislation in the 1980s. Competition for resources (especially land), intergenerational tensions, and friction between tribal and chiefly structures of authority and 'progressive' forms of mobilization like community associations and trade unions were often the result. The UDF's tactics of work stay-aways, as well as school, consumer and transport boycotts, and resistance to the incorporation of townships into KwaZulu put it on a collision course with the Inkatha/KwaZulu government axis. Inkatha became a focus for the fears and discontents of parents who wanted their children to go to school, workers who resented being intimidated into staying away from work, councillors in black local authorities who were threatened and sometimes killed if they did not resign, and owners of businesses, township 'warlords', taxi bosses and 'shacklords' whose status in the community was threatened. However diverse the causes of tension and conflict might be, all could be portrayed by Buthelezi and Inkatha as the result of an out-of-touch, exile leadership of the ANC attempting to stamp its hegemony through its puppet the UDF. This characterization may have slandered the local roots of the UDF and oversimplified the dynamics of the struggle, but it was sufficiently in tune with the ANC's self-proclaimed pretensions to hegemony not to lose all credibility for the IFP's constituency on the ground.

These clashing configurations of the conflict – the ANC's all-consuming, hegemonic ambitions and Buthelezi as tribalist and apartheid collaborator – persisted from the 1980s into the post-1990 period of free political activity, negotiation and transition. Indeed, the lines of conflict hardened as the IFP lost its national leverage with white elites to an ANC that now presented a more moderate image, with its liberal democratic constitutional agenda and abandonment of nationalization. As Buthelezi was forced in this changing balance of power back on to regional ambitions and increasingly belligerent ethno-national mobilization, close ties between the IFP and apartheid security forces were revealed by the media, which by now had much greater licence for investigative journalism and freedom from censorship than before 1990. These revelations confirmed stereotypes long held by ANC activists, and further evidence was provided by Buthelezi's marriages of convenience with the white right and bantustan leaders in COSAG. At the same time, as we have seen, the IFP's straddling of traditional and modern agendas and chronic confusion of federal, confederal and secessionist strategies continued. It was never easy to see whether this was genuine confusion of discourse, crude negotiating tactics in which secession is threatened in order to extract democratic, federal concessions, or a long-term strategy of using federalism as a stalking horse for independence. Whatever the case, this varied menu offered no settled basis for inclusion in the terms of engagement which the ANC and the NP had painstakingly and self-interestedly developed. A self-perpetuating cycle duly ensued in which Buthelezi boycotted talks to protest at being marginalized and thus further marginalized himself. Violence on the ground escalated in incidence, intensity and paramilitary character, and increasingly spread from Natal to the Witwatersrand.

Once the NP and the ANC were closing on a deal, and especially after the date for the first democratic election (27 April 1994) was set in June 1993, these problems could no longer be approached through a combination of containment and opportunistic exploitation; they had to be solved. It was bad enough to contemplate an election boycott of a few hundred thousand white right-wingers; it was quite another issue to face the destabilizing prospect of an IFP boycott, given the demographic weight of Natal and KwaZulu in the overall population and the IFP's unquestioned ability to close off and defend at least the rural areas of KwaZulu. Apart from the immediate prospect of instability and violence, the symbolic implications were very grave. Stubborn refusal of a minority of the white minority to be part of whatever new future for South Africa the elites of the ANC and the NP were improvising could be presented as an aberration and a toxic, anachronistic legacy. This would not be the case with the defection of a large slice of the African population; the implications would be very serious for whatever form of future nation would eventually emerge to carry forward what was by this point was now habitually referred to as 'the new South Africa'.

This problem was much more serious for the ANC than it was for the NP. The concluding stages of the negotiations for the interim constitution and the approach of the founding election forced the ANC to make a final choice on what it understood the IFP to represent. On the one hand it could be regarded as an alternative and taboo form of African nationalism which had to be exorcized as being narrow, tribalist and fissiparous to the integrity of the South African state the ANC was grooming itself to inherit. Or on the other hand its claims to be a legitimate rival in essentially the same space of African popular politics under conditions of democracy could, however, grudgingly be taken seriously. The ANC was not helped in making this strategic choice and choosing from the tactical alternatives that would flow from the decision by the chronic ambiguity of the Zulu factor and how the IFP deployed it. Appropriately enough the ANC's response was ambiguous too. At the level of territorial civil war the IFP was anathema. It was atavistic, an enemy to modernity, to youth, to all that was progressive and the future, as well as a collaborator prepared to do the (white) enemy's work and thus worse than the enemy itself. At the highest levels of the leadership, however, Buthelezi could be treated in terms of diplomacy between the elder statesmen of African nationalism; but however flattering it was to be treated as an African nationalist grandee, to Buthelezi this carried the broad and completely unacceptable hint that he should return with honour to the true fold and not continue to see himself as an independent force. This ambiguity could not continue. If the ANC recognized the imperative of Buthelezi's and the IFP's participation for the legitimacy of the founding democratic election, it would have to recognize the legitimacy of competition with them on terms other than war or reabsorption into the true home of African nationalism. It could not have it both ways. This, inadvertently but fortuitously, raised a wider issue. Deciding conclusively what the IFP represented sharpened the question of what the ANC itself represented. It could not afford to risk ceding the entire corpus of African traditional culture to the IFP and allowing Buthelezi to portray himself as its sole defender.

Both in exile and through its popular-front surrogate the UDF, the ANC acquired a metropolitan and cosmopolitan human rights culture, borrowing much from international organizations as well as from trade unions and social democratic and liberal parties in the West. How deeply embedded this was, was a matter for conjecture given the extent of SACP influence on exile organization and on the movement's ideology and, throughout the 1980s, insurrectionist strategic rhetoric. That the SACP had been deeply Stalinist in character – rather than, say, Eurocommunist – and struggled to overcome this heritage even in the light of Gorbachev's reforms did not help. Enough was known about the disciplinary practices of the exile camps to suggest that the ANC's own internal human rights record was not spotless. Contradictions or no contradictions, however, the progressive and cosmopolitan face was the one which the ANC turned to the world, and the negotiation process seemed to be confirming its authenticity. As the new South Africa beckoned, the question of how to harmonize this progressive persona with actually existing African society presented itself.

In the early 1990s, 47 per cent of South Africans lived in rural areas. The percentage was higher for Africans and in KwaZulu and Natal, at that time the most populous region of the country, the percentage was among the highest. It was not only in KwaZulu and Natal that traditional leaders – tribal chiefs and indunas (headmen) – were a significant factor. The ANC was already allied to an influential lobby group, the Congress of Traditional Leaders of South Africa (Contralesa) which was strongest in the Eastern Cape. The ANC had never denied the importance of tradition altogether. It had made selective use of it, in celebrating warrior resistance to colonialism, for instance. However, there were many reasons for the ANC to be cautious and sceptical. Tradition could mean superstition and patriarchy which were antithetical to progressive ideas and practices in general. In areas of gender and intergenerational relations in particular, traditional influence was a source of conflict. Unpopular, 'reactionary' and 'oppressive' chiefs figured prominently in ANC accounts of the civil war in KwaZulu and Natal. Tradition had the potential to divide along cultural and linguistic lines rather than to unite; it had in any case been compromised and contaminated by colonialist manipulation for the purposes of indirect rule, and used by apartheid to keep black resistance in check.

These sources of scepticism would persist, especially in the most metropolitan and secular elements of the ANC Alliance; but as the likelihood of governing power grew closer and a decision on how to deal with Buthelezi and the Zulu factor became imperative, the prospect unfolded of using tradition as a resource. There was much to be said for this. A movement called the African National Congress could ill-afford to dismiss African tradition lightly, no matter how ambiguous and corrupted a state it was in. As the ANC was discovering in preparing for the election, traditional leaders, of which there were about 800 in the country at the time, could be substantial brokers of electoral and other influence. Some of them, through entrepreneurship and brokerage relationships with institutions of government, were themselves bringers and interpreters of modernization to their communities. This undermined the blanket portrayal of them by ANC detractors as atavistic and reactionary. The ANC, despite its liberation credentials, was short of demotic appeal in those mainly rural parts of the country where progressive ideas had only patchy and shallow cover. By engaging more closely and sympathetically with the force of traditional beliefs, customs, authority structures and allegiances in African life, the ANC would be addressing one of the principal challenges of post-apartheid South Africa; that is, reconciling traditional and modern elements in a new, democratic political culture. By doing so this would also resolve the Buthelezi problem. Acknowledging the authenticity of the beliefs and practices he held dear, they would – indirectly – be recognizing his legitimacy as part of an evolving African popular political culture; but they would also be signalling the ANC's ability and determination to compete with him on those grounds and to locate them in a wider African nationalist context than that of Zulu ethno-nationalism.

As it turned out it was the IFP's own strategies that offered an alternative opportunity to the ANC other than 'one last push' in the civil war on the ground, allied to diplomacy without leverage with this most obdurate of opponents. Language and culture were not enough as a basis for the IFP's mobilization. Many people who spoke isiZulu and adhered to Zulu customs supported the ANC. It was by becoming the champion for the Zulu monarchy in the negotiations that Buthelezi tried to differentiate between Zulus and those who merely spoke the language, through this to establish continuity between present and past and thus seal the compact between nation and political party. This strategy was somewhat ironic since Buthelezi's relations with the king were fraught with past clashes and, on the king's side, humiliations. Nevertheless, neither could look forward with equanimity to the reintegration of KwaZulu into an ANC-ruled South Africa without a strong measure of autonomy for the former bantustan to preserve their privileges. Buthelezi's Constitution of KwaZulu-Natal (December 1992) was strongly confederal and the king went so far (February 1994) as to declare a 'sovereign Zulu kingdom' based on the 1838 boundaries of Zulu territory, an intervention that was as historically problematic as it was constitutionally imprecise and politically fantastical. So despite past differences there were enough common interests for Buthelezi to make the prerogatives claimed by the king the main sticking point in his own differences with the ANC and the NP.

However, by tying his fortunes so closely to the monarchy, Buthelezi exposed a flank that the ANC could turn. If, as part of a general engagement with African tradition and culture, the ANC was willing to propitiate the king and assure him of a place in the new democracy, it could engage Buthelezi on several fronts. By engaging the IFP on its own ground the ANC could undercut its ethnic appeal and make useful political capital out of claims that by manipulating the monarchy Buthelezi was corrupting the heritage of all Zulus for his own opportunistic reasons. While direct appeasement of Buthelezi was politically impossible, generous gestures (though without real political substance) could be made to the king. This could detach him from Buthelezi, counter the IFP's most negotiable asset and in addition set the terms for more flexible alignments and freer political activity in the future. Such gestures were duly made, the most public being the invitation to the king to attend a huge ANC rally to celebrate African traditional culture in Durban in October 1993. Its theme was inclusiveness, its name was 'Sonke' (isiZulu for 'we together' or 'all of us') and the signal it sent was that the ANC was comfortable with African traditional life. Many monarchs and traditional leaders from around Southern Africa attended. It would have been too provocative for King Goodwill to attend, but the invitation recognized his special importance in the region and defined the ANC in terms that encompassed Zulu traditions.

The ANC's open embrace of African tradition did not persuade Buthelezi into the election, but it did reveal the ANC's longer-term thinking on the question of competition under conditions of democracy, and served warning that if Buthelezi left a void by boycotting the election, the ANC would gladly fill it. However, this factor probably played a part in appraisal of the balance of forces just before the election. As with the white right, objective appraisal suggested that for Buthelezi to boycott would be at best futile, at worst lead to bloody disaster. The Bophuthatswana fiasco and the fragmentation of the white right left Buthelezi isolated and exposed in the struggle to force the ANC and the NP to postpone the election and modify the interim Constitution. The declaration (31 March 1994) of a state of emergency in KwaZulu-Natal (as the combined region was now called) showed that the government and the TEC were determined to hold the election and confident that the security forces would remain loyal. Bluntly put, if the white (or at least white-led) army and police did not mutiny for Viljoen they were unlikely to do so for Buthelezi. Perhaps the most telling factor was the knowledge that if the election went ahead, with or without the IFP, KwaZulu-Natal was going to be integrated into South Africa, and Buthelezi's best chance of retaining a power base would be through a division of electoral spoils. Still, it took cliff-hanging diplomacy along the pattern of the engagement of the white right to secure the IFP's participation.

The ANC's principle was the same in both cases: agree (sincerely or not) that there is a case for self-determination, propose that the election be regarded as a test of the strength of support for the principle, promise that the grievances and aspirations of the boycotters would be addressed after the election, and hope privately that the dividends of even partial success in a wider democratic South Africa would salve the grievances and blunt the aspirations to the point where the new government could politely bury the pre-election undertakings in politico-legal nit-picking. With allowance for some shades of emphasis, this is what happened with both Buthelezi and the white right. Both felt that the ANC had negotiated in bad faith and this grievance was added to their original ones. However, neither was aggrieved to the point of threatening instability in the new state under construction, or to the improvised and ambiguous nation that the election crowned on 27 April 1994. The diplomacy of inclusion that led to this point had both long- and short-term effects for nation-building. First and most importantly, in the short term it ensured that South Africa got in one piece to the point of transfer of power by democratic means, and if a nation were to be built in the future at least the elements were intact. In the longer term, by forcing the ANC to come face to face with actually existing African society, rather than the abstracted visions of both its own theoretical documents and the Third Worldism of Afro-Asian solidarity movements, confrontation with the ambiguous Zulu factor would make sure that 'tradition' would be firmly on the nation-building agenda.

## The ambiguities of improvisation

The achievements of negotiation and transition from the unbanning of liberation movements in February 1990 to the adoption of a new Constitution in May 1996 have been rightly celebrated. The breadth and depth of rights in the Constitution, the provision for robust institutions, the rule of law and the justiciable principle embodied in the new dispensation have all been widely praised. The new South Africa, as it came to be labelled, proudly advertised the merits of this democratic polity in a securely unified state. However, the new dispensation was less articulate about the nation and nationalism. It was not clear whether the new South Africa was a nation achieved or a nation-in-waiting, or a democratic polity which had no need of the nation and nationalism as commonly understood.

Afrikaner nationalism had taken the country to the brink of ruin through its determination to bind the achievement of self-determination for the Afrikaner people to white supremacy. It then divested itself of this suicidal baggage, only to go around in ever-decreasing circles and vanish in a maze of mirrored chambers. The 'non-group group' provided a fitting epitaph for this craziness. African nationalism, as constructed and policed by the ANC, resembled the biblical house of many mansions. In order to accommodate everybody – in order in effect that the ANC might *become* the nation – extensions were constantly under construction. Africanists, settlers, minorities, communists, black consciousness advocates and now increasingly from the mid-1990s, traditionalists who might otherwise be tempted in tribalist directions, all had to be accommodated, and all had their own views on the nature and limits of the nation and nationalism, as well as the meaning of 'African'. This meant, however, an accretion of ambiguities, suspicions and unanswered questions.

Among the things that remained unclear about the ANC and the nation were the question of who is an African, the relationship between the African nation and the South African nation and what the status really was of the 'African majority' on whose importance ANC documents historically insisted. Such a majority could be a contingent thing, a temporary collective of the oppressed; or it could be a living, homogeneous, eternal thing, a nation in and of itself. With legacies like these, it was not too surprising that the Constitution, the apotheosis of the new South Africa, treated questions of identity rather gingerly and hesitated to be too explicit about what constituted the nation. The preamble to the Constitution is in fact imbued with a sense of nationhood, but it is not directly stated and not defined beyond the belief, attributed to the 'people of South Africa', that 'South Africa belongs to all that live in it, united in our diversity'. Thus in one line the preamble nods in the direction of continuity by incorporating references to both the Freedom Charter and (obliquely) to the motto of the 1910 Union and the (1961) Republic of South Africa which was *Ex unitate vires*. However, insofar as the sense of nationhood is further expressed, it is focused on the future and as an aspiration.

According to the preamble, the Constitution is being adopted in order to heal the divisions of the past and to establish a democratic society, to improve the quality of life of all citizens and build a united and democratic South Africa able to take its place as a sovereign state in the family of nations. All these are invoked as tasks rather than achievements, and although the preamble does not use the phrase, 'nation-building', it can be seen as a nation-building manifesto. However, nation-building is a rather curious concept in this context. If, as the preamble proclaims, a people insists on its unity in diversity and undertakes a social contract through its freely elected representatives to do the various things to which the preamble aspires, then what is it if not a nation already? The negotiated achievements of 1990–6 were admirably clear on the subjects of rights and institutions, but inevitably they were shrouded in ambiguity and uncertainty in terms of nations and nationalism. There is every good reason why this should be so. In the first place, there is a good argument for saying that nations and nationalism have no place in a democratic constitution, which should be confined to contractual and justiciable matters; national issues are too much matters of the spirit and the emotions to be part of such processes. In the second place, to many, the legacies of Afrikaner and African nationalism were enough to motivate scepticism about the desirability of nationalism in all its manifestations. Lastly, ambiguity about national feelings might not be a bad thing in the political situation in which South Africa found itself after 1994. Lack of clarity about the nature and status of the nation allowed people to see what they wanted in the new dispensation; and within reason this could make for stability under circumstances in which, despite the achievements of 1990–6, there were uncertainties and potential threats.

In this way these achievements could be understood as prima facie evidence for a number of differing positions on the nation: first that it already existed; secondly that there was now a basis for building it, either as an elaborated version of something that was already there, or something different – perhaps along the lines envisaged in all the earlier ANC positions on African nationalism, which, from the Harare Declaration onwards, appeared to have been abandoned, for public purposes at least; thirdly, that the nation was not needed – constitutional rights and democratic institutions were self-sufficient and all else was diversity, which, along with democracy itself might be threatened if a stronger form of nationalism was encouraged. In short, according to taste, South Africa was or was not a nation. For a brief period the first of these positions – the already-existing nation – held centre stage. This was not surprising. The integration or reintegration of all the national territory into a unified state along with, for the first time, common citizenship in a democratic polity was an achievement so miraculous as to camouflage any number of uncertainties. It is easy to understand why there was a widespread belief that this also represented the birth of a new nation.

Some believed it because they did not understand the difference between a state and a nation and assumed that they came as a package. Others subscribed to the widespread, popular delusion that there is an automatic connection between democracy and nationalism. Some perhaps suspected that there was no new nation to go with democracy, even perhaps that it was not necessary or even desirable, but on the whole it was better to keep quiet and indulge others' illusions. Probably the most influential contributor to this belief was a version of 'the medium is the message'; the negotiations, their successful conclusion, the avoidance of several abysses, the election and the transfer of power, were the medium, and the message was that the nation existed. Perhaps it had been there all the time under the greed, follies and fears of the whites. This view was encouraged by journalistic accounts of the negotiations, especially those which, in book form, solidified into what many saw as the standard accounts of the time.

Three elements are uppermost in these accounts. The first is the mutual discovery of common humanity in general and South Africanness in particular; the second is the recognition of trust and interdependence under emergency conditions; the third is seduction. Implicit in all versions is the idea that all three of these things were conveyed by personal networks and by publicity in widening eddies to an ever-growing public, from the tiny numbers of elite participants who directly experienced them. Emboldened by the demonstration effect of their leaders' experiences and, it should not be forgotten, by the removal of sanctions on interracial contact, the public was actively encouraged to replicate them in their own lives. This process encompassed a decade or so, beginning around 1985 with pre-negotiation meetings with Mandela in captivity and in various locations in the ANC's places of exile where white intellectuals, business people and progressives went on what were habitually, but inaccurately, labelled 'pilgrimages', and subsequently accelerated with negotiations proper after February 1990. The discovery of mutual bonds is customarily presented in straightforward psychological terms:

> The NP-ANC instant love affair replicates an experience many South African exiles from different political backgrounds have encountered when they meet abroad. Free of the apartheid framework, they discover their common South African-ness. A psychological explanation of the cordial relations between former arch-enemies would point to the rediscovery of bonds of origin, of a repressed kinship. Children of the same soil realised what they had in common. (Adam 1990: 7)

The interdependence under emergency conditions is symbolized in several accounts by an incident in which, while on a private fishing trip, ANC chief negotiator Cyril Ramaphosa removed a fishhook from the hand of a fainting Roelf Meyer, the NP's chief negotiator. The neat reversal of racial stereotypes contained in the fact that it was Ramaphosa who was the experienced fly fisherman and Meyer the novice gives added resonance to the symbolism. Although the story had wide currency, it is in Alastair Sparks' account of the making of the new South Africa that it is most fully developed. He uses the story first as a prologue, then as a *leitmotif* to highlight the recurring theme of drawing together, both before and after the actual incident itself in 1991: 'As with all the clandestine meetings between white and black South Africans taking place around this time, the bond of the fishing story – of mutual attachment to the same country despite racial and political differences – asserted itself. The men shared jokes and anecdotes and reminiscences and a kind of unspoken fellowship arose among them' (Sparks 1994: 82). Like Sparks, Patti Waldmeir emphasizes the importance of the 'fish hook' story, but goes on to situate it in a wider power balance which is very much in Ramaphosa's favour: 'The National Party was simply on the wrong side of history; nothing Meyer did could change that' (Waldmeir 1997: 209). These first two building blocks that helped lay the foundations for compromise are relatively unremarkable. Indeed the attribution of revelatory power to the discovery of common humanity might have seemed a little overdone to anyone but South Africans themselves or those who knew the country intimately; to them the epiphany-like quality of these encounters became an important part of the mythology of the new South Africa. Seduction, however, is a rather different thing.

The first fully worked version of the seduction thesis was in Waldmeir's account of the negotiated 'miracle'. She saw this as a first draft of history with 'feelings' as well as 'facts', which is certainly an accurate description of her interpretation. Beginning with Mandela setting out to achieve the 'capitulation' of 'Afrikanerdom' by mastering the language while in prison (ibid. 5–19), she continues in a long-established Anglo-Saxon and metropolitan tradition of objectifying and psychologizing 'the Afrikaner' and 'Afrikanerdom'. According to her, unlike the more impulsive and romantic elements in the ANC revolutionary tradition, ANC president Oliver Tambo and his protégé Mbeki, 'were intent on delivering not just the corpse of a defeated nation but the mind and soul of the Afrikaner people to the New South Africa' (ibid. 67). Continuing in the kind of psycho-prescription terms that recommend love as a nostrum for disturbed adolescents, she claims that Mbeki for one, 'was shrewd enough to understand that behind the façade of the Afrikaner bully dwelt an almost pitiful yearning to be understood, loved and accepted by Africa. Only the subtlest of ANC minds could recognize this truth; that petting, coddling and cajoling the Afrikaner would pay enormous dividends' (ibid.). Gevisser's biography of Mbeki goes even further than Waldmeir in using seduction as a metaphor for the personal relationships which, in both their accounts, made negotiation and compromise possible. He devotes a whole chapter (Gevisser 2007: 496–525) to Mbeki as 'The Seducer of the Afrikaners', and chooses to treat the metaphor in an even more highly charged way than Waldmeir does.

What are we to make of this metaphor and what does it tell us about the idea that a nation was improvised, or revealed itself, between 1990 and 1996? At first sight seduction is a problematic and inappropriate instrument of nation-building. Indeed the enthusiastic and durable promotion of this interpretation as part of the mythology of the negotiated transition (Gevisser's version is as recent as 2007) has probably contributed greatly to the disillusion now felt by many Afrikaners towards the settlement which was based on these negotiations. So provocative is this narrative that it might have been perversely designed to have that precise effect. However, it does have its uses, notably in suggesting an essential ambiguity in these years; that is, it may be possible to believe in the improvised nation, but we should not be too credulous about its provenance and durability.

How much does it matter whether or not a South African nation existed when democracy came in 1994, and if it did, whether it came into being as a result of psychological conversion, trickery, a realistic reappraisal of changing circumstances or some combination of all of these? Possible answers include the belief that a nation did exist and had it been there all the time, but could only now express itself after the shackles of racial supremacy had been thrown off. Another possibility is that the end of apartheid was year zero and only then could a nation begin to be created. These considerations were not merely tiresome hair-splitting; what people believed and felt at that time about the nation and about their fellow-citizens-to-be mattered. It mattered because it helped shape expectations of what democracy would mean in the years to come and how citizenship, rights and democratic practices would be understood, applied and contested; and these things in turn would profoundly affect the chances of nation-building in the first 20 years of democracy.

Inevitably, there is a case for scepticism that the negotiated transition was underpinned by any kind of national sentiment. It can be argued that to believe in the improvised nation is to underestimate how bitterly divided the country was and how close to unravelling it came in the final stages of transition. One measure of this is the fact that nearly 20,000 people died in political violence in the 10 years from September 1984 and the election of April 1994 (Johnston 1995: 71). From September 1984 to the end of 1989 – the peak years of the struggle – 6,216 deaths were attributed to political violence. In contrast, from the beginning of 1990 – when 'free' political activity became possible for the first time – to the end of April 1994, more than double that number (13,458) died in political violence. Perhaps an even more striking indication of the country's divisions was the diffuse nature of the violence. There were several fronts in the war of liberation: a campaign of insurgency carried out by MK (the armed wing of the ANC) and a campaign of often violent disobedience in African townships (1984–90) were both met with violent counter-insurgency measures; a rearguard campaign of violence was sponsored by elements within the security forces (a 'third force') aimed at disrupting the negotiations; succession struggles were fought by the ANC and the IFP, mainly in KwaZulu and Natal, for the control of territory and the allegiance of Africans in anticipation of the end of white minority rule (1985–94 with residual actions thereafter); localized conflicts waged by warlords, criminals, hostel and informal settlement-dwellers acquired a political dimension because their protagonists were exploited by (and in turn exploited) third-force operations and ANC-IFP political rivalry. These shocking figures attested to the fragmentation and deadly competitions that were released by the end of apartheid.

However in 1992 alone, a not untypical year for the period, more than 20,000 died in acts of unlawful violence, of which 3,347 were classified as 'political' (South African Institute of Race Relations 1994: 292). This even more shocking statistic reveals that only a relatively small proportion of deaths, in what was probably at the time the world's most violent society, was in fact due directly to political division and competition. Even more significant is the fact that political violence declined dramatically after the April 1994 election: by 60 per cent in the first post-election month, by a further 10 per cent in June and, with only minor fluctuations, the trend stayed downward thereafter (South African History Online).

The reduction in political violence still left a shockingly high incidence of violence overall, prima facie evidence of lawlessness and anomie, both of them hard to reconcile with stable nationhood. Nevertheless, the drop in political killings accompanied another positive sign (to which it was undoubtedly linked), the fact that the secessionist moment had clearly passed both for the white right and the IFP. This meant that the centre, formed out of cooperation between the ANC and the NP government, had not only held, but could count on the state apparatus to remain loyal during the transition, as the conduct of the security forces and the bureaucracy during the election made clear. Of course, factors other than burgeoning nationhood can be adduced for this: calculations of power relations and lack of viable alternatives; habits of obedience and discipline; and the 'Sunset Clauses' agreed in September 1992. These proved the key breakthrough in the negotiations by offering sufficient guarantees to the more than 40 per cent of Afrikaners who worked in the public service, to cement the relationship between the ANC and the NP in what some people labelled a 'purchased revolution'. However, these incentives to pragmatism alone are not enough to account for the remarkable combination of continuity and dramatic change that ushered in the new order with an impressive display of choreographed symbolism, typified by the ceremonies for Mandela's presidential inauguration. In any case such pragmatism left only one viable direction in which to travel – that of inclusive citizenship and, by implication, nationhood.

Even if the idea of the improvised nation can be defended in these ways, grounds for scepticism remain. Who and what did the improvised nation represent? How wide and deep was its coverage? Critics could define it as an elite coup and/or a creation of the liberal media. There is no gainsaying the elite nature of the negotiating process, although it is hard to see how it could be practically achieved any other way. This does not necessarily make it undemocratic. Democracies are able to function well, by and through elites, provided they are open and representative elites. Indeed, democracy is understood by many to be a system for developing, choosing and circulating elites in power, provided that the duration and extent of the exercise of power are both limited. Were the elites in this case representative? The constitution-making process was in fact a rather inelegant compromise between the NP's and the IFP's demand for a closed and speedy negotiation process among participants deemed to have established support and the ANC's countervailing demand for an elected constituent assembly. The agreement had concessions within concessions rather like an arrangement of Russian dolls. In what was probably its largest concession to its opponents, the ANC gave way on the constituent assembly, but insisted that negotiations between the existing protagonists could yield only an interim Constitution which would be finalized by the first democratically elected assembly. The NP in turn secured the provision that the interim Constitution would be accompanied by binding constitutional principles that the final Constitution would have to respect. Having established this kind of process, the question was: who would qualify to take part in it? The answer came from a quickly evolving repertoire of pragmatic strategy, largely driven by the ANC. It was in the ANC's interest to have as broad a base of negotiation as possible for the sake of legitimacy, but as things got down to business, to have progress directed by a condominium of the ANC and the NP government. The logic of this was hard to refute because the ANC was the likely successor to whatever version of governing power the negotiation process threw up and the NP, its present custodian. The ANC and the NP would doubtless argue that this was in everybody's interest anyway, for without the driving force of 'sufficient consensus' of the powerful, endless Lilliputian squabbling and vetoes would bring with them a real threat of disintegration and anarchy.

Thus it was that the constitution-making process began with 19 parties represented in CODESA, a structure that comprised 5 working groups with almost 80 participants in each. At the beginning of the negotiations, the parties committed themselves to a Declaration of Intent, which bore a marked resemblance to the Harare Declaration. This confirmed the ANC's strategic acumen in committing itself to such a bold statement of democratic principles before the negotiations proper started. It was admittedly risky to frontload these concessions to a liberal constitutionalism that it would have deemed totally unacceptable only a couple of years previously; however, the CODESA Declaration of Intent seemed to confirm that the ANC was already on the high moral ground, and that it could invite the others to join it there. Whatever difficulties this may have caused internally, it paid huge dividends with the rest of the world. When the negotiations resumed after the breakdown of CODESA, in the form of the Multi Party Negotiation Process (MPNP), the base had been broadened to 26 parties.

Although the white right and Inkatha defected before long, this served only to strengthen the legitimacy of the majority that remained, especially since it looked as if the defectors were reneging on what they had committed themselves to in the Declaration of Intent. The two main centres of power had their own claims to be representative. The NP had been the clear winner of a 'democratic' general election on a racially exclusive franchise in 1989 and the whites-only referendum of 1992, which asked the question: 'Do you support continuation of the reform process which the state president began on 2 February 1990, and which is aimed at a new constitution through negotiation?' The result yielded a 68.73 per cent 'Yes' vote, which considerably strengthened De Klerk's hand (though the NP went on to overplay it badly). Because its support base had not been tested in democratic elections the ANC had no comparable mandate. However, any accusations that it was thereby unrepresentative were nullified, since it was its opponents that blocked the holding of democratic elections which the ANC had demanded before constitutional negotiations. The last thing the NP and other participants wanted was proof of the ANC's representative credentials. Despite this foolproof alibi for lack of a conclusive mandate, the ANC was very conscious of the need to demonstrate these credentials, at least in terms of its internal democracy. Interviewed in August 1992 about the negotiation process and taxed by the interviewer with the possibility of friction between the negotiators and the grass roots, ANC negotiator Kader Asmal was typically bullish about the ANC's own procedures:

> Well since the ANC's the only organization that every month had 14 regions coming to Johannesburg and there was this negotiation forum it was called, and since in fact every region had discussed the ANC proposals, and this is a matter of record, this idea of revolt and shock and indignation is news to me because I believe very much that the process of negotiation must be open. We said that it should be televised. . . . I would just say also that the fact that the negotiations are highly centralized itself is a fundamental weakness. In the ANC they are decentralized and this is why I reject this idea that there will be large scale dissatisfaction, they are decentralized and I explained to you how they are decentralized. Apart from the fact that the National Party never meets as a conclave to discuss the proposals, we clear the proposals to the point of tedium in our NEC. We discuss these proposals and so there is a very decentralized system of negotiation in the ANC. (O'Malley Archive interview with Kader Asmal: 1992)

Another ANC negotiator, Mac Maharaj, questioned by the same interviewer a year later, gave a similar response:

> I think that the ANC, particularly through Nelson [Mandela] and during the time of OR [Tambo], has been able to sell very difficult packages.

> The importance in selling the package is that the political explanation must be very simple and clean, must not be complicated and larded with all sorts of theoretical formulations. The people on the ground want to understand very clearly how do we go? I believe that an explanation even now which says, as happened on the debate during strategic perspectives, which says OK, along this route and this scenario effective majority rule is realized in five years from 1994. Now you may not like different elements of the package but here it is, can you now critique this package to show whether it has built in blockages of such a nature that could prevent that five years realization of democracy? If it does then let's see how we improve the package. Having done that we now have to address the question, is there another strategy available to realise the same objective in a shorter time and at a lesser price? (O'Malley Archive interview with Mac Maharaj: 1993)

The only thing that is missing from these accounts of internal discussions (bearing in mind the lack of alternatives to taking the informants at their word) is *how* the negotiations were sold in terms of how the achievement of constitutional democracy would match what the ANC had promised in the struggle years; that is what arguments were used to bridge the gap of expectations between CST and African national liberation on the one hand and the Harare Declaration on the other.

If the negotiated settlement was achieved by finely tuned diplomacy of inclusion, heavily influenced by inevitable *realpolitik* and perhaps the occasional confidence trick, it was retrospectively legitimized, to almost universal approval, by South Africa's first democratic election (26–29 April 1994). In the absence of a voters' roll the turnout could only be estimated, but just over 19.5 million valid votes were cast and this was widely accepted to be 86 per cent of those eligible to vote. The representative claims of the ANC (62.5% of votes cast) and the NP (20.4%) were vindicated, as was the principle of 'sufficient consensus', which was revealed to rest upon nearly 83 per cent of votes cast. The Freedom Front, the party formed around Constand Viljoen to contest the election at the last moment, received 2.2 per cent, which put claims to Afrikaner self-determination in perspective (Johnson and Schlemmer 1996: 301–8). The IFP's 10.5 per cent was concentrated in KwaZulu-Natal to the extent that it won the province and was able to retain its patronage base without continuing drama over a thoroughly unrealistic threat of secession. Although the world was quick to endorse the result, to hail the new order and move on, there were substantial doubts about some aspects of the election, notably the existence of numerous 'no-go areas'. All the major parties had serious allegations of fraud and these were dealt with at least in part by high-level haggling. The idea that the result had been manipulated in the interests of peace became the subject of instant mythology. According to one account, 'There seems little doubt that the final figures were at least to some extent negotiated. . . .

None the less there seems little doubt that in a crude sense the election did represent the will of the people. For all the imperfections and irregularities in the ballot, it seems beyond dispute that the most popular party, the ANC got the most votes; that the NP was truly the second most popular party; and that the IFP came a genuine third' (ibid. 334–5).

In the information detailed above there are numerous objective markers of momentous historical change between 1990 and 1996: statements of principle, intent and agreement; the rise and fall in incidence of violent acts; voting behaviour. However, in the interests of understanding the improvised nation, it is necessary to move on from these to ask what sense of themselves the people involved in these things, or who were subject to them, had. We can make this move through the powerful images, iconic figures and memorable words of these days, as well as the interpretations put on them by those who reported them, some of which have been quoted and discussed here. However, because the transition to democracy has not yet attracted much in the way of history from below, the way is open for accusations that such interpretative accounts as we have are essentially elite ones. That is, broadly speaking liberal ones, generally pro-ANC, produced on the whole by people who were conscious of themselves playing a nation-building role, and who were disinclined for the most part to interrogate too sharply what was actually going on. To some extent then, their coverage is narrow and their intention manipulative. However, reportage of this sort reflects as well as creates the spirit of the time; it may be selective and it may be subjective, but often to challenge it on these grounds is merely to substitute one person's subjectivity for another's.

To take one example: the South African journalist Sean Johnson, who extensively chronicled the transition years, wrote in May 1993 about the white people who were leaving and those who would stay. In making the case for 'throwing our talents and energies into building a better new country out of the old' he wrote: 'I am a South African, have never been anything else, and do not aspire to be anything else. This is my home and my history, my skylines and landscapes, my people. I am not afraid of my compatriots being afforded, finally, the basic rights I have always enjoyed; I would be afraid if that were not to happen' (Johnson 1993: 358). No-one can assess with any quantitative authority the size of the constituency for which he spoke; but no-one who experienced these times at first hand could seriously argue that he spoke only for himself or only for an English-speaking, liberal elite, and indeed only for whites.

## The improvised nation and the future

Between 1990 and 1996, South Africans behaved very much like a self-determining people, defining themselves as a polity and sealing a bargain on its institutional form, which in turn was the product of many bargains. It is worth noting how little the forging of this bargain owed to outside brokerage: no peacekeeping forces; no superpower or former colonial power holding the ring; no White House Lawn or Lancaster House. In this sense at least it was an exercise in *national* self-determination and this quality clearly played a binding role. Nevertheless, right up to the end the view that the struggle was a contest between two nations persisted. According to R. W. Johnson, the Democratic Party did so badly in the April 1994 election because it was, 'the voice of liberalism in a conflict between two nationalisms that admitted of little middle ground' (Johnson and Schlemmer 1996: 308). It is true that there was a large measure of historical irony in the fact that the Democratic Party, which alone of the parties had embraced the spirit and principles of the new constitutional order over many years and did not come belatedly to them, polled a paltry 1.75 per cent in the national election, while the NP and ANC, which had rejected them with contempt until the eleventh hour, took over 80 per cent of the vote and two Nobel prizes.

It is also true that more went into this exercise in collective self-definition than the much-publicized spirit of mutual recognition in which black and white found each other. Calculations of collective self-interest and assessments of both continuity and change in power relations played their part. The really novel thing, though, was the virtually universal realization that however collective self-interest and power relations were personified – as Afrikaner or white, as the oppressed black majority or the Zulu nation – they would have to be managed within a larger collective entity. The protagonists differed on how and how soon they came to this realization. The ANC and the NP caught on quite early; the Afrikaner right and Buthelezi only after the election. They also differed between and even within themselves on the extent to which this realization was underpinned and helped along by a common consciousness of belonging, a developing awareness of common experience and even of the possibilities of solidarity. Most of all perhaps, they differed on what the nature and the status of this larger collective entity was, and what claims could be made in its name. However, more of them shared a sense of common consciousness of belonging and common experience at the end than did at the beginning. As ANC negotiator Maharaj put it to his interviewer, 'Trust is a process, not a precondition' (O'Malley interview 1993). And enough of them, and the people they spoke for, shared these things to make it possible to say that the process of transition was accompanied by an improvised nation. 'Improvised' is a fitting adjective to qualify the achievement of at least a minimum framework of common social and political life. It carries with it appropriate connotations of a makeshift, temporary and uncertain response to an extraordinary situation, and for most of the population – even for most of the major participants in the drama – a novel and largely unexpected one. The improvised nation was not deeply rooted and its origins were elusive. It could be seen as a willed delusion driven by relief, hope, the spirit of crisis and, finally, the euphoria of consummation; or perhaps it was a piece of temporary role-playing employed to extricate all concerned from a precipitate and profound existential crisis that threw everything, past, present and future, into question, and to which, each in its own way, all the major political role-players were subject. Many other interpretations were possible, which of course was the source of the improvised nation's short-term strength and long-term complications.

It is one thing, however, to acknowledge the role that such an improvised nation played in getting South Africa through the transition, quite another to agree on where it might go thereafter. There were those who hoped to see it confined to a secular and instrumental polity, a framework for resolving differences based on the assumption of 'many peoples, one polity', but without any bonds of solidarity and fraternity. This would not be a viable proposition. The demographic weight of the ANC's constituency, and the burden of the past obtruding into the present in the form of poverty and inequality, meant that something more would be required than an attempt to prolong the bargaining culture into an era of democratic elections. Without that 'something more', the ANC would have to rely on pure hegemony and it was not used to this. As a liberation movement in exile, the ANC had become accustomed to using 'soft power' as diplomatic leverage, and this had continued to serve it well during the transition. The frontloading of concessions to liberal democracy in the Harare Declaration had increased this stock of soft power; Mandela's charisma and leadership multiplied it; the (not entirely deserved) status of victim in the civil war with the IFP consolidated it; and press coverage that was often uncritical and at times verged on hero worship, for Mandela if not the movement, sustained it. However, the ANC would require soft power to govern, as well as to achieve governing power and, once in office it would need to find fresh sources to renew this soft power. The legacies of apartheid could be addressed in many ways, undemocratic as well as democratic. There were some in the ANC who felt that too many concessions had been made and that the Constitution was unduly restrictive. However, if the ANC leadership had learned one thing it was that that its overriding obsession – creating a South Africa that was united in territory and citizenship – could only be achieved as a democracy. So the legacies of apartheid would have to be addressed democratically. From the ANC's point of view, the 1994 election delivered the luxury of both democracy and hegemony; but democracy would bring frustrations and hegemony would bring temptations. The soft power of solidarity might provide a way of easing both. The idea that the Constitution was self-sufficient, that the bonds created by the equal enjoyment of rights were enough, would continue to influence people who were suspicious of anything more than constitutional nationalism or even saw the future in terms of post-nationalism, ideas for which there was a growing international intellectual pedigree. From this point of view the improvised nation, with its equal rights underpinned by common humanity and South Africanness, might be solidarity enough. However, those who believed this were not the majority. Many doubtless felt that Roelf Meyer was being too sanguine when he said to an audience in Northern Ireland, another 'divided society', 'We in South Africa had basically no differences to resolve. . . . It was almost as simple a matter as colour or race that separated us. We had to remove this problem to reach out to each other as human beings.' But it is likely he spoke a profound truth of great relevance to the transition; colour and race and common humanity *are* simple once you are able to see them for what they are. However, there is a second truth which Meyer did not highlight, but was never far from the minds of the people across the table from him; it is the associated derivatives of 'race and colour', and legacies of unequal power relations, such as poverty and inequality, that are complex. And the extent to which you fully grasp these complexities might depend on which side of the unequal power relations you have spent your life.

Given the electoral preponderance of the ANC, its national liberation pedigree and the tasks it saw itself addressing, it was more likely that it would try to find some formula that moved the improvised nation forward into something that answered the question posed by Craig Calhoun in 'Nations Matter': 'For polities not constructed as ethnic nations, what makes membership compelling?' (2007: 10). Partly answering his own question, Calhoun goes on to assert that democracy requires a sense of mutual commitment among citizens, 'that goes beyond mere legal classification, holding a passport or even respect for particular institutions' (ibid.). The need for something more was particularly acute, viewed from the perspective of the newly elected ANC. Calhoun again provides the answer: 'Nationalism not only expresses solidarity or belonging but provides a rhetoric for demanding equity and growth. Nationalism . . . has underwritten most successful projects of economic redistribution including especially those within European countries' (ibid. 18). David Miller reinforces the point: 'The redistributive policies favoured by socialists are likely to demand a considerable degree of social solidarity if they are to win popular consent, and for that reason socialists should be more committed than classical liberals to the nation-state as an institution that can make such solidarity politically effective' (1997: 92).

Writers like Calhoun and Miller were concerned not only to defend nationalism against the criticism of those that held it responsible for atrocities and excesses like those of the Balkans and Africa in the mid-1990s, but also to confirm its progressive and democratic credentials. It was a conceptualization of nationalism that offered a way forward for the ANC as it sought to address the legacies of apartheid through redistribution. However, conceptualizing the nation in this way would not be easy; the question of reconciliation loomed large. In the days of struggle, it was unproblematic to characterize all whites as beneficiaries of crimes against humanity and not too urgent to name the price for crimes of complicity or commission. Now, however, whites were full and equal citizens with the right not to be discriminated against, and the price had to be negotiated in this context. There was to be chronic confusion over the sum to be paid and the currencies in which it would fall due, which included symbolic acceptance of guilt, rituals of apology and material reparation. There was an area of trackless territory in which to get lost, between voluntary tithing, ransom and collective punishment.

Building solidarity out of a conflicted past would be challenging enough, but this was not the only way to conceptualize the nation and not the only challenge. One source of challenge was the danger of taking too much for granted about the Constitution and the liberal state whose creation it envisaged, as the focus for solidarity. If South Africans could count on the accommodation of cultural diversity, the outlawing of discrimination and the operations of a democratic polity, then perhaps nation-building would take care of itself. The danger lay in complacently assuming the neutrality of the cosmopolitan and metropolitan culture that produced these things. As Calhoun puts it: 'The liberal state is not neutral, cosmopolitan civil society is not neutral. Even the English language is not neutral. This does not mean that any of these three things is bad, only that they are not equally accessible to everyone and do not equally express the interests of everyone' (2007: 17). One of the few things to transcend the divided life experiences of South Africa's racialized society was a profound and widely shared social and cultural conservatism. In some respects the origins of this were similar – organized religion, for instance – and in other respects they were different. However, not the least of the nation-building's tasks was the reconciliation of the culture of the Constitution with a largely conservative, demotic culture.

There were other possibilities for alienation beyond the liberal–conservative divide, in what was often perceived as the generally metropolitan and Anglophone culture of the transition. Some Afrikaners came to see the emerging ANC political and business elite as 'Afro-Saxons', who intentionally or as a by-product of their own upward mobility were contributing to the Anglicization of South Africa begun after the Anglo-Boer War by imperial proconsul Lord Milner. Many Africans and Afrikaners would find resonance in the words of an Irish scholar when he wrote that a type of exile in the latter half of the nineteenth century 'brought many rural peoples into cities and towns, where their children, in the course of ever-extending schooling were made to learn a standardized vernacular. For the Irish who stayed in their own country that language was English, and *a life conducted through the medium of English became itself a sort of exile*' (Kiberd 1996: 2, emphasis added). The vehemence with which aspirant black executives were to react against the 'culture of business' through race-based organizations such as the Black Management Forum (BMF) would later testify to the potential of this alienation as a grievance and source of tactical leverage. In general, the opportunities held out by a globalized, new South Africa often seemed to be varieties of hybridization – Afro-Saxon or Anglokaner. Those who could don these identities and exploit them often resented having to do so. But at least they were insiders. Outsiders, who could not gain access to them and the opportunities to which they held the keys, resented them even more.

Reconciliation, then, was not the only problem. The focus for improvising the nation was the polity and the Constitution. Longer-term nation-building would require embedding these things in and if necessary defending them against more populist understandings of values, rights and identities. One possibility of course was recovery of languages, cultures, values and identities that had been suppressed and denigrated under the varieties of white supremacy that had marked the previous 300-odd years. Doing so would have to cope with four problems however. The first was that pre-colonial South Africa did not offer an unambiguous source of 'Africanness', or if it did, it was only at a high level of generality; the influences and expressions were varied to the point of fragmentation. The second problem was that although the offices and practices of traditional rule had survived colonialism and white supremacy, they had been corrupted and exploited by them for the purposes of indirect rule. That which was authentic enough for the purposes of recovery was often the subject of controversy on this score. Thirdly, harmonizing certain aspects of tradition with the new order would not be easy; apart from obvious clashes between the new rights culture and popular views on gender and sexual orientation, questions of landholding under traditional authority and communal tenure were seen by some African nationalist modernizers as obstacles to economic growth. Lastly, Africanizing the national culture would have to satisfy at least two constituencies: a mainly rural, deeply conservative and traditional one; and a mainly urban, aspirant and mobile one that did not so much want to reject globalization but to Africanize it. To deal adequately with these four issues would require a formidable feat of neo-syncretism.

Such was the extent of the ANC's post-apartheid hegemony that it alone would have the resources to address these various challenges of reconciliation and use them as the basis of solidarity for nation-building. However, in order to do so it faced challenges of its own. The central challenge was familiar – the reconciliation of its twin legacies of non-racialism and Africanism, a duality which was camouflaged in the improvised nation but could not but assert itself under the conditions of majoritarian democracy. Writing in 1999, CRD Halisi described this 'enduring duality' in the following terms:

> Black republicanism . . . is a complex set of ideas that embraces and extols the communal virtues of the African people. Many of the practical and

ideological compromises that liberationists have made over the course of the struggle may only serve to disguise a deeper core of black republican belief. The dichotomy between multiracial union (non-racialism) and black republicanism cannot therefore be too rigidly drawn. . . . In South Africa they are virtually inseparable and clearly complementary. (144–5)

While specifically black republican organizations were in disarray in the aftermath of the ANC's assimilation of black consciousness after 1976, Halisi (ibid. 141) warned that, 'race conscious populism pulsates strongly within the ANC', in the form of aspirations to cultural and national authenticity. Two other challenges overlapped with this one. The first concerned what organizational form the ANC would take as it made the transition from exiled and underground liberation movement to governing authority. This was usually expressed as a choice between becoming a political party and remaining a liberation movement. The ANC always stoutly denied that this was even an issue; being a liberation movement was its past, present and future, and it would reflexively dismiss the views of anyone who questioned the implications of this status for the role of nation-building in a multi-party democracy.

A second and related challenge was to be consistent about the meaning of the negotiated settlement. At times the ANC treated the negotiations as a shared national achievement; at others, with undisguised triumphalism, as a victory over a powerful and devious foe. Sometimes the outcome was treated as an achievement in its own right, at others, as merely a beachhead to 'true' democracy. Underlying and unifying all of these was the challenge that mattered the most, defining the role that the state would play in nation-building and what role the ANC would play in state-building. In the early post-apartheid years, insofar as nation-building was considered, there was a tendency to focus unduly on the polity, the Constitution and civil society, and to underestimate the role of the state. However, if the state were weak in its capacities and reach, the prospects of nation-building would not be enhanced. Similarly if, in a democratic and plural society the state is not trusted because it is not impartial, the chances of a strong nation emerging are reduced. The strength, integrity and impartiality of the state are crucial, particularly if the kind of nationalism which is the basis of redistributive solidarity is to be achieved. This, above all, was the challenge that had to be successfully negotiated if the improvised nation which sustained the transition to democracy were to be deepened and extended.

When considering the achievements that lay behind, once the new Constitution was finalized in 1996, and the challenges that lay ahead, it is always tempting to think in terms of South African exceptionalism. This temptation is available to most peoples and to South Africans, perhaps more than most. However, sometimes a resonant quotation presents itself from another country's history which helps summarize the experience of one's own. The words of Massimo Taparelli, Marquis d'Azeglioi (1798–1866) on the unification of Italy have achieved deservedly wide currency for their insight into nations and nationalism. He said in his memoirs, published in the year of his death: 'We have made Italy, now we must make Italians' (Doumanis 2001: 86–7). The spirit nicely fits South Africa; a new South Africa had been made and now, with all its ambiguities and unanswered questions, it was to be the context for making South Africans.

# PART THREE
# Beyond the improvised nation

# CHAPTER FOUR

# Over the rainbow: From the Mandela moment to the Mbeki project

The conventional narrative of nation-building in the first decade and a half of the new South Africa recounts how Mandela's Rainbow Nation became the neo-Africanist project of his successor as president, Thabo Mbeki. At this point the quality of leadership enters the nation-building equation and with it the question of individual character. There is a marked tendency in popular and to some extent in academic accounts of South Africa's recent history to theorize, or at least to speculate in psychological terms about anything from the character and motivations of individual leaders to collective psychosis at the level of whole populations. As we have seen (and shortly will again), Afrikaners in particular have been subjected to uninformed and somewhat kitsch psychologizing which, if it had been applied to others would be regarded as somewhat suspect, perhaps faintly distasteful and possibly downright racist. This happens less often with Africans, possibly because South African Africans are more obviously heterogeneous (in language, for instance) or possibly because the alleged collective mindset of (erstwhile) masters holds more fascination in popular mythology than that of their victims. Certainly the warning bells of ethno-racial determinism go off earlier if the subjects are black than when they are white, in polite company at any rate.

When it comes to individuals, however, the position is reversed and Mandela and Mbeki have attracted far more in the way of psychological speculation than De Klerk and his predecessors. It is not difficult to see why. History may or may not be written by the victors, but it does tend to be written *about* them. Neither is it difficult to see why the first decade and a half of democracy in South Africa should be written about in such a personalized way. However, that it should is still of some interest because it is symbolic of a profound change in the nature of the ANC, a change with which the organization is still grappling.

Throughout its history the ANC has strenuously promoted a self-image, to both internal and external audiences, as a mass organization whose leaders are servants of a mobilized people. Probably nothing has been more important to its self-understanding than this mythology of collective agency. The movement has an extensive corporate lexicon through which to communicate the selflessness and lack of ambition of its leaders. Nobody who is in the running for a leadership position can announce him or herself in any terms other than that of a humble cadre whose only ambition is to serve at the movement's pleasure and who will wait passively for the call. This was a mythology that befitted an exiled and underground movement with little access to patronage, much exposed to individual danger in South Africa and even, latterly, in exile. What it could offer was a corporate and even familial home to people whose prospects of advancement and community were cruelly stunted by apartheid. Understandably, motivations of personal ambition were regarded with suspicion in this communal atmosphere, in theory at any rate. This was not only mythology but also an operating principle. Although lobbying and caucusing helped to facilitate the emergence of leaders, this was on a factional basis (especially through the SACP) and not on the basis of groups coalescing around an ambitious and charismatic individual. In the exile years the bonds of identification between the organization and its adherents and surrogates at home may have been strong but the links were tenuous. The most important symbol of leadership, Mandela, held no office and was invisible, in jail.

Under these conditions the ANC operated in an uneasy combination of modes between conspiracy and popular mobilization, especially as the anti-apartheid struggle intensified in the 1980s. Popular mobilization was behind a self-defining cause (the overthrow of apartheid) in a self-enclosed movement. Leadership for popular mobilization is not the same as leadership for democratic popular politics which requires leaders in a range of sensitive situations: articulating principles and interests in policy terms; winning support from the uncommitted; compromising by democratic means with rival and opposed forces. Distrust of strong, individual leadership was not only shaped by these circumstances but had deeper roots. Among these is a general aversion to anything that can be labelled 'individualism', which is held to be liberal, 'Western' and un-African. Conversely, strong leadership is also suspect because it can threaten to evolve into a mutant form of African nationalism – the neo-traditional, patrimonial, African 'big man' syndrome. All these conjunctural and ideological factors are discernible in the ANC's history, but it is impossible to assign weight to each in explaining the ANC's disinclination to be led. Indeed, it is also difficult to assess the extent to which they may have been able to provide cover for a simpler and more prosaic explanation: that is, the desire of factions and barons for freedom of action without interference from a strong leader. This factor has been of increasing importance throughout the post-apartheid period and helps account for the revolt against Mbeki and his removal from power.

As in so many other things the years from 1990 to 1994 represented an interregnum in the ANC's attitudes to and practices of leadership. Mandela's release opened up enormous possibilities of charismatic leadership, extending far beyond the enclosed organizational confines of the ANC itself and building on the popular-front tactics that emerged in the mid-1980s; with these possibilities came the problem of how to manage and control the effects within a framework of organizational discipline. At the same time the tasks of the years of negotiation could not be carried through on the charisma and natural authority of someone who had become an elder statesman without ever having truly been a politician. These tasks were tasks for a team: Mbeki, then increasingly Ramaphosa, supported by Asmal, Maharaj and others of lower profile but crucial importance like human rights lawyer Arthur Chaskalson who became democratic South Africa's first chief justice. All the time the ANC was in a high state of mobilization. Much of that changed with the ANC's election victory in April 1994. The ANC now had an executive president who was formally leader of the whole country and the mass movement to which the ANC had been primarily responsible in the absence of a formal democratic mandate was rapidly demobilized. The rival elites who had contributed to the improvised nation were now effectively excluded from power. Although the NP participated in the first post-apartheid government, power relations were so asymmetric in the face of the ANC's massive majority, and power-sharing fell so far short of the NP's (probably unrealistic) expectations, that they considered it de facto exclusion and left in 1997. A path to oblivion followed: this included an unconvincing name change (to the *New* National Party); a brief alliance with the Democratic Party (2000–1); alliance with the ANC (2001–5); electoral collapse from 20.4 per cent in 1994 to 1.9 per cent in 2004; and finally dissolution in 2005.

The ungenerous interpretation of power-sharing and the demobilization of the mass movement were the largely unforced choices of the core leadership of the ANC in which former exiles predominated over the internal anti-apartheid forces. The predominance of 'exiles' over 'inziles' features prominently in most conventional accounts of the ANC after 1994 – especially in those that lament its 'failure' to evolve from a liberation movement into a conventional democratic political party, or loss of its 'soul'. Having made the strategic choice to retain the liberation movement ethos, but to dispense with the momentum of popular mobilization, the new government was left on its own in the face of an expectant black population and a suspicious white minority to make good the many promises of the Constitution. It was also faced with the imperative of giving to the civic cosmopolitanism of this Constitution some enduring foundation of national coherence by cultivating a basis for broad-based emotional attachment to the new order.

These were not by their nature tasks to be addressed by committee; they were too complex and contested to be addressed from within the mythology of collective decision making subscribed to by the ANC. In any case the variety of interests and ideologies now assembled under the banner of the liberation movement was so diverse that collective decision making risked paralysis. In short, resolving the contradictions of South Africa appeared to require the simplifying force of individual leadership and it is not surprising that personal factors began to loom large in the ideas and practices of nation-building. As a result the task of building on the improvised nation came to be interwoven with the personalities, the histories, the world views and the mythologies that grew up around the two men who would be the first presidents of the new South Africa, Nelson Mandela and Thabo Mbeki. Each had a characteristic hallmark; emotional intelligence in the case of Mandela and an analytically based grand vision in the case of Mbeki. In an ideal world the two would not only be compatible but one would enrich and lead seamlessly on to the other. This, however, is not the verdict that has emerged so far.

## The Mandela moment

So extensive, deep and durable is popular appreciation of Mandela's contribution to the transition from apartheid to democracy that it requires a special effort to recall that he held office in government for only five years and that he made his contribution to nation-building to a large extent prior to that. What is more, with the exception of these short five years he did so without the benefit (or arguably, the curse) of formal, popular mandate and accountability. Indeed even this short period in office, which is in danger of being seen as a postscript to his career rather than its pinnacle, was served in a kind of condominium with his executive vice-president, Mbeki. By contrast, if we include this period of effective joint rule, Mbeki had nearly 15 years (1999–2008) to make his contribution to inventing the nation from the seat of government. Such was the brevity of Mandela's presidential career in relation to the length of his service as African nationalist mobilizer, accused-in-the-dock, iconic prisoner and symbol of reconciliation, that ever since his retirement there has been something of the 'lost leader' about him in public perception. Whether that is the case or not, for his brief presidential moment he was a leader unusually well suited to the global temper of the post-Cold War world. In a piquant coincidence, at precisely the moment that Mandela was at the peak of his powers in 1995, 'emotional intelligence' swept the world as a new global vernacular of leadership, far beyond the academic circles of management and organizational studies where it was developed (Goleman 1995).

Its five-point paradigm of self-awareness, self-regulation, motivation, empathy and social skill (Goleman 1998: 95) might have been drawn up with Mandela's approach to nation-building in mind. He was well able to demonstrate this in the first year of his presidency.

## World Cup triumph

The most celebrated example of Mandela's nation-building charisma came during the 1995 rugby world cup (RWC) and centred on the final (24 June 1995) between the Springboks and the New Zealand All Blacks. The RWC was inaugurated in 1987 and is held every four years. The 1995 tournament was thus only the third to take place. This cycle of competition was fortuitous; the second tournament took place in 1991 and at this early stage of the competition's development the choice of host was made at relatively short notice (there is now a five- or six-year lead time). This meant that the South African rugby authorities could make a bid with the full backing of the ANC in 1993. The success of the bid represented a considerable leap of faith for all concerned. The first democratic election had not yet taken place. The ongoing civil war in Natal and on the Witwatersrand, the looming threat of Afrikaner paramilitary resistance and the racial tensions that were stoked by the murder of South African Communist Party and Umkhonto We Sizwe (MK) leader, Chris Hani, in April 1993, were all stark reminders that the stability needed for hosting a major, international tournament could not at that point be guaranteed. Although the RWC was a lesser undertaking than the FIFA World Cup or the Olympic Games, nevertheless at that stage it involved 16 national teams, 32 matches and a total estimated attendance of over 1 million. Thanks to the sports boycott, South Africa had no experience whatsoever of hosting multinational tournaments and precious little experience at all of participating in a rapidly evolving environment of international sport.

Even if enough confidence in the prospects of stability and South Africa's logistical capabilities could be found to encourage sceptical (and competing) administrators from other rugby jurisdictions and to convince nervous supporters from more sheltered countries, there was the problem of rugby itself and its place and role in South African politics and history. Such were the conflicted perceptions of this place and role that staging the RWC in South Africa courted at best controversy and at worst disruption.

## More than a game: Rugby and South Africans

Up to 1990, rugby had defined and emphasized divisions in South African society, and its potential as a reconciling and integrating force was by no means obvious. During the apartheid era, rugby, along with other sports, was principally considered in political terms as a target for international (and for that matter internal) boycott. International isolation of South Africa was one of the four pillars of the ANC's struggle and, given the inherent unlikelihood of achieving universal, mandatory and comprehensive economic sanctions, sporting isolation was one of its most important components. Rugby was the most important target for isolation as a result of the sport's genuinely popular nature in the white, but particularly the Afrikaner community, in the sense that it was broadly based rather than the preserve of an elite (as historically it had largely been in England) or a niche pastime (as it was in Australia).

Rugby was scarcely a subject for serious analysis at all before 1990. Insofar as it was (Coetzee 1978), it was dealt with in terms of a conventional narrative which emphasized its place and role in Afrikaner nationalism. Treated in this way, it was regarded as a colonial import, adopted by Afrikaners, which allowed for expression of hyper-masculinity and controlled, rule-bound violence directed towards physical domination, as well as mutual dependence expressed as team spirit. These were useful components of creating and sustaining Afrikaner nationalism as an identity system directed towards survival needs and ethno-racial bonding. Accordingly, rugby was deeply embedded in Afrikaans-medium schools and universities and these, joined after 1948 by the Afrikanerized armed forces, police and parastatals, became the building blocks of South African rugby. Through them, rugby became one of the key bonding elements in what was coming to be named 'Afrikanerdom'.

More importantly for Afrikaner nationalists, from as long ago as the early twentieth century, rugby offered the twin opportunities of identifying with the wider imperial and colonial world, but at the same time defining white South Africa in independent opposition to Britain, the metropolitan centre of this world. This was never very easy to carry off, and in a changing world of decolonization and increasingly liberal and multiracial societies in Britain, Australia and New Zealand, the balancing act became more difficult. As a result, South African rugby was more vulnerable to boycott. All sports were vulnerable, and in fact isolation developed earlier in cricket, thanks to the precipitating crisis over Basil D'Oliveira in 1968. D'Oliveira was a 'non-white' cricketer from Cape Town who had emigrated to England and played test cricket for his adopted country. The refusal of South African Prime Minister John Vorster to accept D'Oliveira as a member of an England touring side precipitated South Africa's expulsion from international cricket. However, the impact of isolation on rugby was greater, partly because of its broad-based popularity and ethnic significance to Afrikaners. It was also because rugby was the sport at which South Africa most consistently excelled at the very highest level, albeit with a traditional form of the game that emphasized power rather than grace. This neatly fitted the stereotype which, partly through self-ascription and partly as a result of external labelling, had come to characterize Afrikaners.

This narrative was to some extent oversimplified. It tended to treat rugby as a uniquely white obsession and to gloss over the sport's genuine roots in the Coloured community of the Western Cape and among both Coloureds and Africans in the Eastern Cape, coincidentally the heartland of the ANC. The conventional narrative tended to underestimate or ignore the lonely and hard-fought struggles of talented rugby players of colour in anti-apartheid organizations who refused to play 'normal sport in an abnormal society' and refused special dispensations to play with or against whites. Equally ignored were the Coloured and African players who played within the system and formed teams to play against touring British and Southern-hemisphere sides in what were usually notably violent contests. In depicting rugby as the glue of wider white political unity, this narrative omits the bitter ethnic rivalry between Afrikaans and English rugby at levels of province, club and educational institution. Nevertheless, the narrative is substantially accurate, if a little lazily framed and expressed. Clearly to Afrikaners, rugby remained more than a game, even though they were no longer sure precisely what it represented, as the old certainties of political identity crumbled under the pressures of social, economic and political change which we have documented in earlier chapters. Equally clearly, the understandable antipathy felt by substantial elements in the ANC and in the wider black community towards the history and lore of South African rugby in general, and what the Springboks symbolized in particular, was all too genuine. In the years before sporting boycotts put an end to international fixtures, the vocal support for visiting British and other touring teams from the segregated 'non-white' enclosures of Test venues was clear enough demonstration of this, reinforced by widespread anger and opposition when various boycott-breaking tours of rugby and cricket-playing mercenaries visited South Africa in the 1980s.

## Capitalizing on rugby

Although the nation-building episode of the 1995 RWC is rightly credited to Mandela's unmatched qualities of leadership, insight and charisma, even his formidable capacities for single-minded application of personal authority and of political stage-management required favourable circumstances. Two in particular stand out. First, although Mandela had to work very hard indeed to persuade his own supporters of the need to unite behind the Springboks and to preserve the name, badge and colours of the team instead of insisting on a break with the divisive iconography of the past, the ANC had become well aware of the potency of soft-power diplomacy and the politics of cultural symbolism. The negative sanction of cultural and sporting boycott was only part of this. The positive deployment of soft power in the form of iconography and music – much of it centred on

Mandela himself – was important in legitimizing the ANC and its cause to a global audience that would not have understood, or have been repelled by the parochial and sectarian symbolism of African nationalism or Third World revolution. The ANC was nothing if not adaptable in moving from one symbolic register to another, and although Mandela had to work hard to promote the accommodation of what had hitherto been sectarian, white symbolism as yet another terrain of iconography, at least he had a corporate tradition of adaptability to work on. A key issue that is sometimes overlooked is the fact that Afrikaners and whites generally were not the only audience for the RWC. Rugby is not a global game in the way that soccer is, but in 1991 it was played not only in Britain and the former white dominions of the British Empire, but Europe (France and Italy), South and North America (Argentina, Canada and the United States) and Japan. In short, all members of the G7 were represented at the RWC in South Africa with the exception of Germany. If rank-and-file members of the ANC were angry at the sacrifice implied in retaining the Springbok colours and emblem, there were many in the leadership who appreciated that adopting and, in today's parlance, 'taking ownership' of them while at the same time showcasing the country's capacity to preside over a major international sporting event, under the benign tutelage of an ANC government, was a price worth paying.

The second favourable circumstance was that rugby was available for appropriation in the state of flux that characterized the white politics of the day. They were in a state of flux because whatever his qualities of political courage and acumen, De Klerk could not provide the kind of leadership which effectively communicated what his project meant in human terms for those he signed up for it. Neither in character nor in temperament was De Klerk the kind of leader to whom his followers could look for exemplary inspiration and instinctive bonds of understanding and sympathy. In that sense, fittingly enough, he was not a nationalist leader at all, despite the name of the party he led. In any case, the straitened structural political conditions he found himself in would not have allowed him to be that kind of leader. A measure of obfuscation was a necessary part of his project. As a result of this a cloud of ambiguity hung over whites' perceptions of whether the negotiated settlement and the handover of power to the ANC amounted to a shared triumph, a get-out-of-jail card, or a threatening reversal of fortune. This ambiguity communicated itself easily to the ANC, feeding the suspicions of those who were in any case predisposed to regard whites as hopeless reactionaries, intent on sabotaging black rule, and who were alert for any signs that this was the case. Among such portents was the behaviour of white rugby supporters on the occasion of the first legitimate international tour in August 1992 when the Springboks played the All Blacks. By flying the flag and singing the anthem of the apartheid republic a section of the crowd seemed to confirm the stereotypes of rugby and its followers held by many black South Africans. Clearly they had not learned two lessons: the first was that in the interests of peace and reconciliation they should adopt the new shared anthem and flag; and the second was that if they were to enjoy international rugby it was by the permission of and on the terms of the ANC. Fortunately enough whites expressed their condemnation of this boorish behaviour and, crucially, a new generation of younger and more progressive rugby administrators was coming to the fore. In the combination of these factors, Mandela and those on the ANC side who supported him could see both a challenge and an opportunity.

## 'The Game that Made a Nation'[1]

Nelson Mandela's appropriation of the Springbok world cup campaign for the purposes of nation-building was a genuinely cathartic, national experience and an instant global media event. Its durability as an exemplary fable was confirmed by the success of journalist John Carlin's retrospective account (2008) which was made into a Hollywood film[2] starring Morgan Freeman as Mandela and Matt Damon as François Pienaar, the Springbok captain. The outline of the story is well known. The Springboks were marketed as 'one team, one nation'; Chester Williams, the one black player in the squad, lost his place through injury, but by the time he recovered, his (white) replacement had been banned for an act of hotheaded foul play and Williams could play in the final; Mandela met with the team, bonded with and motivated them, wore their jersey at the final and publicly rejoiced with them and the overwhelmingly white crowd at their victory over the All Blacks; there was much rejoicing away from the stadium too, among black people as well as white. This uncomplicated and slender narrative has borne an impressive weight of popular mythology. Carlin's book gives an outsider's gloss on this. A somewhat fevered version of the international journalist's take on South Africa's transition, this, like Waldmeir's and other predecessor versions, objectifies and psychologizes 'the Afrikaner'. Interpreting the crowd's chants at the final, 'Nelson . . . Nelson' Carlin comments: 'They were crying out for forgiveness and they were accepting his, and through him, black South Africa's generous embrace.' This was the culmination of Mandela's long-term campaign to win over whites: 'one after another succumbed as he widened his embrace until the day of the rugby final when he embraced them all' (Carlin 2008: 252–3). This quasi-biblical interpretation – lost, sinful and leaderless tribe is readmitted to humanity by a redeemer representative of prelapsarian Africa – is of course within the legitimate bounds of speculative licence. It is possible that some sort of mass psychological phenomenon of this sort was taking place, if so, probably at a level of consciousness not normally accessible to the average rugby supporter. It is difficult to tell. However, more directly pertinent to the issue of nation-building in South Africa is the claim that the great task of Mandela's presidency, securing the foundations of the new nation and 'Making South Africans', had been accomplished 'not in five years but in one' (ibid.). This is a large claim to make and although Carlin qualifies it later, his interpretation still seems to elevate the events of May–June 1995 to the level of foundation myth.

There is widespread agreement that something remarkable took place around the 1995 RWC, although South African accounts (for instance, Grundlingh 1998) tend to see the effects as more ambiguous and ephemeral than Carlin does. Ephemeral or not, the World Cup Moment invites discussion in terms of the contribution of myth-making to nation-building. Historians and theorists of nationalism find political mythology well-nigh indispensable in understanding their subject. Part of the attraction is probably the concept's flexibility; its parameters are undemanding and encompass many different kinds of story-telling, story-tellers and audiences. Under these circumstances it is not unreasonable to accommodate Mandela and the World Cup within the political mythology of nationalism and try to identify what was distinctive about this South African version of myth-making.

Difficult as it is to generalize about a subject as diffuse and varied as nationalist mythology, the Mandela-World Cup myth and by extension the whole transition-to-democracy myth, diverged quite radically from some of the more traditional elements of nationalist myth-making. One principal difference was that it was developed in a largely top-down way. This does not mean that all genuine nationalist myth-making takes place from the grass-roots up. This is not the case at all; charismatic leaders, metropolitan political classes, state sponsorship and mass media have been driving forces of nation-building for centuries. However, they have generally been supported in fostering and propagating nation-building myths by community-based activist-intellectuals. In many places, stock figures such as nationalist schoolteachers, priests, party organizers and mayors, as well as other local notables contributed – often over long periods and as creators as well as transmitters – to what might be termed the micropolitics of nationalism. These were largely absent from the myth-making of South Africa's hastily improvised nation. Arguably, this is in any case an anachronistic model of nation-building in an age of mediated political societies and globalized media. It had in recent memory indeed been a model that was integral to building Afrikaner nationalism. However, as the Afrikaner coalition divided and fragmented, the micropolitics of cohesion were a principal casualty of various forces of change; urbanization, social mobility and affluence, political secularization and the growing recognition of the costs of apartheid. This is what helped make Afrikaners appear to be rudderless and available for Mandela's brand of directly communicated humanist charisma, which was diffused by all the resources of local and global media and focused on a fortuitous, once in decades opportunity, that of hosting the rugby world cup. However, this still left open the question of what or who would foster, elaborate and sustain this spirit and reinvest the nation-building capital it briefly made available.

The experience of black communities was somewhat different. Apartheid repression drove representative black community figures into acquiescence or for those who resisted, into exile, detention or to their deaths. The work of those who survived underground, or increasingly openly as the 1980s wore on, centred on motifs of resistance and insurrection. The return of the ANC in 1990 came with the turn to negotiations, explicit acceptance of liberal–democratic values and coexistence with the enemy. The result was considerable ideological confusion; it was ironic that at the point where the ANC was at last able to mobilize openly and freely, with the exception of no-go areas controlled by the IFP, there was considerable ambiguity about what it was mobilizing for. One thing was certain; it was mobilizing for the end of apartheid and the installation of democracy but what these things would mean was far from clear. Among the things that were uncertain was the future of non-racialism. It would not have been difficult to read Mandela's world cup outreach as a version of non-racialism in which South African whites were free to express themselves in enjoyment of their advantages without undue interrogation of how they came to have them in the first place. Whatever non-racialism might mean, for most African-South Africans, certainly in the ANC and crucially, for Mbeki, this was not it. Despite this, a favourable combination of factors gave momentum to Mandela's representative demonstration of lived non-racialism. These were the president's own authority and charisma; the ANC's favourable calculation of the costs and benefits of getting behind the Springboks; and the unsophisticated but clearly genuine and ungrudging response of the white players to Mandela, led by Pienaar as captain. These were enough for the moment, but not enough to give the ongoing and self-sustaining traction at the level of communal consciousness, that we associate with the most binding examples of popular nationalist mythology.

## Making sense of Mandela

Mandela's place in the pantheon of late twentieth-century leadership is unchallenged and the verdict is unequivocal that if South Africa's 'miracle' of transition belongs to any one individual it belongs to him. Therefore, it may seem presumptuous or even perverse to interrogate his achievements for limitations, ambiguities and comparative perspectives, especially in the area with which he is indelibly associated, that of nation-building. Any kind of assessment that is more than an encomium is in any case not easy to produce. There are several reasons for this. The first is that there is a genuine quality of mystery about his life and career, despite the availability of an apparently frank and comprehensive autobiography. The ambiguity has been deepened by the release of an early draft of the work, smuggled out of jail in 1977. Such ambiguity is inevitable with a life divided abruptly between the focused glare of public attention, in the dock or in the most highly publicized ever release from jail, and the obscurity of life underground or in a cell. This obscurity was heightened for many years by the determination of the repressive regime which jailed him to ban his name, his words and his story, along with those of the organization to which he belonged, and in its own propaganda versions to distort them as far as possible by branding him simply as a 'terrorist'. Related to the mystery is the magic: it remains difficult to pin down why and how he had such effects on people. Highly wrought accounts like that of Carlin discussed above are an open invitation to deconstruction and even perhaps debunking. It remains true, however, that such interpretations are not the sole preserve of the star-struck. Even such hard-headed and ethnically grounded commentators as Giliomee and the late Van Zyl Slabbert agreed on the 'magic' of Mandela's effect on Afrikaners: 'Afrikaners were captivated by Mandela; he cast a spell that produced a state of charismatic bewilderment' (Giliomee 2003: 648).

Adding to these ingredients of enigma are the facts that he spent only a small portion of his career in the public eye and an even smaller one with his hands on the levers of power. Moreover he left power when he could have stayed on. As a result of all these things, as we have already noted, there is an inescapable quality of a lost leader about him. This affects how we assess him overall and perhaps more importantly how we judge those who followed him. It is tempting to invoke the verdict of the English politician Enoch Powell on political careers, whose half-truths have become a staple of discourse about political leadership: 'All political lives, unless they are cut off at midstream at some happy juncture, end in failure, because that is the nature of politics and human affairs' (1977: 151).[3] By this kind of reckoning, if Mandela had not cut off his own career at such a happy juncture – earning even more plaudits in the process as the man who defied the gerontocratic tendency in African nationalist leadership – we might have had to judge his career differently.

Another difficult question of perspective is how much of his achievement we should credit to others. Verdicts like the following are typical: 'The overriding legacy of the Mandela presidency – of the years 1994 to 1999 – is a country where the rule of law was entrenched in an unassailable Bill of Rights, and where the predictions of racial and ethnic conflict did not come true. These feats, alone, guarantee Mandela his sanctity' (Gevisser 2007: 648). This capsule judgement does credit 'the presidency', but the weight of the approbation is on the individual. On its own, the need for economy pushes such assessments in the direction of the representative individual, even when some of those who make them are well aware of the many significant contributions from across political divides. However, the key issue here is the relationship between Mandela the nation-builder and the ANC. This arises from the fact that in this context there are two

Mandelas: the partisan Mandela and the shared Mandela, both of which were essential for him to have the nation-building impact that he had. For the ANC, Mandela was embedded in the liberation movement family and without this popular and organizational base there would have been no magic. However, he became more than the object of a parochial cult, owned and treasured by an exclusive constituency of African nationalists. This was not a coincidence and not something that a man isolated in jail for 27 years could achieve on his own; it was largely the ANC's own doing. One essential way to understand the Mandela phenomenon is to see it as 'a collectively manufactured achievement – the deliberate assembly of a messianic personality originating in a movement's awareness of its own organizational shortcomings and willingness to compensate for them by directing its ideas through a charismatic individual' (Lodge 2009).

This is clearly an important part of the story, though just what the balance should be between the Mandela who was his own man and the Mandela who was the manufactured icon will always be in dispute. However, part of the political significance of this dual provenance is that while he brought enormous dividends of credibility to the ANC, he was the source of much anxiety as well. The ANC laboured long and hard to create the Mandela myth when its subject was in jail. But even before he was released he was creating his own myth in his negotiations with his captors, and after he was free he showed an alarming inclination to be his own man, despite frequent protestations, which may have owed something to irony at times, that he was no more than a humble servant of the liberation movement.

Leaders who are more popular, or more to the point are more trusted than their parties, are difficult enough for ordinary parties that are not much more than electoral machines; for a liberation movement that saw itself as a nation realizing its destiny, Mandela was more than a handful. The dangerous precedents came not so much from the Big Men of African nationalism, but, ironically perhaps, from the party leaders in Western democracies who appeal over the heads of their parties to wider constituencies. They may do this out of a sense of personal mission or ideological zeal because they can grasp a larger historical reality than the myopic faithful or, more prosaically, just to make them more presentable to the electorate. But in doing so they are insensitive to the dogma which kept the committed together through tough times. Tensions and suspicions of this sort were present even, perhaps especially, when the shared Mandela was at the height of his popularity; however because the ANC was in such a state of ideological flux anyway, and by that time so hungry for the rewards of office, by and large the tensions were containable. Another source of tension was that the ANC having worked hard to give Mandela to the world could be uneasy about sharing him. It is only a superficial irony that Mandela was a global icon before he was properly a national figure; the prohibitions and distortions around his name within South Africa until he was released and the ANC unbanned are sufficient to explain that. The global Mandela posed few problems for the ANC and offered much room for creative exploitation. However, having worked hard to create the shared Mandela, the ANC was touchy about sharing him at home in South Africa with those who did not understand or rejected the political culture of African nationalism in which he grew up and which he had helped to create. Worse still were those who in the eyes of the ANC opportunistically used him against these very values. This area of tension has lasted long after Mandela retired from politics. In early 2013 there was a bitter dispute between the ANC and the DA over the latter's use of photographs which showed Mandela together with the DA's own source of inspiration, liberal anti-apartheid parliamentarian the late Helen Suzman. This was part of a campaign to refute negative stereotyping about the opposition party's 'whiteness' and alleged lack of anti-apartheid credentials. The ANC's outrage at this act of 'appropriation', nearly 20 years after the first democratic election, shows how ambivalent its feelings remain over the shared Mandela.

In this respect striking ambiguities contributed to the clashing images of the partisan and shared Mandelas. To the partisan eye he can be viewed as a distillation of all that the ANC stood for; in the shared political arena he could be seen as a shining example of what it lamentably failed to be. It is certainly true that for many people he was living refutation of Afro-pessimism. However, it mattered greatly whether his humanism was perceived to be his *because of* being African or *in spite of* being an African nationalist. It also mattered greatly whether he was a great man because he was a democrat or because in certain strategic respects he was not. Mandela's democratic credentials are of course impeccable; his respect for the rule of law and his graceful exit from office when he could easily have stayed on, are cases in point. However, according to one of his biographers, Mandela's messianic politics were employed to 'demobilize a popular insurrection in one of the world's most unequal societies' and under such circumstances, 'the institutions of liberal democracy depend on the protection afforded by highly authoritarian forms of charismatic authority' (Lodge 2006: 203). 'Highly authoritarian' might be stretching the point, but there is no doubt that in politics Mandela had his patriarchal side and that this was not the least of his attractions to whites. It was attractive especially to those who did not fear Africans as such, but African democracy, especially when it took populist and nationalist forms. In this sense, Mandela was the dream ticket; democratic rights and a benevolent African patriarch to guarantee them against upstart revolutionaries. To this day when whites bemoan the lack of leadership in the ANC it is this kind of combination that at least some of them have in mind.

However, it would be superficial to assume that only whites were attracted by this side of Mandela. Indeed there is a retrospective tendency to overemphasize how much he meant to whites and to take for granted what he meant to black people. It is worth remembering that in late 1998, as he came to the end of his tenure as president and of his political life, he had the approval of 59 per cent of whites and 80 per cent of all South Africans (Lodge 2002: 17). Many Africans too had an appetite for the exercise of personal authority that promised stability against the liberation struggle's worrying legacy of ungovernability, a threat which was frequently invoked from all political quarters between 1990 and 1994. This side of Mandela played a key role in the ANC's ability to counter Buthelezi's claim to represent stability against ungovernability. The sources of authority Mandela wielded to this end had a wide appeal. He was patrician and despite his loyalty to the ANC he appeared to be unbeholden to cliques or factions within it. He had to be mindful of the movement's internal dynamics but appeared to be above them. This was reassuring both to those who identified with the ANC and to those who did not. His relationship to the cultural and traditional side of African nationalism was similar; he was part of it but not subject to it: 'I respect custom but I am not a tribalist. I fought as an African nationalist and I have no commitment to the custom of any tribe. Custom is not moribund. It is a social phenomenon which develops and changes' (Meredith 2010: 541). This meant that he was rooted but not root-bound, another reassuring trait for people of all races who were overwhelmed with change fatigue. In his autobiography he said of his decision to have a (modest) home built at Qunu in the Eastern Cape: 'I have always believed that a man should have a home within sight of the house where he was born' (Mandela 1994: 599). This is a sense of belonging that can be shared across all sorts of regional, ethnic, racial and language boundaries. At the same time no-one paused to ask exactly what it meant to Mandela to be an African nationalist or what his respect for custom would entail.

In the last analysis, Mandela's contribution to nation-building illustrates both the power and the limitations of individual humanism. The five years of his presidency did not represent a new departure for nation-building but an extension of the principle of improvisation. He met the political needs of the moment with his personal instincts and values, and for the most part he was able to react in calculatedly symbolic ways that satisfied both of them. Personal lapses of judgement in support of comrades whose values fell short of his were the major exceptions. However, his exemplary, lived, humanistic non-racialism was not anchored by any searching and rigorous analysis of the structural legacies of apartheid and how to confront them. Debate continues over whether or not Mandela was ever a member of the communist party and whether it matters if he was. One thing seems clear; if he ever was a communist, then he was not a very good one since apparently he was not at all inclined to think in terms of overarching theories, abstract socio-economic structures and impersonal historic forces, certainly in his post-imprisonment incarnation. Doubtless this was all to the good since he would scarcely have been able to achieve the extraordinary human effects he did if he had been hobbled by party-think. However, sooner or later the improvisation had to stop and nation-building would have to take the forms of vision and policy architecture. As Mandela left office in early 1999 there seemed to be two possible futures for nation-building. The first was that Mandela had bought time for his successor and credit for the ANC which they could spend by building on Mandela's achievements, while addressing the massive material inequalities and conflicted relationships between redress and reconciliation which could not be faced up to under the pressures of Mandela's own time. The other alternative was that Mandela had prematurely taken the country too far down a road of reconciliation that disproportionately favoured whites and allowed them to escape a proper accounting for their own history and their present position. A sharp call to order was required, which might risk, or even require undoing some of Mandela's work. How the next phase of nation-building would go would depend on his successor, Thabo Mbeki.

## Making sense of Mbeki

Mandela published no manifesto or testimony during or after his political career which explained in any detail what African nationalism and non-racialism meant to him and how they guided him. The few words he devotes to African nationalism in his more than 600-page autobiography refer mainly to the African nationalism of Anton Lembede to which the young Mandela was attracted in the 1940s. In the autobiography, he describes this conception of nationalism as 'emotional', 'racially exclusive', 'undiluted', and tells how he 'outgrew' it when he began to associate with a more multiracial society of communists and other progressives and his views matured (Mandela 1994: 101, 106, 112, 215). Thereafter, African nationalism disappears from the text except as an occasional label to describe himself. 'Non-racialism' does not appear at all. We are left to piece together from the testimony of his life that to be an African nationalist means to work to create one nation out of many tribes, overthrow white minority rule, and establish 'real' (that is majoritarian) democracy (ibid. 93). Non-racialism means that a majority should not oppress a minority. However, what makes a majority a majority and what makes a minority a minority and what it is that makes them both part of some larger whole are left as if they are part of the common pool of knowledge that South Africans (and indeed all humanity) are assumed to share. To some extent this is fair enough; we should not underestimate the capacity of ordinary people to understand who is who and what is what, especially if this shared knowledge has a force of common humanity like Mandela's behind it. This is not to mention the fact that part of the key to success in political leadership lies in not being too analytically explicit about everything. However, with the open-ended prospect stretching into the future of living both with the democratic settlement and with each other, South Africans needed more than human decency and folk wisdom.

More might reasonably have been expected in this line of Mbeki as he approached the presidency in 1999. He was self-consciously intellectual, of an analytical cast of mind, a forensic debater and a rhetorician. These cerebral gifts combined – in the testimony of interlocutors and adversaries – to make him a formidable persuader one-on-one and in small groups. Yet, no more than Mandela has he left a direct, uncomplicated, economical and practical testimony as to what it means to be an African nationalist in an era of shared South African citizenship, and to be non-racial in a context both of equal constitutional rights and massive material inequalities between races. In Gevisser's exhaustive 900-page biography there are no index entries for nation, nation-building, African nationalism or non-racialism. That is not to say that Mbeki wrote nothing of relevance to nation-building and identity. On the contrary, he was notably productive on this score. However, the meaning is never distilled and has to be tracked across obfuscations, hesitations, circumlocutions, ambiguities and contradictions. Mbeki on the 'two nations' in South Africa may send very different messages from the justly famous poetry of his 'I am an African' speech. Or it may not: but reconciling the two is an intellectual task which does not make for the kind of instinctive rapport which is the gold standard of nation-building through mass political communication. However, these observations should not be made without sympathetic qualification. In Mbeki's defence it can be pointed out that the assumptions and catchphrases of the Rainbow Nation and the New South Africa were stretched over chasms of inequality and (on the part of whites in particular) deep wells of ignorance about how others lived; someone had to tell the truth about all this. However, at the same time, calculations about how much truth was enough and how much was too much, as well as which truth among several possibilities should take priority, were not easy in a situation where passions were not far from the surface and people on all sides were quick to sense betrayal in the air. It was partly a question of personal style. Mandela defused passions with empathy, kindness, etiquette, chivalry and honour. Mbeki tried to contain them within elaborate theoretical architectures and modulate them with poetry.

Assessments of Mbeki's contribution to nation-building are clouded by uncertainties of this kind about where he really stood. They are also affected by collateral damage from his disastrous espousal of AIDS denialism. Inevitably views differ on whether he had a positive or a negative effect on the prospects of strengthening a sense of nationhood, but the balance is tipped quite strongly to the latter. Before attempting an audit of such judgements it is probably best to begin with what it is generally agreed that he brought – for better or worse – to the question of nation-building. To begin with he is credited with administering a realist antidote to rainbow-era optimism and forcing recognition that material conditions of life are important in shaping identities and affiliations. Allied to this was a reputation – at least at the beginning of his presidency – for rational management and policy architecture. This would complement the soft human skills of Mandela with hard organizational skills; these in turn would deliver the benefits that would ease reconciliation He also injected a strong measure of African identity into nation-building to the extent that he was often given the label 'Africanist' by the media. Finally, he encouraged what was already a pronounced tendency in the ANC to conflate state, nation and party, which greatly blurred and confused his thinking on the composition of the nation.

## A dose of realism: Inequality and the two nations

Mbeki had already made his mark on the subject of nation-building before he became president. In May 1998, a year before he succeeded Mandela, he opened a debate on 'Reconciliation and nation building' in the National Assembly with an uncompromisingly materialistic definition of the nation: 'nation building is the construction of the reality and the sense of common nationhood which would result from the abolition of disparities in the quality of life among South Africans based on the racial, gender and geographical inequalities we all inherited from the past' (Mbeki 1998). These disparities amounted to 'terrible deprivation' and 'dehumanisation' in whose continuing presence 'the concept of nation building is a mere mirage and . . . no basis exists, or will ever exist to enable national reconciliation to take place' (ibid.).

In making a link between the legacy of race-based inequality and nationhood, Mbeki was being quite discriminating. A blanket insistence on equality as a prerequisite for nationhood would strike too socialist a note from a president-in-waiting who as early as 1995 had (inaccurately) predicted that the Alliance left – the communists and the trade unions – would go its separate way within five years, who acknowledged the need for South Africa to be hospitable to markets and free enterprise, who was integral to the ANC government's adoption of the fiscally austere GEAR programme in 1996, and whose plans for economic transformation would include BEE provisions which would allow an unequal opportunity for those who were politically connected to the ANC to become unequal. The only positive reference in the two-nations speech to equality (as distinct from the evils of race-based inequality) was to the need to make equality of opportunity – a classical liberal concept – a real prospect for poor black people instead of being, under current material conditions, wholly incapable of realization.

Mbeki's assault on the progress of nation-building so far should have come as no surprise. The promises of the Constitution are indeed broad and generous and material inequalities render it difficult to make good on them. A call to order was inevitable and could have been salutary. However, much of the speech came as a shock, especially to whites: the vehemence with which he characterized nation-building thus far as dishonest and an illusion; the insistence that all inequality was and would remain race-based and that no other dynamics were at work; the implication that the time span for true nation-building would rival the 350 years of white involvement in South Africa. However, the most potentially damaging aspect of this calculated blighting of the green shoots of the Mandela era was the characterization of South Africa as two nations: one white and prosperous and the other black and poor.[4] At a stroke, everything that had been achieved was invalidated and he proposed a South Africa that was at ground zero. What is more, the lack of success of nation-building thus far was in Mbeki's view, solely the result of intransigence and opposition from whites to the ANC's attempts at transformation.

This forceful recasting of the nation-building question would have made sense as the prelude to announcing a radical change of direction away from conservative, macroeconomic policies and in the direction of a massive programme of redistribution. Since nothing of the sort was on the cards, the tone of the speech, if not the content, looks in retrospect like a political miscalculation. Mbeki, more even than Mandela as president at this stage, was responsible for managing executive power on behalf of a party in government that had won close to two-thirds of the popular vote. By characterizing the state of nation-building in such stark and unpromising terms without offering radical ways of dealing with it, he merely advertised his own and his government's impotence or lack of resolution and opened the way for flanking attacks from left-wing and populist critics. Coupled with this was the characterization of whites as a separate nation. This in itself undermined what little there was in the speech that was positive. There was a rhetorical 'call to rally a new patriotism', a rather random eight-point agenda of desirable things to be secured through 'common fights', 'concerted actions', 'united offensives' and 'all embracing efforts'. This included the goal of:

> a sense of common nationhood and a shared destiny, as a result of which we can entrench into the minds of all our people the understanding that however varied their skin complexions, cultures and life conditions, the success of each nevertheless depends on the effort the other will make to turn into reality the precept that each is his or her brother's or sister's keeper. (Ibid.)

It made an unpromising beginning to this project, to quarantine whites in a separate nation especially when the entire process of negotiation, compromise and agreement that had brought democracy to South Africa was premised on whites' self-revaluation that they were *not* in fact a separate nation. They were of course greatly assisted in this belated awakening from the delusion of their separate nationhood by the considerable persuasive powers of Mbeki himself.

This irony seems to have been lost on the author of 'two nations'. In short, whatever the metaphorical power the speech had[4] in conveying how serious the challenge of inequality was, it was not wise to deploy the expression in a country as literal minded as South Africa. The usage did not revive the notion of white nationhood, but helped to reinforce the self-assigned status of threatened minority and self-justification as having collective rights and interests which received coded expression in the Democratic Party's 'Fight Back' slogan for the 1999 general election, a few months after Mbeki's speech. The slogan was deeply controversial but electorally successful in rallying and aggregating white votes behind the DP.

In addition to its dubious politics, Mbeki's reductionist portrayal of inequality as exclusively racial in nature was simply wrong. 'If Mbeki had attached more importance to social and cultural divides between white and black South Africans he would have probably been on stronger ground, but in emphasizing interracial economic inequality he misunderstands the changing nature of inequality in South Africa' (Nattrass and Seekings 2005: 343). In the first place the trends of declining racial inequality and rising interracial inequality had already begun in 'the final decades of apartheid' (ibid.) and in any case, South Africa's income distribution was simply not bipolar between rich and poor, irrespective of race. Belated recognition of both the political miscalculation and the factual inaccuracy of the two-nations characterization probably played a part in recasting the problem of inequality in the early years of Mbeki's own presidency. According to this new official framework of development economics, rather than two nations, two *economies* existed in South Africa. These were a dominant, first economy, globally integrated and able to export a range of manufactured goods and commodities, and another marginalized economy. Alongside but disconnected from it, was a second economy consisting of large numbers of the unemployed and unemployable in both rural and urban areas and which was incapable of self-generated growth and development. Crucially, 'the communities occupying these conceptual spaces (cannot) be categorized in terms of race and class' (Presidency 2006). This more nuanced approach better captured the problems of poverty and inequality which handicapped the project of nation-building. However, the formulation, 'communities occupying conceptual spaces' is less likely to remain in the mind than the sound bite provided by 'two nations' and in that sense the damage to nation-building was already done.

## Truth, reconciliation and the high moral ground

Parallel to Mbeki's anxieties about how inequality was being perceived – or ignored – was the issue of accounting for the crimes and the crime of apartheid. For many people the Truth and Reconciliation Commission (TRC) process was the defining feature of South Africa's transition to democracy. This was especially true of foreign observers, for whom it was the culminating act of the South African drama, providing irresistible moral theatre for those with nothing invested in its outcome. As a measure of this interest, the TRC's official research website lists over 550 books, chapters and articles written exclusively about the process between 1996 and 2003 when the final report was published. Much more was also written of course in general treatments of the period. Despite, or perhaps, because of this consuming interest, the main protagonists in the transition were far from wholehearted in their approach to the TRC. The ANC and the NP had both recognized the need for amnesty as a condition for negotiation, but differed over whether a general or case-by-case approach was better. This difference was less one of principle, more in terms of the issue's potential for leverage in the negotiations; the ANC began by being in favour of a general amnesty while the NP government insisted on case-by-case. As the balance of power changed in the three years between the unbanning of the ANC and the signing of the interim Constitution, a powerful lobby among ANC legal experts, encouraged by religious and other groups in civil society who were broadly sympathetic to the ANC though not necessarily part of it, argued for a process that would effectively trade individual truth-telling for amnesty in the interests of restorative rather than retributive justice. That is to say in terms of redefining crime as wrongdoing against people rather than against the state. This spirit was duly reflected in a post-amble to the 1993 interim Constitution which declared, 'The pursuit of national unity, the well-being of all South African citizens and peace require reconciliation between the people of South Africa and the reconstruction of society.' Following this, the Promotion of National Unity and Reconciliation Act of 1995 provided for a commission to embody a process in which victims and the community would be involved, perpetrators would make disclosure and take responsibility for their actions. Despite a general acceptance that amnesia was not a viable option, neither the ANC nor the NP were united in wholeheartedly welcoming the TRC and many on both sides would have preferred a general amnesty. Despite this ambivalence the TRC was well resourced; 17 commissioners were chosen by Mandela after broad consultation; they were backed by a staff of over 500 in 4 regional offices and comprehensive, live transmission by the South African Broadcasting Corporation (SABC) of the public hearings that were the TRC's hallmark ensured maximum publicity. The TRC's profile was completed by the appointment as chairman of Archbishop Desmond Tutu who, after Mandela himself, was the most respected public personage in South Africa thanks to his courageous contributions to the struggle against apartheid and the critical independence of mind with which he treated all political parties and personages. The four objectives towards which these resources were directed all concerned 'gross violations of human rights': research would uncover their provenance, nature and extent; victims would come forward, have their testimony witnessed and reparations would be designed for them; perpetrators of politically motivated human rights violations could come forward and receive amnesty in return for full disclosure, while failure to do so could leave individuals open to prosecution; a report based on the findings would stand as a monument to the past and recommendations for the future.

Inevitably, it was a political and logistic imperative that the work of the commission would be defined and delimited. It was equally certain that it would be criticized for having too limited a mandate. The principal grounds of complaint can be summed up in the difference between the crimes of apartheid and the crime of apartheid. The singular and plural usages, 'crimes' and 'crime' of apartheid are not mere quirks of semantics. The commission's focus on gross violations of human rights meant a mandate restricted to crimes of apartheid. These could be understood as acts committed in an undeclared war between supporters and opponents of apartheid, and as such, individual accountability could be achieved, though not guaranteed. Even here there were difficulties of moral responsibility relating to chains of command, clarity of orders and the 'rogue element' in security force behaviour. Much dissatisfaction surrounded the way this issue was handled. For some critics, however, a bigger issue was involved; foregrounding individual acts meant that the crime of apartheid itself went unrecognized:

> The systemic (even genocidal) gross violations of human rights under the apartheid system – mass forced removals, pass laws, the bantustans, the whole apparatus of decades-long territorial 'ethnic cleansing' resulting in mass malnutrition, high levels of infant mortality, abysmal levels of life expectancy, all of this is largely kept largely to the side. (Cronin 1999: 6)

> Victims of apartheid are now narrowly defined as those militants victimized as they struggled against apartheid, not those whose lives were mutilated in the day-to-day web of regulations that was apartheid. We arrive at a world in which reparations are for militants, those who suffered jail or exile, but not for those who suffered only forced labour and broken homes. (Mamdani 1996: 4)

Critics of this persuasion tended to see the TRC as inadequate to or even a betrayal of 'real transformation, real reconciliation and real national unity' (Cronin 1999: 20). However, behind the rhetoric they did little to create a coherent, moral framework to comprehend apartheid in the systemic terms they called for and make it operational across all of South African history. Such a moral framework could be constructed out of crude two-nations thinking along the lines Mbeki took: all whites are guilty, all blacks are victims, but this does not seem to have been the intention of the critics. Any more nuanced framework, especially one to be arrived at through dialogue between white and black (anything else would not really count as 'reconciliation' but as victor's justice) would risk endless subdivision into degrees of responsibility and grades of beneficiary and similar categorization of their counterparts in victimhood.

Like people everywhere, all succeeding generations of white South Africans were, by inheritance, dealt a hand by the previous generation. Critics of the limited mandate of the TRC tended not to apply themselves to what would be the best way of judging how each generation played its hand and how free it was to do so, especially in view of the fact that victims were agents – agents of struggle and conflict – too. What seemed to be required, moreover, was a moral architecture that embraced not only the sample of perpetrators and victims solicited by the TRC within its time frame from 1960 to 1994, but all South Africans across the generations and indeed the centuries. Of course, historians can make such judgements; but historians do not have to act as brokers between legatees of historical acts for which they are not directly responsible but whose costs and benefits they bear and enjoy, and historians do not have the power to apportion costs and reparations on that basis. What is more, historians are free to be as objective or as partisan as they like, but they do not have to participate in an interactive process with those whose actions they weigh in the balance.

Perhaps acknowledging the line of criticism which demanded an accounting of the crime of apartheid, the TRC did make an effort to accommodate a more systematic approach through a number of special hearings. Among them were sessions devoted to business, religious faiths, the media and the health sector.[5] These did not amount to a structured programme; each had its own line of enquiry as well as scope and limitations in pursuing it. For instance, the health sector hearings stayed close to the TRC's limited general mandate by seeking to establish the roles of health professionals and authorities in 'perpetrating, colluding with or resisting human rights abuses during the period under review'. By contrast, Archbishop Tutu's introduction to the business hearings suggested a much wider mandate:

> What we know is that business operated in a milieu, not obviously of their creation where they gained profits as a result of government policies. Cheap labour, the migratory labour system, the system of single sex hostels, the iniquitous pass laws and the severe influx measures that impacted negatively on black family life. The operation of job reservation and the colour bar. I know that some of those in the business sector protested against such unjust laws but many acquiesced at best or positively co-operated. (Department of Justice Special Hearings Transcripts)

However, the business hearings like all the others devoted to sectors of society were voluntary. No representatives of oil companies attended, for instance. Tutu went out of his way to create a non-threatening atmosphere in the interests of coaxing what he called 'critical self-scrutiny', although some of the other commissioners were more aggressive. Under such circumstances it was difficult for those who volunteered to appear to hit the right note, avoiding extremes of self-abasement on the one hand and self-justification on the other. Clearly the commissioners, the ANC and black opinion generally felt that participants in the hearings (especially business and the media) erred on the side of self-justification and missed an opportunity to acknowledge what appeared crystal clear in their eyes at least; that apartheid was enabled by a wide base of morally dubious relationships extending to most if not all white people and institutions. One thing the experience of the hearings did imply was that 'critical self-scrutiny' was not necessarily the best way to demonstrate these things. There would always be a shortfall, it appeared, between the expectations of those demanding (or even merely 'facilitating') a reckoning and what those of whom it was demanded were prepared to offer up. However, although it was almost perversely set up to produce disappointment, it is hard to see what other approach would be viable.

What the special hearings did do was illustrate the complexity of 'white society'. The Afrikaans churches were criticized for being grudging in their submission, while the Anglican Church was so determined to make apologies to everybody that it apologized to the Afrikaans churches as well for affecting moral superiority towards them. The Afrikaans media did not take part at all, but organized Afrikaans business was praised by Tutu and the commissioners for the spirit of reconciliation he believed they embraced, by contrast with their English-speaking counterparts.

Criticism of the TRC's restricted mandate was not the only source of dissatisfaction with the commission's work. Some whites, especially Afrikaners, as well as Buthelezi and the IFP (which boycotted the proceedings) felt that appointments to the TRC were heavily slanted towards ANC fellow travellers. The Afrikaans press generally encouraged the view that the commission's work represented a witch hunt against Afrikaners. Others felt that the TRC's adoption of a restorative justice framework unduly favoured perpetrators and deprived victims of a legitimate expectation of retributive justice. In this view they were being sacrificed for the larger needs of inclusive nation-building. What was intended to give force to the TRC's adoption of restorative justice was the concept of *ubuntu*. *Ubuntu* is a philosophy of human interconnectedness and the antithesis of individualism, frequently translated in terms such as 'a person is a person through other people'. Among its many attributes is a preference for redemption and rehabilitation in the community rather than retribution, even retribution through due process. The extent to which *ubuntu* characterized actually existing African society in the immediate post-struggle period may be arguable.

However, it was in any case taken up and woven through the politico-legal discourse of constitutional formation, reconciliation and nation-building, in the hope of giving it an indigenous, communal and popular quality to ground the somewhat individualistic and universal values that otherwise predominated. Whatever salutary political effects the adoption of *ubuntu* may have produced along these lines, to some critics there were also costs, especially from associating amnesty with *ubuntu*:

> Creating a polarity between 'African' *ubuntu*/reconciliation on the one hand and 'Western' vengeance/retributive justice on the other, closes down the legal space to discuss fully the middle position – the pursuit of legal retribution as a possible route to reconciliation in itself. The constitutional right of citizens to due justice, to pursue civil claims against perpetrators is taken away by amnesty laws which preclude both criminal and civil prosecutions. This was justified in terms of a uniquely African form of compassion or *ubuntu*. By combining human rights and *ubuntu*, human rights come to express compromised justice and the state's abrogation of the right to due process. (Wilson 2001: 11)

The bitterest criticism of the TRC, however, came from the ANC, led by a furious Mbeki. The point at issue was the TRC's finding that the ANC was guilty of human rights abuses through the killing of civilians and the torture of its own members by its security branch in exile camps. So incensed was the organization that it attempted to stop publication of the commission's report through court action, which failed. This politically injudicious application and the harsh rhetoric against the commission which accompanied it tended to undermine the moral standing which the ANC felt belonged to it by right and seemed to confirm its potential for authoritarian intolerance to those who were already worried on that score. Since the TRC had endorsed this moral status by characterizing the ANC's armed campaign overall as a 'just war' in its report, the ANC's fury was quite counter-productive. This is something that Mandela, whose response was typically mature and measured, was clearly aware of.

Inevitably reactions to the TRC were mixed and it is hard to estimate its overall effect on nation-building. White people were on the whole sceptical, although for some who were close to the hearings it was a profoundly emotional experience to be widely shared in reportage, and there is some evidence that for many others the revelations of the hearings brought home to them what had been done in their name. Black people, again on the whole, tended to be more positive with some dissenting views, sometimes bitterly expressed, from victims or those close to them. It seems clear that the expressive combination of religion and theatre that accompanied (but did not wholly define) the proceedings gave affirmation and consolation to the sufferings of many individuals and communities. On the other hand, based on an ethnographic study of communities that had participated in hearings, Wilson argues that the TRC underestimated the extent to which some communities at least wanted retributive justice. Indeed the new constitutional and legal order of which the TRC was part and the nation-building assumptions it served was a 'new hegemony' which required a degree of 'moral coercion' to establish it. Part of this was the manipulation of assumptions about 'African' justice based on a romanticized, static and ahistorical view of African community (Wilson 2001: xvi, 9, 10). It is not possible to say how much this was driven by genuine misunderstandings about the nature, prevalence, coherence and applicability to a modern constitutional state of an African tradition of justice, to idealistic hopes that African traditions would inspire a new moral order, or, more prosaically, to good faith manipulation in the higher interests of desirable political outcomes like peace, stability and nation-building. Whatever the case, Wilson concludes that the institutions of the new moral and legal order like the TRC may have undermined their own legitimacy by association with amnesty.

Perhaps the predominant view among South Africans, looking back at the TRC, was relief that it was over. However, for some this was not unmixed with the sense that there was unfinished business. Prominent on this unaddressed agenda was the view that the generality of whites had not acknowledged to black people the role that they had played in sustaining apartheid. This, it appeared to some, would be a way of demonstrating the horizontal bonds with strangers that constitute an imagined community and would be an essential part of nation-building.

## Home for All: The end of reconciliation?

Insofar as the Home for All campaign is remembered at all today, it is as a rather sad, perhaps embarrassing coda to the TRC. Nevertheless it is worth recalling as a point to mark both the conclusive end of the reconciliation moment and the unfolding of a new political context for post-apartheid nation-building. Home for All[6] was an initiative born of the conviction that it was necessary to go beyond the TRC's selective approach to perpetrators and victims, and demonstrate engagement between all whites as beneficiaries of apartheid with blacks who were all disadvantaged by its various racially defined exclusions, discriminations and repressions. The initiative was jointly led by Mary Burton, president of the women's anti-apartheid movement the Black Sash and Carl Niehaus, former political prisoner and ANC activist who was regarded by many Afrikaans-speaking whites as an apostate, but by some in the ANC as a potential bridge to Afrikaners. Behind the joint leaders was a committee of white progressives some of whom had been involved in the TRC and had transferred this engagement to the IJR, an NGO which was set up to continue to work for reconciliation in the same broad spirit as the TRC. The chief component of Home for All was a 'Declaration of Commitment by White South Africans',[7] which was linked to initiatives through which whites might make contributions to 'development and reconciliation' either by financial donations or transfer of skills. The declaration acknowledged the following things, emphasizing the solemnity of the pledge by the repetition in each case of the words 'We acknowledge': the massive damage apartheid inflicted on black South Africans which 'undermined our common humanity'; the 'white community's' responsibility through the active and passive support of 'many of us'; the debt owed to black South Africans because all whites benefited from apartheid's injustices; that racist attitudes of white superiority and black inferiority still shape 'our lives'. Signatories also acknowledged their failure to accept responsibility for apartheid and their deep regret for 'all of this', while committing themselves to redress.

The declaration was launched in 2000 at a function attended by around 200 people, only half of whom were white and it was eventually signed by about 2,000 people (Matthews 2010: 9). This is only a tiny fraction of the white population, which at the time was around 4 million people. Not only did the campaign fail to attract many signatories but: 'What was striking about the reaction of white South Africans was that the Campaign was not simply ignored or treated with apathy, but that it was met with great hostility' (ibid.). The obvious inference to draw from this was that the reconciliation moment was over; the question was, why? In a review of contemporary comment on the failure of Home for All to attract many signatures, Matthews suggests that hostile portrayal in the media had a role to play: 'The organizers had carefully avoided including words like "apology" and "guilt" in the Declaration in favour of words like "acknowledgement" and "regret", yet it was presented in the media as being an admission of guilt or apology on the part of white South Africans' (ibid. 9–10). This seems rather naïve, or even disingenuous on the part of the framers and perhaps it would have been better to avoid circumlocution. Irrespective of the words used, by a reasonable person's standard the meaning is perfectly plain, and indeed Matthews herself refers to the document a couple of pages earlier as 'an admission of the guilt of most (but not all) South Africans in supporting apartheid'. Aside from alleged misrepresentation by the media, white reaction was explained at the time in several ways, among them; a sign of the deep conservatism of whites and their unwillingness to reach out from their racial zone of security; a symptom of whites' confusion at having their world overturned, akin to the earlier stages in the popular psychological characterization of the stages of grief, with the hope that acceptance would come; wariness that signing the declaration would be a precursor to assuming multiplying responsibilities for reparation.

These largely dispassionate explanations do not include angry reactions which also surfaced at the time, blaming the whites' reactions on an assumed moral indifference and inadequacy, as well as their racism and arrogance.

Some of the reviewed explanations hint at a political context but none of them confront it squarely. That is because there was considerable confusion over the political dimension of reconciliation. That is to say, as the Mbeki presidency gathered momentum and the work of the TRC unfolded, the how and the why of reconciliation could be conceptualized in quite different ways in relation to politics, especially politics defined as the representation of clashing interests and competitive organization to defend and promote them. Effectively there were three ways of looking at reconciliation, all of which placed it outside of politics.

From one point of view, reconciliation was post-political. The successful completion of the liberation struggle had installed the ANC as the embodiment of national aspirations if not in perpetuity then as far as the imagination could run; any manifestation of opposition to it was subversive, reactionary, racist or all three, and failure to comprehend that this was the context in which reconciliation had to take place, for instance, by treating reconciliation as a topic for debate or bargaining, amounted to racist denial. This current ran strongly in the ANC. Running equally strongly, thanks to Mbeki's developing ideas on the subject, was the opposite conceptualization; reconciliation was pre-political, a condition for the resumption, or more properly the initiation of democratic politics. In this view, reconciliation required the achievement of full equality – whatever that meant – and until that happened democratic politics in any full sense was not possible. The third possibility was that reconciliation was transpolitical; that is, it took place in a parallel moral universe to politics. Participants, especially those deemed to be the guilty parties, should deny themselves political agency, or at least suspend it until they are rehabilitated. This last conception is probably what came closest to the intentions of the Home for All. One way or another there was a tendency to treat reconciliation in an un- or anti-political way and to assume that whites' existing conceptions of their political interests and allegiances were either irrelevant to or superseded by the imperative of reconciliation.

There is of course a case for turning this analysis around and arguing that far from denying themselves political agency, in accepting their responsibilities to initiate reconciliation through taking up Home for All's invitation, whites would be dramatically expressing it. They would be doing so in a mature and long-sighted way, making a decisive break with the past and their 'comfort zone'. This would be a rational calculation of their long-term material and security interests as well as their affiliation needs and an expression of the civic values they now (in theory at least) espoused.

There are several problems with this interpretation. The first is that no-one – least of all Home for All – presented the initiative in this light. The declaration and the proposed follow-up approached whites solely as individuals and as somewhere between liturgical statement and charitable endeavour, leaving them on their own to work out what their political interests were and how to pursue them. The declaration contained no vision of who or what might be changed as a result of people signing it. The second problem – which spread across a much wider area than merely the choice to sign up to Home for All or not – was the question of where such a break with the past would lead. It could of course lead into the ANC (and doubtless there were whites who saw the Home for All initiative as a thinly veiled recruiting poster) thus ensuring that the de facto one-party state had total rather than merely predominant coverage. Alternatively it could lead into a brave new world of realignment in which whites who acknowledged their collective guilt but would be otherwise purged of all 'white' associations, would be joined by like-minded blacks to form a multiracial movement to play a constructive role in the new South Africa under terms of coexistence with the ANC which would have to be worked out. Fantasies of this sort have been staple fare since 1994 for those who were anxious about the prospects of one-partyism but repelled by the 'whiteness' of parliamentary opposition; throughout this time whites have been regularly castigated for failing to pursue such fantasies. However, since one of the co-leaders of the Home for All initiative was a prominent ANC politician and others of its backers were (at least at the time) supporters, this scenario for encouraging a multiracial alternative to ANC hegemony, understandably, did not play any part in it. In any case at the time (2000) there was no incentive whatever for black people to turn their backs on the promise held out by ANC rule, not to mention the opportunities for personal advancement through a party which was committed through the cadre deployment policy to place its own supporters in all government and quasi-government jobs, and given the size of its majority and its excellent prospects for maintaining it, had the leverage to do so. In the light of these problems, Home for All was a political dead end and the default mode for whites was to conceptualize their political interests and affiliations in existing modes of party-political organization and competition. This at least would be a holding operation, with the option of later transforming the parties to appeal beyond a white base, which is what the DA did. This however did not count as reconciliation in the ANC's eyes.

The significance of Home for All's failure – and the larger failure of reconciliation which it confirmed – can be better assessed if it is seen against the main political currents of the day, rather than in isolation as a matter between every individual white person and his or her conscience. What Home for All portrayed as a simple and obvious confessional act was, viewed in this light, rather more complicated. One straw in the wind was De Klerk's apology before the TRC. The largely negative – and substantially scathing – response to this may have suggested to some whites the futility of trying to satisfy moral gatekeepers who unilaterally set standards for confession, apology and by implication readmission to common humanity. Another was Mbeki's 'Two Nations' speech. This had decisively shifted the emphasis away from apology and forgiveness. Admission of guilt would not secure reconciliation: only the achievement of material equality which would enable equal enjoyment of the promises of the Constitution. It was not clear how long this would take, what means would be employed, who would decide when enough was enough and how reconciliation would be marked. Most of all it was not clear what the state of relationships between the two nations would be until that happened, only that whites could expect a long period of moral probation. Doubtless Mbeki thought that an apology was a welcome step, but it would only be a reminder of how far there was to go and whites could expect no dividend, other than becoming able to see themselves with greater moral clarity.

A third pointer to the future was the attempt led by government and quasi-government organizations to construct a new moral hegemony around proliferating and ever-more extensive definitions of racism. In this respect the statutory Human Rights Commission (HRC) set new standards of thoroughness, vigilance and self-interrogation for whites in its inquiry into racism in the media: 'Dealing with racism therefore requires being alert to those manifestations of behaviours which have their root in a history of hegemonic relations between black and white people and which continue to be discriminatory in effect, whether intended as such or not. The non-racist approach is to be in continual check of one's assumptions and to test them against other ideas and situations' (2000: 63). According to the HRC, 'Racism is parasitic. It attaches itself often to other defensible, socially acceptable discourse and action. It becomes necessary therefore to prise out the accretions and mutations of racism' (ibid. 65). Clearly exorcism on this scale would require more than a blanket apology, especially as the charge sheet against whites was expanding in the post-apartheid years rather than shrinking.

Significant as these specific instances might have been, it was the developing structures of power in post-apartheid politics that are more likely to have influenced whites' attitudes to reconciliation. By the time the initiative was presented to whites in 2000, there had been two general elections, in which the ANC had won 62.65 per cent (1994) and 66.35 per cent (1999) of the vote. This was close to the two-thirds majority required for unilateral change to the Constitution, a margin the ANC duly went on to win (69.69%) at the next election in 2004. In the years since the Constitution was ratified in 1996, ambivalence about the settlement on which it was based had become apparent in the ANC and the wider Alliance. The settlement was still celebrated by the ANC as a mutual triumph of compromise, shared values and common humanity. However, it was also viewed as the ANC's own victory over a cunning, ruthless and unscrupulous foe. Moreover it was also increasingly referred to as a mere staging post in the ongoing journey to the National Democratic Revolution through which the 'African majority' would come into its own, and indeed at times for some the constitutional settlement was stigmatized as an obstruction in that journey. As always the chronic incoherence of the ANC and the ability of its senior members to move fluently from one register to another, made it difficult to read all these signals; not only did they emanate from different parts of the Alliance, but the same individual was capable of expressing more than one, or even all of these characterizations of the settlement at different times and for different audiences. While the official line of the ANC leadership was that the settlement was safe in ANC hands, indeed that it would be safe *only* in ANC hands, these reassurances were delivered against and sometimes in direct response to background noise which suggested the contrary. At the same time, things on which the ANC always spoke with one voice were the imperatives of fusing party and state, of the ANC ruling in perpetuity and, as the 'leading social force', penetrating and guiding every significant sector of society and the economy. Rather than apologizing and admitting guilt to an undifferentiated population of black victims who, in the nature of things had neither the organization nor the power to make a reciprocal gesture, many whites may have felt with some discomfort that they would be doing these things to this pervasively powerful, ambiguous and potentially sinister force.

This in some respects goes to the heart of the matter. How would an undifferentiated apology to all black people be registered, responded to, make a difference? One possibility of course is that the response of black people was not the point, but the act of admitting guilt would make a therapeutic difference to whites themselves. This somewhat solipsistic view is fair enough, and it might indeed have done something for the moral and psychological well-being of white people. However, what its concrete outcomes for reconciliation would be are hard to gauge. Another possibility is that only through the ANC could such a collective act of whites be registered and responded to. For the most part the ANC has remained inscrutable on what might have been expected had hundreds of thousands or even a couple of million whites come forward. The fact of the matter is that whites have been vouchsafed only fleeting and confusing glimpses of the new selves that they should adopt to fit them for an African future. It seems that no African leader or intellectual has applied his or her mind much to the detail, beyond vague references to privileges, which are never specified and enumerated in detail, and the need to give them up, without much clue as to how the divestment should be made operative. There is always the possibility of course that it would have been difficult for the ANC to calibrate a response to large-scale, white acceptance of the need to show regret and remorse and that this task would not have been entirely welcome. At a minimum it would have complicated the ANC's access to the negative stereotypes of whites that have been so useful for political mobilization and, more importantly for stigmatizing opposition or even merely criticism that had any significant white provenance. It would also have threatened to prolong the 'smug rainbowism' of the Mandela moment that so many of them, from Mbeki downward, were so keen to discredit and jettison. Relief, then, may have been the predominant emotion when the ANC found that it would not be faced with the political fallout from hundreds of thousands of whites expressing their contrition. Whites were not the only ones in South Africa who had political comfort zones, and the ANC had well-exercised political reflexes to help it make capital out of this latest evidence of whites' moral inadequacies.

Perhaps it is unfair to dwell for too long on the Home for All campaign and to ascribe too much significance to it as a turning point. It was in many respects an improvised initiative with little in the way of resources; organizational inadequacies and mistakes – such as failure to build a campaign through enlisting sympathetic prominent whites as role models – did not help the cause. As well as lack of resources, there appeared to be no broad vision as to what the initiative could achieve, other than the assumption that it was a good thing in itself from which other good things would surely flow. The failure to drive and coordinate the initiative may have stemmed from a naïve belief that it would acquire a momentum of its own, driven by a broad-based hunger for atonement or by peer pressure, which would override calculations of political implications. If that were the case, the organizers were out of touch with ordinary whites. There is no evidence whatever that the initiative was set up precisely in order to demonstrate the recalcitrance of whites and to add point to Mbeki's avowed aim to administer a sharp dose of realism and dispel the hazier visions of rainbow optimism. However, as it turned out, it might as well have been, and for many, especially black South Africans, white reactions were read either as a regrettable missed opportunity or a reprehensible snub.

## Mbeki's Africanist dilemmas

One of the most frequently used words in association with Mbeki's presidency – especially in journalistic accounts – is 'Africanist'. It is possible to gain the impression that writers resort to this loose and oversimplified characterization out of frustration at having to convey economically what was a complex, ambiguous and sometimes contradictory project. In one interpretation the ambiguities and contradictions, and perhaps even a somewhat tortuous and enigmatic quality to Mbeki's theory and practice of nation-building, are largely the product of the man himself. Doubtless his character traits as well as habits of mind and expression had psychological roots at least to the extent that those of all leaders have. However, his espousal of AIDS dissidence and denialism from 1999 made him a world figure, though not in a good way. What is more, his stances departed so far from the mainstream science and policy establishments' conceptions of rationality that it made him fair game for speculative interpretation of the presumed psychological turmoil and inner demons that drove him down this path. This was duly forthcoming, usually with race as the principal *leitmotif*. Whatever Mbeki's psychological make-up may have brought to nation-building however, there is no doubt that he faced real problems and dilemmas in how or even whether to carry forward the legacies of the improvised nation that had delivered the settlement and the rainbow moment which, under Mandela, had seen the ANC firmly established in power, albeit with a lingering strain of neurotic insecurity that it has never managed to shake off.

Viewed from the perspective of the incoming president there were serious problems with non-racialism and civic nationalism. Non-racialism had been one of the strongest cards in the ANC's hand in the war of images surrounding the negotiations and in bedding-in the ANC in power during the Mandela presidency. However, it had little to offer the pent-up expectations of the still-excluded majority in a divided society. Few if any of them believed that the natural energies of a newly opened society would address the disparities in material circumstances, as well as the differential access to social and cultural capital which whites enjoyed. By contrast, most whites believed that the removal of apartheid legislation on its own was enough to install non-racialism and equality of opportunity, and that under these circumstances those who deserved it would get ahead. Not surprisingly Mbeki and most other black people regarded this as complacent and superficial nonsense. In any case the ANC believed itself to be the custodian of non-racialism and regarded the vast majority of whites as very late converts to an idea of which they had little understanding. As we have seen the ANC had long experience of juggling non-racialism and African nationalism, emphasizing one or the other according to the needs of the time or audience. For the best part of a decade, from the Harare Declaration to the end of the Mandela presidency, non-racialism had enjoyed a strong run. Perhaps it was now time for African nationalism to receive its due. Fortunately the ANC, although it had accorded a hallowed place to non-racialism in its mythology, had never been too explicit about it and in Mbeki they had a master of the art of ambiguity. Hopes of constructing a credible synthesis of non-racialism and African nationalism rested on this potential for alchemy. Those who insisted on sniffing out contradictions between non-racialism and African nationalism could be safely ignored or demonized as racists and reactionaries.

Civic nationalism also posed problems. As Mbeki had already pointed out in his two-nations speech, the idea of a civic nation in South Africa was open to the classic critique of liberal society familiar to all political philosophy undergraduates. That is, equal rights are a sham in the face of material inequality: the greater the inequality, the greater the sham. To this could be added the lack of rootedness. There was something bloodless, imported and cerebral about the universals of the civic nation. Especially after the demise of the Reconstruction and Development Programme (RDP), which sought growth through state-led redistribution, in favour of the Growth, Employment and Redistribution (GEAR) programme of self-imposed fiscal discipline, it seemed as if in government the ANC was leaning too much in the direction of the nostrums of globalization. While in principle there is nothing un-African about either civil rights or fiscal discipline, it was clear that by the time Mbeki took over as president that something was needed to indigenize them and rid them of what was an unmistakably alien taint.

That something was obviously African nationalism, but producing a remodelled version suitable for democracy rather than liberation struggle, and a world of emerging markets and globalization rather than Third World solidarity, would not be easy. In the first place there were the potential problems associated with all kinds of ethno-nationalism: exclusiveness, the marginalization of minorities and the possibility that African nationalism would emerge as a form of majority racial domination from the camouflage of non-racialism and the civic nation. These were not the only problems. By the mid-1990s, the decay of African nationalism across the continent was too obvious for even a successful liberation movement to ignore. Authoritarian, big man patrimonial leaders, sclerotic liberation movements living on the past, corruption, tribalism and regional conflict were among the pathological symptoms that made continental models unattractive. There was in addition a less obvious source of worry over neo-Africanism as a basis for popular democratic cohesion. That is, South African Africans made up a diverse population with only a weak basis for ethno-national cohesion. Lurking behind the prospects of African nationalism was the perennial problem of tribalism; this left the ANC in its customary schizophrenic state, which was composed of public denial and private anxiety that tribalism was a problem. To pick and choose a package of linguistic, cultural and historical characteristics and attributes as the basis for African identity would risk provoking particularistic rivalries for inclusion and precedence. The most obvious of these was the real or imagined threat of Zulu hegemony in historical narrative, symbolism and iconography. Traditional culture of a pan-tribal sort was likely to be bound up in contested areas like traditional leaders and authorities. In the form of the IFP or Contralesa, traditional authority was a potential alternative source of authority and popular identification, each with disturbing regional associations. This was not to mention traditional authorities' head-on clash with the modernizing, secular and human rights element in the ANC over matters such as gender. There was, however, another possibility for the role of injecting a shared Africanism into a new South African identity. This was *ubuntu*.

## The Constitutional Court and the *Ubuntu* moment

In the mid-1990s there was flurry of interest in *ubuntu*, stimulated, as we have seen, by its appearance in the Constitution and the TRC. There was an element of superficiality and opportunism in some of this, especially in business and management circles. *Ubuntu* was a handy marketing tool for black change-management consultants, who could claim to be experts by virtue of being African, and were sought out by white businesses which were seeking to rebrand themselves with 'genuine' African credentials. Alternatively *ubuntu* could be deployed to give an edge to performance: the article title 'Building competitive advantage with *ubuntu*' (which some might see as a contradiction in terms) captures the spirit of cultural excitement in a transitional time (Mangaliso 2001).

However, the principal boost to *ubuntu* came in the Constitutional Court's 1995 judgement which abolished capital punishment (Constitutional Court 1995). The Court invoked *ubuntu*, 30 times in the 202-page judgement, and several (though not all) of the 11 judges relied heavily on its authority in their reasoning for rejecting the death penalty. The judgement contained several definitions including:

> An outstanding feature of *ubuntu* in a community sense is the value it puts on life and human dignity. The dominant theme of the culture is that the life of another person is at least as valuable as one's own. Respect for the dignity of every person is integral to this concept.

And:

> The need for *ubuntu* expresses the ethos of an instinctive capacity for and enjoyment of love towards our fellow men and women; the joy and the fulfillment involved in recognizing their innate humanity; the reciprocity this generates in interaction within the collective community; the richness of the creative emotions which it engenders and the moral energies which it releases both in the givers and the society which they serve and are served by. (Constitutional Court 1995: 142 and 153)

These definitions, particularly the second, take us some distance from the customary rigour and emotional economy of the typical high-level, legal deliberation. This loosening of the constraints of legal reasoning extended to some of the claims made by some of the justices on behalf of *ubuntu*. One of them referred to the concept as 'a notion that is now coming to be generally articulated in this country' on the basis that it was a 'shared value and ideal' which, despite the divisions, strife and conflicts of the past, 'runs like a golden thread across cultural lines' (ibid. 170). These are remarkable claims to make in the face of the accumulated horrors of South African history. Another justice claimed that 'a spontaneous call has arisen among sections of the community for a return to *ubuntu*', though this call was 'largely without explanation of the concept' (ibid. 143). This degree of conceptual uncertainty was echoed by another judge who noted that *ubuntu* was 'not defined in the constitution', in contrast to the enthusiasm of yet another who thought that *ubuntu* was 'so well-enunciated in the constitution' (ibid. 148, 142). Confusion and a degree of vagueness on the part of the learned judges is a clue to the utility of *ubuntu* for the Court's purpose at the time of the judgement, as it is to the later fate of *ubuntu* as an organizing concept in the new South Africa.

There was not much doubt that the Court would rule against the death penalty. The punishment was clearly a violation of the bedrock principles of the Bill of Rights and the judges by any reasonable interpretation would have found themselves bound to abolish. However, in the year that the Court heard the matter, there were nearly 27,000 murders in South Africa. In itself this was an indication that *ubuntu* had only limited leverage in actually existing South Africa as was the fact that public opinion favoured drastic punishment. To limit the legal and moral justification for abolition to the Constitution alone would be to place the legitimacy of the decision and of the fledgling Court itself at risk. The Chief Justice Arthur Chaskalson, who wrote the principal judgement, was closely involved in the negotiations which produced a constitution that, whatever its undoubted merits, had all the hallmarks of an elite pact. To allow the impression that the Constitution, the Court and the TRC were products of a self-enclosed elite, out of touch with popular will on a life-or-death matter like capital punishment, would have been very dangerous for the prospects of stable democracy. The invocation of *ubuntu* gave the decision to abolish a measure of popular and demotic provenance that it probably did not deserve, for all its grounding in sound moral and legal principle. Although the *S vs Makwanyane* judgement raised the profile of *ubuntu* and at least one of the Constitutional Court judges later wrote that *ubuntu* could 'become central to a process of harmonising all existing legal values and practices with the Constitution and . . . become central to a new South African jurisprudence' (Mokgoro 1998: 23), this did not in fact happen. Instead the courts and especially the Constitutional Court itself were reluctant to develop such a jurisprudence. Before long, according to one review, 'the concept of *ubuntu* as a constitutional value seemed to have withered away to a historical artefact of a newly-born democracy' (Bekker 2006: 335). It was never very clear whether what was required was to interpret existing statutes and practices in the spirit of *ubuntu*, a recommendation too vague and discretionary to be much use, or for *ubuntu* to underwrite a whole new set of statutes and practices. Clearly no-one in a position of power and authority had the appetite for this latter task. This is not surprising since it would involve systematically transplanting and codifying *ubuntu* from its historic rural, face-to-face-communal and oral-tradition setting, in order to make it operational across a society and economy that were increasingly complex, urban, modernized and diverse. *Ubuntu* has not become irrelevant; it lives on as a ubiquitous nostalgic metaphor, as an inspirational model for how individual South Africans ought to behave in their interpersonal relations and as an essential part of the opportunistic repertoire of personal or corporate reinvention. However, it was clear by the end of the 1990s that it was not going to make the grade as a template for the Africanization of nation-building in South Africa.

## Mbeki's synthesis

Mbeki's response to the perceived need for a new approach to nation-building was to perform a delicate balancing act between African nationalism and non-racialism, attempting in effect to restate the former more assertively without abandoning the latter. In principle there was nothing new about this. The ANC had lived with the difficulties of conceptualizing a nation that would combine the two since the 1950s. However, until faced with the challenges of office, making a credible synthesis was not urgent. As a result, non-racialism and African nationalism could for the most part be kept in parallel – perhaps separate-but-equal – conceptual universes. Under Mbeki, the delay which had hitherto been sustained by Mandela's humanist charisma and the effects of settlement euphoria was no longer tolerable. His solution was to build on the national democratic revolution idea, via his own 'two-nations' speech. This meant boldly defining South African Africans as a nation in order to give shape to the tasks of reconstruction and renewal which, obvious as they were in some respects, had to be addressed in a structured and not haphazard way. By nationalizing them as it were, they could be focused, delimited and given priority.

This was a drastic and risky simplification of a reality that was getting more complex – in respect, for instance, of inequality between Africans – the greater the distance travelled from apartheid. Nevertheless, a case could be made for dramatizing the situation in this way; anything less reductive would risk dilution of purpose in the face of the sheer inertial weight of white economic and cultural power, as well as offer opportunities for hair-splitting, defensive and delaying tactics in favour of white privilege and, moreover, risk unnecessarily setting Africans – who at the end of the day had much more in common than divided them – against each other. Even if such rationale were accepted, however, this was still a risky project which courted division and conflict. Two linked features of Mbeki's restatement of African nationalism should have hedged against such risks.

First, for Mbeki, African nationalism did not refer to bonds of cohesion which set off South African Africans from the rest of the population, with typical ethno-nationalist markers such as race, kinship mythology, culture and religion. Instead it set off *all* Africans, in South Africa, the continent and the diaspora, with markers of inferior status including poverty, exclusion, cultural denigration and psychological damage. These were not the work of 40 years of apartheid alone, but of centuries of colonialism and imperialism, of which apartheid was no more than a short-lived, parochial version. This helped to hammer home the essential point for Mbeki that getting rid of apartheid was not going to be enough. In addition, by raising the sights of African nationalism to far historical and continental horizons, Mbeki was hoping to lower the stakes of parochial, South African antagonisms. In this way he could dissipate the risk, inherent in his conceptualizing two nations, of provoking a repeat of South Africa's dismal history as a contest between two nationalisms. This was one among several motivations for his grand plan for a continental African Renaissance, which he would go to considerable lengths to elaborate as part his overall nationalist project. Secondly, it followed from this that the point of reconceiving this victim nation was not its self-realization as a self-sufficient and eternal entity in the classic national vision, but to transcend it as soon as possible. Its destiny was not so much self-expression or even self-rule, but to be folded into a larger South African nation. This would still be 'African' demographically and morally, in ways that would be hard to elucidate in advance, but it would be composed of black, brown and white people equally equipped to enjoy the promises of the Constitution and to treat each other with equal respect. The exclusively African nation of the downtrodden would become the non-racial, African nation of equality.

These subtle distinctions were not meant to camouflage the simple idea at the heart of Mbeki's Africanism, which was that the interests of Africans come first. Mbeki stated and restated this too often and too directly for camouflage to be the purpose. It was one of the few things that he did communicate simply and directly. The subtleties were intended to get round the manifold difficulties of conceptualizing South African Africans as a full-blown nation in any classical sense of the word, without at the same time losing the mobilizing force of the idea. There was something else at stake. It was all too apparent that if Mbeki did not sufficiently allow expression of African identity then others would, probably in populist and racial forms that might be destabilizing rather than productive, not only in terms of keeping minorities on board but within the African population itself. To judge by the way he treated questions of African nationalism and identity it is probable that he, like others before him in the ANC, saw it as something to be tamed and disciplined as much as encouraged.

All of this can be understood as a response to the real pressures Mbeki was under. However he, like some of his interpreters, may have overestimated his compatriots' appetite for and capacity to appreciate subtlety when he opted for this version of African nationalism. In one interpretation, it eschewed race as its basis but nonetheless carried 'strong racial inflections'. This established, 'perimeters and conditions for inclusion that were not strictly racial while at the same time pivoting on the interests and histories of the African majority' (Marais 2011: 417). While this doubtless well-meaning account is sensitive to the subtleties – or some might feel casuistry – of Mbeki's thought, no-one should really be surprised if South African minorities failed to spot the difference between 'racial inflections' or conditions of inclusion that were 'not strictly racial' and the real thing – full-blown racial nationalism. Or for that matter if some black South Africans failed to spot the modulations with which Mbeki sought to qualify Africanist racial assertiveness and assumed he was advocating racial nationalism.

The idea whose purpose was to bridge the gap between the theory and practice of prioritizing African interests was and remains 'transformation'. Given its ubiquity in government discourse and that it is the subject of numerous, wordy ANC and Alliance documents, which are updated every few years, transformation is surprisingly elusive. Such documents tend to deal in cloudy generalizations such as 'Transformation involves a fundamental change of society in an effort to create a non-racist, non-sexist, democratic and prosperous society.' Even the Broad-based Black Economic Empowerment (BBBEE) Act, in its only substantial reference to transformation states merely, in a rather circular way, that the objective of the Act is to 'facilitate broad-based economic empowerment by promoting economic transformation in order to enable meaningful participation of black people in the economy' (Department of Trade and Industry 2003: 1). Alternatively, transformation often makes an appearance as an all-purpose word of justification, slipped in to buttress many specific ANC goals such as the need for party members to occupy all significant state offices. In working terms it generally signifies the reduction of material inequality and the increase in the participation of black people in the economy at all levels, to reflect their demographic weight in the population, in ownership, employment and, in particular, positions of seniority, authority and influence especially in the public sector. Transformation has become a one-word sound bite to cover all actions taken – legislated and informal, transparent and opaque – to bring this about.

The principal vehicles for realizing the nation-building vision of transformation are programmes which promote racial preference in employment (employment equity) and use the state's leverage to extend black ownership of productive entities. The latter, BEE has been pursued through statutory requirements for the direct transfer of negotiated percentages of equity, as well as through compulsory black participation in state tenders and other forms of stipulation, including a new regime for licensing mining activity. Such programmes are broadly endorsed by the Constitution, which states in the Bill of Rights (Constitution 9 (2)), 'Equality includes the full and equal enjoyment of all rights and freedoms. To promote the achievement of equality legislative or other measures designed to protect or advance persons or categories of persons, disadvantaged by unfair discrimination may be taken.' In order to comply with the next provision of the Constitution, which prohibits 'unfair' discrimination, the legislation, particularly the employment equity provisions, is hedged around with procedural requirements intended to establish its fairness.

The benefits and costs of transformation for nation-building are not easy to calculate, particularly because criteria for success and failure are in general only sketchily drawn and there is no widely shared consensus on what its priorities should be. It would be easy to assume that by delivering tangible benefits to black people and by clearly signalling that their interests take priority that transformation ought to anchor the settlement and the constitution in popular attitudes. However, there is room for scepticism on this score. Transformation has delivered little except perhaps hope to the 35.9 per cent of the working population who, by the extended definition, are currently (2013) unemployed. Another possibility is that transformation by requiring white people to make a contribution (symbolic if nothing else) to redress for the apartheid past, would go some way to appeasing those who were disappointed and angry at most whites' attitudes to the TRC and the insouciance, or outright rejection, with which they responded to opportunities for voluntary making good. This is balanced by those who feel that transformation simply has not gone far enough and that ways should be found of compelling whites to give up more. This attitude is most sharply expressed in the area of land reform.

Criticisms of the nation-building effects of transformation as it is defined and practised generally fall into one of five types. First there are arguments that transformation is wrong in principle: it is discriminatory and it requires the re-racialization of society through the need for racial classification and headcounting; in addition it encourages the unhealthy and divisive practice of 'playing the race card', that is drawing attention to an individual's racial background or the racial composition of any corporate entity for reasons unrelated to goals of principled redress, including personal advancement, the settling of scores and as a shield from questioning and criticism.

Secondly, transformation is flawed in design. This is principally argued because race is too crude a yardstick of disadvantage to designate appropriately where redress should be directed and the result is to help create a narrow class of beneficiaries. The distinctively South African neologism 'previously disadvantaged' captures some of the problems. A fairly substantial class of black people has acquired advantages of their own since the end of apartheid, many of them thanks to transformation. The problem of whether and how to distinguish them from black people who are '*currently* disadvantaged', mainly through being unemployed, and from white people from a modest background, by adding an element of class to race is simply not addressed. This is because the ANC as a working organization is principally made up by a mixture of people from this currently advantaged class, and those who aspire to join it. As a result their own interests are uppermost in its corporate priorities, in practice if not in theory. Unfortunately there is in addition a self-limiting logic to transformation, partly created by the safeguards designed to prevent its abuse, such as the provision that no-one should be employed under equity provisions who does not have the qualifications to do the job. Where these provisions are adhered to, the process favours black people who have already received some sort of comparative advantage in access to quality education, skills and social capital and it is difficult to break out of a narrow pool of 'insiders'. Critics argue that transformation is also flawed by inappropriate measures of success. Every year there is a ritual outburst of indignation that the 'black' equity ownership of the Johannesburg Stock Exchange (JSE) listed companies (itself something very difficult and contentious to measure) has increased by a disappointing margin. Rather than linking transformation measures to real-world indicators such as growth and employment, racial headcounts are treated as ends in themselves and as the measures by which the health of the nation should be monitored.

A third line of criticism is that transformation is poorly executed in its own terms. Overzealous interpretation of the purposes of transformation, venality, incompetent management of recruitment and simple failure to understand the legislation are among the reasons cited for poorly executed transformation. This means that the stipulations which are meant to ensure the integrity of affirmative action – such as the requirements that racial preference should not override the need for qualification and that posts should not be left vacant when there are no qualified black people to fill them – are often flouted. In the case of BEE the widespread practice of 'fronting' – by which black and white interests collude to corruptly manipulate BEE requirements in tender processes – is another instance of poor execution. Reactions to fronting vary; the government insists that higher penalties and ever more vigilant policing will remedy the situation, while critics argue that BEE by its very nature multiplies the opportunities and incentives for corruption.

Fourthly, unintended consequences of transformation are cited as a reason for criticism. South Africa is not well endowed with skills and human capital and, it is argued, stringent transformation requirements exacerbate the situation. According to this line of argument, instances of failure to make the best use of what capabilities South Africa has include the heavy use made of consultants to cover for lack of capacity in the public service and the incentive to emigration of skilled white people. Above all, stagnating or declining indicators of quality in public health and education, as well widespread corruption and mismanagement in local government, point to a malaise of entitlement and decay which is the result of elevating criteria other than task-related capability in recruitment and tendering.

Lastly, the ANC has made little or no effort to make transformation a national project – in the sense of making it something that can unite people of differing ethnic provenance, social class or political persuasion – but has tied it to the realization of its own self-proclaimed mission and destiny to lead and to rule. By making itself the sole interpreter of transformation and making it a monopoly and partisan project, the ANC demonstrates its intention of monopolizing nation-building. To question or criticize the ANC is to be against transformation, to reject nation-building and to deny reconciliation. This is not only a theoretical issue; the practice of transformation dovetails with the ANC's policy of cadre deployment, aimed at party control of all significant centres of power and influence in and around the state. The ANC's official line on this somewhat Orwellian (in the sense of 'doublethink', disguising, distorting or reversing the meaning of words):

> Transformation of the state entails, first and foremost, extending the power of the NLM (national liberation movement) over all levers of power: the army, the police, the bureaucracy, intelligence structures, the judiciary, parastatals, and agencies such as regulatory bodies, the public broadcaster, the central bank and so on. *This is not in contradiction to the provisions of the constitution which characterise most of these bodies as independent and non-partisan.* Control by democratic forces means that these institutions should operate on the basis of the precepts of the constitution; they should be guided by new doctrines; they should reflect in their composition the demographics of the country; and they should owe allegiance to the new order. (1998, emphasis added)

In practice, transformation, cadre deployment, politically connected patronage, cronyism and factionalism have all become fused in a semi-anarchic system. This, ironically enough, functions in ways more akin to the 'amorphous markets'[8] so distrusted by the ANC than to the highly ordered, interlocking model of state, government and party envisaged by Mbeki and the ANC ideologues and government bureaucrats who supported him in developing it. In this idealized and updated iteration of generations of ANC and SACP strategy documents, the ANC in government and in society would be an operational command centre, the true location of sovereignty, which would discipline and exploit the talents and energies of dedicated cadres to galvanize the nation behind transformation.

This is quite unlike what has transpired. The ANC itself, despite regular calls for self-renewal from ANC Secretaries-General and others, is a passive instrument exploited by ambitious individuals and factions, rather than the purposive and controlling arbiter of the nation's unfolding destiny as it appeared in Mbeki's imagining. Naturally enough, interpretations of how this came to pass vary according to perspective. For diehard ANC and fellow-travelling romantics, the ANC had 'lost its soul'. For liberals it was not a fall from grace, but a predictable unfolding of what was built into the movement's DNA: a quasi-soviet mindset and a package of Third World nationalist assumptions already long out of date when the ANC came to power. Central to these were one-partyism and the fusion of party, state, government and nation, wrapped up in liberation movement mythology. For leftists it *was* a fall from grace, the result of a Faustian pact with capitalism, masterminded by South African and international business interests, which were never interested in redistribution beyond the politically connected insiders who would safeguard the future of capital accumulation. In this version the deal was sealed in the '1996 class project', thus dubbed from the year the GEAR macroeconomic stabilization package was adopted.

Many strands of thought and experience went into the effort of nation-building, with transformation at its core, as it developed in the Mbeki era. However, two sources of pressure and influence are worth highlighting. In the first place it would be unwise to underestimate the simple and rather banal fact of pent-up expectations on the part of the ANC elite to emulate the living standards of (some) whites. Two quotations which have come to epitomize this tendency have received such wide currency that they might reasonably be described as 'notorious'. In 2007, the then principal spokesman for the ANC, Smuts Ngonyama, said when questioned about allegedly questionable financial dealings on his part, 'I didn't join the struggle to be poor' (*The Economist* 3 June 2010). Further back, Phumzile Mlambo-Ngcuka, the then Minister of Trade and Industry (and future deputy-president under Mbeki) said while addressing a group of black businesspeople, that 'Blacks should not be ashamed to be filthy rich' (Adam et al. 1997: 201).

This might have been a crass but nevertheless unexceptionable remark in a society which ranked individualism and capital accumulation highly as organizing values, but it was distinctly out of harmony with the ANC's ethos of communal African values and self-sacrificial struggle. What is more, she was speaking as a leading figure in a party that had the reduction of inequality as its principal goal and as the minister in the department responsible for the development of BEE codes, which offered a morally dubious short cut to riches for a few. Whether unguarded or deliberate, Mlambo-Ngcuka's remark undermined the credibility of transformation and obligingly left flanks exposed to attack from both liberals and leftists. It would be a mistake, however, to see Mbeki as simply bowing to an unseemly feeding frenzy that he could not hold back. His conceptualization of transformation was much more strategic, amounting to a determination to remodel the ANC with the emerging black middle classes as its centre of gravity. Mbeki, like the rest of his party was in thrall to the idea of 'the commanding heights of the economy', believing them to move at the direction of shadowy and anonymous forces that threatened to render all governing power impotent. If the government could not occupy the commanding heights by taking them into state ownership, the next best thing would be to occupy them by stealth and through the proxy of a 'patriotic bourgeoisie'. This phrase is a strong contender for the least-articulated and most-unexamined slogan of the post-apartheid years (although there is stiff competition for the prize). Although it was commonly deployed in the Mbeki years, it was never accompanied by even the most rudimentary analysis of how a patriotic bourgeoisie would differ from a bourgeoisie. This left open the possibilities that it was either a disastrous misreading of how politics and economics interact in a democratic society or merely a flimsy camouflage for greed. In this case, the patriotic bourgeoisie would be, so to speak, the centre of gravy as much as the centre of gravity.[9]

Mbeki's conceptualization of transformation was also influenced by the ideological vacuum which surrounded him. The collapse of actually existing socialism, which helped precipitate the end of apartheid in South Africa, was followed by a prolonged, if forgivable, failure of the imagination and will on the left of the ANC Alliance. There was no socialist alternative with the moral and intellectual force to convince at the level of the ANC leadership or in popular politics. In any case, the Left was not going to take the risk of presenting itself separately to the electorate, preferring the embedded comfort of the Alliance. The nearest thing to an alternative economic policy was produced for the ANC as it stood on the threshold of power by a left-wing research group composed of South African and British academics. According to an ANC policy insider, it was marred by contentious disagreement leading to a muddled final report, and in any case it did not differ markedly from the ANC mainstream (Hirsch 2005: 54–7). However, socialism was not the only casualty of the end of the global political economy of the Cold War. 'Third Worldism' had largely provided the ANC with its ideas in the years of late apartheid. This was a loose-knit, largely rhetorical stock of attitudes and positions which had emerged: 'out of the activities and ideas of anti-colonial nationalists and their efforts to mesh highly romanticized interpretations of pre-colonial traditions and cultures with the utopianism embodied by Marxism and socialism specifically, and "Western" visions of modernisation and development more generally' (Berger 2004: 1). Mbeki had too much concern for continuity simply to jettison this now-outdated baggage; instead he worked hard in both visionary forms (the African Renaissance) and institutional architectures (New Partnership for African Development and African Union) to update Third Worldism for the era of emerging market trade and investment opportunities, debt forgiveness, continent-wide infrastructural rehabilitation and regional conflict resolution. This dovetailed well with his aim of lifting African nationalism from a parochial to a continental frame of reference.

Ideological woes were to be found outside the ANC Alliance as well. South African liberals struggled to make sense of their own diversity and of the 'Ironic Victory' (Johnson and Welsh 1998) in which their principles and values had triumphed in the form of the Constitution, but at the hands and to the advantage of others. At the same time, the only party-political expression of liberalism, the Democratic Party, went on to electoral near-oblivion in 1994. Reconstructing liberalism to fit over South Africa's racial identities and divides among the wreckage of apartheid was going to be a long process. This was especially so in the teeth of withering contempt from Mbeki and the ANC generally, who, from the comfortable heights of their electoral majority, worked hard to give the impression that liberalism was as great an evil as apartheid.

Mbeki had to deal with the get-rich-quick aspirations of those around him, although to his credit he distrusted and feared the mentality that bred them. One thing he could do to distract himself and other South Africans from the grubby reality was to indulge himself in lofty rhetoric and grand schemes of nation-building. The ideological vacuum offered more freedom to do so than was good either for him or for the prospects of nation-building. The absence of robust bodies of ideas to challenge him meant he could indulge his penchant for centralizing and monopolizing truths about nation-building in an overbearing and top-down way, as well as closing down debate and scornfully discrediting such dissenting voices as there were. Where there were none, he was happy to invent them, and his speeches were full of references to shadowy conspiracies and underground subversion. Without the need for the disciplines of focus and economy, there was every temptation to construct an eclectic nationalism from words that would accommodate everyone.

Thus he could go from teetering on the edge of exclusive Africanism, to the far continental horizons of the African Renaissance, to the austere and unforgiving portrayal of divisions in the two-nations speech, to the inclusive, evocative mysticism of the much-praised 'I am an African' speech which he delivered to the National Assembly at the adoption of the Constitution in May 1996. This included sharply outlined images of landscape and poetic invocations of history. It succeeded in its presumed intention of not making any South Africans feel alien, but in such a curiously unspecific way – the speech was not confined to South Africa but ranged freely across the continent – that while listeners could feel they belonged, to *what* they belonged was wrapped in a kind of heroic opacity. The general impression is of the passing images of a powerfully evocative slide show. The speech has attracted more than its share of exegesis (see, for instance, Chipkin 2007: 99–102), but the point that should not be missed is that the greater the intellectual effort required to interpret it, the more likely that it has missed the mark as a piece of enduring nation-building communication.

## From Mandela to Mbeki: An appraisal

According to one popular narrative of nation-building in post-apartheid South Africa (subscribed to by most whites but numbers of Africans too), Mbeki betrayed or squandered Mandela's priceless gift of non-racialism and reconciliation.

In one version, Mbeki revealed African nationalism in its true colours of crude racial nationalism. In another – which is probably closer to the truth – he applied a correction to the rainbow optimism which followed in Mandela's quasi-regal wake, an optimism which was unsustainable in the presence of gross material inequalities and historical injustices. However, he did so in an overzealous, politically ham-fisted and needlessly racially inflected way. His fatal inability to communicate anything at all with clarity and economy did not help.

There is something to be said for this narrative, although its weakness is a habitual failure to take seriously the challenges which would have been faced by anyone in sustaining Mandela's approach to nation-building. Arguably, however, there is something that both Mandela and Mbeki have in common to tell us about nation-building in post-apartheid South Africa. It is that both exemplify the limitations on the contributions of individual leaders to nation-building. Something that is greatly underappreciated in post-apartheid South Africa is that nations do not invent themselves, nor can they be sustained by the magical power or intellectual exertions of extraordinary individuals. In general, nations are invented by strong states and/or by political movements which mobilize populations in a synergy of top-down and bottom-up initiatives combining spontaneity and centrally directed strategy. Both of these are missing in South Africa. The reach and capacity of the state are poor and the ANC's determination to dominate it means that it is suspect as a focus of nationhood in the eyes of anyone whose political choices and allegiances lie somewhere other than with the National Democratic Revolution and Colonialism of a Special Type. The ANC cannot play the role of nation-builder across the whole population because it is the dominant player in a partisan and adversarial polity, and it is in any case chronically unsure about which nation – Black African or civic – should take precedence.

As a result, an undue burden fell on the first two presidents to fill the institutional void, Mandela because he was capable of dominating public discourse with his extraordinary personal qualities and Mbeki because – until he overreached himself – he intellectually dominated a movement in which he did not have a great deal of competition. Whatever the strengths and weaknesses of both men – and sooner or later more critical accounts of Mandela will likely appear – individuals do not invent nations.

One possible answer to the question of who or what should take up the slack was to emerge in the technocratic visions of social cohesion prepared in the Presidency from about the mid-2000s onwards.

# CHAPTER FIVE

# From reconciliation to social cohesion

Somewhere around the tenth anniversary of South Africa's first democratic election it began to be openly recognized in and around government that the principal task of nation-building was not to resolve how whites – 8 per cent of the population – would fit into the new South Africa but whether and how Africans – 80 per cent of the population – would cohere as the moral and demographic centre of a citizen nation. The belief that African-South Africans did not constitute a nation (indeed were not even 'South Africans') but rather a miscellaneous collection of tribes which could be elevated into nations with sufficient tutelage from whites was absolutely central to apartheid ideology. It followed from this that it was taboo for opponents of apartheid to inquire too closely into the nature and limits of the nation which opponents of apartheid assumed Africans to constitute. This taboo remained strong, but although Africans affirmed in attitude surveys that their primary identification was South African, there were grounds for concern about the progress of nation-building. These concerns were pursued under the rubric of 'social cohesion' which has come to dominate official discourse on the subject of nation-building first in the guise of making moral citizens and then in pursuit of a benign cycle of social cohesion and economic growth.

## Making moral citizens from crooked timber

Especially under Mbeki, nation-building as conceived by the ANC came to be expressed in the need to address material inequalities and to achieve levels of prosperity, welfare and socio-economic self-realization that would allow blacks to enjoy the promises of the Constitution on equal terms with whites. However, from the beginning, hopes for a new nation were accompanied by persistent concerns for the moral and spiritual health of the population of citizens that would constitute it. Such was the degree of anxiety with which these concerns were expressed that it was as if the prospects of nation-building were being haunted and the earnest efforts of the nation-builders mocked by Immanuel Kant's gloomy prognostication: 'Out of the crooked timber of humanity nothing straight was ever made.' Mandela and Mbeki expressed their anxieties in characteristic ways; Mandela expressed the magisterial disappointment of the humanistic patriarch whose people did not live up to his deceptively simple example; agonized poetic images of inhumanity stalked Mbeki's 'I am an African' speech, highlighting the evils of colonialism and racism without sparing other forms of depravity. Significantly, despite their differences of style, neither Mandela nor Mbeki confined himself solely to a sociological framework of brute facts detailing the pathologies of social disintegration which underlined the nation-builders' tasks. By insisting on a moral and spiritual dimension to these tasks they were not alone, but drew on and represented deep currents in South African society, and the ways in which many representative figures habitually portrayed its history and present condition.

There were several reasons for the ANC to tap into this spiritual vein. The first was that the organization has long traded heavily on the cultural stereotype of Africans as innately spiritual beings, particularly by contrast with the 'West's' alleged materialism, individualism and general lack of humanity. This has been part of a much wider need to indigenize itself and its project. It may seem absurd that a movement which arose out of indigenous resistance to alien oppression should have to indigenize itself, but the ANC spent so long in exile, absorbed so many transnational influences, identified with so many transnational causes and participated in a settlement that owed more to international human rights discourse than to African nationalism, that the point is not as fanciful as it first seems. These characterizations of African spirituality and the soulless West did not owe a great deal to reflection or to rigorous analysis. The West thus portrayed was something of a straw man, caricatured in Mbeki's case with florid literary denunciation, and by much of the rest of the movement in vulgar Marxist clichés. Interrogation of the idealized image of the spiritual African was not much practised or encouraged. None of this mattered very much. Such essentialist judgements on the difference between Africa and the West were delivered by ANC leaders who had personal experience of being on the receiving end of apartheid, a system which summed up a good deal of what could go wrong with 'Western' values. They also spoke for all Africans and other black people who could say the same and this was generally enough to secure them the high moral ground, a vantage point which bestowed a certain complacency of perspective. In any case, African spirituality as deployed by the ANC was flexible enough to be extended to white South Africans (especially Afrikaners) if they deserved it; the 'I am an African' speech again provides an example. On the other hand it could also be used to remind whites – as Westerners – of their comparative moral and spiritual bankruptcy, for example, when they declined 'Home for All's invitation to contrition. A handy bonus accruing from this practice of juxtaposing African spirituality with the empty materialism of the West was the fact that the only significant electoral challenge to the ANC has been the DA, whose liberal origins made it an easy target for accusations of being 'un-African' and representative of all the various manifestations of the West's spiritual deficit including excessive individualism.

The ANC went far beyond making a generalized case about the spirituality of Africans, however; an essential part of its own self-conceptualization is that it represents much more than a coalition of coincident interests, but is a repository of spiritual values as well. There were sound strategic and tactical reasons for this characterization. One of the ANC's 'four pillars of struggle', adopted at the Morogoro conference in 1969 was the mobilization of the international community against apartheid. Crudely put, the ANC was asking individuals and civil society bodies all over the world, as well as states and international organizations to take sides. Naturally, especially after committing itself to armed struggle, it did not want this choice to be between black and white identities in a racial war or between rival nationalisms in a violent parochial power struggle, with all the messy details and complexities that would get in the way of moral clarity. It was better for the purposes of international solidarity that the conflict be conceived in terms of a world historical drama and the choice as being between humanity and anti-humanity. This inevitably raised the ANC's claims beyond that of being the legitimate representative of the oppressed majority, important as that was, to being the custodian of essential values of the human spirit. In addition, the ANC had of necessity to ask its own members to risk and to sacrifice a lot with, until late in the game, very little apparent prospect of success. The claim to be serving higher purposes on behalf of humanity, rather than individual or even national self-interests, was essential to maintaining morale and reproducing commitment. The ANC's cultivation of this spiritual dimension to its mission gave rise to one of the most durable clichés of post-apartheid political discourse – 'the soul of the ANC' – a term much loved by journalists and others who habitually portray politics as a moral drama, and especially those who take the ANC to task for 'losing its soul' (e.g. Gumede 2005).

This need to conceptualize nation-building in moral and spiritual terms did not end with apartheid: indeed, it intensified with the transfer of power. This is because the destructive effects of apartheid and of the struggle extended far beyond material damage and the blighting of prospects and opportunities of African people. The tendency to see apartheid – and by extension racism, colonialism and imperialism – as vehicles of spiritual degradation was with the ANC from the beginning, but it was probably intensified by the absorption of so many Black Consciousness recruits from the late 1970s onwards BC's tendency – as the name makes clear – to emphasize the spiritual and psychological aspects of racial oppression and the need for spiritual rearmament to combat it was absorbed into the ANC along with the post-1976 recruits. In addition, the destructive effects of the migrant labour system, forced removals and other aspects of apartheid also went far beyond material deprivation to undermine the primary cradles of values in family and community.

The struggle itself also had its dehumanizing effects; it was a war not only against white policemen but also against collaborators, spies, and in the shape of the IFP, rivals, to define the post-apartheid shape of African aspirations. All of these fronts in the struggle had their share of violence, and they were if anything even more traumatic than the violence of the identifiable oppressor. The phrase 'black-on-black violence' may have been a cynical and opportunistic mislabelling by the white government in its last phase, but this does not alter the nightmarish quality of real experience of internecine violence, however labelled. Other forms taken by the struggle, summed up in the slogans, 'ungovernability' and 'liberation before education', however much they contributed to liberation, were a poor preparation for democratic national citizenship, especially for those whose formative years were influenced by participation in violence which was inspired in these terms.

Two other concerns emerged after the ANC took office as government and helped motivate it to insist on a spiritual dimension to nation-building. One source of anxiety was that undiluted promotion of black advancement to the commanding heights of the economy, especially using the extensive leverage of state patronage to get them there, risked being an open invitation to cronyism and corruption. This would in turn contaminate the whole project and undermine the integrity of the ANC as its orchestrator. A second was that although the ANC was determined that the state would be the principal driver of the economic and social change that was essential for nation-building, the ANC in government worried from the beginning about encouraging dependency, passivity and an undue culture of entitlement to rights and rewards that paid insufficient heed to citizen duties. These worries escalated from about the mid-2000s.

It was one thing to register this amalgam of cultural assumptions, historical legacies and policy dilemmas, deducing from them that there was more to nation-building than the material imperatives of socio-economic transformation. It was another to find ways of expressing this recognition in practice. The first initiative to do so, the Moral Regeneration Movement (MRM), had its origins in Mandela's appalled reaction to what he saw as a 'spiritual malaise', composed of cynicism, pessimism, fear and self-centredness whose compound effects expressed themselves in greed, egoism, cruelty and ultimately in crime and corruption (Rauch 2005: 9). Although the MRM was on the government's agenda after the election which brought Mbeki to the presidency in 1999, it took a moral panic in the media over child rape in late 2001 to bring it to launch in April 2002 as a non-profit company, funded by the government and overseen by the Department of Arts and Culture (ibid. 11). The MRM has been a caricature of ineffective window-dressing, whose only achievement has been the promulgation of an eight-point Charter of Positive Values, which took it six years until 2008 to produce. The points do little but repeat the values of the Constitution, adding vague and bland goals such as 'ensuring harmony in culture, belief and conscience' and 'protecting the environment'.

What is more, when the Department of Arts and Culture belatedly reported on the MRM for the first time to its parliamentary portfolio committee in March 2010, the members of parliament found themselves none the wiser as to what the movement actually did, but better informed as to its governance deficiencies, which included the absence of an audit committee. This omission meant that the MRM had not been able to account for its expenditure since its inception (Parliamentary Monitoring Group 2010). The inadequacies of the MRM have been variously attributed to the following: underfunding – it receives only R4 million a year; its inability to find focus in what is an ill-defined and potentially huge area of activity; the overtones of organized religion which attended its early years (the ANC's commission of religious affairs was a prime mover) and which may have dissuaded more secular activists (Rauch 2005: 12–13); and the ironic patronage of Jacob Zuma, given his rape trial and the shadow of corruption investigations over him.[1]

If the MRM illustrates the difficulties of finding an institutional expression for spiritual renewal in society, the RDP of the Soul illustrates the limitations of striving for moral renewal without one. Once again the inspiration was Mandela's. The RDP was the ANC's short-lived flagship economic policy after it took power in 1994. By 1999, although it had been superseded, Mandela was using it as a metaphor and was talking about the 'reconstruction of the soul of the nation, the RDP of the soul'. He was concerned about societal indiscipline ('teachers or students go to school drunk') and an imbalance between freedom and responsibility. A work ethic, respect for life, pride and self-respect as South Africans had to be restored. Mandela's metaphor has since been taken up as a recurrent reference point for moral citizenship, notably by Mbeki (2006) as well as in an ANC discussion document for its 2007 national conference. The dominant themes are familiar: the rejection of materialism and the evils of the West; the tainted inheritance of apartheid which entrenched even among the oppressed, 'the deep-seated understanding that personal wealth constituted the only true measure of individual and social success' (ibid. 9).

In Mbeki's scourging and exhorting rhetoric the powers which betray social cohesion and solidarity are positively supernatural:

> Thus, everyday, and during every hour of our time beyond sleep, the demons embedded in our society, that stalk us at every minute, seem always to beckon each one of us towards a realizable dream and nightmare. With every passing second, they advise, with rhythmic and hypnotic regularity – Get rich! Get rich! Get rich! (Ibid. 12)

The ANC's discussion document (2007) aims beyond this to a kind of higher fusion of 'secular spiritual understanding':

> Transformation extends spiritual understanding from the religious world to the whole secular creation. It recognises that spiritual strength lies in human communities as such and not necessarily in religious institutions. The RDP of the Soul which moves us from the Liberation to the Transformation of our society is a secular activity of the spirit of ordinary people, not reserved as a religious activity for saints. Its proclamation and practice by some transformed experienced progressive religious and theological people is a huge bonus. (ANC 2007: 5)

In this haunted moral wasteland, the ANC saw itself as central to the creation of a new moral order of citizenship, beginning with the fostering of what have been variously called 'new cadres and mandarins' and the 'New Person'. These servants of the revolution are not well defined, except in terms of their 'tirelessness and boldness' but:

> Failure to build a New Person, among revolutionaries themselves and in a more diffuse manner in broader society, will result in a critical mass of the vanguard movement being swallowed in the vortex of the arrogance of power and attendant social distance and corruption, and ultimately, themselves being transformed by the very system they seek to change. (ANC 2000)

Behind the wordy and, certainly for non-members, alienating jargon, this is a clear and perceptive warning of what has in fact happened to the ANC in the decade or so since it was delivered. However, whether or not relying on the development of the 'New Person' was the best way to try to avoid it, may be another matter. The core of the problem is more likely to be that the ANC cannot bring itself to choose decisively between the revolution and capitalist society.

It is hard for outsiders to know what to make of South Africans' preoccupation with matters of the soul and spirituality in connection of nation-building. This should perhaps not be the case: many, perhaps all nations, have claimed to possess just such attributes at some time or another, especially in the Romantic era and in struggles to obtain independence; Ireland and Poland are cases in point. Other nations have claimed a presiding 'genius' of some sort or another, France and imperial Britain being two contrasting examples. However, under present global conditions there is something anachronistic about claims on a nation's behalf to possess a soul and spirituality; especially a nation as problematic in its contours and even its very existence as South Africa. Westerners in particular may find this difficult, but in a sense this is the whole point. As a South African theologian and former research director of the TRC puts it:

> To talk of a soul is to talk of an epicentre, an essence, a seat of passion, a heart, a fire and a drive that constitutes the very being of something or someone. The nature of the South African soul is too complex to reduce to a single essence or source. It is a soul of striving and strife, impacted by brutality, oppression, resistance, dominance, liberation, greed, globalisation – *and a hankering to be different*. (Villa-Vicencio 2007: 150, emphasis added)

This sums up well the conviction of South African exceptionalism that is well diffused across the South African political class and is by no means confined to the ANC or to Africans – indeed some South African whites are even keener than Black Africans to differentiate themselves from the soulless West. This exceptionalism expresses itself in a conviction that South African society possesses well-springs of spiritual depth that defy articulation but are a source of strength in adversity, though this resource is inevitably dissipated in better times. Though this kind of belief is widely shared and is a central part of the new South Africa's foundation myth, its sources can differ; for some it is likely to be a sincerely held belief in a heroic fallacy, for others a shrewdly deployed piece of mythology to get over rough times. For most it is a proud source of distinctiveness, even for those who are conscious of sharing aspects of Western heritage. For all of them, however, there is probably an element of dread at the consequences of there being nothing beneath the new dispensation after all, but a void.

## Broadening the base: The National Planning Commission and the National Development Plan

In November 2011 the government's NPC released a comprehensive NDP which contained a 'Vision for 2030' and a 'roadmap' for realizing it. The NPC was set up in 2009 with a brief to carry out long-term planning for the country. It is based in the Presidency under the leadership of former

Minister of Finance Trevor Manuel as chairman and as deputy chairman, Cyril Ramaphosa. In some respects the commission carried on established patterns of policy making, in others it was a departure from them. In this combination of continuity and change the NDP represents the present state of thinking on nation-building in the government.

The Presidency is, in addition to being the office which supports the president and deputy-president, the department at the heart of the executive with the responsibility for the integration and coordination of policy and the monitoring and evaluation of performance across government. In the current vocabulary of governance, it is responsible for 'evidence-based policy' and 'joined-up government'. Largely at the initiative of Mbeki, the Presidency expanded greatly in size and responsibilities from 2000 onwards, carrying out substantial policy research, much of it commissioned to consultants. As a result, Mbeki was often accused by his critics in the ANC and Alliance of trying to monopolize policy making in his own hands and in the hands of technocrats, while sidelining the ANC and its Alliance partners. In this way the Presidency became a second focus of tensions between 'popular' and 'technocratic' policy making, the primary focus being the National Treasury. Many in the coalition, which elevated Zuma to the presidency of the ANC (2007) and of the country (2009), subscribed to this negative view of the Presidency's role in policy making and it was an important factor in the ANC's rejection and then ejection of Mbeki from office. Despite this, far from being cut down to size under Zuma, the centrality of the Presidency was reinforced. This enhanced role was confirmed by the appointment of Manuel, whose long service as Minister of Finance, as well as his popularity and leadership role in the ANC and high international reputation, made him a real political heavyweight. Zuma also personally declared his commitment to the NPC's role in future policy. Twenty-four commissioners were appointed to serve under Manuel and Ramaphosa, many of them experts in specific policy areas who had worked for the government before. The group also included a couple of prominent business people and the economic adviser to the labour federation Cosatu. Although this was far from representative of South African society and there was a certain in-house quality to it, nonetheless it was reasonably broad-based and expertise rather than partisanship was the qualification.

In government, the ANC has been from the beginning committed to the principle of long-term planning along the lines familiar from the five-year plans of socialist states, but more recently and directly inspired by the so-called developmental states of Asia, among which Malaysia has been a fertile source of influence – in theory if not in practice. However, relatively little progress had been made in macroplanning between the demise of the RDP under conditions of economic crisis and bureaucratic confusion in 1996 and the appointment of the commission in 2009. Even the grouping of government departments into functional clusters proved difficult to manage, and much of the energy of the Presidency and the

National Treasury, the only sites of governance where expertise and even basic capacity could be consistently relied on, was taken up with ad hoc measures to support weak departments by the Treasury and attempts to monitor their performance by the Presidency. However, this latter function at least provided a body of work on which the NPC could build, because from 2000 onwards, the Presidency produced a number of reviews and reports that evaluated government performance and identified problem issues and areas (Presidency 2003, 2004, 2006, 2008). Something that these reports made clear was that there was reason for concern about social cohesion and the threat of fragmentation, and the need for a unifying sense of national purpose to underpin hopes for a civic nation and economic growth to sustain it. Reconciliation did not disappear as a desirable goal of nation-building, but it tended to be subsumed under the general issue of social cohesion.

This was in some respects a curiously uneven body of work, clearly torn between the dangers of complacency and self-congratulation on the one hand and the desire of government to take the credit it felt was its due (and was in any case a political necessity in an adversarial electoral system). As a result the reviews and reports, whether produced by the Presidency or for it, tended to oscillate between celebration and warning, especially on the subjects of social cohesion and its effect on nation-building. Something of this quality is caught by the report 'Social Cohesion and Social Justice in South Africa' produced by the HSRC for the Presidency (Presidency 2004: viii). According to this, challenges to social cohesion, social capital and social justice arise from 'forces contributing to social disorder, lawlessness, entropy and decay' from both historical and contemporary sources. From the past, 'Colonialism, apartheid, patriarchy and capitalism have all contributed to the erosion of social cohesion, the destruction of social capital and to conditions of social injustice' in a pattern which continues to dominate our country today. In the present, 'new challenges, including ongoing and often increasing inequality, national reconciliation, regional migration, globalisation and the HIV and AIDS pandemic . . . are layered upon the sediment of the past dispensation that functions as part of the foundations of the new order' (ibid.). At the same time:

> Yet no matter how significant the challenges we face as a country, ours is a success story. We recognise that people all over the world look to South Africa as a model, an example and even as a 'political miracle'. This clearly points to a degree of social cohesion and to social capital that allows for the functioning of a society despite the social justice situation. (Ibid.)

There is little to quarrel with in any of the individual components of these passages and there is every reason to sympathize with anyone who has to pin down the complex realities of South Africa's nation-building situation.

Nonetheless, as a synthesis on which to base further progress, 'the glass is half-full and half empty at the same time' leaves something to be desired.

When the Presidency confronted nation-building directly during this period, in 'A Nation in the Making' (2006), for instance, it tended to follow closely the world view put forward in Mbeki's speeches of the period. It is true that this version did not quite match Mbeki's apocalyptic vision of Mammon devouring the Revolution's children, nonetheless it shared the sententious moralizing tone and the Manichean vision of 'the-survival-of-the-fittest . . . the market jungle . . . premised on cut-throat competition' versus the 'alternative value system of human solidarity . . . and . . . humane and just social relations' which are locked in eternal struggle (Presidency 2006: 86–91). The document also echoes the spirit and style of the Mbeki era 'New Person' and 'New Cadre' themes. For example, the alternative value system of human solidarity

> requires conscious individuals determined to propagate human values – in government not enticed by the arrogance and illicit rewards that power can bring; in business not mesmerized by the glitter that purely selfish pursuits can harvest into the personal purse; and in civil society not fazed by mindsets that pour scorn on the humble lifestyle of an honest day's work. (Ibid. 88)

In general 'A Nation in the Making' conceptualizes the challenge of nation-building in terms of tensions between individual and collective goals: 'between encouraging individual self-advancement and collective development' and 'between encouraging individual excellence and social equity' (ibid. 94). Resolving these tensions depends on the 'successful regulation of social behaviour' and the state 'is the pre-eminent authority charged with leading this process'. However the report strikes a note of resignation, again reminiscent of Mbeki's quasi-philosophical musings: 'there is in our country a dominant collective social aspiration to fashion a society that cares, an aspiration informed by the ideals of equity, compassion for the most vulnerable, gender sensitivity, and honesty in individual and collective behaviour. . . . The truth, however, is that aspiration and reality do not necessarily, and not always, coincide. Real life, even if it may jar with ideals, influences social behaviour in the here and now' (ibid. 91).

Just over a year later the Presidency produced its review of progress since 1994, a little ahead of the 15-year anniversary. In 'Towards a Fifteen Year Review' the warnings have a harder edge. The achievements of government were duly noted but deemed not to have been enough. In language which echoed the scenario-building exercises that played a prominent role in South Africa's transition, the Presidency summarized the current trajectory:

> South Africa could continue along this path, barely denting structural ills such as massive unemployment among the youth and unskilled

workers, the structure of the economy, inequality, poor quality in some social services and trends in violent crime. With this, society would plod along with occasional social instability and periodic spurts of growth. (Presidency 2008: 115)

This was not simply a matter of government policy and capacity, however. The review asked: 'Is there a possibility for a big push based on broad, *national* consensus and focused on a few catalytic *national* initiatives, propelling the totality of *national* endeavours?' (ibid., emphases added). There was now less emphasis on the moral hazards of capitalism and the need for moral renewal to avert them: one emerging focus was on the imperative of growth and a second was on the shortcomings of state capacity to achieve government objectives. This was not something separate from nation-building but linked to it in a positive loop: 'A cohesive society whose citizens are well endowed with human capital is both a goal and a driver of development. For that reason, attending to the stresses in social cohesion that have become evident needs to be given priority' (ibid. 117). While the message was muffled somewhat by the government's need for self-affirmation and to avoid giving too much ammunition to the political opposition, it was clear enough. Government policy makers were aware of a nightmare scenario composed of a weak state and an absent nation, which threatened stagnation in a country that had to move forward (principally in accelerating economic growth) to avoid further decay. Standing still was not an option. Perhaps a South African nation did exist, the Review implied, but only in the minimum sense of a people that identified with the territory and paid lip-service to its values without living them to any meaningful extent. What was missing was for people to conceive of the nation as the vehicle for individual or collective aspirations and for which they might make sacrifices. Maybe there were no threats to the integrity of the South African nation, but this was not the basis, in terms that increasingly entered the Presidency's discourse at around this time, for a *successful* nation.

'Towards a Fifteen Year Review' pointed the way clearly to the NPC: 'The state should have the capacity to give leadership in the definition of a common national agenda and in mobilizing all sectors of society to participate in implementing that agenda' (ibid. 119) and provided substantial clues as to what the priorities should be in this national agenda. The NPC began by producing a series of 'Diagnostics', which were analyses and interpretations of the main challenges in governance, the economy and human and material conditions. One was devoted to 'Nation Building'. It begins with a blunt statement of civic nationalism: 'The aim was to use the Constitution as a foundation for the building of a new national identity through a common citizenship and equal rights and the avoidance of ethnically defined federalism.' The Constitution's shared values and vision of a prosperous, non-racial society not only provides a common identity but 'a common destiny' (NPC June 2011: 2). It is not only shared values, however, that hold the country together. The Constitution is also a written, social compact (presumably in the form of its property rights clause) which allows the 'former colonisers' to retain ('by and large') 'the ownership of the factors of production and their wealth', in return for 'universal franchise and some form of redress' for the 'former colonised'. The fact that this trade off was consummated and the package of shared values was agreed amounts to a 'usable past, the creation of a national history', which is at the centre of all subsequent nation-building efforts and the grounds for optimism in the future: 'The starting point for the "new" South Africa is that the country's people managed to walk away from the precipice of war and bloodshed, to create peacefully through negotiations, a democratic society' (ibid.). What was achieved once could be achieved again.

Like the Presidency's previous body of work, the NPC tends to conceptualize nation-building challenges in terms of pairs of opposed elements. But for the NPC the opposition is not irreconcilable; it is not so much the resolution of tensions that is important, but the recognition that the opposition is in fact superficial and the real relationship is one of interdependence. The plan tends to express these aphoristically. For instance, 'unity and redress': 'Without unity, the nation cannot hope to redress the wrongs of the past. Without correcting the wrongs of the past, unity would be superficial' (ibid. 1) and 'growth and redistribution': 'Redistribution and equity are not only a constitutional imperative, but are good for growth, development and stability. Without effective redistribution, growth itself becomes unstable. However, it is also true that without faster growth, effective and sustainable redistribution programmes are likely to be pyrrhic and tenuous' (ibid. 14).

After a period of public consultation and discussion on the diagnostic reports, the analyses were carried forward into the main report (NPC November 2011), a comprehensive and weighty document, running to nearly 500 pages and covering all areas of government responsibility. The final one of 15 sections ('Transforming society and unifying the country') deals explicitly with nation-building. But effectively the whole document can be seen as an exercise in nation-building on a grand scale. The Plan begins with a lengthy statement envisioning the desirable state of South Africa in 2030. As part of this it gives a ringing answer to a question posed by the Presidency in 'A Nation in the Making'. This was whether the various racial, ethnic, linguistic, class and religious identities of South Africa should 'fuse in a melting pot of national identity . . . or coexist in a variety of multiple combinations with an overarching common identity' (Presidency 2006: 85). According to the NDP, by 2030, South Africans should be able to say, 'We are a community of multiple, overlapping identities, cosmopolitan in our nationhood. Our multiculturalism is a defining element of our indigeneity' (NPC November 2011: 24). This sidesteps what is, for some, a most pressing question: what should be the common, or more likely the dominant culture? There was a degree of post-colonial *angst* in 'A Nation in the Making':

> There is . . . a continuing struggle to affirm an Afrocentric consciousness against a mindset to glorify everything in developed countries as invincible and infallible. This in part reflects a social pathology to seek affirmation from other nations and thus to view ourselves through the prism of other countries' opinions. (Presidency 2006: 98)

This has given way to the NDP's cool, post-modernist paradox: 'The key to the country's unity is that all South Africans have many identities' (NPC November 2011: 472). This can be viewed, according to taste, as the welcome onset of mature, national self-confidence or a betrayal of the essential Africanness of the people and country. It is true that the nation-building diagnostic report does pledge to reverse the eurocentrism of the past and give back pride to Black, Indian and Coloured South Africans in part by 'state efforts to teach children about African heroes and Africa's contributions to world history and culture' (NPC June 2011: 3). It remains to be seen whether Africanism can be folded so gracefully into 'multiple identities'.[2] The Plan reaffirms the commitment to civic nationalism based on the Constitution and warns against the 'wrong' kind of nationalism in an oblique, but none the less pointed reference to the outbreaks of xenophobic of violence in 2008: 'We must constantly guard against narrow nationalism, dislike of "others" or the development of a superiority complex in relation to people from other countries or continents. Nationalism, taken to an extreme, engenders new forms of racism, discrimination and chauvinism' (ibid. 462).

In some respects the NPC's prescriptions for nation-building show substantial continuity with past government thinking on this subject. A case in point is redress, which is not only seen as absolutely central to building national unity, but is also treated unproblematically as race-based: 'Given that disadvantage was racially defined for decades, the nature of that redress will by definition be race-based' (ibid. 2). Although this is treated as a matter of simple fact, or indeed fiat, there are concerns: 'The risk of getting this balance wrong is enormous. Erring on one side implies building a unity that is superficial; erring on the other means deepening the divides' (ibid.). Although there is no hint of it in the body of either of the NPC's documents, the case for substituting class for race in redress measures is boldly set out and appended as a 'key question for discussion' to the diagnostic report in the NPC's public engagement process. This suggests that some at least of the commissioners might have been in favour of a rethink, but since no more was heard of it, presumably there was no public support or that anything other than race as a basis for redress was deemed politically unfeasible.

In other respects the Plan offers fairly mainstream ideas on nation-building which could qualify for the label, 'motherhood and apple pie'. Children should be imbued with the values of the Constitution in both the family and in education; open displays of opulence are divisive ('a scourge') and there should be balanced and appropriate incentive systems; it would be good for more non-African-South Africans to speak an African language; there should be more common, public spaces; middle-class people should not opt out of public services since their social capital is essential for critical and active citizenship. Given the level of dysfunction in public health and education provision, the last of these is particularly difficult, although in fairness elsewhere in the Plan much stress is laid on the need to improve these as a priority. However, the question of which will come first for these dysfunctional public services, the chicken of middle-class participation or the egg of improving standards, is unsurprisingly not addressed.

Beyond these rather conventional prescriptions, the main thrust of the NDP's thinking goes into the idea of a social contract.[3] This, especially in South Africa, features prominently in the nation-building repertoire, and can thus be labelled a 'conventional' or 'mainstream' solution in itself. However, it is this very lack of novelty and innovation that confirms the NDP's recommendation, which amounts to a call to revisit a tried and tested formula, the 'usable history' on which the future can be based. It would be easy to criticize the NPC for resembling generals who prepare to fight the last war, rather than the next one, but it would also be unfair. The prescription of a social contract is not so that (as we noted earlier) 'South Africans can walk away from the precipice of war and bloodshed', but to 'help propel South Africa onto a higher development trajectory as well as build a more cohesive and stable society' (NPC November 2011: 457). Effectively the founding myth of South Africa's democracy is brought up to date by situating it in the burgeoning literature of why nations succeed or fail at achieving high levels of inclusive and sustainable growth. It may or may not be a problem that there is no immediate abyss for South Africans to look into and to concentrate their minds on agreeing to the terms of a compact. However, there are other differences between then and now that complicate the intention of importing the idea of a compact into the present.

In the first place, there is the question of 'ownership' of any compact of the sort which the NPC recommends. When the negotiations took place for the transition to democracy, which became the founding compact, there was no legitimate government. In this vacuum of legitimacy, all parties involved in the negotiations could claim ownership and none could claim to be the legitimate authority that brokered and underwrote the settlement.[4] It is from this quality that the settlement derives its symbolic power. This condition no longer applies, which poses a number of problems. The ANC is at the same time the legitimate government and the leading participant in an adversarial system of democratic, electoral and parliamentary politics.

As the government it is well placed to claim credit for a compact; as a contestant in party politics it will certainly want to do so. Any other party or group participating in a social compact will have to weigh carefully the chances of merely being co-opted into broadening the basis of the ANC's support. On the other hand it is possible that the NDP is being used by some elements in the ANC to canvass broad support for policy alternatives on which they cannot prevail within the ANC and Alliance. If so there will be those within the Alliance who take a dim view of the policy-making prerogatives of the ruling party and legitimate government being circumvented in an alternative, political theatre under the guise of nation-building.[5] One normally essential principle of compacting is that not every party gets everything that it wants. It is very hard to see how the ANC, the winner of massive electoral majorities, will be able to handle this without alienating its own support base. The other alternative – that the government plays the role of broker, persuading others such as business and labour to make concessions without making any of its own – is not an attractive position for anyone else.

Another issue is who should take part in such a compact. As we have noted, the ANC is compromised by being both a participant and legitimate arbiter; other political parties risk compromising their competitive positions; churches and civil society do not have much to offer other than rhetoric and moral support. Effectively, the key players are business and labour, and in fact the NDP acknowledges this. However, there are several difficulties with this. One problem is that there is a question mark over whether or not each 'social partner' can speak with one voice and deliver a constituency. Business is an activity, not an entity. In South Africa 'it' is composed of small, large, multinational, 'black' and 'white'. Black CEOs of 'established' business may see things differently from the equity beneficiaries of BEE deals. Since some of the largest South African businesses are now listed in London or New York, it is difficult to say exactly what defines a South African company, never mind what a 'patriotic' business is. All that can be said with confidence is that size and race count; the political leverage of black business and the general economic leverage of the biggest businesses are influential. Until 2012 it was possible to view organized labour as, if not monolithic, then at least coherent. In the second half of 2012, however, rivalry between established and newly formed unions in the mining industry, as well as deep rifts in labour federation Cosatu over the nature of the relationship with the ANC and government, shattered this coherence and put in jeopardy the whole system of ordered labour relations, which had been a source of relative stability for nearly 20 years.

A second problem is the appropriateness of allowing the interests of business and labour – even a synthesis of them – to be proxies for the national interest. However much realism may demand recognition of the influence of business and labour, their interests do not necessarily coincide with those of the unemployed and otherwise economically marginalized (such as informal traders, for instance).

Finally, there already has been a compact between government, business and labour, and in the eyes of some this has been part of the problem, not the solution.

## A partial and selective contract

In the four years of negotiation and the first two years after the 1994 election the various challenges of economic reconstruction were distilled into a single imperative: to reduce poverty and improve equity without sacrificing growth. This in turn meant that the political and economic fundamentals that underpin markets had to be preserved and where necessary rescued from the old regime's distortions, but at the same time a substantial degree of redistribution had to be built into policy. The implicit position was that redistribution was essential for reasons of social justice, political necessity and the sustainability in the long run of market-led growth itself. This last point meant that redistribution would involve income rather than assets (land being an exception), and would in all cases be characterized by due process, consistency and predictability, in conformity to constitutional protection of property rights and other relevant provisions. Lastly, it would be paid for in large measure by the dividends of growth and depend on changing relative shares of wealth and stakes in the economy more than absolute reduction of the wealth of the white minority.

The conventional understanding of how this imperative of redistribution through sustainable growth came to be the dominant theme of economic policy is that it arose from a historic compromise between the ANC, business and labour. That this social contract would function as the economic correlate of the political settlement was confirmed by Mbeki (2003):

> In crafting the Bill of Rights, the founders of our democracy knew too well that political rights without a socio-economic foundation would be unsustainable. They knew that a political settlement without an enduring contract among the economic role-players for growth and development would, in time, collapse on a foundation of sand.

In essence this compromise reflected an acceptance by both the ANC and business that the sheer scale of the challenges of reconstruction could only be tackled under contemporary global economic conditions through market-led growth. However, the corollary which would make this politically feasible was that the mere removal of apartheid barriers to participation in the economy would not be enough. The closest to an institutional expression of this compromise is the act of parliament setting up the National Economic and Labour Council (Nedlac) composed of representatives of organized business, organized labour, community and social organizations and the state (Nedlac Act 1994). The act mandates the council to 'strive to promote the goals of economic growth, participation in economic decision-making and social equity' and consider draft labour-market legislation as well as all significant changes to social and economic policy before it is implemented or introduced in Parliament'. In this sense the compromise is about process in the interests of avoiding damaging conflict. There is no formal statement about the principles to be followed in striving for growth and equity, no statement of national plan or vision, never mind detailed working agreements, on price and wage restraint, for instance. The compromise has no popular mandate to give it status or authority. It is commonplace for business, labour and government to refer to each other as 'the social partners' but what is involved in this partnership is left extremely vague. It is possible that the partners themselves have a working understanding, but how the partnership works to modify, restrain or motivate behaviour cannot be audited against any set of public agreements.

That does not mean there are no public agreements. There are several, usually arising from 'summit meetings' such as a Jobs Summit in 1998 and a Growth and Development Summit in June 2003, or in crisis-driven measures such as the Framework Response to Economic Crisis (February 2009). The content of the summit documents typically includes visionary statements of a very broad sort, as well as open-ended and non-specific commitments which are difficult to monitor, never mind impose. Typical of the first of these is that partners should strive to make South Africa 'The leading emerging market and destination of first choice for investors whilst retaining and expanding social equity and fair labour standards.' What the documents avoid and what on the whole the social contract is not explicit about is any statement of value about the type of economic system South Africa should follow, and no statement of shared commitment to such values – except for agreements to work together cooperatively and avoid damaging conflict. There is no sense that hard choices and competing priorities have to be faced – when there are two priorities which might conflict with each other, they are simply aggregated as in making South Africa the 'destination of first choice for investors while retaining and expanding social equity and fair labour standards'. President Mbeki greeted the Growth and Development Summit in effusive terms. 'It should not be seen as an isolated event', he said: 'It is a major step forward in a protracted process that should in time culminate in a People's Contract for Growth and Development' (Mbeki 2003). What he had in mind by a people's contract for growth and development was not clear, but the Summit documents did little to bring it any closer.

Perhaps it would be naïve to expect anything more from a social contract on economic policy in a country marked by such inequality, poverty and with such a conflicted history. In addition, it could be argued, a fuller contract – in the sense of a shared endorsement of a comprehensive package of economic values – is not necessary. Each constituency has a kind of guarantee in some form or another for what it values. Property rights are guaranteed in the Constitution: business believes that the threat of fallout from changing the Constitution significantly in this area is enough to protect them. Labour rights are enshrined in statute: organized labour interprets a social contract to mean a veto for itself against significant changes to labour-market legislation.

What this means, however, is that each side defends its own and has only a very limited conception of shared, economic values. More significantly, there are crucially important areas of policy that are neither guaranteed in these ways nor covered by a contract of shared values. When hard choices reach a critical stage, as the government decided in 1996 when it adopted the GEAR package of fiscal restraint, the so-called social contract simply did not work. For organized labour GEAR was a double violation: first of its position in the ANC Alliance and secondly of the social contract. If the social contract did not cover something as basic as fiscal discipline it might reasonably be asked, what matter of substance did it cover at all? Or indeed what matter of process, since Cosatu was particularly exercised that the government insisted GEAR was non-negotiable.

Business and labour settled for essentially defensive positions. In the case of business the core interest was fiscal discipline and macroeconomic policy generally. For labour it has been legislative protection in the labour market. Each makes forays on the other's territory without real hope of success, at least in the formal institutions that supposedly express the terms of the contract, Nedlac and the periodic summits between business, labour and government. Nedlac largely functions as a spoiling chamber in which labour can change or kill legislation introduced by government pragmatists seeking modest, labour-market reforms. Each party tries to lobby government for its wider agenda. There are of course substantial differences in the options open to them. Labour and its ally the SACP can hope to achieve its goals by 'capturing' the ANC and changing economic policy that way. Quite what such a 'coup' would mean for the present or a future social contract is not clear. In the eyes of the Left this would not in any case be a coup but a 'counter-coup', since it is an essential part of the Left's narrative of the post-apartheid years that the ANC was 'captured' on behalf of capitalist and 'neo-liberal' interests in the mid-1990s. At least (in their eyes) such a counter-coup would be legitimate for having used the democratic structures of the ANC and the privileges of membership.

## 'Social partnership': A building block or a stumbling block?

Essentially what the NDP has in mind is to give expression to Mbeki's 'People's Contract for Growth and Development'. Leaving to one side for a moment the inconvenient detail that 'the people', whatever it means, means more than business and labour, there are two ways of looking at this conceptualization of nation-building. From an optimistic perspective, the habit of joint consultation and the acknowledgement in rhetoric of common interests, no matter how grudging in practice, offer much to build on for a more concrete, lasting and comprehensive contract that would spill over from the partners themselves to a broader sense of renewed, national purpose. A more measured, and perhaps more realistic perspective, might point out that any progress towards such a People's Contract would not involve blue-sky thinking and a new agreement, but the renegotiation of an existing one that has given the partners something to defend. For business (and probably by extension most whites), this is everything they thought they had preserved during six years of bruising negotiation. For labour, it would be putting in the balance all the gains that they thought were the fruits of liberation. It would be a somewhat naïve view that presumed all parties could take into the new social compact everything they had in the old and merely build on it. This could only be done by pre-restricting the agenda and excluding legitimate, but potentially destabilizing alternatives which have minority but significant support. Among these are nationalization – a chimera that the ANC spent several nervous years grappling with before banishing it in 2012, and land reform that looks north to Zimbabwe for inspiration. Both of these lurk in the populist imagination. An agenda for a compact that is restricted to tweaking the privileges of business and labour, on the grounds that anything more radical is 'populist' or 'extremist', in a country where only 41 per cent of the working-age population has a job, where the discontent of the marginalized regularly erupts in violent protest and where there are many views on economic alternatives, is unlikely to be inspirational on a national scale. On the other hand, one that is genuinely inclusive would be extremely difficult to manage.

To be fair to those who drafted the NDP, the plan does not ignore at least some of 'the complexities that make the crafting and implementation of a social contract difficult in South Africa' (NPC November 2011: 476). Prominent among these is the lack of trust between labour, business and government. Another problem is that the state may be neither willing nor able to 'punish' parties who break the letter or spirit of a compact: 'State capability issues bedevil the chances of success' (ibid. 477).

## Social cohesion and the limits of technocracy

The NDP is in some respects a continuation of Mbeki's conceptualization of nation-building but in a much more inclusive form, without the grating rhetoric and obsessively Manichean quality he brought to all questions of race. There is room to wonder whether if the NDP had followed Mandela without Mbeki's abrasive interlude, the Plan might have continued the constructive momentum of the Mandela years.

Be that as it may, if Mandela and Mbeki showed the limits of the individual, the NDP and its antecedents point to the limitations of technocracy. Despite a preludial attempt to dress itself up in inspirational nation-building poetry, the Plan is couched largely in consultant-speak, which is overanxious to express itself in chain reactions of benign relationships between growth and cohesion, tailor-made for the PowerPoint presentation rather than the pulpit or the soap box. It is true that there was a public process of consultation and feedback, but however sincere in intention it was, this had the air of a one-off formulaic marketing exercise. Once again, without the extensive organizational framework we associate with previous exemplars of nation-building, capable of doing the week-in week-out demotic graft of raising national consciousness, it is hard to see the 500-page plan as the inspiration of a new wave of progress. However in one respect at least, it is possible that the Plan may make a significant contribution to nation-building. The NDP makes a stronger and clearer diagnosis of state weakness than previous official documents (though it could still be accused of pulling punches) and offers firm prescriptions for improvement. Given that state weakness is a hindrance to nation-building, if the Plan is taken seriously and acted on it will have made a significant contribution to removing this obstacle.

## PART FOUR

# South Africans today: Coming together or pulling apart?

# CHAPTER SIX

# Do South Africans have a shared life?

Whatever else might be said about the official preoccupation with social cohesion which was discussed in the previous chapter, it is not misplaced. The concerns that 'South Africans' live in fragmented enclaves, are reluctant to assume citizen responsibilities and are prone to social deviance are real ones, and the possible effects of these things on nation-building need to be taken seriously.

The task of dissecting the raw material of nation-building in terms of conventional markers such as race, language and ethnicity which was undertaken in Part One is a necessary but not sufficient condition of successfully exploring the state of nation-building in a democracy like South Africa. Two other things are relevant: the degree to which citizens enjoy a shared social existence and the degree to which social behaviours that support or undermine nation-building are prevalent. Even nationalisms that rely for their binding force predominantly on contractual and consensual adherence to civic bonds, rather than mythologies of common descent and literal kinship, are not entirely bloodless agreements between atomistic individuals. In a democracy, national identity involves both vertical and horizontal relationships. Vertical relationships between the state and individuals as citizens within the framework of a polity, largely involve consensual allegiance. Horizontal relationships between citizens as individuals, grouped in both formal, associational ways and in informal, shared patterns of behaviour, can reinforce (or subvert) these relationships of consensual allegiance by virtue of the degree of affinity they express. In this sense it is meaningful to ask not only 'Who are South Africans?' but also 'Do South Africans have a shared life?' As we have already seen, there are many markers of difference among South Africans, measurable in terms of race, language, ethnicity, cultural practices and social attitudes. These can be correlated with material and status inequalities of many kinds. It is widely believed in South Africa that such differences threaten the prospects of nation-building, especially if they encourage the development of separate or segmented public spheres. Equally however, it is hoped that such effects can be mitigated by experiences of shared life. In other countries, experiences usually perceived as positive for the purposes of creating or reinforcing national identity include formal associational life (what is frequently labelled 'civil society'), a shared, media public sphere, shared consumption of public services, shared sporting experiences and shared participation in the polity.

## Civil society and associational life

The number and variety of civil society bodies in South Africa is frequently cited as a major factor in shaping the country's democracy and helping to make it sustainable. In the eyes of many South Africans it is the distinguishing feature of South African democracy. The scope and reach of the many thousands of non-governmental organizations (NGOs),[1] professional and business associations, trade unions, charities, research, lobbying and constitution-supporting organizations is indeed impressive. In March 2012, 85,000 non-profit organizations were registered in terms of the (1997) Non-Profit Organizations Act. Less formal organizations also flourish. Among them are *stokvels*, small-scale, informal savings and rotating-credit unions, whose origins go back to the nineteenth century and which have been influential in organizing African social and community life since at least the early 1930s. According to the government's NDP, in 2011 there were 811,830 *stokvels* and 11.4 million *stokvel* members, with a total savings value of R44 billion in South Africa (NPC November 2011: 377). The purposes of *stokvels* include saving for burials, birthdays and increasingly for investment. They do not have functions outside their members' finances and social lives. However, although they are often classed as 'informal', many have constitutions, office-bearers and monthly meetings which combine social functions with managing the organization's business. In this respect they are important community building blocks and vehicles for socialization and financial education. A mark of their importance is that there is a National Stokvel Association. Although they are historically associated with lower-income groups, an indication that *stokvels* are keeping pace with upward social mobility is the growing number of *stokvel* investment schemes. The origins of the movement – like those of the African Independent Churches and other manifestations of African organizational vitality – lay in the restricted opportunities for Africans in the mainstream of South African social and economic life. Such is their current economic power, and hence their attractiveness to the financial services industry, that interesting challenges lie ahead; whether they maintain their communal distinctiveness, or become a bridge to their members' involvement in the mainstream financial sector.

More generally, the sources of South Africa's vigorous associational life are numerous, varied and not always complementary. At its simplest the web of civil society organizations is an outgrowth of the fact that South Africa is a complex and developed society with many functions – most obviously professions – which require self-regulation. There is also a very strong historical legacy from the liberation struggle of civil society activism, which has remained an inspiration in the first 20 years of democracy. One of the most potent weapons in the liberation struggle was the fusion of local-level grievances – typically rent increases or poor services – with the larger issues of apartheid oppression. Ambiguity and contest remain over the extent to which this civil society movement was an independent expression of resistance and how far it was at the initiative and under the management of the ANC in exile and underground. There is also ambiguity and contest over whether and how far the ANC was responsible for deliberately demobilizing the civil society organizations that supported it, once it came to power in 1994. These ambiguities have ensured that although many believe civil society activism is the distinctive, inherited quality of South African democracy and should be the foundation of civic nationhood, the relationship between civil society and the governing ANC is at times a fraught one.

A third source of encouragement for civil society is the Constitution itself. The Constitution's broad recognition of civil and political rights obviously rewards and builds on the legacy of these civil society struggles. However, the Constitution encourages civil society in less obvious ways. It recognizes broad social and economic rights that the ANC government has found difficult to make progress in enacting, and even where it has been able to devote resources to realizing them, it has often fallen short of the capacity to deliver them. This has stimulated activist associational life in two ways: first by motivating lobbying groups whose purpose is to hold the government accountable to the Constitution in matters of social and economic rights and secondly in the growth of a service industry of non-profit organizations in support of the government's existing social welfare programmes. In terms of the latter, the NDP notes that: 'In social welfare services, the state has adopted a partnership model of social welfare provision and relies mainly on non-governmental welfare organizations to provide professional social services' (NPC November 2011: 377). Fourthly, the vitality of civil society activism has to some extent been crisis-driven. The most obvious example of this has been the Treatment Action Committee (TAC), which was founded in 1998 to agitate for change in the government's response to the HIV/AIDS pandemic. Very much inspired by the UDF example of activism and counting among its leaders some of its veterans, the TAC was not only successful in its own right, but held out a model of non-sectarian association which pointed in the direction of the kind of civic nation-building sketched in the Constitution and the improvised nation of the transition period. Fifth and last, civil society organizations received significant international encouragement and considerable funding, not only during the final years of struggle and transition, but also well into the democratic period as well.

No-one should underestimate the variety, and in many cases, the vitality of the contributions made by civil society organizations to South Africa's public sphere, and the role they play in structuring society and underpinning democracy. On the other hand it would be overly idealistic to ignore strong elements of antagonism and segmentation within the public sphere itself and between some of the more activist organizations and the ANC government. Government and civil society often seem to be operating according to quite different conceptions of democratic citizenship and nation-building. It remains an open question whether South Africa's public sphere of democratic citizenship transcends the segmentation and divisions of South African society or reproduces them.

Inevitably transformation is one area of tension. The anomalies of civil society in South Africa are highlighted by the continuing presence of organizations that have a racial basis of association. Among them are the Black Management Forum (BMF), the Black Business Council (BBC), the Black Lawyers' Association (BLA) and the Association for the Advancement of Black Accountants (AABA). Such organizations are not numerous, nor do they have mass membership, but individually and collectively they enjoy a high-profile, privileged access to policy makers and over some issues such as BEE, they have been influential. None of them is explicit about racially exclusive membership requirements; indeed to do so would violate the equality provisions of the Constitution and anti-discrimination legislation. On the contrary, most of them explicitly refer to themselves, despite their titles, as non-racial organizations. In this respect they are illustrative of South African doublethink about race, which is by no means confined to organizations of this sort. They are concentrated in business and in the professions most closely associated with business. However, not all black professionals choose this racially autonomous route – for instance, black South African doctors apparently do not feel the need for a separate organization and work for non-racial transformation through the genuinely non-racial South African Medical Association (SAMA). Although exclusively black organizations profess broad transformation aims on behalf of all black people, critics see them as lobbying groups for the further advancement of middle-class black people who have already been advanced by affirmative action and Black Economic Empowerment (BEE).

Black business and professional organizations justify themselves by arguing that a non-racial society will not be possible until economic power (a somewhat opaque and flexible concept) is wrested from whites, and that to achieve this it is essential to intensify affirmative action and BEE measures. The concentrated lobbying that this requires is best undertaken by organizations that boldly define themselves and the interests they seek to promote in racial terms. Another underlying self-justification for organizations defined in terms of blackness is the view that non-racial organizations are vehicles for 'white' interests because such is the preponderance of 'white' power, including organizational culture, in the economy that white interests can shape the agenda of such organizations without having to announce their 'whiteness' explicitly. In this respect, black organizations claim to present a more honest reflection of South Africa's realities. To critics, this kind of reasoning merely confirms the somewhat Orwellian flavour conveyed by the principle that in order to work for non-racialism, you have to organize yourselves along racial lines. None of the civil society organizations that identify themselves in explicitly racial terms devote any significant intellectual energy to visualizing a future in which racially conceived organizations will be irrelevant. The absence of any coherent vision of what a non-racial society might be like naturally leads to suspicions that they are no more than self-interested lobbying groups.

Whatever the merits of civil society organization along racial lines, its attractiveness is not diminishing. In 2003, in what was hailed as a historic advance of non-racialism, white and black business organizations that had their roots in the forced segregation of the apartheid years joined together as Business Unity South Africa (BUSA). This was an unhappy marriage which lasted only until 2011 when black businesses reformed the Black Business Council, claiming that BUSA could not adequately represent the interests of black business. At present business interests are represented by BUSA, which has both black and white members, and the Black Business Council. This does not make for coherent definition and articulation of these interests.

Even where civil society organizations do not define themselves explicitly in racial terms there is room for debate over whether they represent a unified or segmented public sphere. South Africa's highest profile civil society organizations share a concern for the integrity of the Constitution, but they interpret threats to the constitutional order in different ways and they have different priorities. As we have already noted, one major civil society concern has been to hold the government accountable for the realization of social and economic components of the Bill of Rights. Paradigmatic of this approach is 'Section 27', a public interest legal advocacy organization established in 2010. Section 27 takes its name from Section 27 of the Constitution which enshrines in clause 1 the rights of all South Africans to healthcare services, sufficient food and water and social security. Clause 2 lays on the state the responsibility to: 'take reasonable legislative and other measures, within available resources, to achieve the progressive realisation of each of these rights'. Section 27 builds on a vigorous and substantial tradition of legal advocacy and social activism, much of it developed to counter the government's response to the AIDS crisis during the Mbeki presidency. It specializes in, but is not confined to, health issues and it complements the work of other legal advocacy organizations, as well as that of radical, social activist movements on behalf of squatters and other marginalized people.

This form of civil society activism, of which Section 27 is one example among many, tends to see itself a kind of purifying and standard-setting opposition to the current institutional form of the ANC, from within the traditions of the organization itself. It provides a meeting point for those that are wary of the authoritarian potential of the ANC's fusion of party and state, those who are concerned that the ANC may be abandoning non-racialism and developing a race-based nationalism, those who think that the organization is sliding towards organizational decadence and decay and those who merely believe that it needs to be constantly goaded into meeting its responsibilities. What they have in common, however, is reverence for the ANC's sacred documents – the Freedom Charter in particular – and a conviction that it is unthinkable to compete directly with the ANC for political office. This conviction is reinforced by strong identification with direct democracy and popular mobilization, as well as a general disdain for the conventional politics of electoral competition and parliamentary opposition.

A second form of civil society activism which takes the Constitution as its touchstone, operates from the rather different premise that the Constitution is principally a safeguard against the abuse of governing power, and that the ANC has to be watched very closely in areas like the separation of powers and judicial independence, property rights, land reform and expropriation, language rights and media freedom. Some, though not all civil society organizations of this sort, take an explicit stance on what they conceive to be minority rights in the Constitution. The trade union Solidarity, which claims 130,000 members, most of them white, had its origins during the apartheid years in the extreme right-wing, white miners' union. Purged of all such associations – though still vulnerable to taunts from the ANC on the grounds of its origins – and committed to the new constitutional order, Solidarity and its civil society activist offshoot, Afriforum, take minority rights as their chief concern, albeit within a wider concern for the constitutional order. Afriforum and numerous other organizations that operate in this general area have to perform a difficult balancing act between what can appear to be special pleading for a racially and/or ethnically defined group and concerns which affect the whole population. A notable case in point is the campaign to highlight murders of farmers and their families and to lobby for better rural security, within a wider context of high crime levels and inadequacies of security policies. The point at which special lobbying for a group deemed to be particularly at risk becomes a divisive rather than an integrative campaign is in practice difficult to define, and is of course prey to highly charged political opportunism of various sorts. Similarly, when organizations such as Solidarity mount legal challenges to what they claim are breaches of legislative guidelines for affirmative action and other redress measures, their claims that they are opposing only breaches of codes of practice and not the legitimacy of redress per se do not always ring true with Black South Africans.

The various groups that use extra-parliamentary mobilization and mount legal challenges to affect government priorities and spur more effective action, or to place limits on its operations, tend inevitably to focus on those specific rights they believe to be unrealized or threatened by abrogation. They tend to operate in their own spheres are wary for the most part of cooperation outside them and emphasize different ends that the Constitution might serve. However, they mostly share a concern for the overall constitutional order, wisely seeing that whatever their different priorities, their freedoms to pursue them stand or fall together. In this sense, activist civil society groups do contribute to a diverse but integrative associational life.

This, however, is not a view shared by elements in the ruling party, including at times its leadership. The ANC's attitude to civil society activism is permanently wary and tense, and frequently verges on the paranoid. Not all these tensions come from the same source. Some in the ANC take the organization's self-assigned description as 'the leading social force' literally to mean that all 'independent' social action should be subject to ANC leadership and directed to goals identified and approved by the ANC. Others are outraged, on the one hand by those who take it upon themselves to lecture the ANC on is own values and traditions and to use the Constitution and the courts to enforce their interpretation, and on the other hand by those who (in the ANC's eyes) use the Constitution to protect special interests from the essential task of realizing the National Democratic Revolution. A third source of exasperation comes from those in government who recoil in technocratic frustration at not being allowed a freer hand to make and deliver policy.

In general, the ANC sees itself as the target of a two-pronged attack by meddlesome progressives from one direction and from the other, by obstinate reactionaries defending past privileges. Unsurprisingly, the ANC points in all cases to the more than 60 per cent of votes cast which it has managed to win in all elections since 1994. ANC cadres of all persuasions draw from this the conclusion that far from being the embodiment of democracy and the citizen nation, activist civil society obstructs and frustrates democratic nation-building, at least in the images preferred by the ANC itself.

## Media consumption and the public sphere

For many people the central truth about nationalism is the fact that nations are communities whose memberships extend far beyond what first hand experience can do to recognize and foster kinship and fellow-feelings. In this sense, in Benedict Anderson's celebrated phrase, nations are 'imagined communities' (1983). It would seem to follow from this designation that the further a community is from literal kinship and the greater the degree of diversity and division that is incorporated into it, the greater the task of imagining a metaphorical kinship and the greater the role for a wide range of communication media, which provide essential support for the process of imagining. They do this by inviting members of a putative national community into national consciousness, by helping them to recognize themselves and their fellows in portrayals of presumed national characteristics, values and ideal types of citizen or subject. In this sense, especially in the contemporary world, consumption of media in common is a useful marker of the shared life that can contribute to nation-building.

It is worth noting that some national communities are closer to literal kinship than others. Although Afrikaners developed as a community out of a melting pot of settlers from various European countries, principally the Low Countries, France and Germany, kinship among them could have quite a literal quality. This was bestowed by a degree of geographical isolation, intermarriage and social distance between themselves and English colonists, and themselves and black people. Nonetheless, despite this relative closeness to literal kinship, much hard, nation-building labour was needed in the cultural, linguistic and mass communication fields to imagine the Afrikaners into the potent and cohesive national community they were at their peak. By contrast, in terms of the raw material for imagining a community, it would be difficult to conceive of a community further removed from literal kinship than the black and white people of South Africa, legatees of colonialism and apartheid.

This fact alone suggests that the task of imagining a new South Africa through shared consumption of media which encourage recognition of metaphorical kinship would be a particularly challenging one. As if that were not enough, however, there are two sources of contention which complicate this kind of nation-building. The first is over the actual and desirable nature of South Africa's information order and the second is over defining the place and role of the public sphere in nation-building. Such has been the intensity of dispute over the public sphere and in particular the degree of hostility shown by the government towards sections of the media that it is an open question whether there is enough common ground to imagine a community by this route.

## An unequal and segmented information order

What is meant here by the information order is patterns of regulation, ownership and access that characterize the production and consumption of information through mass media of communication. In this regard South

Africa entered the democratic era with a mixed legacy but reasonable grounds for optimism. In the first place, the Constitution set a broadly enabling context for open and shared communication. This was articulated by the development of public policy in the first years of post-apartheid government. The aim was to entrench values supportive of a vigorous public sphere, including a model for public broadcasting which sought to avoid the excesses of state control that characterized the broadcasting services of the apartheid years. At the same time the position of the existing commercial media was left largely intact. Market-oriented print media and an embryonic commercial broadcasting sector, which would rapidly expand thanks to deregulation, had up until that point largely served the tastes and assumptions of white consumers. There were of course strong political expectations not to mention commercial motives for transformation of staffing, management, ownership and orientation.

In the years since the new media dispensation was shaped, it has not been easy for either the commercial or public service media to deliver on the expectations of the first years of democracy. The confidence with which the SABC can claim to be an independent public broadcaster is greatly compromised by its entanglements with the ANC government. Predictably, the pace and extent of transformation in the commercial sector has been marked by bitter controversy. Changing the personnel of the newsroom has been the least problematic, although the point at which enough has been done can never be set to universal satisfaction. Ownership is still the subject of much contention. Even where there has been progress however, controversy remains. Black editors and journalists soon found themselves subject to demands from in and around government over how a 'transformed' press should conduct itself, and at times to vilification as 'puppets' if they did not toe the line. However despite these growing pains, South Africa has a reasonably well-populated and diverse stable of media sources which between print and broadcasting achieve quite a high level of penetration.

The six-monthly All Media Products Survey (AMPS) of the South African Audience Research Foundation (SAARF) is the standard industry measure of consumption of print and broadcasting media. In 2012 AMPS covered 22 daily and 28 weekly newspapers. The average readership in mid-2012 was 10.8 million for dailies (30.9% of the adult population) and 11.5 million (32.8%) for weeklies. Calculation of readership is far from an exact science,[2] but it can be said with reasonable confidence that these figures are low by world standards. According to the 2012 World Press Trends Report of the World Association of Newspapers and News Publishers (WAN-IFRA), more than half of the adult world population reads a daily newspaper. Readership is declining, but still very high in Europe and North America; in Asia, readership has increased by 16 per cent over the past five years. In South Africa readership has grown from about 8 million a day and 31 per cent in 2003 (Johnston 2005: 26), but this increase has not kept pace with population growth and the percentage has been stagnant for a decade. If all newspapers, including those that are distributed free and the very smallest community newspapers are totalled, readership has been calculated as high as 15 million. However, it is debatable how much such small-scale titles contribute to shared experience and hence to nation-building.

Inevitably this market-driven consumption of newspapers is segmented. It is first of all segmented by language. The key fact here is the dominance of English-medium daily newspapers which, based on AMPS data, are read by 22.5 per cent of the population, that is, more than two-thirds of the total readership; this is an impressive figure given the minority status of English as a home language. The corresponding figures for other languages are 6.5 per cent for Afrikaans and 2.5 per cent for isiZulu. English may provide a common language for the newspaper-reading public, but there is no such thing as a national daily newspaper in South Africa, never mind a newspaper of record. Daily newspapers in English which are identifiably regional are read by 6.5 per cent of the population; 69 per cent of daily newspapers are sold in Gauteng (effectively Johannesburg, Pretoria and the metropolitan and industrial area to the east of Johannesburg). However, despite the dominance in sales of Gauteng-based papers, none of them have more than patchy cover outside their home province, thanks among other things to poor distribution systems; effectively they are all regional titles with dubious national pretensions. Inevitably the question of racial segmentation of consumption arises. The clearest example of this is the *Daily Sun*, a tabloid aimed at working-class (but aspirant) African people. Its readership of 16.2 per cent of the population is over half the total daily readership and nearly three and a half times its nearest rival, the *Sowetan* (4.7%) which is also aimed at an African readership, though a more middle-class one. Despite its target market and the selling point which distinguishes it from all other titles – a disposition to take seriously the role of witchcraft and the supernatural in daily life – the *Daily Sun* is owned by media conglomerate News24, the lineal descendant of the main, apartheid-era Afrikaans newspaper group. With the exception of the Sunday newspaper, *City Press* (5.3% of the weekly market), which is aimed at middle-class Africans, all the other English titles aim for a multiracial audience, and without access to their commercial data it would be difficult to estimate the racial breakdown of their readership.

The penetration of broadcasting is greater than that of print media. According to the 2011 census, 10.7 million households had a television set (StatsSA 2011: 99). With an average household size of 3.4, this means about 70.5 per cent of the whole population is exposed to television broadcasts. According to SAARF data, an estimated 89.5 per cent of the adult population listens to radio regularly. In contrast to print media, which is almost entirely market-driven, the balance of broadcast consumption is on the side of the public sector. The SABC owns 18 radio stations broadcasting in all 11 official languages. As a result of deregulation, 13 private-sector commercial radio stations have been licensed.[3] The SABC takes 42 per cent of the radio audience. Four stations, all of them owned by the SABC, are listened to by more than 10 per cent of the adult population. Three of them broadcast in African languages, including the largest at 20 per cent, Ukhozi FM (isiZulu). The fourth (and second largest overall at 17%) is Metro FM, a commercial station aimed at urban, predominantly African and younger audiences, which broadcasts in English. The SABC has three domestic TV channels (it also beams two channels externally in Africa), each of which broadcasts in a wide range of languages. There is also a free-to-air, private enterprise channel, e.tv and a subscription satellite service, Multichoice. The SABC accounts for 69 per cent of the television audience, e.tv for 22 per cent and Multichoice has 1.6 million subscribers.

This brief sketch of patterns of media consumption in South Africa's information order suggests that there is a diverse programme of offerings in which South Africans can see themselves and their world reflected. Coverage can be patchy, depending on command of language, geographical location and financial threshold of access. Not all media products are accessible to everyone. Despite this, few if any South Africans are denied access altogether. Nevertheless, concerns about the information order are politically quite salient. They tend to be focused on three things: segmentation, ownership and access.

Concerns about South Africa's 'highly segmented media market' (Wasserman 2010: 23) reflect fears that by defining audiences racially, commercial media reinforce old stereotypes. For instance, when the *Daily Sun*, the country's biggest-selling newspaper, trades on a daily basis in stories of witchcraft, superstition and miracle cures, this may 'serve to further essentialize the imposed ethnicities of apartheid, rather than acknowledge the ways in which African identities are constantly in flux' (Wasserman 2010: 77). Fears of this sort tend to be expressed by critics who are deeply suspicious of commercial media in particular and of market forces in general. Since, however, they are generally prescient enough to be aware of the dangers of overweening state provision, of overregulation and the fiscal limitations on increased public funding, such concerns on the whole lead to impasse rather than suggestions for fruitful, policy initiatives. In any case, whatever else may be said about the media segments in which South Africans find themselves, both the public and the commercial providers that cater to them are equally convinced of the legitimacy of the South African state and constitutional order, and do not question the reality of a South African nation. They may host opinions that do so from time to time, and themselves agonize over the problems and progress of nation-building. However, they contribute to what Michael Billig calls 'banal nationalism' by helping to establish the idea of nationhood as routine and familiar, and constantly reminding South Africans that whatever market segment they belong to, they are 'situated within a homeland which is itself situated in a world of nations' (1995: 9).

In this context it is important to note that there is a substratum of nation-building communication beneath the direct discourse in newspapers and broadcasts. This direct discourse includes news reports of 'national' events such as commemorative holidays, state occasions like the opening of parliament and elections: news is supplemented by opinion pieces and letters which, whatever their differences, tend to take the nation for granted. Beneath this direct discourse, the 'commercial technology of nation-building' includes advertising, soap operas, talk shows, chat rooms and blogs. In sharing this, 'proliferation of discursive patterns, images and objects . . . South Africans will come to believe that collectively they constitute "a nation" which exists, as it were, "outside themselves"' (Narunsky-Laden 2008: 136).

This is a worthwhile reminder that commercial interests and those of state authorities can coincide in promoting nation-building, whether the motivation is reproducing state legitimacy or selling products. Large corporations deploy nation-building imagery extensively in advertising and in self-promotion of their corporate social responsibility activities. One of the best-known practitioners of this kind of advertising is the former South African Breweries, now global company SABMiller, one of the world's largest brewers. Strong association with South African national identity is important for SABMiller because, although it is a truly global company, South Africa (where its share of the beer market is 90 per cent and of alcohol overall, 72%) remains extremely important. In addition, having moved its primary listing to London in 1999 the company has chosen to associate itself with a strong South African identity to brand itself as a nationally based global champion, a useful image to define itself in the world and to ward off criticism at home that it is merely another footloose, capitalist MNC.

Alleged deficiencies in the capacity of South Africa's information order to provide the kind of shared experiences that allow full expression of citizenship and national identity are frequently expressed in terms of ownership and access to media. Such has been the political salience of these concerns that a statutory body, the Media Development and Diversity Agency (MDDA) was set up by act of parliament in 2002, funded partly by government and partly by a levy on broadcast licence holders and print media companies. The official rationale for the agency is the need for strong and diverse media to support nation-building, democracy, social cohesion and good government. To these ends the MDDA is mandated to encourage ownership and control of, and access to media by historically disadvantaged groups and inadequately served communities. The MDDA is greatly preoccupied with the question of black ownership of commercial media, lamenting the fact in 2009 that its own research showed that 'the print media landscape in post 1994 South Africa has not transformed much in terms of ownership and control' (*Mail & Guardian* 30 July 2009). However, the agency does not articulate clearly how the quality of nation-building and information democracy would be improved by greater black ownership of commercial print media than the average of less than 26 per cent (over the four biggest companies) which it revealed in 2009. For instance, it does not spell out in what ways commercial broadcasting – which has a much higher percentage of black ownership – plays these roles better than print. Like many other proponents of greatly ramped-up BEE, for the most part, it simply assumes that many good things will flow from changes in ownership patterns without being greatly exercised to spell out what these good things will be. However, the MDDA is not unaware of the financial challenges in the commercial print media industry. Considering the slim possibility that it would ever receive the kind of funding that would underwrite new entrants (its present annual budget is R45 million), it has probably settled beneath the rhetoric for the role of palliative agent at the community end of the media sector.

It is also worth noting that the assumptions that underlie the MDDA initiative are open to question. For instance, the link between access to and use of media and citizen enjoyment of democratic rights may not be as simple as the MDDA and other critics of the information order assert. The rationale for the MDDA is that historically disadvantaged communities are deprived of access to information which is essential for effective participation in democratic processes. Yet, one account of political communication in post-apartheid South Africa points out, based on survey data, that whites 'display high levels of news media use, but their rates of voting, campaign activity, community activity, and contacting political parties are far lower than either Africans or Coloured citizens' (Mattes and Glenn 2011: 11). The implication is that either the degree of denial of access to Africans is not as great as critics of South Africa's information order claim, or that difficulties of access do not impinge on the quantity of democratic activity as much as the critics assume.

## A contentious public sphere

The concerns about segmentation, access and information equality can be viewed at one level as straightforward policy issues capable of being addressed by the kind of developmental strategies involving resources and their distribution which are followed by the MDDA. However, underlying them are more fundamental clashes of value about how the public sphere in which the nation will be imagined should itself be conceptualized. These clashes have greater potential to stall or derail nation-building than wrangling about racial headcounts in the newsroom or equity ownership in newspaper groups; wrangling that in some respects is a surrogate for deeper (and arguably darker) ideological differences.

What is meant here by 'public sphere' is Habermas's classic definition: 'a domain of social life in which such a thing as public opinion can be formed', especially on matters of general interest which have an orientation to practices of state, that is a political public sphere (1997: 103). In the context of post-apartheid South Africa, the public sphere is the virtual or metaphoric arena in which the rights and freedoms of the Constitution are enjoyed and practised. The media are only a part of this sphere, but an important part; for large populations, as with the general case of imagining the nation, means of mass communication capable of dissemination and dialogue are essential for any sort of public sphere to function. The contest revolves around a central point: what the freedom of expression which is enshrined in the Constitution actually means in the context of nation-building. This includes opposing views on what sort of national values and codes of behaviour should, either formally or informally, limit this freedom.

What might without exaggeration be labelled media wars over this disputed territory have been fought without respite, but in periods of varying intensity ever since the late 1990s. While 'war' is a reasonable, figurative description, it has been a war of manoeuvre and siege rather than all-out strikes. It has been waged by the ANC Alliance, principally against the commercial print media, often described with the qualifier, 'mainstream', which is an unsubtle 'dog whistle' designator of 'white' or at least, 'serving "white" interests'. The significance of this relationship lies not only in the existence of hostility and a measure of disdain on both sides. By and large in democracies with free presses, governments and media do not much like each other. Arguably democracy can be all the healthier for that. However, in South Africa's de facto, one-party democracy, where the ruling party is approaching its twentieth, unbroken year in office with majorities close to or at the two-thirds level throughout, the tensions have a particular quality. The press feels more keenly the danger of overweening state power and the responsibility of keeping the government accountable. The government resents all the more keenly the encroachment on what it feels are its prerogatives to govern with a free hand, given the size and the durability of its mandate, and chafes at the restraints on what it believes is its revolutionary task. These are difficult tensions to contain within a framework of building national unity and sustaining constitutional rule.

It is possible to summarize the hostile view of the print media that emanates from the ANC Alliance, but it is important to bear in mind that not all the views are held all of the time by all the various constituent parts (and factions) in the government, the ANC and its alliance partners. Nevertheless there is a coherent, hostile portrait that is expressed often enough and widely enough, both at the grass-roots level and by enough very senior people, to call into question whether a shared public sphere can make a strong contribution to nation-building.

In this view, the ANC considers that the print media – or at least the sections that are targeted – obstruct nation-building by being at one and the same time subversive and reactionary. Criticism, investigation and attempts to hold authorities to account are viewed as evidence of opposition to the National Democratic Revolution, motivated by defence of established (white) interests and incorrigible racism, the latter subliminally manifest in perceived Afro-pessimism and alleged refusal to believe that a black government can govern competently. In addition, the press, in ANC eyes, represents inappropriate values for a developing nation. It is in thrall to liberalism, individualism and Western orientation, sceptical of the state and insufficiently deferential to 'African' values. This last deficiency is manifest in a lack of respect for the privacy of ANC leaders, as in outrage (2013) at the press's 'intrusion' in investigating the building of a R200-million 'compound' for President Zuma in his home village with public funds and criticism of the government's lack of transparency on the issue on 'security' grounds. This, in the ANC's eyes is only one particular manifestation of a general refusal to grant deference to the ANC, its leaders, its history, its mission and its overwhelming mandate from the voting public.

The ANC's hostility has several sources: scepticism about liberal values – especially the ideal of objectivity in media reporting and analysis; profound insecurity, despite its unassailability in electoral competition (in the short term at least), and a disposition to believe it is beset by conspiratorial forces that make up for lack of numbers in cunning and shadowy economic power. To these discontents is added a powerful sense of grievance that the press did not do enough for the liberation struggle and since achievement of democracy has not done enough to apologize for this omission. Last but not least, in the eyes of liberal critics, is another source of hostility, a collectivist urge to control and unwillingness to tolerate any genuinely independent and critical forces which have competing views on how society should be organized. Unsurprisingly, the press and its supporters view this hostile portrait as evidence of creeping authoritarianism which must be resisted.

Given the intensity of the hostility that the ANC displays towards the print media it is remarkable how few concrete actions against it have resulted. Threats to tighten regulation, which at one point appeared to threaten censorship, have eventuated in a system for dealing with complaints against the press that both sides appear able to live with. Similarly there was a three-year battle (2010–13) over a bill for the protection of state information, in which the government at first sought extremely wide definitions of the kind of information to be protected and draconian penalties for those possessing it. This would have made investigative journalism (and 'whistleblowing') impossible. As with the regulation issue this has been resolved in what appears to be an acceptable compromise. These cases raise the possibility that the media wars are 'phoney wars', all rhetoric and no action. Members of South Africa's political class (of all persuasions) like to reassure foreigners that this is the South African way; that South Africans have a unique capacity to salvage compromise out of what appears to be irreconcilable hostility. Clearly there is something to be said for this point of view because the foundation of South Africa's transition to democracy followed this narrative. However, it is not a propitious way of engaging for the long haul of building and imagining an accommodating nation.

# Do South Africans have a shared sporting life?

## *Legacies of sporting identity*

Sport is widely believed to have a close relationship with national identity. This is partly because particular sports can be made to symbolize ethnic, cultural and national characteristics, partly because sporting clubs and associations are useful building blocks of the integrative life that helps make nations and partly because, traditionally, sporting competition at the highest level has been organized on an international basis. Viewed in this light, sport can be seen as a potential resource for national movements and for governments. However, its effects cannot be taken for granted, since while 'sport possesses a powerful symbolism that can be exploited on occasion to great effect, the malleability of sports symbolism often undermines its capacity to have a lasting effect on national identity' (Houlihan 1997: 113). Certainly in South Africa there is a widespread reflexive belief that sport is an essential part of nation-building. This is encouraged by a hyperbolic self-image common to both black and white South Africans, probably influenced by a history of isolation, that theirs is the 'most sports-mad' nation in the world. However, there are more solid reasons for sport to be regarded as an important part of nation-building in post-apartheid South Africa. As we have seen, the Mandela moment at the 1995 Rugby World Cup was a high point in the improvised nation that emerged from apartheid, where sport had its status as a metaphor for shared existence confirmed and extended at that time. Part of this metaphorical power came from the understanding of how important sport, especially rugby, was in creating the fraternal cohesiveness of Afrikaner nationalism. In very different circumstances, soccer had considerable influence in organizing African social life under apartheid. According to a historian of African soccer:

> Football functioned as a mobilising force that shaped urban social identities and influenced political organisations. Sport became bound up with both formal and informal politics. Football clubs expressed street, neighbourhood and township identities as well as territorial rivalries often linked to the activities of gangs and migrant workers' associations. Recognising football's magnetic attraction among ordinary working people, criminals and activists alike used the game to construct patronage networks and alliances and to legitimize their activities at the grassroots level. (Alegi 2004: 3)

These two sports represented a decidedly mixed heritage, but it seemed logical that if they could be purged of unsavoury associations and their positive power harmonized and shared, then the resource potential of sport could be realized. For South Africans who were prepared to look outwards, there were inspiring examples overseas, in the United States in particular, of black people who were able to use sport as an opportunity to excel and by doing so undermine racism. Football has contributed greatly to making the United Kingdom much less racist over the past 20–30 years, partly by providing positive black role models and partly by addressing the problem of racism within the sport itself. It is possible that the hopes for sport's nation-building potential were also underpinned by the presumed ease with which progress could be made. The repeal of apartheid laws could not by itself undo the massive economic and developmental inequalities bequeathed by apartheid and colonialism. But the removal of restrictions on who could play with and against whom would allow blacks to excel, and black and white together to test themselves against other nations. In this sense, sport had the potential to be one of the 'easy wins' of the new South Africa.

## Transformation and representation

In reality, sport's hoped-for effects on the prospects of common nationhood have been more difficult to achieve. The dividends have been real, but limited and sporadic and they have been offset by as many dividing moments as displays of unity, which in turn have tended to come only when the eyes of the world are once again on South Africa. Other than these transcendent moments, sport has been for much of the post-apartheid period just one more terrain of struggle over transformation. Unsurprisingly, transformation has principally meant battles over the racial make-up of national (and to some degree subnational) teams and of administering bodies. While more even racial representation has been supported in principle by everyone with any vested interest of any kind in sport, its place in the hierarchy of sport's purposes has been hotly contested among other aims which include success in competition, making money and allowing free expression of individual excellence. Also contested have been the acceptable limits of government action to define and demand targets for transformation, and to what degree punitive sanctions for failing to meet them are acceptable, and for that matter enforceable. The parliamentary portfolio committee on sports and recreation under a notably abrasive and interventionist chairman (ANC member of parliament Butana Khomphela 2006–11) was a focal point for extreme demands and intimidatory statements. Typical of these regular clashes was Khomphela's threat in 2007 that he would persuade the Minister of Home Affairs to cancel the passports of the Springbok rugby team prior to the world cup that year because the team was too white. He also threatened to have the (black) Zimbabwean player Tendai Mtawarira deported because the Springboks capped him after he had been resident and playing in South Africa for five years on a skilled work permit, but before his permanent residence had been processed. Khomphela and the then Minister of Sport also tried to have the Springbok emblem removed in 2008, forcing the ANC leadership to intervene.

Cricket has also known its tensions, which have arisen at grass roots as well as national levels of administration. A study of the KwaZulu-Natal Cricket Union found that 'abiding non-racialism' was an elusive goal and its pursuit had 'fuelled tensions between Indians and whites, between Indians and Africans, and among Indians of various ethnic and religious backgrounds. This indicates quite strongly the challenges involved in building a common national identity while pursuing redress' (Vahed et al. 2010: 254). At national level, legacy tensions have been complicated by the changing nature of the sport. In 2008, the president of the governing body Cricket South Africa (CSA) vetoed the selectors' choice of the international team on the grounds that it did not include enough black players. The president was able to force a quota on the team, but at the expense of unhappiness on the part of both white and black players (some of whom resented being token selections), who, it transpired, had other options to pursue outside the country. Having lost the confidence of a majority of CSA affiliates, the president resigned a short time afterwards. In the aftermath, transformation targets remained, but have been pursued more circumspectly and the president's right to veto the national team was taken away. This controversy marked the high point in the influence of a generation of anti-apartheid sports campaigners in cricket, mostly based in the Cape provinces and often talented players themselves, who had gone into national administrative bodies after 1994. In one account, this signalled that the old campaigners were 'out of kilter with the new age of professionalisation, commodification and mediatisation of sport' (Desai and Vahed 2010). The changing nature of cricket brought its own problems, however, and a scandal broke out when it emerged that the CEO of CSA, Gerald Majola, took undeclared bonuses for himself and other members of staff. This was as a result of a deal with the enormously powerful and lucrative Indian Premier League (IPL), which in 2009 staged its tournament in South Africa as a last-minute-emergency measure because of security fears for Indian venues. The findings of an independent judicial enquiry into the bonus scandal, commissioned by the Minister of Sport, have been the basis for considerable restructuring within CSA.

## Professionalization and identity

Cricket's difficulty in dealing with the increasingly transnational marketing of sport, introduces the possibility that it has not only been South Africa's predictable legacies and divisions that have limited the nation-building potential of sport. South Africa's return from international isolation coincided with, and in some measure contributed to, profound changes in the structure and organization of sport. The Mandela moment at Ellis Park came just a few months before the international rugby authorities recognized rugby as a fully professional sport. 'Shamateurism' had been rife in South African rugby before 1995, but it took open professionalism to transform it in ways that diluted and compromised its nation-building potential. The average pre-isolation amateur Springbok team was made up of farmers, miners, policemen, teachers and the occasional minister of religion. In terms of national cohesiveness and fraternal solidarity, they were representative teams in a very deep sense of the word. In the post-professional rugby world, the pool of players (about 200 strong), from which the national team is picked, is earmarked in teenage years, along with several hundred others who will not make the grade, to enter a world of preparation rather different from the normal educational and occupational worlds. The forcing ground for this talent is overwhelmingly private or semi-privatized schools with superior resources. It is commercially and politically essential for such schools to provide scholarships for talented rugby players from poor and/or black backgrounds. However, the quality of representativeness that the 'old' rugby gave has gone in a world of celebrity sportsmen (and women) bred like mercenary gladiators and distanced from the communities from which they came.

If one by-product of professionalism is the transformation of the players into a mercenary elite, a second is dilution of the presumed association between ascribed ethnic qualities and particular sports. The traditional recipe for success in Springbok rugby during the years of colonialism and apartheid was an implacable collective drive for domination achieved through superior physique and relentless exercise of will, rather than virtuoso, individual athleticism. The nation-building potential of this association between sporting strategy and ethnic essentialism was easily grasped and consciously cultivated, not only from above but also from below. With the demise of Afrikaner nationalism, the utility of this association has been greatly reduced, but to a surprising extent it remains; to some extent all Springboks become Afrikaners irrespective of their ethnic and racial backgrounds, and assumptions about masculine physicality are certainly shared across racial lines. However, the imperatives of professional competition, the absorption of transnational influences (especially in the Super Rugby Southern Hemisphere tournament), and the advent of black players have changed the nature of how South African rugby is played, as well as diluting and confusing the ethnic associations of the sport.

The same influences have partially changed South African soccer. Historically, African soccer in South Africa was the polar opposite of rugby. What was of cultural value was 'the spectacular display of individual talent . . . often more enjoyable, and ultimately, even more desirable than the final score' (Ndebele 1994: 47). Alegi describes this as an enduring aesthetic legacy, born in the 'Africanisation of football' under conditions which brought Africans into cities and the industrial economy in the twentieth century:

> The contemporary black working-class South African aesthetic continued to place more value on the cleverness and beauty of feinting and dribbling. These stylish moves elated audiences and, at the same time, symbolized the cultural importance of knowing how to get around difficulties and dangerous opponents in an oppressive society with creativity, deception and skill. (2004: 61)

Whether or not soccer is able to carry the full weight of this author's interpretative ambition may be moot; however, the principle he advances will strike a chord with anyone, right up to today, who has watched (or played in) any formal or informal game of soccer involving African-South Africans. Nevertheless, as with the worship of physical power attributed to the Springboks and their followers, this principle of aesthetic satisfaction over pragmatism has been considerably diluted by the imperatives of transnational, commercialized professional competition. To sum up then, the most typical and popular South African sports have retained weaker versions of their ethnic associations, but have on the whole become homogenized versions of the global sports. This (doubtless fortuitous) blend of old and new probably helps make sport's associations with presumed national characteristics more easily shared across South Africa's continuing ethnic divisions.

A third by-product of commercialization and global professionalization is familiarity of the spectacle. Between 1921 and the end of 2013, the Springboks will have played the New Zealand All Blacks 85 times: in the 71 years between 1921 and 1992 there were 37 matches (the boycott was a factor between 1981 and 1992); in the 21 years between 1992 and the end of 2013 the total will be 50 matches. The Springboks now tour the United Kingdom every northern-hemisphere autumn, whereas in the whole decade of the 1960s there were only 3 tours of Britain. One or other of the British or European sides tours South Africa every year. An annual Southern Hemisphere tournament involving Australia, New Zealand, South Africa and, since 2012, Argentina means that international rugby has reached saturation point. None of this means that international rugby has been robbed of its interest or support, but it seems fair to argue that probably the intensity, and certainly the quality of contribution to national cohesiveness through community representativeness, has changed greatly.

Both cricket and rugby have been affected by transnational possibilities open to players. Like other cricket-playing countries, South Africa faces the prospect of the financial attractions of IPL cricket clashing with international selection. Other opportunities have been opened by the Kolpak ruling (2004).[4] By 2010, around 50 South African cricket players had taken advantage of the Kolpak ruling to play in English domestic cricket (Desai 2010: 200). Given that the pool of fully professional cricketers in South Africa is no more than about 200, this is a large number. Although by no means all of these players were white, the Kolpak opening has been seen by some as a means for whites to 'cope with transformation' (ibid.). Another transnational route, followed by both cricketers and rugby players, has been to use claims to British citizenship to play in (and for) England. This can be done either through ancestry or the relatively undemanding residential qualification of four years. The current England cricketer, Kevin Pietersen, is the most celebrated of these players. The extent of this phenomenon is illustrated in the Lords cricket ground in London. At Lords there are honours boards in both the home (England) and visitors' dressing rooms. On the visitors' board the names of seven South African players appear who have scored a century in a Lords test match since South Africa's readmittance to international cricket in 1992. In the England dressing room the names of five South African-born players appear who have performed the same feat for England over the same period.[5] The Kolpak and Pietersen phenomena help to further muddy the relationship between sport and national identity which once was so clear. Which country a player represents can seem less a matter of national obligation and more of a career choice.[6] This combines with the conflicted politics of transformation and the treadmill repetition of international sport to dilute and confuse sport's contribution to nation-building.

## Relaxing in diversity

The sporting life of South Africa is shared to the extent that representative teams are increasingly mixed as, to a more limited degree, is support. Racial representation remains an issue with the potential to divide, but it has developed more nuanced concerns. A current preoccupation is with addressing the situation whereby many young African players are chosen for age-representative Springbok rugby teams, but only a much smaller number go on to establish themselves in top-level franchises and the senior Springbok squad. In general the imperative of remaining competitive in a highly commercialized context tends to put a brake on assertively interventionist approaches. There has been a marked change of atmosphere in the parliamentary portfolio committee on sport and recreation. At a meeting in February 2013, the South African Rugby Union (SARU) claimed that half a billion Rands had been spent on transformation and development since 1992 and its current budget for transformation was 'about ten per cent' of annual turnover. The ANC chairman was reported to have commented that 'the leadership of SARU was on track. Waiting for the results of the next ten years would be exciting; it took time to reap the fruits of development. The process did not happen overnight; it took time' (Parliamentary Monitoring Group 19 February 2013). This attitude is considerably more relaxed and accommodating than in the past.

While South Africans are free to play and watch sport together and the divisions of transformation, while real, are being pursued in more constructive ways than in the past, South Africans tend to exercise choice in highly segmented ways. Rugby and cricket are largely the preserve of the white, Coloured and Indian minorities, although considerable effort is put into marketing them to the African population – while soccer is overwhelmingly the sport of choice for Africans.

Unsurprisingly given the different historical and socio-economic profiles of the population groups and their historical sporting legacies, these sports inhabit very different worlds. One contrast is illustrated by comparative attendance figures. The Premier Soccer League (PSL) is a purely domestic competition, contested by 16 teams. Average attendance at games is around 7,000; this figure is considerably distorted by a handful of games between the biggest clubs. For instance, the highest attendance for a single game in the 2012–13 season was 80,000. The minimum ticket price is generally R40. While the average attendance figures do not reflect the sport's popularity, the broadcast rights do. In 2011 a pay TV channel secured the rights for five years for over R2 billion. The premier rugby competition, Super Rugby, is transnational, involving 15 franchises (5 South African) drawn from Australia, New Zealand and South Africa. Average attendances are much higher for rugby in South Africa than for soccer. In 2012, the 5 South African, regional franchises averaged 25,600 for their home games whose ticket prices were roughly double those of the PSL. The highest average attendance for a franchise was 42,729 and the lowest 19,033. The highest attendance for a single match was 52,000. In 2011 the average attendance for the most important domestic competition (the 59-game, interprovincial Currie Cup) was 15,873. This indicates that rugby attendances are distributed comparatively evenly across the country, while the very few soccer games that attract large crowds are all in the Johannesburg area, and attendances elsewhere are derisory. Cricket follows the pattern of all cricket-playing countries, in that domestic competitions are relatively poorly attended, but the regular international matches attract large crowds.

The international arenas in which the different South African sports compete are quite different. The national soccer side plays in a virtually exclusively African setting. There is the Africa Cup of Nations to qualify for every two years and 53 African countries compete for 5 places at the FIFA World Cup finals every 4 years. As a result, there is a constant round of inter-African soccer and very few fixtures against non-African sides. There are also very few transnational club games, and those that exist take place in Africa. In contrast, rugby still emphasizes historical axes of competition with British and more particularly New Zealand and Australian sides. These coincide with the burgeoning post-apartheid emigration routes taken mostly, but not exclusively, by whites.

Although rugby and cricket on the one hand and soccer on the other are almost literally worlds apart, there are strong parallels, mainly due to professionalization, sponsorship, broadcast money and celebrity culture. All major sports are sponsored by essentially the same commercial interests, with banks and mobile phone companies well to the fore. In a sense then there has been convergence in the way that South African sports are run and the purposes which they serve: high-quality spectacle for consumers mounted by highly paid celebrity performers; privileged access for corporate sponsors, their clients, administrators and politicians; seemingly limitless marketing opportunities. In this respect, sport in South Africa is no different from sport in many other places in the world. This, in the eyes of some critics, is the problem. Billions of Rands are spent on salaries for players and coaches (of which the national soccer team has had 21 since 1994), perks for administrators and stadia which, in some cases, having had their moment in the global limelight, rapidly become white elephants. Yet:

> If a government that is spending billions to host the 2010 FIFA World Cup of Soccer cannot ensure that school kids in the most needy of communities have decent soccer facilities and equipment, or that meaningful development programmes are in place for players in these communities where soccer is one of the most basic forms of social relations and recreational activity, then it should be clear that things have gone horribly wrong. (McKinley 2010: 97)

Effectively, the argument of these critics is that sport has become hollowed out into a passive, spectator culture and, in addition, is nothing more than another example of the gross material inequalities between the combined ranks of the old and new privileged elites and the excluded majority. In the light of these criticisms, it is perhaps ironic that the strongest and most insistent claims made for sport as a nation-builder in South Africa arise from this high-level, commercialized, transnational version of sport.

## A talent for hosting: Showcasing the nation

South Africa's record of success in international sporting competition since its readmittance has been uneven, though not without distinction. The soccer team (Bafana Bafana) has won the Africa Cup of Nations once and been a beaten finalist once. The Springboks have won the Rugby World Cup twice. The national cricket team (the Proteas) is currently (2013) ranked number one test-playing team, but it has failed to win any of the (increasingly numerous) international tournaments in the shorter forms of the game. South Africa's Olympic medal tally probably represents underachievement for a country of its size, but such are the effects of inequality and developmental anomalies that it is difficult to benchmark the country in comparative terms of what might be typically expected. Putting these not-insignificant achievements in the shade is South Africa's post-apartheid record of hosting major international sporting competitions. South Africa has hosted the Africa Cup of Nations soccer tournament twice and is the only country so far to have hosted the cricket, rugby and soccer world cups.[7] There are two straightforward reasons for this remarkable performance. The first is that the ANC, both before and after becoming the government, made a conscious decision to showcase the country's stability, organizational capacity and economic potential for tourism and investment. It has also astutely leveraged the idea that the African continent deserves greater international recognition; the 2010 FIFA World Cup slogan was 'Ke Nako: Celebrate Africa's Humanity' (Ke Nako means 'It's Time' in the Sotho languages). The second reason is the international community's wish to reward South Africa for its (relatively) peaceful transition to democracy and the international sporting bodies' desire to capitalize on South Africa's climate and infrastructure.

It is difficult to quantify how much South Africa has indeed gained from being a sporting host. Experts differ on quantifying economic benefit or lack of it, and soft-power benefits are simply unquantifiable; boosters and sceptics alike make what they can of slim evidence. As we have seen, critics worry that the hosting role has distorted spending priorities away from grass-roots development aimed at increasing and providing for mass participation in sport. However, it would be difficult to make a case that was negative across the board. Nevertheless, none of this has anything much to say about nation-building in the sense of horizontal relationships and the shared life. Bearing this in mind, the South African government commissioned a large-scale study on the impact of the 2010 World Cup on social cohesion, nation-building and reconciliation to be carried out by the statutory, social science research body, the HSRC (2011). Based on focus groups, the annual South African Social Attitudes Survey (SASAS), and a sample of press coverage, the study found that the effects of the world cup hosting were very positive, but might be difficult to sustain. A key finding stressed the importance of 'simply placing people in common spaces on trains, in buses, in fan parks and walkways' (ibid. 255), as a way of breaking down the divisions between 'us' and 'them'. However, respondents pointed out the limitations of these beneficial effects. Mere recognition of common humanity is not enough:

> As some focus group participants pointed out there is a difference between mixing and integrating. While South Africans shared common *public* space during the World Cup event, this seldom translated in to the sharing of *private* social space. After the event South Africans of all races and creeds went back to their 'racially separate publics'. Significant efforts will be required to draw South Africans back out of their safety zones to participate actively in a shared expectation of citizenship. (Ibid.)

In order to achieve this ambitious goal, '[e]normously innovative, creative and sustained interventions will be required'. This is a conception of nation-building to which we will return later.

## Sport and the shared life in South Africa today

Relationships between sport, society and nation have so many strands that it is hard to pull them together for an assessment of sport's contribution to shared life in South African society today. Historical legacies, class, commerce and many other things all play their part. Two other problems get in the way of a neat summing up. The first is the question of how much weight to assign to the fact that identification with different sports corresponds quite closely with racial, ethnic and class differences. Perhaps, there is a danger of being oversensitive and ascribing too much importance to this. After all, in Britain, identification with rugby or soccer still goes quite closely along class and regional lines. Though this may be changing with professionalization, many, perhaps most, top English rugby players are privately educated (the greatest marker of social division in Britain today), while virtually none of their soccer equivalents are. Rugby and soccer supporters are generally indifferent to the other sport and often aggressively dismissive of it. Scottish people share nationality and citizenship with English (for the time being at least), but sporting rivalry with the 'Auld Enemy' can reach extremes of tribal xenophobia. There is doubtless something to be said for the argument that these things are more tolerable in the context of mature and well-rooted nationhood and citizenship. In South Africa's more fragile and uncertain context, where racial and ethnic differences so closely mirror wealth and poverty, perhaps a more assertive cultivation of shared sporting experiences is called for.

This counter-argument leads to another issue. It is possible that the expectations of sport in South Africa are too high. The HSRC report on the 2010 World Cup lays out the case for sport as a cure-all of social ills: 'The South African government has consistently argued that sport can be used as a tool to support and help realise social and economic development, including the achievement of the Millennium Development Goals (MDGs); and it can encourage constructive social behaviour in individuals and promote social cohesion, tolerance, peace and security, as well as nation-building' (HSRC 2011: 6). These assertions fall squarely within a familiar ANC mindset of ambitious social engineering, which it has sought to apply in many areas of South African life, with delivery falling well short in every case. The report goes on to strike another familiar note, one which implies powers to command that the government simply does not have and probably no democratic government should aspire to: 'Government has explicitly stated that social polarisation in sports is unacceptable insofar as it would continue to create racially separate "publics", with different benefits, rights and obligations and fragmented experiences of citizenship' (ibid.).

Such statements of intent as these two examples, with their rhetorical overreach and in the second case vaguely minatory implications, threaten to distort the perspective from which the contribution of sport to shared social life and nation-building is assessed and in doing so, to set up expectations that are doomed to disappointment. It is not only the government that overplays the potential of sport to unite; this is something that runs throughout South African society. It is present in calls from the political Left for 'a return to a collective discipline, motivation pride and passion that is at the heart of a progressive society and the game of soccer itself' (McKinley 2010: 101).

Invocations of illusory past golden ages and improbable future people's utopias are likely to carry no more weight than hopes for sport-led, social engineering. Sport has changed and society has changed. The nation-building successes that sport has had around the world in the past – at least in terms of providing the building blocks of associational life – are likely to remain in the past. Whether it was the contribution of sport to Afrikaner nationalism, the contribution of the Gaelic Athletic Association (GAA) to Irish nationalism, Corinthian values to British imperial identity, patriotic sports associations to the nationalisms of Nazi Germany and Soviet Russia, the relationship between sport and nation was anchored by some ethnic, religious or ideological identity. It is very difficult to see anything with that sort of binding strength emerging in democratic South Africa. Perhaps it is just as well. Recent examples of the association between supporters of football clubs in Italy with the extreme nationalist and xenophobic right and their counterparts in Croatia and Serbia with ethnic war are not encouraging examples of synergy between sport and nation.

The contribution of sport to nation-building in post-apartheid South Africa has been uncertain and somewhat unstable. High points have included the major multinational hosting exercises which did much to enhance South Africa's image across many fronts. Among other things, they also united many white and Black South Africans in justifiable anger against the hostile, Afro-pessimist, pre-World Cup coverage led by the British tabloid newspapers and followed, as tends to happen, by much of the world press. As the official report on the 2010 World Cup pointed out, however, it is not clear how consistent and sustainable these effects will be. Low points have included wrangles over the meaning and content of transformation in sport, the ignominious fall of a Springbok coach as a result of making unguarded racist remarks, corruption scandals in soccer and cricket and a general sense of malaise in high-level sports management. However, it should be noted that these things are no worse in sports than in many other areas of corporate life in South Africa, nor are they worse than sports management in many other countries. All this is taking place against a global background of intensive commercialization of sport, which is hollowing out sport in South Africa, diluting the relationship between sport and nation and setting up powerful, transnational interests as competitors to national bodies. Not all of this is negative. There are opportunities, notably for sportsmen and women, in transnationalism and even national bodies can profit, as the relocation of the IPL tournament to South Africa demonstrates. If broadcasting can encourage people to spread their interests across several sporting codes and countries, allowing, say a Johannesburg township dweller to share his or her support between Orlando Pirates, Tottenham Hotspur, Bafana Bafana and, when they are not playing, the England soccer side, then this is no bad thing. South Africa will certainly remain divided for the foreseeable future into what the government calls 'racial publics'. However, it is not clear why this should be as bad a thing as the government assumes. Part of the reason for this uncertainty is that the racial make-up of the country is so heavily weighted towards African-South Africans. Whichever is the most popular sport is going to look overwhelmingly African. It is also possible that the government has not applied itself seriously enough to thinking through why people attach themselves to different sports.

Despite sport's chequered post-apartheid history, there are hints that progress is being made towards a new and more relaxed normality. Mandela and the World Cup success of 1995 remain securely part of national mythology, although as with all national myths, the story means different things to different people. However, the Springboks won the title again in October 2007 and once again their president was there to encourage them and share their success. Yet few if any South Africans remember this as a momentous event. Without the sheer physical presence and natural authority of Mandela, the diminutive Mbeki, thanks to the inclement Paris weather, unable to wear the jersey, but wrapped in a Springbok parka over his sober business suit, looked happy and relaxed as he was hoisted on giant shoulders among a vividly multiracial group of players and officials. The point surely was that this was the new normal and there is no need to craft nationalist mythology out of what people take for granted. To reinforce the image created in Paris, Mbeki's ministers wore Springbok kit to their next cabinet meeting after the victory. It appeared that South Africans could live with both the fractious squabbling about the racial composition of the team, which was their inauspicious send off and the national euphoria of returning as winners. What is more these happy scenes took place against a general context of Mbeki's tortuous (and to whites, threatening) efforts to redefine African nationalism. The only point of controversy surrounding the victory was whether or not the defeated English players had been inadequately briefed to acknowledge Mbeki as a head of state, rather than, from their insular heights of sporting celebrity, as just another anonymous African personage in the milling crowds. As many (perhaps more) whites as African-South Africans noted and responded angrily to this alleged, national slight.

## An afterword on sport: 'Sies! wat 'n kafferpak!'

On Sunday 23 June 1974, during the British and Irish Lions rugby tour of South Africa, the Afrikaans Sunday newspaper, *Rapport*, at that time the second biggest-selling title in the country, carried a banner headline on its front page: 'Sies! wat 'n kafferpak!' The headline referred to the Springboks' heavy defeat in the second test (the Lions went on to be unbeaten on the tour, winning three of the tests and drawing the final one). The headline could be translated as 'Ugh! What a hiding!' but this English rendition lacks the intensity and the peculiar quality of self-flagellation of the Afrikaans version. The key word is, of course, 'kafferpak'. Some authoritative dictionaries merely translate this in terms such as, 'a thorough thrashing, sound beating, whipping' (Van Schaik 1981), leaving out the obvious fact that the compound word includes the derogatory and contemptuous term of address or description used by racist whites (and others) for African-South Africans; that is, 'kaffer' (English, 'kaffir'). Other sources are more direct and give 'lit. kaffir beating' as part of the translation (Branford 1980). Three linked things are significant about this affair. First, the fact that the headline appeared in larger than normal typeface as the lead story on the front page of the biggest-selling Afrikaans newspaper shows graphically how important rugby was to Afrikaners at that time and for what reasons of national identity. Afrikaner nationalism is frequently and erroneously understood to be a matter solely of self-definition in the face of South Africa's black majority; however, of equal or greater importance, certainly in earlier periods, was self-definition in the face of metropolitan and imperial British identity. The second point of significance is the depth of national self-disgust that is revealed by the implication that the Springboks had been reduced to the status of no more than a rabble of natives that had been thrashed by their masters. The third is the way that rugby was intimately bound up with ingrained, casual racism, which could be deployed with impunity (there was criticism of the headline from liberal Afrikaners and in the English-speaking press, but this incurred no significant costs for the newspaper).

Although *Rapport*'s outburst was nearly 40 years ago it would be a mistake to regard it as no more than a quaint, distasteful, historical footnote. It is worth revisiting, partly for the fact that it lies comfortably within the memory of much of South Africa's current political class. As such it helps to put in perspective the magnitude of Mandela's gesture in rallying black South Africans behind him and the Springboks in 1995, and Mbeki's in duplicating it in 2007. It also places in context some of the raw emotions that have accompanied transformation in sport. Finally, this digression also helps to measure the distance sport has come in South Africa. There may be legitimate doubts about the extent to which sport has fostered a shared life of horizontal relationships across South Africa's other divides. Relatively small numbers of those who wish to do so, travel across cultural and ethnic lines to play or spectate with reasonable comfort and to do so in an atmosphere of mutual tolerance of differentiated sporting tastes. This, spiked with occasional intense demonstrations of shared allegiance and mutual enjoyment on the world stage, defines sport's modest progress. Even if that is all that can be claimed, however, it is no small journey to have successfully undertaken away from the shameful, racist starting point that *Rapport*'s headline exemplifies.

## Religion and shared life in South Africa

South Africa is de facto a Christian country with a large majority of self-declared Christians. However, the Constitution does not recognize this predominance and public policy reinforces religious pluralism. In education, for instance, insofar as religion is part of school syllabus and practices, it is in a determinedly multifaith context. The Constitution expresses a firm commitment to religious freedom and diversity, the general principle being that of religious pluralism in a secular state. Despite the numerical preponderance of Christians there is significant diversity among them in forms of belief, worship and church organization, within the overall meaning of 'Christian'. While the divisions are very largely expressed in benign ways and do not lead to conflict, the different denominations do tend to live within their own worlds, shaped by different historical legacies and the present life circumstances of their constituencies.

## Religious affiliation

Recent figures on religious affiliation in South Africa are not readily available because the 2011 census dropped the question which in previous censuses registered adherence to religions and denominations.[8] However, both the 1996 and 2001 censuses recorded high levels of religious identification. In both of them, around a third of respondents identified with 'mainstream' Christian denominations (Anglican, Roman Catholic, Dutch Reformed Church, etc.) and by 2001 another third (rising from 27 per cent in 1996) with African Independent Churches[9] (AICs). With the addition of Pentecostals and other charismatic churches and 'other Christians', the total claiming to be Christian was 74 per cent in 1996, rising to 80 per cent in 2001. On this basis it looks as if the percentage claiming to be Christian rose at a higher rate (19%) than did the increase in population (10%), but the two censuses are not strictly comparable.[10] It is probably safer to say that the Christian share of the population held its own as the vast majority with perhaps modest growth and some redistribution away from mainstream denominations towards AICs, and Pentecostal/charismatic churches; the latter grew fastest of all from a modest base of 2 million in 1996 to 3.4 million in 2001. The main non-Christian religions maintained their tiny shares virtually without change between the two censuses. In 2001, Judaism was professed by 0.2 per cent; Islam by 1.5 per cent and Hinduism by 1.2 per cent. Twenty-five per cent of Indian South Africans that identified with a religion were Christians.

## Christianity in South Africa: Forms and legacies

The diversity of Christianity's forms in South Africa today is reflected in the mixed historical legacy of religion in the country. The overall effect is less that of Christianity shaping a homogeneous people, more that of the religion itself taking on its various forms from the experiences and needs of those that professed them. In this way the Dutch Reformed Churches were as integral to Afrikaner nation- and state-building as the Roman Catholic Church was to Irish and Polish nationalism. These churches, especially the majority NGK (Nederduitse Gereformeerde Kerk) gave theological justification for apartheid and were an essential part of the organizational spine of Afrikaner nationalism, a legacy it is still struggling to resolve. African peoples' experience of dispossession, repression and exploitation found expression in a variety of Christian ways which gave consolation, but more importantly support for non-racialism, Black Consciousness and resistance. AICs provided space for authentic African leadership and initiative but the example was at best an ambiguous one; this may have been 'freedom' of a kind but only within an overall imposed racial order. Mainstream denominations (other than the Dutch Reformed Churches) with their substantial white congregations made 'Periodic affirmations of dissent' (Davenport 1987: 561) during the apartheid years. Formal dissent rather than direct protest, never mind resistance, remained the corporate response of the mainstream churches, though they became more active and critical during the 1980s as the struggle intensified and the implications of the fact that the majority of Christians were black began to dawn on them. Even in the NGK, Coloured and African believers were in a majority, though they were organized in two separate 'mission' churches, the Dutch Reformed Mission Church (DRMC: Coloured) and the Dutch Reformed Church in Africa (DRCA: African). Not the least of these implications was the rise of black clergymen to national leadership positions, the most notable of course being the charismatic Anglican Archbishop Desmond Tutu, who was fiercely committed to ending apartheid (but equally fiercely independent) and who became a potent symbol of resistance.

The ANC itself had a pragmatic relationship with religion. Several prominent Ethiopian (AIC) church leaders were involved in the formation of the ANC in 1912 (Anderson 2001: 59) and the connection was never lost; there was always representation of the devout and even the ordained in the membership. However, the close relationship that developed between the ANC and the South African Communist Party (SACP) from the 1950s, the armed struggle and in the 1980s the call for sanctions against South Africa all compromised the ANC in the eyes of many Christians, a rift which Buthelezi tried to exploit. The liberation movement's conscious strategy of broadening the struggle into a united front against apartheid in the 1980s went some way to ease these contradictions as did the ANC's conversion to rights-based constitutionalism and the rule of law.

Despite this mixed legacy, the shadow of apartheid has not obtruded greatly on religion and the churches in post-apartheid South Africa. The stance of the churches during the apartheid years may have been morally and politically flawed (and in the case of the NGK mortally compromised) but many individual clergymen and believers went much further than their churches in opposition to apartheid, and Christian principles provided the motivation for many of the small minority of whites who became active resisters. Those in the individual churches who may have chafed at corporate conservatism found other outlets for activism: 'A high degree of unity of purpose was forged between the churches, coalescing most visibly in the work and witness of the South African Council of Churches but also in many other local ecumenical and fraternal networks and organizations' (De Gruchy 2005: 283). For the rest, corporate apology was an option. The Anglican Church made a submission to the TRC which acknowledged that 'there were occasions when, through the silence of its leadership or its parishes, or their actions in acquiescing with apartheid laws where they believed it to be in the interests of the church, deep wrong was done to those who bore the onslaught of apartheid' (SAPA 1997). The submission also acknowledged that: 'This moral lethargy has been bolstered in part by the fact that the church had, over the years, developed its own pattern of racial inequality and discrimination.' As we have already noted, the apology was even extended to 'the Afrikaner community' to whom white Anglicans had extended an 'attitude of moral superiority' (ibid.).

However, it has not yet proved possible to resolve all the outstanding business of the apartheid years. Unity has not yet been achieved between the formerly white NGK and its Coloured and African counterparts, the two 'mission' churches, which united to form the Uniting Reformed Church in Southern Africa (URCSA) in 1994. The churches are not segregated of course, but until the NGK adopts as a statement of fundamental belief the Belhar Confession (adopted by the DRMC and DRCA in 1986) which rejects 'forced separation on grounds of race' and stigmatizes any grounds used to justify it as 'ideology and false doctrine' without theological validity, the URCSA will not contemplate unity. At its General Assembly in 2011, the NGK undertook to begin a process of negotiating acceptance of the Belhar Confession with its constituent churches.

Although AICs account for 32 per cent of South African Christians and one of their number, the Zion Christian Church (ZCC), is the largest single denomination in the country (4.97 million members in 2001), they occupy a much less central position in society than their mainstream counterparts. They are much less forthright on social and political issues and indeed on this score they could be reasonably described as somewhat enigmatic. In the apartheid years the conventional wisdom was that they were socially conservative and preached acquiescence to the civil power, irrespective of its unjust basis. Much was made at the time (1985) of the ZCC's invitation to the then president P. W. Botha to the church's seventy-fifth anniversary celebrations. Anti-apartheid activists were shocked and angry at Botha addressing an African crowd of an estimated 2 million people who applauded him frequently and warmly. However, the ZCC's preference for prayer rather than activism rested on a rejection of violence rather than acceptance of white supremacy and, as Anderson points out, as soon as they were able to do so openly, ZCC members joined African nationalist movements and parties in large numbers. One year after the unbanning of the ANC, 42 per cent of ZCC members were members of the ANC and a majority were members of one or another nationalist group (Anderson 2001: 106). The sheer size of the respective shares held by the ANC and the AICs of the allegiance of South Africa's African majority make it clear that there is very substantial overlap. A more recent study claims a sociopolitical role for AICs, arguing that: 'local religious communities vitally sustain broadly-held popular expectations of obtaining the as yet unrealized benefits of social justice and full citizenship that were the promise of the liberation struggle' (Bompani 2008: 665). Although it is based on a study of only five AICs in one suburb of Soweto, this claim makes intuitive sense, since under contemporary South African conditions it would be hard for any church to confine its offerings exclusively to the spiritual world and to ignore its members' material circumstances and worldly aspirations. However it is worth noting how decentralized the world of the AICs is. Although the ZCC was the biggest single denomination in 2001 with 11 per cent of the population, this was only a little over one-third of the AIC's 31.8 per cent share. StatsSA's Summary Code List for religion in the 2001 census contained over 4,500 names of individual AICs (De Gruchy 2005: 245). This suggests that a large part of whatever supportive role is played by AICs in social cohesion and nation-building, it is highly localized, fragmented and in terms of public profile and links to mainstream socio-political currents, effectively underground.

## Religion and values

High figures for religious affiliation do not necessarily tell us a great deal about societal values and their relationship to nation-building. This is true even when one religion is as dominant as Christianity is in South Africa. It is not easy to generalize because there are liberal and conservative, cosmopolitan, African traditional and fundamentalist versions of Christian beliefs and values. However, in South Africa, the evidence of social attitude surveys reliably associates South African Christians not only with high degrees of religiosity but with conservative and traditional versions of Christian belief and with conservative social attitudes (Rule and Mncwango 2006: 252–76). The 2004 round of the SASAS[11] reported that 51 per cent of South Africans claimed to attend regular church services (excluding weddings and funerals) every week and

**TABLE 6.1** South Africans' doctrinal beliefs

| Question | Response |
| --- | --- |
| I know God really exists and I have no doubt about it | 74% 'yes' |
| Praying a lot is a waste of time | 89% disagree |
| When we die we all go either to heaven or hell | 64% agree |
| Jesus is the solution to all the world's problems | 77% agree |
| The bible is the actual word of God, literally word for word | 64% agree |

Source: Human Sciences Research Council (HSRC) South African Social Attitudes Survey (SASAS 2004) reported in Rule and Mncwango 2010: 189–90.

another 25 per cent at least once a month (Rule and Mncwango 2010: 189–90). Since respondents to survey questions like this may overreport in order to conform to perceived social norms, it is possible that these figures do not reflect people's behaviour with strict accuracy. However, at the very least they indicate a high degree of social desirability attached to regular religious observance. In addition, most South Africans hold highly orthodox doctrinal beliefs (see Table 6.1).

These highly conservative and traditional theological convictions are linked to strongly conservative social attitudes on social and human rights issues like abortion ('right to life'), sexual orientation and capital punishment; there are strong majorities for conservative positions on all of these social issues. For instance, the 2003 round of the SASAS reported that 78 per cent of respondents thought that 'it is always wrong for two adults of the same sex to have sexual relations' (Rule and Mncwango 2006: 260). In some respects this may not be entirely surprising, given that same-sex sexual relations are illegal in more than half of African countries. However, this widespread rejection is only partly linked to questions of Africanness. In a 1995 HSRC study only 35 per cent of respondents agreed that homosexuality was 'Un-African' and a higher proportion of whites than Africans disapproved of same-sex sexual relations (ibid. 256).

In many countries there is a degree of disconnect between elite-driven values on social issues which are enshrined in legislation on the one hand, and popular beliefs on these issues on the other. In South Africa there appears to be a particularly wide distance between a secular state which expresses the most progressive positions on individual rights to choice on social issues, as well as the right to be free from discrimination on a very wide range of generously defined grounds, and a citizen population which exhibits a high degree of religiosity of a particularly orthodox and conservative kind, linked to highly conservative social attitudes. These attitudes if given expression in law would negate many of the rights currently protected in the Constitution. It is one of the many paradoxes of South Africa's passage from racial authoritarianism to democracy that the Constitution which enshrines this transition should be internationally hailed as one of the most progressive in the world, while its citizenry rates at or near the top of several international league tables of conservative religious belief and social attitudes (ibid. 252–74). The fact that the Constitution is so squarely at odds with the most fundamental values and beliefs of the electorate should have profound consequences for nation-building. This is especially so, since in the absence of ethnic solidarity or any other form of non-voluntary kinship, commonly shared historical experience, egalitarian traditions or a convenient 'other' to assist in national self-definition, the Constitution and its values loom large in the hopes of nation-building. Perhaps the greatest irony of all is that in a country where racial divisions are widely perceived to be an enduring obstacle to nation-building, the only things which reliably and verifiably transcend the boundaries of race are the fundamentalist Christian doctrine and conservative – even authoritarian – social attitudes that flatly contradict the country's national, statutory value system on which elite hopes of nation-building are pinned. In short the most significant thing that black and white people appear to have in common is rejection of many of the values which are supposed to bind them and which doubtless appear to many of them as the product of a liberal coup during the negotiation process.

In some accounts this leads to a kind of population-wide cognitive dissonance:

> In most instances, citizens are confronted with a set of human rights entitling them and their fellow countrymen and women to engage in practices that are contrary to their upbringing, socialization or religious beliefs. They will continue to hear specific values propagated within the context of their religious meetings and teachings that criticise these practices and values, and will be faced with regular dilemmas about whether to follow their beliefs and consciences or whether to abandon these in favour of the state's enshrined Constitutional values. (Ibid. 273)

This appears to be somewhat exaggerated; after all the Constitution does not require citizens to avail themselves of all the rights it recognizes. What is required for the most part is inaction in the form of tolerance, although some conservative believers might chafe at the legal requirements that enforce tolerance. Chief among these is restriction of free speech on the grounds of prohibiting 'hate speech', a somewhat ill-defined category of discourse invoked by the Constitution itself and an Equality Act which has equality courts to uphold it, the Promotion of Equality and Prevention of Unfair Discrimination Act, no. 4 of 2000. Exaggerated or not, any dissonance effect caused by disparity between constitutional and popular values is more complex than it might at first appear. This is suggested by the absence of any strong and sustained attempt to close the gap from below. There is a political party which attempts to do this. The African Christian Democratic Party (ACDP) exists to uphold and promote the conservative values that are apparently held by substantial majorities of the population. Its 2009 general election manifesto included promises to amend 'liberal and humanistic' policies and legislation in the interests of moral regeneration with specific reference to pornography, access to contraception and abortion on demand, and also made promises to restore corporal punishment in schools and capital punishment for specified categories of murder. Despite the overwhelming preponderance of Christianity as the religion of national conviction and the widely shared conservative views on social issues, the ACDP's best performance in the four general elections since 1994 has been the 1.6 per cent it polled in 2004 (7 seats out of 400 in the National Assembly), from which it declined again to 0.81 per cent in 2009 (3 seats).

## The polity and shared experience of citizenship

In considering whether South Africans have a shared way of life that encourages nation-building, a key area to examine is the polity. At issue is whether the ways in which South Africans practise and experience citizenship have qualities conducive to developing and sustaining civic nationalism; that is, to developing a form of metaphorical kinship based not upon ascribed characteristics such as race, ethnicity or language, but on freely chosen attachment to a shared set of political ideas and practices. The absence of ascribed attributes that could credibly bond the whole population makes it clear why civic nationalism should be so central to nation-building in South Africa, and why it should have been the essential element in the improvised nation which saw the country through the negotiated transition. There is also a pervasive, circular logic which underlies much political discourse in South Africa along the lines: 'South Africa is a nation because it is democratic and it is democratic because it is a nation.' The implication (which is in fact sometimes clearly stated) is that if it ceases to be democratic, the nation will be exposed as fraudulent, and if the nation does not cohere sustainably, then democracy itself will be unsustainable. Historians and theorists of nationalism differ on whether or not there is a necessary connection between nation and democracy, but in South Africa it is a given of mainstream discourse that the two are mutually dependent.

Ways in which citizenship can be experienced and practised which might be evaluated in terms of the relationship between democracy and nation include the following: identification with and interpretation of the state's fundamental legitimizing ideas; the exercise of rights, especially that of voting; engagement with the state through public services; identification with the state's symbols; and discharge of citizen duties.

## The Constitution and shared citizenship

Two key principles of South Africa's constitutional order are rights and justiciability. As one recent study admits: 'The extent to which the Constitution has become part of people's lives is difficult to measure in any quantifiable way', but it then goes on to claim that there is 'growing awareness of constitutional rights in South Africa, an increased activism in bringing cases to the court and the entrenchment of the Court as an institution in our democracy' (Segal and Cort 2012: 228–9). This view is based partly on the fact that in its foundation year there were 26 applications to the Constitutional Court and in 2010 there were 118, and partly on judgements of the Court that required the government to progressively realize the socio-economic rights in the Constitution (ibid.). This is certainly a legitimate interpretation, but as we shall see there are those, mainly in and around the ruling party, who believe the opposite: that such activism is a sign of weakness, not of strength in South African democracy.

We have already noted that the Constitution's broad and generous recognition of rights is in some respects in advance of more conservative public attitudes. It is all the more important then that public views on justiciability and the rule of law are taken into account in any assessment of shared citizenship. In 2010, one such survey-based assessment recorded that 59 per cent of South Africans agreed that 'the rulings of South African courts should be consistent with the Constitution even if they go against the will of citizens' (IJR 2010: 6). At the same time, 49 per cent *disagreed* that 'it is sometimes better to ignore the law and solve problems immediately rather than wait for a legal solution', and 59 per cent *disagreed* that it is not necessary to follow the laws of a government that they did not vote for. These findings support constitutional order and the rule of law, but not without some equivocation and they hardly amount to a ringing endorsement.

Another survey tested levels of confidence in various state institutions among an 'elite' sample and a 'public' sample of the population (Kotzé and Steenekamp 2009).[12] This could be viewed as a useful proxy for sharing founding values and experience of citizenship. In the elite sample, 88.4 per cent expressed confidence in the Constitutional Court compared to 66 per cent in the public sample (ibid. 105). This is a considerable difference, but even the lower figure suggests widely shared values. However, the same source also reported major differences in the confidence levels expressed by the four officially recognized race groups in a group of key state institutions.[13] A composite confidence index registered 73 per cent for Black Africans, 52 per cent for Coloureds, 38 per cent for Indians and 33 per cent for Whites. Compared to measurements made in 2000, black confidence had levelled out, Indian levels had declined and those for Whites and Coloureds had increased. The most noteworthy result was the increase in white confidence from a very low figure of 22 per cent in 2000 to the still low but substantially higher figure of 33 per cent in 2006 (ibid. 98–104).

The results of these and other surveys suggest that people's attitudes to and understandings of their experience of citizenship fluctuate over time and according to which institution is in focus. However, the main determinant of difference is race: there is a relatively strong sense of shared citizenship and of having a stake in the polity among Black Africans (who constitute 79 per cent of the population) which does not extend to the minorities. This poses difficult problems for state-led efforts at nation-building. Important as it is to try to assess the extent of support for democracy as an element of shared national life through survey evidence of this sort, a degree of caution is essential. An authoritative study of support for democracy in Africa based on 'Afrobarometer' surveys in five African countries, including South Africa, urged caution about assuming depth to expressions of democratic commitment (Bratton et al. 2005: 85–94). These expressions were characterized in the study as 'wide but shallow', and the widespread popular support for democracy which Afrobarometer recorded as 'loose, sometimes contradictory, formative, perhaps temporary'. Unsurprisingly, among the reasons for this caution was the fact that respondents meant different things by democracy, some emphasizing rights and the rule of law and others delivery of material benefits and services.

Certainly there is reason to believe that survey data do not always capture what are quite clear contradictions in the status of constitutional values and institutions in the day-to-day workings of the South African polity. For instance, Kotzé and Steenekamp record a confidence level in the Constitutional Court of 92.7 per cent among declared ANC supporters in their elite sample. Yet, it is from this quarter that the most pointed challenges to the justiciable principle and the performance of the Court are levelled. ANC reservations about the Court are situated in wider suspicions of the judiciary and legal system, located in the more populist elements of its support. Such suspicions range from perceptions of 'racist white judges' to the belief that the legal system has been manipulated in order to pursue factional competition in the ANC. The latter suspicion tends to reside in the minds of those who are losers in such contests. The government recognized this (albeit in somewhat overdelicate and circumlocutory phraseology) in a review of governance issues in 2008: 'Some public ambivalence and debates around some judgments seen as reflecting racial or gender stereotypes, or as having political motivation, have found more vocal expression in the recent period. Particularly when linked to party-political dynamics, such challenges could be beginning to detract from the popular legitimacy of the courts' (Presidency 2008: 47). Among other things the Presidency was probably referring to the populist demonstrations mounted by the ANCYL, trade union federation Cosatu and the SACP in support of Jacob Zuma in his three-year battle with the courts (2006–9) on a rape charge (which resulted in his acquittal), and corruption charges which in the end he did not have to face. These demonstrations and the fiery rhetoric that accompanied them had a definite intimidatory quality to them, and were widely perceived to be a threat to the rule of law. This agitation subsided when Zuma emerged victorious from his contest with the prosecuting authorities and one (white) judge whose ruling was central to the abandonment of the case against Zuma briefly became a populist hero. However, the concerns of Zuma's supporters were immediately replaced by other fears on the part of those who felt that in the case of the corruption charges, due process had in fact been manipulated in Zuma's favour.

Whether in fact the two things are linked or not, this spectre of populist pressure on the rule of law inevitably lurks behind the ANC's increasing expressions of displeasure at what it sees as the undue role of the Constitution and the Constitutional Court in South African politics. Deputy Chief Justice and Constitutional Court judge Dikgang Moseneke summarized this displeasure as arising from feelings of grievance at, 'the will of the people frustrated by the supremacy of the Constitution'. The result, in this perception, is that the government has a large majority that yields only empty executive and legislative power and is frustrated by constitutional restraints in its goals of delivering social equity. The origin of this grievance is the belief that 'the Constitution is an awful bargain shaped by inapt concessions during the negotiations in 1993' (Moseneke 2011: 2). In the robust defence of constitutional supremacy which follows his summary of ANC discontents, Moseneke makes it clear that he is responding to ANC Secretary-General Gwede Mantashe (ibid. 13–14). In an interview given to the *Sowetan* newspaper (August 2011) Mantashe accused Constitutional Court judges of being politically partial and hostile to the ANC, of being willing to be 'used' by NGOs and opposition parties as an instrument of opposition, of being counter-revolutionary and blocking transformation.

Mantashe, in common with all other senior ANC leaders who pronounce on such matters, deplores the infringement of what they feel is the ANC's legitimate autonomy to govern by the misuse of the Constitution. We have already noted in the discussion of shared associational life that the ANC government believes itself to be the target of attack by misguided progressives from one direction and unscrupulous reactionaries from another, both using the Constitution as a weapon. At the same time, conscious of the high stakes involved, the ANC affirms its commitment to the Constitution and the integrity of the Constitutional Court. Proposed measures which have caused consternation in the judiciary, civil society and the parliamentary opposition are defended by ANC ministers as necessary innovations for the better working of the legal system. These include the Superior Courts Bill, passed by the National Assembly in late 2012 after five years of controversy and reworking, and a proposed review of Constitutional Court decisions to determine their effect on transformation (ongoing in 2013). In these and in other cases involving matters of constitutional principle, the government has been mindful of opposition to its original plans and has adjusted them in this light. For some ANC leaders these adjustments will have been grudging concessions extorted by their natural enemies; for others no doubt they represent a willing return to constitutional rectitude. The ANC Alliance is so ideologically amorphous that it would be difficult to assess the balance between these two positions in the internal dynamics of the organization.

Inevitably it is difficult to assess how far identification with the foundational values of the new South Africa provides a shared basis for civic nationalism. In the first place, an authoritative empirical audit of who believes what is difficult to produce. In addition, the overall meaning and purpose of constitutional democracy can be interpreted in quite different ways: to limit the power of government or to set standards of material provision and access to which the government of the day can be held. These are not necessarily incompatible; there is a good case for saying that a well-rounded democracy will harmoniously combine the two. However, this is not easy to achieve, especially in a country with as divided a legacy as South Africa. When contending political actors choose to mobilize exclusively behind one or other of these interpretations, with the government caught in the middle, then the overall balance of just what is being shared in attachment to the Constitution is placed in doubt. An additional danger can be glimpsed when the government seizes on the Constitution as a scapegoat for failings of performance that might have quite other causes. Mantashe's complaints and Moseneke's response afford us such a glimpse.

Overall, South Africa has survived tensions caused by conflicting interpretations of the Constitution quite well. This has certainly had something to do with a principled attachment to shared values, but it is difficult to say how much. Possibly it has more to do with a realistic appraisal on the part of constitutional sceptics in the ANC Alliance of the costs – inside as well as outside the Alliance – of departing too much from the constitutional settlement. Whether or not this will be enough to sustain democracy in its present form and foster civic nationalism is equally difficult to tell and may depend on generational factors. A generation – some would say a golden generation – of activists, many with legal backgrounds, who fought the liberation struggle as much if not more as secular democrats than as African nationalists, is entering the twilight of its political influence within the ANC Alliance. Much will depend on whether this generation is replaced by another which was born politically, if not literally, into the values of the constitutional settlement. In the meantime, that settlement survives as the medium through which to manage South Africa's legacy of divisions and the post-1994 transmutations of them: this is no small achievement. However for many, perhaps most, South Africans the divisions of race and class are an integral part of attitudes to and interpretations of the Constitution: these attitudes and interpretations remain to a large extent instrumental rather than transcendent.

## Voting and shared citizenship

Arguably the liberation struggle in South Africa was above all a struggle for the vote. It is likely that many of its veterans would agree with Dikgang Moseneke: 'When I was a young activist, bent on destroying the monster of apartheid, we shouted many demands. However I can't recall a demand of the struggle that resonated with my revolutionary zeal more than "one person, one vote". It was and remains a primal demand for that essential element of democracy that effect must be given to the will of the majority' (2011: 3). One of the defining images of the late twentieth century is of long queues of black and white South Africans waiting patiently together to vote in the country's first democratic election in April 1994. Since that day South Africa has successfully held four national and provincial elections and the defining image of the first one resonates in the national self-consciousness. South Africans of all colours are quick to express responsibility for and pride in a reputation for exercising this democratic right and to share memories of the first time they availed themselves of it. On the whole this is justified, but the reality is a little more complex that the triumphalist imagery: 'Broadly, percentages for voter registration and voter turnout reveal that South Africa has witnessed a general decline in electoral participation in terms of both these criteria' (Schulz-Herzenberg 2009: 24). While the number of registered voters increased between 1994 and 2009, this did not keep place with the growth in the voting age population (VAP) which went up by 7 million people. The turnout of registered voters in 2009 was a respectable 77.3 per cent, but this was a decline from 89.3 per cent in 1999 (there was no registration in 1994), and turnout of the VAP slumped from an estimated 86 per cent in 1994 to 59.8 per cent in 2009 (ibid. 25).

South Africa's registration figures are not high in comparative perspective. A 2009 study of registration rates in seventeen countries (Rosenberg and Chen 2009) had Argentina at 100 per cent and all but three of the rest in the 90s (including Mexico, Peru and Indonesia). The three lowest were South Africa (77%), the Bahamas (75%) and the United States with 68 per cent (ibid. 3). This is not necessarily an authoritative measure of citizen interest in participating since much depends on whether governments take an active part in registering voters or leave it entirely to citizen initiative as in the United States. Rosenberg and Chen regard South Africa as a hybrid of these approaches: citizen initiative is the basic approach, but as elections approach thousands of temporary workers are taken on by the Independent Electoral Commission (IEC) to encourage and facilitate registration and 16-year-olds are encouraged to pre-register (ibid. 30–1). In the end it is difficult to apportion responsibility for comparatively low and/or falling registration figures between procedural arrangements and voter disengagement. However, it can be reasonably said that despite a national self-image of 'vibrant democracy' (which is carefully fostered by government communication), South Africa's groundwork for electoral participation is unremarkable at best and at worst unimpressive.

This respectable but undistinguished pattern of participation neither strengthens nor particularly weakens South Africa's claims to be a civic nation. However, arguably it is not the quantity but the quality of participation that is important in this context. From the very beginnings of South African democracy a persistent concern has been that what voters have been doing while exercising their democratic rights has not been asserting membership of a civic nation but affirming their racial identities. The main source of this concern has been the nature of the ANC's electoral majority.

In the first place there is the size and durability of the majority. The ANC has won all four elections since 1994: its largest percentage of the vote was 69.7 (2004) and its smallest was 62.6 (1994); it currently stands at the 65.9 which the ANC achieved in 2009 (Schulz-Herzenberg 2009: 23). Secondly, there is its racial composition. Between 1994 and 2004, the ANC attracted the votes of over 80 per cent of Africans who cast their votes; in 1994, 2 per cent of whites voted ANC, in 1999, 5 per cent and in 2004 less than 1 per cent (Ferree 2010: 6).[14] Thirdly, the ANC and the movements with which it is in alliance cover a very broad, ideological range, well beyond any predictable coincidence of interests of identifiable socio-economic groups. Fourthly, it is clear that many Africans vote for the ANC while at the same time being profoundly dissatisfied with the party's performance in government. Rather than vote for any alternative party, however, they express their disaffection in direct-action protest which is often violent and invariably takes place in areas with very large ANC electoral majorities. All of this implies that there is some binding force in the ANC's majority which transcends interest-based choice and hardens allegiance to the point that transfer is unthinkable. An obvious candidate to be this binding force is ethnic or racial identity.

Suspicion that this might be the case is broadened and strengthened by the voting choices of whites: in 1994, 90 per cent of votes cast by whites were for parties that had their origin in the pre-democracy polity; by 1999 this had gone down to 81 per cent and in 2004 it reduced further to a still substantial 74 per cent (ibid.). These figures seem to suggest that the coming of democracy may have created equal voting rights, but a shared electoral space shaped by civic identity has not developed and voting choice is cast in a racial mould: 'Voters line up with their racial groups, seemingly without thought to issues, performance, or any of the other politics-as-usual factors that drive elections in other countries. Indeed elections look so deeply racial that one wonders if politics has anything to do with it at all' (Ferree 2010: 1).

This outcome, commonly labelled 'ethnic census', was widely anticipated before 1994. Indeed the prediction was a key element in the NP's unsuccessful bargaining position in favour of some form of power-sharing, consociational arrangement. American political scientist Donald Horowitz warned that permanent majorities based on demographic weight would deny the essential character of democracy, that of 'rule by temporary majorities', and that black majority rule in South Africa would mean white exclusion (1991: 96). Writing of the 1994 election, Giliomee and Simkins were in no doubt what the outcome represented: 'The system that was negotiated produced the "ethnic census" which Horowitz anticipated and with that a permanent black majority and a permanent white exclusion from political power' (Giliomee and Simkins 1999: 40). The designation of ethnic (or racial) census, though not necessarily the 'white exclusion' inference derived by Horowitz and others from it, had been earlier adopted by other accounts of the 1994 election, albeit with modifying and cautionary notes (Johnson 1996: 145–6).

The interpretation proved controversial, both academically and politically. For some it was a slight on the ANC which, at that time was particularly keen to emphasize its commitment to non-racialism, and a slur on black people which implied that they were incapable of 'ordinary' rational voter choice. This political outrage tended to ignore the fact that the ethnic census interpretation applied to white people and parties too. For others the 'white exclusion' interpretation carried with it unjustifiable hints of undemocratic practices and even echoes of statutory discrimination. In any case it seemed to assume, equally unjustifiably, that the only way whites could meaningfully participate in the new democracy was as 'whites'. In general, those who deployed the ethnic census interpretation were accused of being incapable of explaining the politics of the new democracy in anything but the categories of the old racial tyranny.

As the racial pattern of voting was apparently confirmed in succeeding elections, fresh objections to interpreting electoral choice in this way were found. Given the demographic weight of Africans in the population and of the ANC politically, discussion tended to focus on them rather than on whites. The diversity of the African population is invoked, along with the fact that Africans tend to put race rather low on the list of available identities presented by attitude surveys. The affirmative action and BEE policies that were elaborated during the Mbeki presidency favoured all Africans, in principle at least. In practice, BEE was skewed towards an insider elite and affirmative action mostly favoured the educated and the skilled. However, in the same way as the American Dream inspires many more people than those who are able meaningfully to live it, these redress policies could give perfectly rational reasons for Africans to choose the ANC. In any case, the broad social welfare programmes that accelerated after 2000 could find favour not only with those who depended on them but also those who did not, on grounds of solidarity with the poor, irrespective of ethnic or racial considerations. It is true that the opposition DA has not neglected social welfare. In fact, like Cosatu, it has favoured a universal social payment (the Basic Income Grant or BIG). However, the DA's reservations about redress policies such as affirmative action would more than cancel this out. It might be objected nevertheless that there have been manifold failures of policy execution by the ANC government which should have invited punishment at the polls. However, the social welfare system has on the whole been well managed and those who aspire to benefit from redress measures are not always concerned about how well they function in terms of the wider economy and society. In short, there have been reasons for Africans to vote for the ANC because they are poor and/or aspirational, reasons that are linked to racial identity only in secular, causal terms with past disabilities and discriminations and not necessarily with emotional ties of ethno-racial kinship. As one summary of the debate put it, a 'growing consensus' was emerging that the 'broad correlation' of race and party support was owed 'to the experience of apartheid that structured individual interests' (Davis 2003: 4).

From about 2002 there has been a change of emphasis in explaining electoral behaviour. There has been a tendency to accept the durability of apparent racial patterns in voting, but to place responsibility for their perpetuation on parties rather than voters themselves. Based on a 2001 survey by the HSRC of identity choices, which found that only 11 per cent of respondents defined themselves primarily in racial terms, Habib concluded that the electorate was more enlightened on race than political parties, and that the 'citizenry' held out greater hope for the consolidation of democracy than the elites who obstructed it. This was because party leaders of both the DA and ANC too often played 'the race card', campaigns tended to be governed by 'simplistic racial assumptions' and 'the national surveys of public opinion suggest that their campaigns are at odds with the prevailing identities among the populace' (Habib 2002: 5). This may be true, but if so, the dissonance did not do the ANC much harm. Habib was writing midway between the elections of 1999, in which the ANC raised its share from 62.6 (1994) to 66.4 per cent of the votes, and 2004, in which it raised its share again to an all-time high of 69.7 per cent. Writing in 2003, Davis confirmed Habib's verdict on parties and campaigns: 'strongly influenced by racial considerations', 'strategize in terms of racial arithmetic', but without the Pollyanna-ish assumptions about the wisdom of 'the citizenry' who, 'remain susceptible to racial rhetoric' (4–28). The most fully worked exposition of the identity problem in South African voting is that of Ferree. In her interpretation the ANC's large and durable majority is a function not of racial identity but of a ruthless political strategy to discredit and delegitimize the opposition:

> Race and identity are therefore red herrings: an exclusive focus on them ignores the hard political work underlying the racial-census outcome in South African elections. What seems organic, a natural expression of a pervasively held social identity, is in fact *politically engineered*, the end result of a negative framing strategy employed by the ruling party to neutralize its competition. (Ferree 2010: 2, emphasis in original)

As Ferree points out however, a key part of discrediting and delegitimizing the opposition is to 'keep it white', and so racial identity retains its leverage in electoral terms, even if it is in indirect ways. Even the most casual observer of South African politics is aware of the relentless barrage of racially inflected abuse directed by the ANC at the DA. This has increased in direct proportion to the opposition party's strenuous efforts to diversify its leadership and profile, and its success in winning elections in the city of Cape Town and the Western Cape Province. Whatever attitude surveys say about the low priority given to race in primary identity choice, there seems to be ample evidence that political parties resort to racial electoral strategies both of the overt and more often subliminal 'dog whistle' types. This in turn suggests that whatever else the successful holding of free elections tells about post-apartheid South Africa, it does not point unequivocally to the emergence of a civic nation.

## Citizenship and public services

The values and goals of the South African Constitution and the policies through which ANC governments since 1994 have tried to realize them, presuppose a strong role for the state and government. This vision bears a strong resemblance to the 'social' state in post-1945 Europe (Judt 2005: 77), at least in aspirational terms. Indeed the South African version sets out in even broader and more constitutionally explicit terms than its European counterparts, the government's responsibility for the well-being and improvement of the condition of its people by providing 'the institutions and services for a well-regulated, safe and prosperous land' (ibid.). It is not only the purposes of justice and fairness that are to be served in this way but, as in post-1945 Europe, for the state to be 'a vital source of community and social cohesion' (ibid.). By facilitating universal access to high-quality social services, notably health and education, the ends of fraternity, solidarity and common identity through ongoing social contact are served, all of them contributing to civic nationhood. The most obvious examples of these services are health and education, although in some specific instances – the United Kingdom is the best – public broadcasting has an overt nation-building purpose.

It is important to note that this is not a universal phenomenon and it is not essential to nation-building: for instance, the premises of successful, civic nation-building in the United States are quite different. The problems of sustaining the European social state are also well known, but this is the model that South Africans have chosen. As we shall see, its problems in its home setting notwithstanding, its influence is intensifying rather than slackening in South African government policy making. However, the lives of South Africans today are very far indeed from the ideal of shared citizen access to high-quality services. This verdict applies across the board, but the best examples again are education and health. The discussion of inequality earlier in this book makes it plain that there are two educational systems and two systems of health provision, and life chances depend very much on which of each an individual finds him or herself in. A citizen's experiences are shaped greatly by race and income, but geographical location plays a large part too. Even for those wholly dependent on state provision, experiences can vary greatly depending on the province and urban or rural location.

## Taxation and shared citizenship

Democratic governments frequently legitimize themselves with reference to a hypothetical social contract. A key, practical element of this is redistributive taxation. For instance, the connection between tax and the responsibilities of shared citizenship has been explicitly emphasized by South Africa's finance minster, Pravin Gordhan: 'Let me therefore applaud the many millions of our country's taxpayers who respect their side of the social contract which has allowed us to continue our vital social and infrastructure investment without over-burdening ourselves and future generations with unmanageable levels of debt' (*Mail & Guardian* 29 October 2010). One of the notable governance achievements of the democratic era in South Africa has been to expand greatly the scope and level of government expenditure without dramatically increasing the percentage of GDP in government tax revenue.[15] The ANC inherited a fiscal dispensation in which both personal and corporate taxes were high by international standards, and they did not wish to penalize their own supporters by raising the regressive VAT: 'Instead, the new government decided to focus on improving the performance of the revenue collection machinery under the existing tax dispensation' (Hirsch 2005: 74). The South African Revenue Service (SARS) has done this with such success that it has been a model of how to combine transformation with efficiency. Along with the National Treasury, it remains virtually the only large-scale, corporate success story in the history of South African government and public service since 1994.

However grudgingly citizens pay taxes, a fiscal regime that combines efficiency with integrity can strengthen the social contract; only those who are unreachable by citizen consciousness anyway and, in particular, deaf to South Africa's need to redistribute are likely to deny this. Such things are very difficult to assess, but it is probably fair to say that Gordhan was not whistling in the dark when he spoke of a social contract around taxation. Despite this, the social contract which Gordhan was celebrating is narrowly based, and noticeably skewed, characteristics which limit its contribution to shared citizenship and nation-building.

In the first place, the poor and in many cases deteriorating quality of public services funded by taxation undermines the prospects of the kind of burgeoning social contract that Gordhan had in mind. Middle-class taxpayers are conscious of paying for services in education and health that they do not trust and have to supplement with extra payments such as voluntary extra fees in education, and out-of-pocket payments in health, or resort to full-blown private provision in education and medical insurance. The enormous growth in the private security industry sine 1994 is a measure of the distrust in the police and criminal justice system, and a further instance of taxpayers paying twice to be served.

Secondly, the numerical balance between beneficiaries of social welfare grants and taxpayers is heavily skewed. South Africa has a well-developed system of non-contributory child support, disability and (means-tested) old-age pension grants. The individual payments are for small sums, but their cumulative cost is high. By the end of 2012–13, nearly 16.1 million people out of a population of just 50 million were beneficiaries of grants of one sort or another. This was up from 2.5 million in 1998 and the number is expected to rise to 17.3 million in 2015–16. More than half of all households benefit from social assistance and for 22 per cent of households this is their main source of income. In 2011–12 this cost 3.4 per cent of GDP and accounted for nearly 10 per cent of government expenditure (National Treasury 2013: 84–7).

Virtually all South Africans are taxpayers thanks to VAT which accounts for 34 per cent of government tax revenue. Corporate taxes account for 19 per cent, but it is the 34 per cent collected as personal income tax which is problematic in terms of the social contract. In 2008, 5.2 million people were registered to pay income tax. In that year SARS required employers to register their employees for tax irrespective of how much they earned. As a result 13.7 million people are now registered for the purposes of income tax. However, it would be disingenuous to claim that these are 'taxpayers'. This could not be the case when 60 per cent of South Africa's workers earn below the tax threshold. In fact, the Solidarity trade union has claimed, based on an analysis of SARS' 2011–12 data, that the burden of income tax, 34 per cent of all government tax revenue, is borne by a very small number of people. In 2011–12, 'only 4.6 million actually filed personal income tax returns and paid tax. Of these 4.6 million, a further 1.3 million (those earning R10–R90,000 a year) contributed only one per cent of the total income tax take. That leaves 3.3 million taxpayers who were responsible for 99 per cent of all personal income tax revenue on 2011–12' (*Financial Mail* 11 March 2013).

One obvious reason for this state of affairs is South Africa's high rate of unemployment. However, the brute fact of unemployment has tended to obscure the problem of the 'working poor'. South Africa's median wage rate of R3,000[16] a month is low, given the cost of living and high dependency rates (*Financial Mail* 4 October 2012). In the face of these figures and given the fragile economic prospects of many working people, hopes of strengthening the social contract by broadening the base of taxation appear slim.

There are very strong moral, political and historical reasons to support South Africa's social welfare system, which has contributed very substantially to whatever gains have been made in poverty reduction in recent years. However the sheer size of the system, the disparity in number between those who benefit from it and those who disproportionately pay for it, as well as the fact that the old age pension[17] and child support are not universal, all tend to make the experience of social security a divided rather than a shared one. All redistributive social security systems are beset by moral hazard and unintended consequences, as well as controversies around issues of dependence, disincentives to work, fraud, and so on. However the peculiarities of the South African system give these debates a particular sharpness which undermines and loosens the social contract.

## Tradition and shared citizenship in democratic South Africa

We have already seen how, when the ANC emerged from exile and banning in 1990, it was confronted with several challenging aspects of actually existing South Africa. One of these was the phenomenon of traditional authorities and leaders in rural South Africa, notably in the Bantustans or 'homelands', the lineal descendants of native reserves, and the proto-independent states which apartheid architects hoped would solve the problems of race relations and legitimize 'white' South Africa. Initially the issue of traditional leadership presented itself in two forms. The first was the competitive and antagonistic form of Buthelezi and the IFP, which the ANC dealt with by a mixture of high-level diplomacy and confrontation on the ground. The second manifestation was in the guise of 'progressive' chiefs who had formed themselves into the Contralesa in 1987, under the auspices of the UDF, usefully adding a traditional element to the ANC's broad-front strategy in the anti-apartheid struggle. The ANC was happy to laud 'progressive' chiefs in the context of fighting white minority rule, but in fact the label was something of a misnomer, certainly in the context of the ANC's modernizing and somewhat metropolitan, recently adopted, human rights culture. In fact, in terms of its atavistic celebration of pre-colonial African culture, its defence of the prerogatives of the traditional leaders who at the time represented this legacy and its claim to be able to bring modernity and development to the rural areas, Contralesa had much more in common with Buthelezi than it cared to admit. However, the 'progressive' chiefs calculated that there was much more to be gained from cooperating with the ANC than by competing with it. It is also likely that they were not attracted by the prospect of an alliance with Buthelezi, who would doubtless at a minimum have demanded precedence and prerogatives of leadership. Conceivably they would also have suspected him of using the general claims of tradition as a means of advancing Zulu ethnic hegemony.

Contralesa successfully lobbied for participation in the CODESA negotiating forum although in the Congress's own account, in which a hint of ancestral expectations of entitlement can be detected, this is the point at which relations with the ANC began to deteriorate: 'Before they were eventually invited to the talks, traditional leaders had to undergo the humiliation of appearing before a committee to justify their call for inclusion in the negotiations on the future of their fatherland' (Contralesa 2012). Thanks to the dual, if contrasting leverage of Contralesa and Buthelezi and in the prevailing atmosphere of celebrating diversity, traditional leaders received substantial recognition in the final Constitution. However, how this recognition was to be institutionally expressed and how the Constitution's understandable stipulation that traditional leadership had to be exercised in ways compatible to the Bill of Rights was to be realized were left to future governments to work out. From the beginning Contralesa was aggrieved at this, complaining that the final Constitution was a substantial dilution of what had been promised to them in the interim version and that: 'Chapter 12, the chapter dealing with the matter of traditional leadership, is often ridiculed by commentators, as the shortest and vaguest in the Constitution. It says virtually nothing about the role and powers of traditional leaders' (ibid.). This assessment is not entirely inaccurate but it naively underestimates the ANC's need to recognize that much of public opinion did not support the prerogatives of chiefs, that the ANC itself was divided and it would be impractical and inappropriate to deliver a full package of institutional architecture and powers under the conditions of constitution-making and without broader public participation. However, the Constitution did invite national legislation to enable traditional leaders to play a role in local government and the administration of justice and for there to be provincial and national houses of traditional leaders. Until such institutional arrangements were made, traditional leaders would carry on administering customary law and other existing duties, and would be paid by the state for doing so.

## Traditional authorities today

In South Africa today there are 11 recognized kingships (Department of Cooperative Governance and Traditional Affairs 2012: 80); estimates of the number of traditional leaders vary but more than 2,000 is a likely figure (Williams 2010: 1). As many as 10,000 people take part in the various local-level councils that support the institution of traditional leadership. Nomenclature in English also varies and sometimes depends on the vagaries of translation from several African languages; titles include kings, chiefs, paramount chiefs, 'senior traditional leader', headman; often African language (especially isiZulu) titles are used in English, *inkosi* (chief), *induna* (headman). Unsurprisingly, given the way white minority governments manipulated traditional authorities by dismissing chiefs who were deemed insufficiently compliant, disputes concerning boundaries, succession and status are endemic to the institution of traditional leadership. According to President Zuma there were 1,244 contested issues of boundaries, succession and status lodged with the Commission on Traditional Leadership Disputes and Claims in January 2011; 139 had been dealt with by late 2012 (Presidency 2012). What the traditional leaders claim in common is the hereditary right to exercise authority and to represent a consensual tradition of decision making in communal African life. This authority is exercised most importantly in the allocation of land, to which there is no individual title in the former homelands, and resolution of disputes under customary law. Another important function is to provide over ancestral rituals: 'the chief's authority is based not only on what he does in the material world but his connection with the supernatural world' (Williams 2010: 8).

It is difficult to estimate how many people live under the authority of traditional leaders. Rural population figures provide an indication, though not an exact one. Current estimates of urbanization suggest that about 38 per cent of South Africa's population lives in the countryside. However, figures are higher for Black Africans, as nearly all whites, Coloureds and Indians live in towns. Based on 2001 census figures, urbanization rates were lowest in Limpopo, Mpumalanga, North West, KwaZulu-Natal and Eastern Cape; these are the provinces where former homelands were situated and traditional leaders are most influential (StatsSA 2006: 23, figure 2). Thanks to high levels of circular migration, 'urban' and 'rural' are fairly fluid concepts in South Africa and numbers of people who are classified as urban in surveys are affected by traditional authorities. The government department responsible for traditional authorities, the Department of Cooperative Governance and Traditional Affairs (Cogta) estimated in 2009 that areas under the control of traditional authority accounted for approximately 20 per cent of the country's land surface and 21 per cent of the population (Cogta 2009: 36). Other estimates are considerably higher. Based on 2001 census data, Williams estimated that 14 million people – 31 per cent of the total population at that time – lived under traditional authorities. Addressing the National House of Traditional Leaders in late 2012, President Zuma said that 18 million people – 36 per cent of the 2012 population – lived, 'within the ambit of the traditional justice system' (Presidency 2012). This suggests that despite continuing migration to cities, the number of people affected by traditional authorities is not declining. Thanks to male preponderance in internal migration to the cities, a clear majority of the people thus affected are women, a fact of some significance given the patriarchal nature of the culture interpreted and administered by a virtually all-male cadre of traditional leaders. A figure of 59 per cent of women in traditional areas appears to be generally accepted (Parliamentary Monitoring Group 24 October 2012).

## Government policy on traditional authorities

The thrust of government policy on traditional authorities is set out in the White Paper on Traditional Leadership and Governance (2003) which establishes a framework of norms and standards, 'in order to support the institution in accordance with Constitutional imperatives and to restore the integrity and legitimacy of the institution in line with African indigenous law and customs subject to the Constitution' (Cogta 2011: 75). A hierarchical suite of institutions has been created in pursuit of these objectives. At grass-roots level there are traditional councils, which are revamped and partly democratized versions of the colonial and apartheid-era tribal authorities; 40 per cent of their members are elected and 30 per cent have to be women. Above the traditional councils are provincial houses of traditional leaders and a national house. The members of these houses are chosen by elected colleges of hereditary leaders from among their own number. Their powers are advisory and ceremonial only.

Despite the creation of this institutional architecture there is no coherent articulation between the new constitutional order and traditional authorities. Through their representative organizations traditional leaders have engaged in a long-running power struggle with the ANC and the government which began with their unsuccessful efforts to have customary law and the right to practise traditional culture exempted from the Bill of Rights, and continues to this day in dogged efforts to defend and extend their prerogatives. The ANC and the government themselves are divided between those who welcome, or are at least prepared to acquiesce in a special dispensation for traditional culture and authorities, and those who are firm on the need for uniform application of rights, justice and accountable administration across the entire national territory.

There are three main areas of dispute: local government, the administration of justice and land tenure. A further point of contention is direct confrontation between certain specific traditional customs and practices – mainly to do with the status of women as brides and widows, for instance – which contradict constitutional rights.

## Traditional authorities and local government

Traditional leaders have claimed right from the beginning of negotiations for a democratic dispensation that they should provide the basic unit of local government. This was met by the ANC's initial determination to impose a uniformly democratic dispensation across the entire territory. Neither side has been able to achieve its maximum goals, and the two are left in uneasy coexistence with no clear roadmap for the future. Traditional councils form part of this compromise along with rights of ex officio membership of rural municipalities for traditional leaders. Despite being enshrined in legislation the relationship between traditional and elected elements of local government is far from clear and it depends to a large extent on local dynamics. The situation is not helped by the chronic weakness, skills deficit and corruption of elected local government structures outside the main metropolitan areas, which strengthens the hand of traditional authorities who are able to exploit such weaknesses.

Such has been the lack of coherence that an assessment of traditional leaders' place in governance commissioned by the Presidency in 2008, 14 years into the post-apartheid period, came to the remarkable conclusion that 'there is still uncertainty as to whether government sees itself as having superior authority over traditional leaders or sees traditional leaders as a parallel governance system' (Sithole 2008: 43). The presidential review of governance to which this paper contributed pondered whether the exercise of traditional power and authority 'reflects the spirit and letter of the Constitution, without the emergence of two classes of citizens; those ruled by democratically elected institutions and those ruled by unelected traditional leaders' (Presidency 2008: 9). The Presidency was still unsure when in late 2011 it produced the NDP: 'confusion emerges when traditional forms of authority are legislated as traditional structures may displace or duplicate the role of the state' (NPC November 2011: 233).

## Land tenure and the administration of justice

Seventeen years after the Constitution was enacted in 1996, the fate of two key pieces of legislation confirms the lack of progress made in harmonizing constitutional and traditional values and structures. The Communal Land Rights Act was passed in 2004 in order to give effect to a constitutional obligation on parliament to legislate secure tenure for people and communities whose landholding was insecure by virtue of past racial discrimination. The Act sought to do this through a suite of tenure possibilities ranging from individual through family and community holders of title through which 'old order' land rights would be converted to 'new order' rights. However the legislation was never implemented thanks to a legal challenge brought by four rural communities affected by it. In 2009 the North Gauteng (Pretoria) High Court declared 15 of its key provisions invalid, and in the following year the Constitutional Court struck it down in its entirety. As it stands, people living in communal title areas remain dependent on traditional leaders for access to land, with women being especially vulnerable to discrimination and abuse.

The expressed aim of the Traditional Courts Bill is also to discharge an obligation under the 1996 Constitution, that of harmonizing customary law with the Bill of Rights. It was introduced to parliament in 2008, withdrawn the same year and reintroduced in 2011. As of 2013 it remains mired in controversy relating to both substance and procedure. This is all the more remarkable since the reform process on the juridical functions of traditional leaders which preceded the bill began as long ago as 1999. By 2003 the government was explaining that one of the reasons the process was delayed was because the first round of consultations had not sufficiently taken into account the views of women. In 2012, nine years later, one of the principal objections which halted the bill's process through parliament was precisely the same: insufficient consultation of women's groups. In the 2012 public hearings on the bill, 57 critical submissions were made by NGOs community groups and trade unions. Tellingly, the government's own Department of Women, Children and People with Disabilities (DWCPD) made a highly critical submission. Among the criticisms were that the bill did not do enough to ensure that women could participate effectively in courts, that it prohibits legal representation in traditional courts and restricts access to justice by denying the rights of persons to opt out of the traditional justice system (Parliamentary Monitoring Group 20 September 2012). The DWCPD submission directly confronted the clash between the Constitution and traditional values: 'in its current form, it perpetuated harmful practices such as *ukungena* (customary practices relating to marriage rites and often involving unprotected sexual intercourse between the widow of a deceased partner and another man – usually a relative of the deceased – chosen by the deceased's family) and *ukuthwala*, or the abduction of potential brides, usually without consent.'

## Witchcraft: Tradition, culture and modernity

Numerous references to witchcraft in the public and committee hearings on the Traditional Courts Bill signal an aspect of South African value and belief systems that may have an important bearing on issues of nation-building. Witchcraft is notoriously difficult to define in a context of widespread belief in the ontological status of the supernatural, and where the borderline between good and harmful deployment of the occult can be difficult to discern. However, a useful working definition of witchcraft as it is perceived in the general population is causing another's illness or death through supernatural means (Ally 2009: 1). It is widely accepted that witchcraft in this sense is a pervasive factor in the lives of many South Africans, attested to by several anthropological studies.

Witchcraft has a variety of destabilizing and debilitating effects for secular nation-building. In the first place it is a motivating factor in killings, usually of elderly women, in which the victims are accused of being witches. It is also the reason for so-called *muthi*[18] (sometimes *muti*) killings in which organs and other body parts, often of children, are harvested for magic potions. Fatalities in both these categories are extremely difficult to quantify; it is generally believed that witchcraft killings are seriously underreported, but the police do not list them in a separate category of murders in annual crime figures. Such killings do appear to be pervasive and persistent, however. Niehaus estimates that there were more than 389 witchcraft-related killing in the Northern Province (now Limpopo) between 1985 and 1995 (2003: 93). In *muthi* killings at Mzamba in the Eastern Cape (2007–8), 'seventeen or eighteen people were killed, including at least one suspect, victim of vigilantes' (Petrus 2009: 106–10). Witchcraft killings are a stubborn part of (mainly) rural life, partly because they do not present a straightforward law and order problem which can be eradicated by devoting enough policing resources to it. In the first place, it is difficult for law and order policies to address witchcraft since the paradigm of state authority on which the maintenance of law and order depends does not recognize the ontological status of the problem. For this reason, citizens cannot obtain police protection from the malign use of the occult. As a result there is a fatal relationship between witchcraft and vigilantism since those who feel themselves threatened by witchcraft have to seek redress through their own resources in all cases other than those where an offence that the state recognizes, such as murder, has taken place. An alternative is to make use of chiefly authority. Although the mandate of chiefs to hear witchcraft cases is uncertain (ibid. 38), it is common for them to do so. This means that the manifestation of authority closest to the problem of witchcraft is often highly compromised. According to several studies cited by Petrus, chiefs are 'traditionally' believed to be the main instigators of *muthi* killings and, 'whether directly or indirectly were often instrumental in using witch killings and muti murders as political weapons to eliminate rivals or legitimate their own authority' (ibid.).

Gauging the extent of witchcraft belief and practice (even defining it) is not easy. Ashforth approaches the problem indirectly by estimating the numbers of traditional healers and AIC *maprofeti* (prophets) who devote at least part of their time to counselling those who believe they are the victims of witches. Based on reports to post-1994 parliamentary select committees, he estimates that around 500,000 people are regularly active in working against 'evil forces'. A significant feature of Ashforth's study is that it was carried out in Soweto (population about 1.3 million), South Africa's largest urban concentration of African people. Most other studies concentrate on rural areas which are often remote and undeveloped. On the basis of his research, Ashforth concludes that spiritual insecurity arising from fear of witchcraft 'informs virtually every aspect of social life and thus impinges on every aspect of politics . . . through changing distributions of social jealousy, the pervasive presence of injustice, the presumption of malice in community life, and habits of interpretation conducive to the distrust of power' (2005: 19).

This set of effects directly confronts some of the values which are vital to the official conception of the citizen nation. In this conception a 'better life for all' (the ANC election slogan since 1994) will be secured through evidence-based policy grounded on confidence in scientific rationality, mediated through planning and executed by a Weberian bureaucracy which manages state-led growth, development and redistribution. The widespread belief that individual fates are determined by malign supernatural forces directed by witches versed in the occult, at the behest of jealous neighbours or colleagues not only undermines rational-bureaucratic and citizenship-based conceptions of the nation but also crucially erodes the horizontal ties of trust and fellowship on which any conception of the nation depends, whether it is ethnic or citizen.

## Tradition and nation-building

The ANC government's attempts to accommodate traditional authority and customary law in the new constitutional dispensation have pleased no-one. Traditional leaders opposed the Traditional Courts Bill and they regard the various councils and assemblies that are supposed to embody their status and give them meaningful roles as merely decorative. Contralesa contemptuously refers to them as 'toy telephones'.[19] On the other hand human rights groups and constitutionalists reject the entrenchment of traditional authorities. Some of them believe they could be made fit for purpose under the rights-based Constitution if they were reformed, especially to accommodate women on equal terms. This would require such changes that it is hard to see what would remain 'traditional' about them. Others simply believe that mixed, hybrid or syncretic systems of law and authority cannot be effectively regulated in a system that is based on equal constitutional rights. In this view, the hereditary principle and blatant patriarchy should not be allowed to determine access to land, especially when compounded by courts whose decisions are often based on uncertain sources and principles at the discretion of traditional leaders, and are strongly affected by local power relations. All of these things violate equal citizenship. The government and ANC themselves are divided among traditionalists who uphold customary prerogatives and would like to extend the powers of chiefs, pragmatists who believe that tradition and traditional authorities can be put to useful purposes – one of which is nation-building – and progressives who believe that semi-autonomous traditional authorities will inevitably be in conflict with the principle of equal rights in a citizen nation.

There are good reasons why these fault lines have proved durable and why the accommodation of tradition in nation-building has proved a slow, contested and attritional process. Despite the ANC's official commitment to the Constitution's version of human rights, the influence of tradition is tenacious and grounded as much, if not more, in current political dynamics as it is on ancestral claims. As we have seen, one of the main operating principles of the ANC is to absorb and co-opt interests and influences that might oppose or rival in any way its claim to embody and advance the aspirations of all South Africans. This was especially marked in the late-apartheid years and the fluid years of negotiation and transition, when the ANC was striving first for as broad a united front against apartheid as possible and then to insert itself into extensive areas of rural South Africa to which it had been denied any but clandestine access for decades. Traditional leaders were key assets for both these tasks and for delivering votes when democratic elections were established. This gave traditional leaders a strong base to build a formidable and well-organized pressure group. Their position has been enhanced by several other factors. The weakness of the South African state in rural areas extends from local government to the administration of justice, and traditional leaders can with some justification point out that the equal rights guaranteed in the Constitution are not reliably available to poor, rural African people. The argument then is that traditional structures should be treated as assets for the management and development of rural areas that the state simply cannot afford to do without. State weakness may also narrow the options for the government in dealing with traditional leaders. Hard-line interpretations of the Constitution's injunction that traditional structures must be subordinate to it could be politically difficult to enforce.

There is of course a more positive side to the political strength and resilience of tradition. The wide-ranging spirit of diversity which animates the Constitution proved far stronger than any premonition that with diversity might come clashes of essential values (although the exiguous treatment of tradition in the document itself might hint at inhibition on these grounds). The determination to restore the dignity of anything that might plausibly be labelled indigenous and African, however uncertain its provenance, also helped to make the case for tradition, and this determination became an essential, though difficult to articulate part of the nation-building project. The sympathetic identification of high-profile ANC leaders with traditional authorities and the African democracy they claim to represent also had an effect. Nelson Mandela's aristocratic bearing and measured reverence for the culture that shaped him were the very epitome of African nobility. It is true that, as is often the case with Mandela, there is an element of ambiguity about his relationship to tradition: 'At times he crossed a reconstituted concept of Thembu political tradition with the conventions of modern Western democracy; at others he pitted the aggressive, go-getting energies of urban modernity against the primitive stereotypes that were favoured under apartheid' (Boehmer 2010: 12). Despite this, Mandela's image probably did much for the prestige of traditional leaders although at the grass roots, they more often than not fail to live up to this ideal type. Jacob Zuma's charisma is of a different kind, though for the right audience just as effective; unapologetically demotic, assertively masculine, in his person he suggests not so much the compatibility of Western and African democracy, but an assertion of the latter's independence and perhaps superiority. Zuma was reported as speaking in this vein about the traditional Courts Bill to the House of Traditional Leaders in late 2012.[20]

> 'Let us solve African problems in the African way, not the white man's way', Zuma said, to cheers from the traditional leaders. 'Let us not be influenced by other cultures and try to think the lawyers are going to help. They will tell you they are dealing with cold facts. They will never tell you that these cold facts have warm bodies', he said. . . . He slammed Africans who had become 'most eloquent' in criticizing their cultural background. 'We are Africans. We cannot change to be something else.' (The Presidency 2012)

In the end the place of tradition in nation-building remains open and contentious because there is an irresolvable ambivalence over whether traditional authority represents no more than a defence of the interests of a reactionary, atavistic and patriarchal pressure group or whether it can claim to be a broader-based, legitimate expression of cultural rights. There is another and deeper ambivalence over the cultural content and processes that Zuma summarized in terms of 'African problems' and the 'African way'. There is no consensus over the place of traditional leaders, never mind of witchcraft, although *muthi* murders are universally condemned, notably by professional associations of traditional healers. This lack of consensus can be seen as a particular manifestation of a general problem: 'South Africa's transition to democracy in 1994 instated a formal political regime of secular, rational, liberal individualism while the majority of citizens hold views – about communal rights, values, the nature of the self, the reality of the magical – which are challenging to that official state narrative' (Vincent 2008: 48). This assessment is probably a bit overconfident in attributing such a specific list of values to 'a majority' but it nonetheless points to a real problem of dissonance.

It is difficult to see how this dissonance can be constructively managed. Traditional culture does not come as a coherent package. It is not a self-sufficient atavistic enclave within an otherwise modernized and secular society. Traditional beliefs, customs, practices, structures – including witchcraft – are woven into the fabric of a modernizing society at many levels and in many ways. Arguably just as the linguistic practice of code switching is an essential part of functioning in a multilingual society, so code switching between traditional and modern, secular and magical is essential to a country like South Africa. However tradition is defined, it is hybridized and syncretized in the South African context. Academic literature tries (arguably too hard) to normalize it and bring it into the ambit of late capitalism and globalization, treating syndicates of *muthi* murderers as entrepreneurs, robbing their actions of their outlandish and cruel associations: 'Rather than an aberration in South Africa's dominant narrative progress then, muti murders are to be understood as a feature of the present period' (ibid. 46). All of this is doubtless a valuable corrective to media-fuelled moral panics. However, as long as this ambivalence remains, the composition of the nation and the place of up to 36 per cent of the population in it remain ambivalent too.

## Half full or half empty?

Any assessment of where South Africans stand in relation to indices of shared life and what this measurement means for the prospects of nation-building naturally depend on what yardstick is used. If the standard is that of the apartheid past, then the answer is clearly that the glass is considerably more than half full. If the measure is some ahistorical ideal of where the country should be by now, then the answer is that it is disappointingly more than half empty. Such considerations bedevil all assessments of democracy, nation-building, transformation and any other measure by which post-apartheid South Africa is to be judged.

Another feature of South Africa deserves mention in this context. That is, assessment of the extent to which South Africans can and should share lives depends on what model of 'shared life' (and by implication non-racialism) is preferred. Well-meaning outsiders tend to think of South Africa, consciously or unconsciously, in terms of European or North American models of race relations in which black minorities become integrated into majority mainstream social and economic life.

South Africa differs in two crucial ways. In the first place, demography decrees that there are not enough whites and other minorities for the African majority to share their lives with. Whatever happens, a majority of Africans, especially those who live in rural areas, will live in neighbourhoods where there are no white people: their children will go to school where there are no white pupils or teachers; all authority figures in their lives will be African. Measures of shared life have to take this into account. Aside from the fact that there are not enough whites to go round, there is the problem of what constitutes the mainstream of economic and social culture, in other words the question of what sort of life is to be shared. There are enough grounds for resentment when black minorities have to 'lose their culture' in order to be absorbed into majority mainstreams in the West: those grounds are multiplied when it is the majority that is being granted access to the mainstream, which has been shaped by a previously dominant and racially exclusive minority – a significantly transnational one at that.

It is difficult to assess how much these factors affect the quality and quantity of the shared life that South Africans enjoy. Demography will always set limits and ensure that there will always be a significant constituency available for mobilization around an exclusive African identity. That potential will depend on whether this is not only an African constituency, but an excluded one as well. As far as contest over mainstream culture goes, this has probably caused less trouble than might be expected. Regular warnings from the BMF and others that the culture of business must be Africanized are warnings against complacency, but failure to articulate what such a cultural shift would entail in practice blunts them somewhat. Certainly whites are lazy, complacent (and sometimes openly dismissive) about learning African languages and respecting African culture, beyond incorporating *ubuntu* into their vocabulary. However, there is enough about African traditional culture (whether true, or distorted in the form of *muthi* killings, for instance) that is alien not only to 'white' culture but to the values of the Constitution, to make it suspect in white eyes. In the light of these things, it is probably inevitable that South Africans will continue to live lives that are partly shared and partly divided.

# CHAPTER SEVEN

# The spectre of anomie: Deviance and national citizenship

As the preceding discussion has shown, there is a range of positive indicators of shared life in South Africa. All of them to one extent or another have the various segmentations of divided South African life built into them, but they still make a contribution to transcending these divisions. However there are indicators of another type, markers of deviance and social fragmentation, which are widely recognized as obstacles to the social cohesion which is part of any nation-building project. So pervasive is the perception of fragmentation and deviance that the condition is sometimes described in terms of anomie – in the sense of a deficit of authoritative social norms and values and an absence of effective social regulation. One study which sought empirical confirmation of this in survey data (Huschka and Mau 2005) claimed to have found, 'that feelings of disorientation, powerlessness and estrangement, in short anomic tendencies are very widespread in South African society' (ibid. 25). This the authors attribute (following Durkheim) to the destructive effect of rapid social change on social regulation and as a result, individuals 'being left to their own devices'. This kind of argument receives indirect confirmation in the literature on witchcraft in post-apartheid South Africa. The dominant approach to explaining beliefs and practices classified as witchcraft emphasizes exactly the same effects of disorientation, powerlessness and estrangement that Huschka and Mau claim to have found. Although the distribution of anomic tendencies in the population is significantly influenced by race and economic inequality, the authors found a 'huge' amount of anomie apparently affected by neither of these things and which they attribute to the overall absence or weakness of normative regulation.

Certainly such findings correspond with a public mood that has been present from the beginning of South Africa's democratic era. It is not only civic and religious leaders and the general public who have expressed concern. Some of the deepest anxieties have been expressed by ANC leaders who, from the point at which it became clear that the task of governing a country in the throes of transformation would fall to them, feared that they would inherit a population so morally compromised by apartheid and by the struggle to overthrow it, and so deracinated by social change, that it might prove ungovernable. Such fears underlie the sentiments expressed by President Mandela in 1998 when he spoke to a 'moral summit' of religious leaders:

> The symptoms of our spiritual malaise are only too familiar. They include the extent of corruption both in the public and private sector, where office and positions of responsibility are treated as opportunities for self-enrichment; the corruption that occurs within our justice system; violence in interpersonal relations and families, in particular the shameful record of abuse of women and children; and the extent of tax evasion and refusal to pay for services used. (Mandela 1998)

The moral summit led, as we have seen, to the establishment of a Moral Regeneration Movement (MRM) early in Mbeki's presidency. Ironically enough the MRM fell under the responsibility of the vice-president Jacob Zuma who was shortly to be embroiled in investigations for corruption and a rape trial. Despite ongoing, official recognition of the problem, concerns about deviance and social fragmentation have continued unabated. These concerns will be illustrated, summarized and discussed for their effect on citizenship and nation-building under four headings: crime, corruption, public disorder and civic disobedience.

## Crime

Crime and corruption can affect nation-building prospects in several ways. They can undermine horizontal relationships between citizens by diminishing senses of shared experience and trust. When one section of the population, however defined, feels that it is being disproportionately victimized by criminals or when another is disproportionately blamed for crime – either in explicit or coded terms – these debilitating effects are exacerbated. Crime and corruption can also undermine vertical relationships between citizens and the state: confidence and trust in state agencies and government leadership are eroded if they fail to guarantee a context of personal security in which citizens can enjoy the rights which legitimize the state and the polity. When citizens lack confidence in being able to enjoy rights to personal security, live in fear of fellow citizens and distrust in the state and government, these things act upon each other to close down social space. People retreat behind whatever measures for their own safety they can improvise: these may be precautionary in the case of gated communities or retaliatory/deterrent in the case of vigilante violence. In short, the way people experience crime and respond to it can have serious negative effects on both the horizontal and vertical relationships that are the building blocks of the nation. There are both quantitative and qualitative dimensions to these experiences and responses.

Since the end of apartheid, South Africa has acquired an unenviable reputation for high levels of violent crime. Labels such as 'murder capital' and 'rape capital' of the world are commonplace in the global media. All crime statistics are uncertain: this is a universal rather than a specifically South African problem. The uncertainties are due to political sensitivity and manipulation, methodological instability and problems of coordinating data on different aspects of crime and from different parts of the criminal justice system. Above all, they are due to the divergence between reported crime (the customary basis for official measurement) and crime that is unreported. This problem is particularly evident in the case of rape. Statistics that attempt to place any given country in comparative status to the rest of the world are most uncertain of all. As a result it is scarcely surprising that any serious analysis of crime in South Africa should come hedged around with user warnings.

Nevertheless there are some generalizations about crime in South Africa which are not seriously contested: since 1994, levels of all crime have been very high, particularly murder and rape; the overall trend has been of significant reduction in crime since a peak in 2003–4 – a decrease of 32.2 per cent in the recorded violent crime rate and of 54 per cent in the murder rate (South African Police Service (SAPS) 2013). Despite the improving situation, there is still much that remains alarming about the crime situation in South Africa. The least potentially misleading international benchmark of comparison is murder; there were 15,609 murders in South Africa in 2012 (an average of close to 43 per day); this figure gives a murder rate of 30.9 per 100,000, which is four and a half times the international average of 6.9 per 100,000. There has been no significant reduction in the number of rapes reported in recent years; in fact there were small increases between the recording years 2008–9 and 2010–11, before a decrease of 1.9 per cent to 55,201 in 2011–12. Despite a reduction in crime, there is no reliable evidence of an improvement in abysmally low conviction rates (Lancaster 2012: 1–4). The reduction in crime has been accompanied by sharp increases in reported police misconduct as well as deaths in police custody and as a result of police action.

Viewed from the perspective of debates about policies for the criminal justice system, these generally agreed figures are a serious concern. They are also treated as a matter of serious concern for nation-building and citizenship, sometimes leading to the assumption that in such a violent country, perhaps one that is inherently so, the social fabric has been torn beyond the point that nation-building is a viable prospect. However, both international comparison and domestic analysis tend to suggest things are more complex than this dramatic (and despairing) viewpoint. The fact that the grounds for international comparison are so fragmentary and unstable has not halted their opportunistic deployment, usually by critics of the ANC government, but occasionally in its defence.[1] However, this tends to lead to confusion and angry exchanges rather than clarity. For instance, South Africa's official rate of reported rape is 94.9 per 100,000 (SAPS 2013: 30). This is only marginally greater than that of Australia (91.9 per 100,000), which is considered to be a stable, cohesive and progressive state, and while it is half as much again as Sweden (58.6), an even greater difference might have been expected between a country with South Africa's history of violent upheaval and one which is a byword for Scandinavian social-democratic cohesiveness (Civitas 2013: 4). However, Australia and Sweden are outliers among OECD countries; there is a difference of 61 between Australia and third-placed New Zealand (30.6 per 100,000 reported rapes) and 28 between Sweden and New Zealand (ibid.). As a result it is difficult to interpret the comparative significance of South Africa's rate with complete confidence and the highly contested area of reported versus unreported incidence of rape deepens the controversy further.

Incarceration rates provide another example of confusion (International Centre for Prison Studies). In terms of absolute number of prisoners, South Africa ranks tenth in the world. Given that among the others in the top ten states, countries with very large populations such as the United States, the Russian Federation, India, China, Brazil and Indonesia appear, this suggests that South Africa's prison population is abnormally large, and that this is an indication that its social fabric is under great strain. However, in terms of incarceration rate, South Africa ranks only fortieth in the world. On closer investigation, this is because many of the states above South Africa by this measure are mini states (such as Caribbean islands) with comparatively large numbers of prisoners in relation to tiny populations. If only the incarceration rates of the top ten by absolute numbers are compared, then South Africa (286 prisoners per 100,000 population) moves up to fifth place. What then is a valid comparison? Perhaps it is no surprise that South Africa's incarceration rate of 286 is close to that of Brazil at 276 given the similarities of inequality rates in the two countries. Certainly it is nowhere near as high as that of the United States at 716 per 100,000. However, all this may mean is that the criminal justice system is very bad at catching and successfully prosecuting criminals by comparison with its US counterpart.

In addition to the levels of crime experienced by South Africans, qualitative characteristics of criminal acts may well be important, for instance, in terms of the shock value of their deviance. Certain crimes may affect levels of alienation from fellow citizens and government more than others. In this respect, arguably it is not only the overall quantitative incidence of rape that is significant but also the inclusion of what are believed to be significant numbers of four kinds of rape in the overall figures: gang rape; violation of children and infants; rape of presumed virgins as a 'cure' for HIV/AIDS; and so-called corrective rape, in which lesbians or alleged lesbians are subjected to rape (often by multiple assailants) in order to 'cure' them of their sexual orientation. The status of the myth linking sex with a virgin and a 'cure' for HIV has been the subject of academic dispute (Leclerc-Madlala 2002), as is the actual incidence of baby and infant rape. However in 2011–12, 25,862 sexual offences against children (under-18s) were reported to the police, 40 per cent of the overall total of sexual offences. This in fact was a significant decrease over 2010–11, when 28,128 were recorded (SAPS 2012: 36–8). Similarly, authoritative figures for gang rape and corrective rape are not readily available, but high-profile cases are regularly reported in the press, leading to much public outrage and in the case of corrective rape, to campaigns by lesbian and gay rights groups for official recognition of the seriousness of this crime and better policing. Media reports (usually based on information supplied by NGOs) put the incidence of corrective rape as high as 500 cases a year (De Silvio 2011: 1471). In 2013 the Medical Research Council reported to parliament on the basis of data collected from 8,000 patients over 9 provinces that '[r]ape was prevalent where groups of boys, particularly in gangs, or in rural areas, collaborated to trap vulnerable girls' (Parliamentary Monitoring Group January–February 2013). It would be fair to say that irrespective of specialized debate and sometimes in the absence of detailed figures, all four of these categories are unequivocally part of public consciousness of the experience of crime in South Africa.

In any case these niche categories of rape are situated not only within what is an already high overall rate of rape, but also in a wider context of abuse of women. This includes very high rates of violence against spouses or partners and a pattern of sexual exploitation of young women by older and (comparatively) economically powerful men. In March 2013 the health minister Aaron Motsoaledi released figures for HIV prevalence which revealed that 'at least 28 per cent' of schoolgirls in South Africa are HIV positive. The figure for the general population is around 10 per cent. Motsoaledi added that 94,000 schoolgirls became pregnant in 2011 and 77,000 had abortions at state clinics, saying that, 'it is clear that it is not young boys who are sleeping with these girls. It is old [sic] men. We must take a stand against sugar daddies' (*Mail & Guardian* 14 March 2013).

Similar points about niche categories of crime which may be particularly destructive of public trust and morale in the context of nation-building can be made about categories of murder. *Muthi* murders are not categorized separately in official statistics, but as we have seen they are treated in public discourse as a small, probably underreported but persistent and high-profile subgroup of killings, capable of generating shock, revulsion and cultural bewilderment out of all proportion to their numbers.

Other subversive categories are counted separately and give the impression not only of crime but of a general condition of lawlessness, not least on the part of the guardians of law and order themselves. In 2010–11, SAPS research identified 12 per cent of 'murders' as taking place in self-defence, that is, 'as a result of law enforcement, in the line of duty or in retaliation' (SAPS 2011: 6), and 7 per cent as a result of 'group behaviour such as vigilantism, gang wars and taxi-related violence' (ibid.). In the following year these categories were disaggregated to 5 per cent each for vigilantism and self-defence and 1 per cent each for taxi and gang-related, group violence (SAPS 2012: 21). This means that around 1,500 violent deaths occurred in 2011–12 in frontier-like conditions of lawlessness which create an impression of lynch mobs and police violence. This impression is supported by the rising annual volume of complaints to the Independent Claims Directorate (ICD) which processes allegations of police misconduct. In 2011–12 the ICD received 720 notifications and complaints about the police which involved the death of a citizen. This was in a total of 4,923 complaints about the police (ICD 2012: 25–30). The overall impression of lawlessness is strengthened by the figures for police officers murdered while on duty. Between 2001 and 2010, 1,130 were killed (Newham 2011). This figure, taken along with the figures for annual killings by police, suggests that the phrase 'war on crime' has more than metaphorical significance.

If we are to assess the significance of crime for nation-building, it is important to register how both the quantitative and qualitative aspects of crime are recorded, interpreted and used to construct official and unofficial narratives; these in turn become the basis for response, whether in the form of public outcry or policy initiative. In the first place it is important not only how many victims there are, but also who they and the perpetrators are. In this respect, official accounts of crime in government statements and SAPS reports lay great emphasis on context and relationships. According to police research in the decade 2000 to 2010, '70 per cent–80 per cent of murders, 60 per cent of attempted murders, 75 per cent of rapes and 90 per cent of assaults . . . involve victims and perpetrators who know one another . . . as family members, friends, acquaintances or colleagues. . . . Alcohol and to a lesser extent drugs frequently play a role in these crimes' (SAPS 2010–11: 6). The message which the police (and the government) wish to convey is clear: although 3,000 to 5,000 South Africans a year are killed by anonymous fellow citizens, there is much more to fear from partners, acquaintances and neighbours who will account for 10,000 to 12,000 deaths. Policies for law and order can only do so much; social incoherence at the level of close relationships is the problem and socio-economic policies can do much more.

In South Africa racial or ethnic attributions are never far from the surface in the construction and contestation of narratives; indeed sometimes they are made explicit. Three typical examples are 'farm murders', family murders and rape.

Farm murders have been a controversial law and order issue since the late 1990s when it became apparent that the rate of murders committed during attacks on farms had escalated sharply. Controversy has centred on several themes: methods for enumerating farm murders and whether or not they should be considered as a separate category at all; whether motivation for the murders was 'ordinary' crime (as in theft-related assaults) or racially motivated revenge, ethnic cleansing or even in extreme versions, genocide (Burger 2012). Policies for rural security have fluctuated from first emphasizing the safety of farmers (1997–2005), then denying that they are specially vulnerable, to once again (2011) acknowledging that farm murders constitute a special problem requiring tailored policies. This latest development is in the light of calculations that claim that the murder rate for farmers is over 3 times the South African average, 14 times the global average and twice the rate for South African police officers (ibid.). The significant point for nation-building is that the contending narratives about farm murders have not simply been about policies for rural security; they have been interwoven with references to the historical legacy of ill treatment and abuse of black farm workers, the tenure insecurity of black workers on the land today, the failures of land reform and the fear of many white Afrikaner farmers that they have been singled out for a coordinated programme of racially motivated revenge which the government refuses to recognize.

Another subset of violent crime in South Africa that receives publicity from time to time is family murders, in which a parent, usually the father, kills partner and children before committing suicide. In the 1980s it was frequently speculated that Afrikaners were particularly prone to this pattern of violence on the grounds that authoritarian and rigid social structures and patterns, involving child-rearing, education, religion and politics, created a favourable ethnic context for this. As rapid social and political change challenged the notions of male dominance and racial superiority that were part of this world view, so the speculation went, the resulting stress caused breakdown and violence, of which family murder was the most extreme example. This narrative of ethnic attribution has persisted into post-apartheid South Africa, despite what little research there is suggesting that all population groups in South Africa are prone to high levels of male violence against women and children, family murders included (Marchetti-Mercer 2003: 84). The durability of this mythology was demonstrated when the Minister for Women, Children and People with Disabilities, Lulu Xingwana, said on Australian television in February 2013: 'Young Afrikaner men are brought up in the Calvinist religion believing that they own a woman, they own a child, they own everything and therefore they can take that life because they own it.'[2] Public sensitivity to the destructive potential of this kind of thinking was demonstrated by the subsequent uproar, in which Xingwana was forced to apologize, and President Zuma released an unusually comprehensive statement deploring ethnic explanations for crime.

Given the destructive potential of combining racial sensitivities and sex, explaining and interpreting the high rate of rape in post-apartheid South Africa has sometimes led to tense confrontation. A case in point was the rape in 1999 of a (white) journalist, Charlene Smith, who used her experience as motivation to embark on a vigorous public campaign to publicize what she and others termed South Africa's rape crisis, and in doing so to correct underreporting of rape and to demand specific measures, including the provision of antiretroviral drugs to rape victims. In the course of her campaign Smith wrote that rape had become endemic to Africa and was a prime means of spreading HIV/AIDS to women and children. This was at the height of the controversy over Mbeki's AIDS denialism and he reacted angrily. He had already on other occasions expressed his anger at what he saw as white racist assumptions in the construction of a mythology about the supposed sexual incontinence and predatory instincts of African men. This led him to accuse Smith of being 'deeply offensive' and 'blinded by racist rage' (Gevisser 2007: 738).

It is probably safe to suppose that these examples of racial and ethnic attributions in the public debate about crime, whether they are explicit or implicit, real or imagined, constitute the tip of a very large iceberg of public attitudes, submerged for the most part by inhibitions about being branded racist. Indeed much discourse about crime in South Africa is conditioned by the accusation that any concerns expressed by white people about crime are manifestations of displaced racism. Unsurprisingly this accusation comes mainly from within government and ANC circles, but others are also keen to expose racism's demonic shape-shifting powers: 'old, overt, explicit racist discourse is no longer possible', so the fears on which white racism is based 'are now expressed in a less overt, more implicit racial discourse based on crime, corruption and incompetence' (Maylam 2001).

It would not be surprising if the consistently high levels of violent crime in South Africa affected levels of public confidence in institutions. In fact, survey evidence concerning this important marker of the progress of civic nation-building is somewhat ambivalent. The 2010 and 2011 rounds of the SASAS (HSRC 2012) contained a module on confidence in the police. The mean level of trust in the police between 1998 and 2011 was 42 per cent with a high of 47 per cent (1999) and a low of 39 per cent (2000, 2006 and 2007). The level of confidence in 2011 was 41 per cent, effectively where it was in 1999 (42%). By contrast, confidence in the courts increased from 42 per cent in 1999 to 51 per cent in 2011, with a mean over the period of 50 per cent. In a different measure, satisfaction with police crime reduction efforts increased sharply from under 20 per cent in 2009 to just over 30 per cent in 2011; crime levels did fall in this period, but reports of police brutality and deaths as a result of police action rose substantially at the same time. The same survey also reported that 66 per cent of respondents believed that corruption was widespread in the police force, by far the highest percentage of the 11 categories of politician and public servant that were measured. An element of ambivalence is introduced by the most recent StatsSA Victims of Crime Survey (StatsSA 2012: 3) which contradicts the SASAS fairly consistent picture of institutional distrust. This survey found that 65.7 per cent of households believed that the police were trustworthy and that '[a]bout 60 per cent of households were satisfied with the way in which police and courts were doing their work'.

The dissonance between the SASAS' 41 per cent confidence level and the Victims Survey's 65.7 per cent measure of trust is difficult to resolve. Both measured attitudes at a time when crime levels were dropping but evidence of police brutality and corruption at the highest level was increasing steeply. SASAS confidence findings were consistent over more than a decade; Victims Surveys in 2003 and 2007 found that 52 per cent thought police were doing a good job in 2003, declining to 49 per cent in 2007 before rising again to the 2011 levels.

Clashing evidence of this sort should induce a proper level of caution in using surveys of public mood to gauge the status of nation-building. However, in the face of what are probably methodological vagaries and instability of public perceptions, it is possible to look for corroborating and contextual material to put the resulting contradictions in perspective. For instance, a third large-scale longitudinal survey, Afrobarometer, is closer to SASAS than to the Victims Survey: 42 per cent expressed confidence in the police in 2008, rising to 49 per cent in 2012, but the police were by far the lowest in public esteem of all of the five state institutions rated. In addition, the percentage of respondents who thought that the police were corrupt increased (Afrobarometer 2012: 14). In terms of context, the persistence of vigilantism does not suggest increasing confidence in police. In addition, the exposure of corruption at the highest level of the police in recent years makes some of the figures for trust and confidence in the police in the Victims Survey somewhat counter-intuitive. The fact that the last two national commissioners of police have been removed from office for misconduct makes 66 per cent public confidence in the force they led a little hard to explain. In 2010, Commissioner Jackie Selebi was jailed for 15 years for corrupt dealings with gangsters[3] and his successor was fired after a judicial commission found him unfit for public office by reason of irregularities in the procurement process to acquire headquarters offices for the police in Pretoria. These high-profile cases raise the general question of corruption in public life in South Africa.

## Corruption

According to corruption watchdog, Transparency International (TI), corruption is one of the most damaging consequences of poor governance, characterized by lack of both transparency and accountability. Corruption hinders economic growth and human development by limiting access to basic social services, as well as increasing the cost of their delivery. It also increases poverty, subverts the financial system and undermines the legitimacy of the state. Thus, according to TI, corruption is anti-poor, anti-development, anti-growth and anti-investment (Lambert-Mogiliansky 2007: 351–67). The financial, human and political costs of corruption are very high with debilitating effects on nation-building.

In South Africa, a partial measure of the impact of corruption on development and government delivery can be gauged from the activities of the Special Investigating Unit (SIU), an independent statutory body directly accountable to parliament. According to the SIU's annual report for 2010–11, up to 20 per cent of the government's annual procurement budget (R25–R30 billion) is lost to corruption, incompetence and negligence. The SIU is currently conducting 60 investigations into 18 government departments (Parliamentary Monitoring Group 11 October 2011). Thus it appears that corruption in South Africa has become endemic despite government attempts to combat it. It is true that there are pockets of excellence. The office of the Auditor-General provides timely and comprehensive information on unauthorized, irregular, fruitless and wasteful expenditure. The current Public Protector, Advocate Thuli Madonsela, has begun to transform a potentially powerful but hitherto ineffective instrument to confront corruption into a force to be reckoned with. In doing so she has demonstrated that if able and determined people are appointed, existing laws can be made to work. However, it is not clear that there is the political will to support her in following through a promising start. The general outlook is not encouraging. According to Willie Hofmeyr, who until 2011 was head of the SIU, good laws and policies are in place but the state's ability to apply them is ineffective, with the result that they are broken with impunity. Lack of coordination between 11 institutions designed to tackle corruption and lack of skilled personnel are problems in this regard. Launching the SIU annual report in October 2011, Hofmeyr said that in order to address corruption effectively, the number of dedicated anti-corruption investigators should be increased tenfold from 700 to 7,000 (ibid.). Since the SIU's remit is limited to the public sector and to matters referred to it by presidential proclamation, figures for its investigations and prosecutions, while providing a valuable indicator of how serious corruption is in South Africa, inevitably underestimate the problem. Relying solely on the SIU's figures also has the inadvertent effect of defining corruption solely as a public-sector problem and omitting private-sector contributions to the problem.

Growing public concern about corruption has led to two recent civil society initiatives, one by the Council for the Advancement of the South African Constitution (CASAC) and the other, Corruption Watch, a trade union-backed watchdog organization. Speaking on behalf of CASAC, chairman Sipho Pityana said: 'Corruption and patronage are so pervasive, rampant and crippling in our society that we are on the verge of being deemed a dysfunctional state' (CASAC 2011). On behalf of Corruption Watch, the general secretary of trade union confederation Cosatu, Zwelinzima Vavi, has said: 'We face a nightmare future of a South Africa up for auction to the highest bidder where no-one will be able to do business with the state without going through corrupt gatekeepers' (Vavi 11 December 2011). Vavi has also spoken of 'a corrupt and demagogic elite of political hyenas using the state to get rich' and turning South Africa into a 'full-blown predator state' (Vavi 23 September 2011). Initiatives such as CASAC and Corruption Watch, as well as zealous watchdog efforts by the parliamentary opposition, have raised the public profile of corruption but the problem is not diminishing. A report prepared by a major Johannesburg law firm (Allwright 2013), which reviewed Public Service Commission (PSC) documents and findings, concluded that corruption was widespread (1,135 cases were reported to the PSC in 2009 and 2010), was underreported, had no meaningful consequences for perpetrators in the vast majority of cases investigated, and was growing rapidly.

## Crime and corruption

Corruption is capable of spreading malaise across society and the polity beyond its direct economic effects. In the case of South Africa, suspicions that an increasing number of whistleblowers are being murdered, as has been reported in the province of Mpumalanga (*Mail & Guardian* 22 October 2010), add to impressions of lawlessness and impunity created by vigilantism and police killings. It is clear that corruption allegations, investigations and disciplinary procedures are being selectively used in factional wars and even personal feuds in the government and ANC. Corruption lay behind much of the three-year controversy (2010–13) over threats to constitutional freedoms of information and expression in a draft Protection of State Information bill. Opponents of the bill in the opposition, civil society and the media believed that the government was determined to entrench a 'culture of secrecy' in order to cover up corruption by, among other things, heavily penalizing whistleblowers even when there was public interest in obtaining unauthorized information.[4]

In these respects, corruption may be said to have the same effects as crime in undermining trust and confidence in institutions and in the horizontal and vertical relationships among citizens and between them and the state, which create and sustain national citizenship. In the case of corruption, as we have already seen with crime, such debilitating effects are hard to quantify and the evidence produced by surveys may be contradictory or ambiguous. However, the seriousness with which all government, political and civil society organizations and leaders regard the problem makes it clear that they consider corruption as they do crime, as a threat to nation-building. Despite this, it is possible that such large-scale problems of deviance have countervailing effects, by rallying defenders of constitutional values and active citizenship and motivating them to work together on a broader basis than orthodox party politics do. This can mean a critical stance towards government or one of partnership with government agencies, sometimes a combination of the two. A well-established example of the partnership model is Business Against Crime (BAC), which channels support from businesses in the form of expertise and material resources to the police and other agencies in the criminal justice system. There is definitely something to be said for the counter-intuitive view that crime and corruption can have positive effects on nation-building, but it would be too much to hope that they outweigh the negative.

Again like crime, corruption has corrosive, indirect effects on the prospects of national cohesion through the ways in which contending narratives about the scourge are constructed. Racial and ethnic imputations, both open and submerged, colour the discourse on corruption as they do with crime. The same ritual is enacted in which accusations of racially motivated Afro-pessimism are met with counter-claims of complicit denialism. These sterile exchanges have become so predictable and institutionalized that it is possible to wonder whether they might have lost some of their disintegrative power. At the very least, however, they are unhelpful.

## Public disorder

Measured by the regular holding of free and fair elections, though not yet by peaceful party alternation in power via the ballot box, South Africa's democracy has been well entrenched. However, from about 2004–5, around the ten-year mark of the democratic period, outbreaks of public violence have become endemic and, along with continuing high levels of violent crime, have shaken confidence in democratic consolidation. Such disorder has taken three principal forms: violent protest, usually in municipalities, often provoked by deficiency of service provision and unresponsive, often corrupt local government (Atkinson 2007: 58); violence accompanying strikes and endemic low-level xenophobic violence, which in 2008 erupted in large-scale riots in several cities.

### Service delivery protests

Variation in definitions of disorderly events and lack of disaggregation in official figures make it difficult to chart the frequency and intensity of categories of disorder with complete confidence. However, there is widespread agreement that violence of this sort has increased since 2004–5. In that year the Ministry of Safety and Security recorded 5,085 legal protests and 881 illegal ones (ibid.); in 2011–12, the SAPS registered 10,748 instances of 'crowd management (peaceful)' and 1,214 of 'crowd management (unrest)'. The figure for peaceful protest was an 8 per cent drop on the previous year; that for 'unrest' was a 24 per cent increase (SAPS 2012: 92–3). These demonstrations, peaceful and violent, have come to be known as service delivery protests. They have become emblematic of grass-roots discontent with the failure to realize a big enough material dividend from the achievement of democratic freedoms. The repertoire of violent protest includes the destruction of government and sometimes private property, mob intimidation and occasionally murder of councillors and other local authority figures, confrontations with police and creation of temporary no-go areas. Although these symptoms of instability have become endemic, casualties are not high: only a tiny percentage of the many hundreds who are killed by the police every year die in unrest situations; the proportion that is attributable to rioters of the 15,000 or so violent deaths a year is even smaller. The impact is also lessened by the fact that disturbances take place mostly in outlying areas, with minimal disruption to the mainstream economy. This is partly a result of apartheid's spatial legacy of dispersed settlement and partly, of course, because the lack of significant economic activity is one of the main reasons for the riots to take place where they do.

Despite these mitigating factors, this pattern of unrest undermines official versions of democratic and national citizenship and suggests that they are seriously out of alignment with the experiences of many citizens who, as a result, subscribe to alternative and contradictory conceptions of moral and political order. One of the notable ironies of post-apartheid South Africa is that the struggle for democracy was widely portrayed as a struggle for the vote, but having achieved it, many citizens exercise it in ways that undermine rather than strengthen the legitimacy of the overall constitutional order. That is, the vote is often less an instrument of choice to reward or sanction competing claims to leadership, management and delivery, but part of a destructive, experiential cycle in which the vote is an instrument for affirming unchanging loyalty to the ANC, an act of loyalty which is met by perceived betrayal, leading to frustration, anger and destructive outbreaks.

There are various ways to explain this destructive cycle, including racial identification between voters and the ANC and the durability of the ANC's liberation struggle dividend. These probably do count, but the effects are hard to pin down, the dynamics are hard to disentangle and the alleged causal relationships (especially between race and voting) are often contested. Another possibility is to point to the difficulties the opposition DA has had in gaining a foothold in the areas where unrest typically occurs, whether through assumed lack of fit between the DA's liberalism and the deprived communities in question or through the remorseless racial profiling which the ANC employs to discredit the DA as guardians of 'white privilege'. These points are not so much untrue as irrelevant, since they wrongly assume that the only possible competitor for the votes of unemployed township and informal settlement-dwellers is a liberal party whose core constituency is among affluent whites, and Coloureds who feel marginalized and threatened by the ANC. Far more important in the perpetuation of the debilitating chain reaction of affirmation followed by betrayal, frustration and anger is the absence of a credible, left-wing electoral alternative whose natural constituency ought to be the unemployed and marginalized of the unrest areas. The South African Communist Party (SACP) and labour federation Cosatu are committed to alliance with the ANC for a variety of strategic and tactical reasons, not least to guarantee access to state patronage for their upwardly mobile leaders. Their own gloss on this strategy is that the marginalized are indeed their constituency, but the Left can better serve them in cooperation with the ANC, rather than by presenting voters with an alternative.[5] The fact that violent protest has become institutionalized in areas which have massive ANC electoral majorities suggests otherwise.

A recent analysis (Von Holdt et al. 2011) of eight case studies of collective violence sparked by community protest and xenophobia in South Africa borrows the term 'insurgent citizenship' from James Holston's study of São Paulo (Holston 2009), which explores the destabilizing consequences of citizenship that is universally inclusive, but differentiated by massive inequalities and as a result is challenged from below. 'Insurgent citizenship' is an elegant sound bite which economically expresses some of the paradoxes which complicate nation-building in South Africa. It also puts a gloss of legitimacy on what many people would regard as deviant behaviour, given the availability of formal, democratic rights and freedoms in post-apartheid South Africa. This again follows Holston, for instance, when he writes of Brazil that insurgent citizenship is not derived from ' incomplete modernity, dysfunctional citizenship, ineffective law, deficient nationality or failed democracy' (ibid. 14). Similarly in South Africa: 'Community protest movements are not inchoate mobs but are characterised by an explicit discourse about human and democratic rights and constitute an insurgent citizen struggle against the differentiation of citizenship rights' (Von Holdt et al. 2011: 25). Legitimization is further implied by placing insurgent citizenship today in the tradition of the 'violent practices' of the 'insurgent civil society of the struggle against apartheid', so that it, 'it is not surprising that similar repertoires of violence are apparent in current insurgencies over citizenship and exclusion' (ibid. 7).

Notwithstanding the smoothness with which 'current' and 'apartheid' exclusions are run together for the purposes of legitimizing violence, even this account is clouded by paradox and contradiction. The authors concede that insurgent citizenship has its 'dark side'. It is corrosive of associational life and politics and 'is not simply and unproblematically a struggle to expand the meaning of and access to democracy', partaking as it does of 'local hierarchies and prejudices' – like xenophobia and patriarchy – not to mention violent, corrupt and criminal local elites (ibid. 31–2). A further twist is added by the fact that some community protests are organized by one faction of the local ANC to unseat another. A certain amount of analytical confusion is forgivable in an attempt to unravel such a thoroughly confusing phenomenon as violent community protest, into which this study has drilled admirably deeply with grass-roots research. Whatever else is revealed by this accumulation of paradoxes, however, it is further evidence that competing conceptions of what it means to be a citizen, especially when violently expressed, do not make for a stable platform on which to build civic nationhood.

## Strikes and violence

South Africa has a highly regulated labour market with legislation entrenching many workers' rights. Despite this, a strong current of threatened or actual violence against property and people frequently accompanies industrial action. The negotiation of South Africa's labour relations regime took place after 1994, rather than as part of the transition from apartheid to democracy, although the contribution of the unions to the anti-apartheid struggle in the 1980s gave them a strong negotiating platform. Nevertheless the labour relations regime is generally regarded as an essential part of the new state's founding settlement, and by many as an equal or greater achievement than the recognition of democratic rights and equal citizenship. In the first dozen years of democracy these verdicts seemed justified. Helped by political stability and modest but sustained economic growth averaging 3 per cent, industrial peace was the norm until 2006–7. From this point in time, however, annual losses of days to strike action have see-sawed wildly, with much higher peaks and a much higher average than in the earlier period.

However, the relative number of days lost does not on its own adequately reflect the state of labour relations. Even in times of relative labour peace, trade unions habitually express themselves in aggressive and often warlike rhetoric, and in times of heightened tension this is often translated into action, which is met by (and sometimes provoked by) security measures by companies and police. It is generally understood, and far from universally condemned, that workers – and sometimes, tacitly, unions – see violence as part of their legitimate repertoire. However, such violence is hard to quantify. For instance, in a two-month strike of security guards in April–May 2006, an otherwise quiet year for industrial relations, an estimated 20–30 'scabs' (non-striking workers) were murdered. The figure is imprecise because the victims were killed in individual assaults, typically in plain clothes, travelling to work and often thrown from moving trains. This pattern made it hard to distinguish strike-related deaths within the daily average of 52 murders reported between April 2006 and March 2007.

Until late 2012 the security guard strike stood out as an extreme case. This was possibly because non-striking workers had learned their lesson and possibly because a high proportion of security guards are immigrants from neighbouring African countries, and there may have been an element of xenophobia in at least some of the killings which was not present in other strikes. Although there were no losses of life to match 2006 in subsequent years, small numbers of strike-related violent deaths were not unknown, and damage to property in the course of strikes was commonplace. The death toll in the security guards strike was surpassed in dramatic fashion in 2012 when 44 people lost their lives in 5 days of violence (11–16 August) at and near Marikana platinum mine near Rustenburg in North West Province. In this case most of the casualties were among striking workers. Thirty-four miners were shot dead by police and 78 wounded on 16 August after several days of confused fighting involving rival unions, police and company security in which 10 people had been killed, including 2 police officers hacked to death. Clearly many things contributed to these violent events over and above the far-reaching wage demands and wildcat strike that triggered them. Among them was rivalry between the established National Union of Mineworkers (NUM) and a new rival, a grass-roots, worker-led initiative called the Association of Miners and Construction Union (AMCU). Leaders of the NUM had been able to use the union's status under the labour relations regime and political influence in the ANC Alliance to become quintessential, upwardly mobile, politically connected, worker-insiders of the new South Africa. The AMCU presented a militant, grass roots, sometimes violent challenge on behalf of miners who still lived with aspects of the apartheid-era migrant labour system and resented the privileged position of the NUM. This volatile situation was exacerbated by serious structural and conjunctural failings of public order policing.

A judicial commission will report on the interplay of factors which produced the Marikana tragedy; aside from the specific and local factors at work, it will be necessary to consider a general context in which violence is viewed by many to be a structural feature of labour relations. A survey of Cosatu members by the National Labour and Economic Development Institute (NALEDI), a trade union-funded research organization found a high level of acceptance of violence as a necessary strategy to take strike demands forward (NALEDI 2012: 17). The findings, summarized by another trade union-supporting organization, confirm other indications that civility under the democratic Constitution cannot be taken for granted: 'There appears to be a generalized acceptance of violence. Workers appear to find it acceptable to resort to violence to further strike action or demands, but they appear to accept violence by other role players like employers and the police' (Labour Research Service 2013: 18). Once again the metaphor of war, so liberally used across South African political discourse, seems to take on a more than figurative meaning. Certainly it seems clear that a formal, comprehensive, progressive and worker-friendly regime of labour relations, which is widely seen as an essential foundation of the post-apartheid settlement, has only patchy and fragile cover and has not yet played its part in delivering a stable foundation of democratic citizenship.

## Xenophobia

Outbreaks of xenophobic violence which spread in a chain reaction across several of South Africa's main urban centres in May 2008 constituted in human terms the most costly episode of public violence in the post-apartheid period. Sixty-two people were killed and 100,000 were displaced in 135 sites of unrest, requiring a major relief operation. Most of the dead were immigrants – both legal and irregular – from other African countries or were mistaken for them. Arguably these events were also the most damaging contradiction to assumptions that the new constitutional order rested on a platform of shared values and civility. Certainly they struck a serious blow to South Africa's international reputation as a human rights-based democracy and the country's reputation, particularly in Africa, suffered greatly.

For some time before the outbreaks, migration experts and human rights groups had been warning that levels of intolerance towards African foreigners were dangerously high. Certainly public awareness of this was high, as illustrated by the widespread currency of the derisive term *makwerekwere* for African foreigners.[6] These warning voices cited survey evidence and a long-term pattern of violence – including the murder of over 20 Somali shopkeepers in individual incidents in and around Cape Town – as well as well-documented intimidation, extortion and other abuses against foreigners by police and other officials. In the aftermath of the violence, further studies were published which documented and analysed the unrest (for a brief review and list see Centre for Development and Enterprise (CDE) 2010: 39–41 and note 125). One of them went so far as to claim that 'South Africa exhibits levels of intolerance to outsiders unlike virtually anything seen in other parts of the world' (Southern African Migration Project (SAMP) 2008: 1).

The same study (ibid. 14–15) noted several typical explanations for the uncompromisingly negative views and attitudes towards immigrants which are held by large majorities of all racial groups in South Africa as follows: a toxic legacy from colonialism and apartheid whose pathological tendencies to stereotyping and intolerance have (in ways that tend to be glossed over) been bequeathed intact to South Africa's black majority and transferred to other Africans; conditions of virtual anomie, shaped by material deprivation and inequality, as well as feelings of betrayal at government failure and vented in rage at convenient scapegoats; competition between economically marginalized South Africans and large numbers of irregular immigrants for economic opportunities and amenities like housing and other services. Amid the list of explanatory possibilities there is one significant omission. None of the studies emphasizes that South Africa's intolerance of foreigners in word and deed is set in a general context of intolerant attitudes and in an extremely violent society. This omission can probably be explained by the fear that if South Africa's xenophobia is placed in this kind of context it will somehow minimize its effect and to set the scene for exculpating those who are responsible for it, both in the narrow sense of committing the xenophobic acts themselves and more particularly in the broader sense of creating a climate conducive to prejudice by being passive, permissive or even complicit (as not only officials and police, but also politicians, are sometimes accused). The result contributes to a general impression that xenophobia is a regrettable departure from a generally liberal and tolerant norm. Nothing could be further from the truth.

## Civic disobedience

The frustration and feelings of betrayal that lie behind spasms of public disorder testify to a feeling on the part of an appreciable number of citizens that a social contract has been broken. This mood has been a subject of growing concern, both inside and outside of government since about the tenth anniversary of the achievement of democracy. However, this concern has been paralleled from the very beginning by a fear that a disquieting number of South Africans are unable or unwilling to fulfil the citizen's side of any such social contract. Mandela's words, quoted earlier, about the 'spiritual malaise' that he felt was all too familiar to his compatriots, did not lose their relevance in the years that followed. Whether or not 'spiritual malaise' is a strictly accurate characterization, Mandela was referring to a broad area of civic deviance or non-compliance which is a powerful, if ill-defined, factor in subverting hopes of a well-ordered society and responsible citizenry. Markers of this deviance include failure to pay for municipal services, electricity and water theft, non-compliance with drivers' and TV licences and non-conformity with reasonable requirements for road safety in the general interest. This is a wide, analytical grey area between civil disobedience (of which there is some) and common crime (of which there is much). In this area of uncertainty, classification and explanation are further clouded by the effects of poverty and deprivation on people's capacity for compliance. Despite this uncertainty there is a strong and widespread belief across political divides that in South Africa much behaviour which is neither civil disobedience nor crime nonetheless contributes to social fragmentation and exemplifies social decay. Civil disobedience is an articulate and purposive, non-violent response of non-compliance to some legal or civil requirement, on a matter of principle which might involve the infringement of a right or some dereliction of a state or government responsibility. The much more widespread deviant behaviours which are such a matter of official concern in South Africa– and which, in the absence of a generally accepted designation, might be called *civic* disobedience – lack the articulation of principle and purposive orientation to change that characterize civil disobedience. At the same time, although civic disobedience necessarily involves the transgression of some law or regulation and is sometimes (though far from consistently) punished as such, it is not generally considered by the authorities, and certainly not by the perpetrators themselves, as having the status and motivations of crime.

Central to the doubts and fears about the appetite of South Africans for citizenship's responsibilities is the topic of payment, or rather non-payment, for municipal services. Non-payment was an essential part of the anti-apartheid struggle and in the immediate aftermath the new ANC government feared that a culture of non-payment had become entrenched and reinforced by a sense of entitlement to services as the material fruits of democratic struggle. As a result of these fears, a campaign – called *Masakhane*,[7] the first of numerous initiatives of this sort – was launched in February 1995 to encourage and educate people into the civic responsibilities of democratic citizenship, including, specifically, paying for services. Judged by this narrow criterion the campaign was not a success: payments increased only for a short time or not at all (Askvik and Bak 2005: 88). Nearly two decades later municipal debt remains a serious problem. In 2011 research by the Financial and Fiscal Commission[8] (FFC) concluded that 'non-payment is crippling service delivery in South African municipalities' (2011: 1). Although debt levels had been declining since 2004, they remained 'alarmingly high' and 'a serious challenge to the financial health of municipalities'. According to the National Treasury, aggregate municipal consumer debts amounted to R87.2 billion in September 2012, and the growth in consumer debtors over the fourth quarter of the previous financial year showed that 'serious intervention is required to arrest further growth' (National Treasury 2012b).

Inevitably such a high level of non-payment is a complex, contested and sensitive political issue in which some explanations favour inability to pay and others a culture of non-payment. Explanations which rely on poverty as a reason are weakened by the fact that payment levels can vary substantially within and between communities that have similar socio-economic profiles but different histories. In addition, government initiatives to provide a level of free services for a class of 'indigent' consumers have further undermined the poverty argument. On the other hand, rising unemployment in the wake of global recession and steeply escalating utility costs (particularly for electricity) have coincided with rising consumer debt to municipalities and brought affordability back into focus.

As with municipal consumer debt, debt owed directly by consumers to electricity supply parastatal Eskom poses problems of interpretation. Over much of the country Eskom supplies municipalities which distribute (at a profit) to consumers. However, in Soweto, South Africa's largest township, Eskom supplies consumers directly.[9] In late 2012, Eskom revealed that the rate at which it received payment for supplies to Soweto was only 20 per cent and that Soweto consumers' historic debt to the supplier (excluding interest) had reached R3.2 billion. In other townships where it supplies directly, Eskom claimed an 80 per cent recovery rate (*Financial Mail* 11 December 2012). In addition to non-payment for scheduled supplies, theft via illegal connections is an important problem. While acknowledging problems of rising prices and affordability, Eskom clearly takes the view that a culture of non-payment is at work. A turnaround strategy, for Soweto, 'will focus on persuading Soweto customers to voluntarily change their behaviour and become legal power users' (Eskom 2011: 88). This is easier said than done, since Eskom technicians installing prepaid meters in Soweto as a way of ensuring payment, customarily have to be accompanied by an armed escort.

One review of survey data on poverty versus culture of non-payment as explanations for municipal consumer debt (Askvik and Bak 2005: 88–94) added another potential factor, that of social trust. Something which the surveys reviewed had in common, irrespective of the differing conclusions they came to, was responses which indicated that there was little stigma attached to non-payment, that many respondents believed that political leaders did not care whether or not people paid for services, and that trust in others to pay, including neighbours and municipal councillors, was low. A fourth factor has gained ground in more recent years: that is the inability of many municipalities to put effective systems for billing into place (FFC 2011: 162). In the end, while it clearly suits differing political agendas to emphasize one factor or another – a partisan tendency which risks exacerbating the already disintegrative effects of non-payment itself – it would not be difficult to imagine the four factors combining and working to reinforce any decision not to pay (or non-decision to pay). Indeed the combination could be seen as contributing to a piece of inarticulate civil disobedience on the part of someone who is poor, resentful of continuing inequality, distrustful of both neighbours and rulers, frustrated by a weak and ineffective state and able to look back on a history of community resistance as inspiration and justification.

The issue of non-payment for services also arises in the case of television licences. In common with other countries that have publicly funded broadcasters, there is a statutory requirement for owners of TV sets to pay an annual licence fee, which currently stands at R250.[10] The issue of non-payment is clearly a matter of great concern to the SABC, since it devotes considerable resources to campaigns encouraging payment. The corporation does not publicize a figure for payment, but this can be calculated from the SABC's income statement in its annual report and the census figures for household ownership of TV sets. Licence-fee income in 2012 was R892.6 million (SABC 2012: 33). According to the census, 75 per cent of households have access to a TV set, yielding a figure close to 11 million. If all owners of television sets paid the licence fee the income would be over R2.7 billion. This means that only about one-third of the people who should pay for a TV licence do so. The various factors discussed above to explain non-payment for utilities probably play a part in non-payment of TV licences.

Driver-related issues add to a general picture of casualness towards civic obligations. South Africa has a particularly high rate of road accident deaths. With around 14,000 fatalities each year and a ratio of 33.2 deaths per 100,000 people, South Africa was ranked one hundred and fifty-ninth in the World Health Organization's global status report on road safety for 2012 and ninth highest for absolute numbers of deaths. This was against a global average of 20.8 per 100,000 and figures like 7.5 for France and 7.8 for Australia (*Financial Mail* 21 January 2013). By 2013 the ratio had declined marginally to 31.9 per 100,000. According to South Africa's Road Traffic Management Corporation there is a pattern of reckless behaviour behind these figures: 'About 90 per cent of road accidents in South Africa are linked to speeding, dangerous overtaking, drunken driving, reckless driving or other violations of road safety rules. In addition, many vehicles on the road are in an unroadworthy condition' (Jeffrey 2012: 22). To add to this, there is widespread concern over driver licences. In 2005 a senior department of transport official caused great consternation by stating that 50 per cent of driver licences in South Africa were probably fraudulent or acquired in an irregular manner (IOL News 15 May 2005). This was not properly supported with research evidence and was probably a considerable exaggeration, but there is enough solid, if fragmentary, evidence to suggest that there is a major problem. The anti-corruption agency the SIU was mandated to investigate Driver Licence Testing Centres (DLTCs) in the aftermath of the 2005 allegations. In 2011, the SIU reported that it had found 53,668 invalidly issued or fraudulently converted licences in the DLTCs investigated (SIU 2012: 26). Indications that this is only part of the problem are that the Minister of Transport revealed in 2012 that there were 600,000 more cars registered in South Africa than there were licensed drivers (IOL News 17 January 2012). More than 26,000 unlicensed drivers were stopped by Cape Town metropolitan police in the three months from July to September 2012 (IOL News 13 October 2011).

## Deviance and trust

The official concern with social cohesion in general and deviance in particular reflects a more mature phase of nation-building in post-apartheid South Africa, reflecting the need to focus on 100 per cent of the population and not merely the past misdeeds and present insecurities of 8.9 per cent of the population. Given the limiting factors noted in the previous chapter, there has been some success in maintaining the shared sense of civic identity which supported the country into and through the period of transition to democracy and in warding off the more obvious threats to it. There has also been some progress in developing a pragmatic shared social identity to go with it, even if this requires Africans in particular to switch from one cultural register to another.

However, the indicators of deviance and fragmentation which were discussed in this chapter remain causes for deep concern. They threaten the horizontal attachments of trust between citizens on which further development of shared identity partly depends – trust not to harm each other and trust that others will fulfil their civic obligations: they invite explanation in terms of racial and cultural stereotype – and even when stereotyping is not being deployed, the suspicion that it is, is equally damaging; perhaps most importantly, such high levels of deviance erode trust in the state – the vertical attachments which are essential for nation-building – even, perhaps especially, among those that identify at the ballot box with the party that runs the state.

# PART FIVE

# The problem of nationalism in South Africa today

# CHAPTER EIGHT

# Nation-building 20 years on

The NDP is in many respects the most comprehensive statement on nation-building to have been produced in South Africa in the past 20 years. However, it is not yet possible to say whether it is broadly accepted as a culmination and a synthesis of previous efforts, or merely one of a number of competing alternatives. That is because the ambiguities and unresolved status of African nationalism are not addressed in the document, except perhaps indirectly.

The NDP's vision sees social cohesion, growth and redress for past exclusions in a self-sustaining, developmental cycle. The envisaged mobilizing agents are active citizenship, and social compacts which will combat the deviance, entitlement, selfishness and dependence which undermine social cohesion. This is a social democratic and technocratic vision within the general framework of the civic nation, inspired by the rights and diversity provisions of the Constitution. In this respect it is largely non-committal on the subject of the binding importance of culture; it cautiously registers the 'complexity' of the relationship between traditional leaders and values and 'constitutional' authorities, and strongly argues for the better integration of traditional healers into the health service. Otherwise the plan does not greatly concern itself with questions of 'indigenous' culture and in its injunction against 'narrow nationalism' there may be a coded warning about ethno-nationalism. It hedges its bets somewhat in the preamble of rather poetic aphorisms with which it envisions South Africa in 2030:

> We have come far with our cultural, religious,
> And ancestral traditions.
> Contemporary citizens that we are, we are
> conscious of the intimate relationships
> between tradition and change.
>
> NPC November 2011: 19

## Enduring Africanism

However, 'Africanism' as a strong political force, even if it is a poorly defined and diffuse one, has not gone away. Clearly it is rooted in many people's allegiances and political consciousness – where it is expressed indirectly as well as directly, for instance, in the disdain expressed by many black opinion-makers for the parliamentary opposition for being too 'white'. It is expressed pervasively in the celebration of the alleged moral superiority of 'African values' over Western ones; it is also a handy lever of self-advancement. The most important repository of Africanism is, however, the insistent portrayal of Black Africans as the demographic and moral majority in South Africa and as a 'victim nation' on whose restoration nation-building in any broader sense must wait. There is substantial continuity between the ANC's pre-1990 formulation of African nationalism, Mbeki's two nations and the NDP with its non-negotiable insistence that race must forever be the basis for redress. To put it bluntly, if a wealthy, black person (or his or her children) is to receive preferential treatment because of his or her race, then it can only be because Black Africans constitute in some sense a nation different from the South African one. However, the question is in *what* sense? There are two sources of confusion. The first is that no more today than in the past is there any clarity on whether this victim nation exists within, parallel to or above the other South African nation. There is also confusion as to whether and to what extent white women or Indians and Coloureds can be designated as victims of discrimination and disadvantage. Some Africanists bitterly reject the idea that white women can qualify for this status and they also put Africans above other blacks whose disadvantage under apartheid they deem to have been lesser. The other source of confusion is whether or not members of the victim nation have any attributes in common other than their 'previous disadvantage' and if they do, whether or not they are exclusive or can be experienced by whites, Coloureds and Indians. The official government and ANC line is that they do not possess such attributes; the line is the promotion of the civic nation and the prohibition of ethno-nationalism. So the predominant official view is that Black Africans both are and are not a nation. However, this is not the only official view, as the following quotations from the Department of Rural Development and Land Reform's (DRDLR) Green Paper on land reform (2011) would seem to suggest:

> National sovereignty is defined in terms of land. Even without it being enshrined in the country's supreme law, the Constitution, land is a national asset. (DRDLR 2011: 1)

> All anti-colonial struggles are, at the core, about two things: repossession of land lost through force or deceit; and *restoring the centrality of indigenous culture*. (Ibid., emphasis added)

> Any attempt at restoring *ubuntu* without a concomitant land restoration would be futile. Land is a fundamental means to *ubuntu*, the end! (Ibid. 2)
>
> Fundamentally, therefore, social cohesion, just like development, is a direct function of land access and ownership – the basic tenet of, or requirement for, the exercise of *ubuntu* in traditional African society. It is not just about allegiance to national symbols, e.g. the National Anthem and Flag, important as these are in the modern state context. It is part of a people's expression of themselves, for themselves. It is a way of life integrally linked to land. If you denied African people access to and ownership of land, as has been the case under both colonialism and Apartheid in South Africa, you have effectively destroyed the very foundation of their existence. (Ibid.)

For good measure the Green Paper also attributes nation-like collective attributes to 'the African majority' and ascribes a collective 'political will' to it:

> Our effort to bring about the corrective measures necessary to tone down the anger, bitterness and pain of those who have been subjected to this brutal treatment must be collective. The Truth and Reconciliation Commission . . . has adequately demonstrated the capacity and political will of black people in general and the African majority in particular to forgive. But this goodwill should not be taken for granted, because it is not an inexhaustible social asset. It is an asset around which we should work together to build our collective future.

This vision of land reform as full-blown, anti-colonial ethno-nationalism contrasts sharply with the NDP's vision of 'an integrated and inclusive rural economy' (NPC November 2011: 217–34), which looks to agro-processing, value chains, skills development, entrepreneurship training and job creation to realize it, and in which land reform will 'unlock the potential for a dynamic growing and employment-creating agriculture sector' (ibid. 226), rather than, as the Green Paper would have it, 'restore the centrality of indigenous culture' and traditional African society, as well as re-establish access to land as a 'people's expression of themselves [sic] and for themselves [sic]'.

Given South Africa's racial demography, apartheid legacy, history of struggle and ambiguous negotiated settlement, it should come as no surprise that there would be some incoherent, cultural noise as background to the government's efforts to keep to a consistent line in promoting the idea of a civic nation. However when, as is the case with the land reform green paper, the discordant voices are coming from within the government itself, then perceptions of nation-building may be thrown into confusion. To keep the matter in perspective it is worth noting that DRDLR is a relatively minor player in government. It is chronically underfunded for the size of the tasks assigned to it (the redistribution of 30 per cent of South Africa's land to African people); its lack of skills and bureaucratic capacity has been a major factor in failure to meet targets; it has been subjected to major policy U-turns, as when Mbeki changed the priorities from small-scale subsistence farming to the creation of a class of African large-scale commercial farmers. Nevertheless, in the green paper the department is expressing a widespread, collective sensitivity among black South Africans to a major historical injustice and looking for ways of expressing it in ethno-nationalist terms. In the midst of this kind of confusion there is an understandable tendency to look for signs that the kind of African nationalism which the land reform green paper expresses is realizing itself on the stage of national politics. This tendency has been especially marked since the emergence of Jacob Zuma as leader of the ANC and state president.

## Zuma and nation-building

Looking back at the journalistic reports, opinion pieces and academic analyses which followed Zuma's rise to the presidency, it is remarkable how often the assumption was that his emergence was somehow part of a logical progression (or in the eyes of some, a regression) that the third ANC president of South Africa should be a man with deep, rural roots, deep attachment to patriarchal, traditional culture, polygamous family life and considerable talent for demotic, political communication with the grass roots. The positive side of Zuma's appeal rested not only on his palpably greater comfort in vernacular and informal communication, but also his ease of manner with ethnic minorities – especially Afrikaners, to whom he extends the rather clichéd recognition of being 'true' Africans compared to the more alien English speakers. However, there was a darker side to the populist coalition that brought him to power: extravagantly warlike language; shows of strength outside court proceedings where his cases were being heard; thuggish abuse of the victim of the alleged rape, of which he was acquitted. In the combination of positive and negative, there was a sense in the air that some evolutionary trajectory of African nationalism was being followed.

It is true that some accounts make it clear how contingent his rise to power was. Zuma and Mbeki were associates and allies in the liberation struggle and the negotiations. The relationship soured while Zuma was vice-president to Mbeki's president, and the cloud of suspicion over Zuma following allegations of corruption gave Mbeki the incentive and opportunity to fire him. Zuma probably calculated that his best chances of staying out of jail were to mobilize a constituency of support in the ANC and regain high, or better still, gain the highest office. This coincided with increasing disaffection with Mbeki, from the Alliance Left over his 'neo-liberal' economic policies and from provincial grandees who were threatened by Mbeki's attempts to centralize and modernize the ANC. The question of succession to Mbeki as ANC president and president of the country turned these clouds of disaffection into a perfect storm. Under the South African Constitution the president is chosen by a simple majority of the National Assembly after a general election and can serve for no more than two terms. Given the ANC's electoral dominance, it is the party's conventions and practices that determine who the president shall be. The convention has been that whoever is elected president of the ANC at its five-yearly national conference, usually about 14 months before a general election, will be voted in as president by the ANC majority in the National Assembly. As Mbeki's second term drew to a close and the ANC's 2007 national conference approached, Mbeki's intentions regarding the succession were not clear. He made it known that he would stand for a third term as ANC president, which would not be unconstitutional; however, this was seen by his opponents as a technicality and seeking a third term at the head of the ANC as a transparent ploy to indirectly prolong his executive power by controlling whoever would be the ANC nominee for state president after the 2009 general election. This turned disaffection into revolt and coincided neatly with Zuma's own ambitions. The result was the installation of Zuma, the defeat of Mbeki and his subsequent, forced resignation from the office of state president. For good measure the 2007 conference passed a resolution hardening the convention that the ANC president would be the movement's candidate for the state presidency.

Some accounts of this transition duly recognized a fortuitous coincidence of interests in the emerging anti-Mbeki coalition and the role played by the president's own bad decisions. Nonetheless Zuma's emergence triggered a general sense of a politico-cultural shift and indeed a tendency to talk in terms of the 'Zuma watershed' (Piper 2009). In this tendency to see Zuma as representing a break with the past, populism and tradition are recurrent themes. In conventional portrayals written around 2007–9, Zuma offered a potent combination of emblematic experience and the common touch. This was spiced with hopes (or fears) of a turn to the Left based on the support of trade unions for him in his struggle with Mbeki or even a turn to ill-defined populism, spearheaded by his other great supporters, the ANCYL. All of this was reinforced by his identification with robust, traditional values, assumed to be more in tune with ordinary Africans' world view than the metropolitan discourse of non-racialism and human rights that underpinned the Constitution, and which was subscribed to by the leadership elite that guided the ANC through the negotiated transition. In this sort of account, Mbeki is treated as an aberration and an enigma, while Zuma represents a more authentic strain of African nationalism:

> In 2009 Jacob Zuma won the endorsement of Nelson Mandela and the overwhelming support of voters, thousands of whom wore '100 per

cent Zulu boy' T-shirts to celebrate the approaching end of an enigma, namely Thabo Mbeki's technocratic (and some say authoritarian) rule over the ANC. Indeed, Jacob Zuma is admired at home because, unlike his inscrutable predecessor, he is a recognizable man of tradition and struggle. Decades ago, the young Zuma left his reserve for work and activism in a South African city, sharing a formative experience with millions in his country, including his idol Mandela. (Carton 2010: 34)

Leaving aside the fact that the aristocratic Mandela's formative experience in the city – study at an elite and at the time multiracial university before embarking on the practice of law – had much more in common with Mbeki than with the unlettered Zuma, this is a fair enough summary. An analysis of the significance of Zuma's trademark song *Umshini Wami* (My Machine Gun) reinforces the point about cultural authenticity, when alluding to: 'A longing in the body politic for a political language other than a distancing and alienating technocracy' (Gunner 2009: 27). However, the problem with Mbeki's lack of demotic authenticity was only partly that of 'alienating technocracy', accurate though that charge might be. Mbeki's demonstration of high cultural and intellectual pretensions by weaving large chunks of Shakespeare, W. B. Yeats and the Bible into speeches, not to mention Marx, Polyani and Adam Smith, also created a hunger for plain speaking (and not only among the ANC grass roots). Identification of this politico-cultural strain in Zuma's appeal sometimes came with warnings. One such treatment (Vincent 2009) referred to the danger of the 'politics of culture, with its narratives of the return to the true Africa, which Zuma has publicly embraced, and through which he is legitimized as the benevolent patriarch'. In this version, the danger is the rise of an 'anti-rights' populism framed in Africanist terms as the basis for an 'oppressive conformism' (ibid. 213). This warning was an academic version of a common popular concern at the time and which has not diminished since.

Whatever the interpretations of the significance of Zuma's emergence may have shared, or the points on which they may have diverged, few if any paused to consider whether Zuma, just as much as Mbeki, may have been an enigma and even an aberration, even if only in the sense that there has not been a 'typical' African nationalist leader in South Africa so far, nor is there likely to be as long as African nationalism remains an enigma, or at least a work in progress itself. To put it another way, no-one appeared to consider whether the Zuma phenomenon might be a demotic interlude, rather than African nationalism showing itself in its true, popular cultural colours and unfolding in some kind of programmed cultural atavism. Two criteria by which this issue might be assessed are whether Zuma is likely to be succeeded by someone like him and whether his tenure has revealed a project to define African popular politics in terms of vernacular culture and traditional beliefs, and to install these terms of discourse above those of diversity and the civic nation.

In addressing the succession question, it is worth considering at length this account of Zuma on his home turf:

> His 'tribal' birthplace is located on the deeply rural southern fringe of the old Zulu kingdom, where polygamous homesteads raise livestock and hunt *izinyamazane* (buck), and people *ukukhonza* the *amakhosi*, offer loyalty to their chiefs. In Nkandla King Cetshwayo lies buried in a sacred grave. Candidate Zuma, the son of this hallowed region, reminded crowds that he developed the resilience to survive the trials of public life by herding unruly cattle, trapping wily game, and hearing of Zulu opposition to the white man. He learned an enduring moral, patriarchal respect (*ukuhlonipa or inhlonipho*), from elders who said that attaining manhood meant *ukwakha umuzi*, accepting the challenges of 'building the homestead' – from abiding the absence of loved ones during migrant labour to managing the obligations of a patriarch with wives and children. (Carton 2010: 34)

Given the patterns of generational experience and of building political careers in the ANC over the past 30 years, it is unlikely that anyone who fits this somewhat lyrical, but doubtless basically accurate portrait will emerge to lead the ANC in the future. The election by a massive majority of the suave, secular and trout-fishing figure of Cyril Ramaphosa to the vice-presidency of the ANC at the national conference in December 2012 underlines the point. Despite occupying what has hitherto been pole position for the presidency, Ramaphosa is not guaranteed the succession on or before 2019, when Zuma's second term will end (at the age of 77) because internal ANC politics are a lot more fluid than they used to be. However, if the succession is not his, then it is likely to be for someone far more like him than like Zuma. A university-educated career politician, trade unionist or BEE tycoon (or like Ramaphosa a combination of all three) is a more likely prospect. The plain fact of the matter is that there is no-one like Zuma in the upper ranks of the ANC from which the candidate will emerge. Doubtless whoever does emerge will have learned from Zuma that demotic talents, authentic or rehearsed, should feature in any leadership package, but the idea that there could be substantial continuity with Zuma's trajectory in life is far-fetched. The question of whether Zuma embarked on his ascent to the presidency with a project to put a demotic African stamp on the country is also likely to be answered in the negative. It is true that there have been cultural tensions during his tenure, but some at least have been brought on as much by provocateurs pre-emptively testing the limits of African tolerance for freedom of expression rather than by a systematic drive on the part of Africanists to suppress it.[1] What has been more characteristic of Zuma's approach has been a scatter gun of quotations, often in an African language and in a spontaneous departure from a script which may or may not have lost or gained something in translation, along the general lines that traditional African culture is to be valued, while at the same time displaying scepticism or denigration about 'Western ways'. Patriarchal views on women and views on sexual orientation, seemingly at variance with non-discrimination provisions of the Constitution, have also figured. Media reporting and opinion pieces in English see these views as divisive, bigoted, patriarchal and sexist, undermining nation-building and posing a threat to constitutional rights from cultural essentialism. This sort of opinion is typically followed by 'clarifications' and rationalizations by Zuma's spin doctors. Two things are worth noting about this phenomenon, which has become a regular part of the South African political cycle. The first is that these pronouncements appear to be largely personal in origin, and although they strike a popular chord they do not appear to be linked to a systematic attempt from within the ANC to change the terms of political discourse in an Africanist direction. It is hard to distinguish any group in the upper reaches of the ANC or government whose purposes this might serve, although lobby groups such as Contralesa and the MK military veterans association would approve. In any case, it is hard to see how this could be done without wholesale changes to the Constitution and harder to calculate what sort of payoff might make such drastic steps worthwhile.

On the other hand, careless expressions from the highest office in the land that can be interpreted or misinterpreted as culturally essentialist and/or reinforcing prejudice should not be taken lightly in a social landscape that is blighted by 'corrective' rape, rampant gender violence of all kinds, *muthi* killings and racist slurs on both black and white members of 'white' political parties. Perhaps the various exchanges that have characterized Zuma's presidency so far should be interpreted not so much as cultural wars of domination but anxious and bad-tempered skirmishes of coexistence, which are the result of South Africa constituting a highly diverse and overcrowded public, cultural space.

Something similar could be said for the marathon task of finding an appropriate place for traditional authorities and culture in legislation that recognizes both the diversity and the human rights goals of the Constitution. This has continued during Zuma's tenure, without the ANC apparently deviating from its long-term goal of trimming and appeasing to accommodate traditional leaders as an undeniable source of interest, allegiance and value in African life without conceding anything essential. Even given the importance of tradition to Zuma, there is no real sign that under him the ANC is doing more than it has to, to find a modus vivendi with a force that even the most secular and progressive of ANC supporters would probably agree can neither be ignored nor extirpated from national life.

Arguably, then, in terms of nation-building, Zuma is as much of an enigma as Mbeki was said to be and not a harbinger of African nationalism's true colours. He has identified himself closely with the NDP and has expressed the hope that the ANC can unite the country behind its vision of growth, social compacts and civic nationalism. On the other hand, there are the flashes of cultural Afro-essentialism, tempered however by willingness to listen to and discuss minority concerns – especially the plight of poor, white Afrikaners. In the end, he is an instinctively communicative politician, a shrewd and capable tactician who presumably learnt much about the sources and uses of power from his period in exile as the head of ANC counter-intelligence. However, the only project on which he puts these talents to use is Zuma himself. As this has become apparent during his tenure of the presidency, concerns about the direction in which he might take African nationalism have shifted from fears that he might preside over the emergence of cultural essentialism that would conflict with the rights in the Constitution, to warnings that he might be turning into the 'Big Man' patronage leader symbolic of the decay of post-liberation, African nationalism in much of the rest of Africa. Such concerns were stoked in 2013 by controversy over the construction of an extremely expensive family compound for him from public funds in his home village of Nkandla, as well as the close relations between members of his family and a family of Indian tycoons, the Guptas, who wielded undue influence with public officials by trading on Zuma's name. Whatever his contribution to African nationalism or to wider nation-building, the Zuma interlude will have made no lasting impression on either, and certainly not to achieving some synthesis between them.

## The ANC and non-racialism today

In February 2011 a political storm broke out over some remarks made in a television broadcast by one Jimmy Manyi who, at the time he made them, was director general (DG: civil service head) of the Department of Labour (DoL), a post he combined, somewhat controversially, with being president of the BMF. The Manyi affair highlighted the unfinished business of non-racialism in post-apartheid South Africa.

In his DoL post, Manyi was responsible for drafting amendments to the Employment Equity Act. One direction he took was to propose that racial headcounts – the principal criterion for success of transformation in employment – should be assessed on a national, not a provincial basis. That is, race groups in each province should conform for the purposes of employment equity to the national demographic profile, irrespective of the fact that there are significantly different concentrations of whites, Coloureds and Indians in all nine provinces. During the course of a television broadcast the question arose of how Manyi's amendments would affect the employment prospects of Coloureds in the Western Cape, where according to the 2011 Census they constitute 48.8 per cent of the population, but only 8.9 per cent nationally. He replied in the following terms:

> I think it is very important for Coloured people to understand that South Africa belongs to them in totality, not just the Western Cape. So this over-concentration of Coloureds in the Western Cape is just not working for them. They should spread in the rest of the country . . . so they must stop this over-concentration situation because they are in over-supply where they are so you must look into the country and see where you can meet the supply [*sic*].

In cold print this does not make much sense, but he reinforced the point later in the broadcast when he said that the rest of the country should be looked at 'to see where there was a demand for Coloured workers' (*Mail & Guardian* 24 February 2011). The clear implication was population transfer in order to Africanize the Western Cape. In fact Manyi made these pronouncements in March 2010, nearly a year before the controversy which broke when trade union Solidarity posted a clip of the broadcast on YouTube in February 2011.[2] Solidarity did this when it came under fire as defenders of white privilege for opposing the legislative amendments. When the clip of Manyi's crass remarks received wide publicity, the ANC soon disowned him and Cosatu sharply criticized him. The clearest denunciation came from the then Minister of Finance Trevor Manuel who in an open letter to Manyi labelled him 'a racist in the mould of H F Verwoerd'. Manuel said:

> The just and constitutionally obligated provisions for redress are not and can never be an excuse to perpetuate racism . . . in the light of the utterances you made when you were the DG of the Department of Labour, and given the fact that the amendments to the Employment Equity Act were drafted during your tenure, I have a sense that your racism has infiltrated the highest echelons of government. (IOL News 2 March 2011)

Manuel was not entirely successful in portraying the amendments and Manyi's gloss on them as acts of freelance folly.[3] Folly they certainly were, given the electoral demography of the Western Cape. Municipal elections were held country-wide in May 2011, and while it would not be possible to assess how much Manyi's racist remarks contributed to the sweeping gains made in the Western Cape by the DA at the ANC's expense, it is safe to say he did not help the ANC cause. Probably concern that this would happen helped focus Manuel's anger, given that he was chairman of an ANC National Executive Council (NEC) committee deployed to regroup the party in the Western Cape after losing the province to the DA in the 2009 general election. However, Manuel's lament that 'we should have been more vigilant' at an earlier stage of Manyi's career does not entirely dispose of the matter. As DG of the labour department, he was a political appointment, a 'deployee' in ANC jargon, and he had never been one to hide his hard-line views on the racial aspects of transformation: anyone who was surprised that they found their way into draft legislation on Manyi's watch had not been paying attention. If Manuel meant literally, 'your racism infiltrated the highest levels of government' – to mean that Manyi had proceeded by stealth – then he is not to be taken seriously. In any case the offending amendments were not drafted in secrecy; they had been around for over a year and indeed had been defended by the ANC and Cosatu following criticism by Solidarity and others. Whatever the merits of Manuel's riposte there is a sympathetic constituency in the ANC for Manyi's views as counter-criticism of Manuel made clear. The leadership conspicuously failed to unite around Manuel, as a terse and somewhat mysterious statement from Secretary-General Gwede Mantashe, reacting to the open letter, indicated. In the end, while it is difficult to feel sympathy for Manyi, it is worth pointing out that it was by taking literally the implications of the amendments in a somewhat ingenuous way, and defending what were in their own terms perfectly logical consequences, that he landed himself in trouble.

One inevitable by-product of the Manyi affair was to bring once more to the foreground a question that had been posed regularly since Mbeki took over from Mandela – inside the ANC as well as outside: 'Has the ANC betrayed its heritage of non-racialism?' This is an extremely difficult question to answer because, as we saw earlier, the terms of engagement on which non-racialism is discussed in South Africa are so slippery. In short, since no-one is really sure what the ANC's heritage actually is in this respect, it is difficult to know whether or not it has been betrayed. According to one typical account, '[t]he dominant motif of the ANC's politics ... centres on the inclusion and accommodation of people of all races' but 'the ANC has never articulated the detailed terms of this political inclusiveness' (Mangcu 2005: 116).

In this ill-defined space, many variations on the theme of inclusiveness and non-racialism jostle for attention. For instance, in an ANC-leaning publication, Ben Turok, ANC and SACP struggle veteran and member of parliament since 1994, posed the question: 'are the imperatives of black empowerment and affirmative action eroding the vision of non-racialism?' He found the answer to be affirmative, but the symptoms, dangers and the cure he cited were not the predictable ones. According to Turok the main symptom was that the upper reaches of the ANC were too African and did not 'adequately symbolize the non-racial vision of the ANC': his remedy was affirmative action within ANC leadership structures to promote members of minority races. The danger was not a matter of principle or any other concern with nation-building, but it was a strategy to keep the ANC in power. Minorities 'have the potential to create a great deal of mischief

... progressive forces can never relax their vigilance, nor take their power for granted . . . the middle strata must have no excuse to go into active opposition to the ruling party' (Turok 2008: 5). In short, the vision of non-racialism is less a matter of political ethics, more a matter of dealing with the dangers to permanent ANC hegemony of 'ignoring the non-African middle strata'. This is an individual and possibly somewhat eccentric view, certainly it is further from policy making than Manyi's was, but it still usefully illustrates the flexibility with which non-racialism is discussed and promoted in ANC ideological circles.

A recent review of the ANC and non-racialism, carried out for a foundation close to the ANC, summarized this intellectual void: 'there is no distinct reference point detailing the party's post-apartheid approach to non-racialism', and ANC pronouncements on non-racialism 'provide little substantive guidance for ANC members on how to instrumentalise a vision of non-racialism', or indeed what in practice a non-racial society would look like (Ahmed Kathrada Foundation[4] 2013: 9 and 10). In practice the ANC is more concerned to justify continued racial differentiation in the interests of redress for previous racial discrimination than it is to set out a vision for a non-racial society. The nearest it comes to the latter is to conceptualize a non-racial society as one in which such race-based measures are no longer necessary. However, the bar is set rather high for the achievement of this situation, for instance, in the ANC's 1991 Constitutional Principles for a Democratic South Africa:

> A non-racial South Africa means a South Africa in which all the artificial assumptions which kept people apart and maintained domination, are removed. In a negative sense, non-racial means the elimination of all colour bars. In positive terms it means the affirmation of equal rights for all . . . the Constitution must provide the positive means to reduce progressively the imbalances and inequalities and to ensure that everybody has an equal chance in life.

This kind of understanding justifies the following lines of thought. The essential meaning of non-racialism is to fight against racism. A non-racial society is one in which people are not differentiated by racial criteria (which in any case have no ontological status). However, a society from which statutory, racial differentiation has been removed is not non-racial. To act as if it is so, is to be in denial of the persistence and resilience of racism, and to fail to understand the nature of 'real' non-racialism. Not only do the structural effects of past racial discrimination persist, but under conditions of political freedom which outlaw its overt expression, racism is forced to express itself in new, covert and coded ways. This opens new fronts of struggle to define, expose and confront these mutations of racism. This struggle is without limit and without foreseeable end. At the same time, 'real' non-racialism requires continued racial differentiation in order to bring about a situation in which racial differentiation will no longer be necessary. No-one knows how long this will take, by what criteria 'everybody has an equal chance in life' will be judged and who will do the judging. It is hard to say whether any of this betrays a legacy of ANC non-racialism since there is no body of thought, writing or practice that these things specifically contravene, and past texts are sufficiently flexible to be interpreted or reinterpreted to legitimize them.

Nonetheless, the somewhat doublethink formula of anti-racist racism (Cachalia 2012: 58) causes unease, not only among the ANC's opponents – who see it as 're-racialization', the 'race card' or 'neo-apartheid' – but among its sympathizers and even in its own discussion documents. At this level the unease tends to be expressed along the token lines of 'we must be vigilant to avoid giving the wrong impression' rather than holding out the slightest possibility of any kind of substantial rethink. Nonetheless it is there in such passages as: 'Racial classification cannot be avoided if we are to ensure representivity in the state and society generally but we must acknowledge that this creates the risk of freezing racial and cultural categories rather than allowing for organic development' (ANC 2005).

Aside from such matters of principle which may bear upon nation-building, all interventions, 'to ensure representivity in the state and society', carry with them the risk of unintended consequences. They may distort incentives and create expectations of entitlement; they offer fertile opportunity for patronage and the stricter their requirements, the greater the risk of introducing a further layer of distortion through practices such as 'fronting', which in turn require an extra layer of policing. Although 'anti-racist racism' is open to criticism on a number of wide fronts, the ANC generally prefers to turn defence into attack on a single narrow one. It does this by choosing to interpret all questioning of its policies in this area as accusations of discrimination against whites, aggressively turning the argument round by pointing to the wide discrepancies between white and black unemployment rates, and demanding further ramping up of race-based redress. In fact few if any serious criticisms come from this quarter, except those that allege breaches of codes of conduct and statutory requirements that are supposed to govern affirmative action and BEE. Examples of these are the cases Solidarity brings on behalf of its members, especially in the security services and parastatals. Despite this, the ANC does its best to close down all discussion of redress policies by branding those who question their application, never mind their principle, in the kind of terms used by Secretary-General Mantashe to describe those who criticized Manyi's employment act amendments, as 'those who hate transformation'.

Ironically perhaps the most vulnerable aspect of 'anti-racist racism' has little directly to do with whites (or other minorities), but has its greatest relevance among those categorized as African. This is the question of targeting redress measures and the relation between race and class. As we have noted, the NPC included this issue in its questions for public engagement, between the publication of the diagnostic reports and the completion of the NDP. It did so in the following terms: 'Can class be used instead of race do drive equity and the nation-building project, or is it too early in spite of the presence of the black elite? Should the focus be on social equity rather than on the continual use of these divisive elements class or race? Does it matter, because class by and large still mirrors race?' (NPC June 2011: 17). The final question goes to the nub of the matter. Either race *is* co-terminus with class, or very close to it, in which case any negative side effects for nation-building from using race as the only basis for redress can be avoided by using class instead. Or race is *not* co-terminus with class, in which case anyone who insists on making race the only basis for redress is buying into racial chauvinism and encouraging intraracial inequality by arguing that all members of a race (a marker which we should recall has no ontological status) are equally deserving. The result of the NDP's invitation to public engagement on this matter appears to have been a deafening silence.

## 'Not white enough, not black enough': Coloureds and Indians in the new South Africa

The sense of not fitting comfortably into any template of South African nation-building which is common to both Coloured and Indian South Africans is summed up in the wry verdict freely offered by members of both communities: 'Under apartheid we were not white enough: in the new South Africa we are not black enough.' The quip is usually deployed in the context of affirmative action and BEE because although Indians and Coloureds are eligible for these programmes and some have done well out of them (certainly enough of them to anger African populists), there is a widespread feeling among both communities that there is a definite hierarchy of advantage where redress is concerned and they both lose out.

Although the 'not white enough, not black enough' characterization distances these 'black' minorities from whites, in many respects they occupy similarly ambivalent and unstable positions in relation to the new South African nation as whites do. The ambiguities of African nationalism and of non-racialism bear on them as much as on whites, but from different perspectives. Added complications in the cases of Coloureds and Indians are that they are black and previously disadvantaged as well. However, these affinities with Africans, rather than making for unambiguous inclusiveness, tend to be translated into questions of 'how black?' 'how African?' and 'how disadvantaged?' in ways that affect the statuses of Coloureds and Indians in the various versions of post-apartheid nation-building. Whether or not the humiliations of apartheid bore down as heavily on Coloureds and Indians as on Africans is something that at times is sharply contested between the various groups. What is incontestable is that in some ways Indians and Coloureds were better off than Africans. Their relative 'privileges' included comparatively secure access to urban areas and employment opportunities, as well as higher per capita expenditure on education and health for them than for Africans. These differences feed into in contests over 'blackness', 'Africanness' and redress issues generally.

Despite some essential similarities which Coloureds and Indians share with whites, only a tiny fraction of the research effort and column inches that have been devoted to the position of whites in post-apartheid South Africa has been devoted to the other two minorities. This is despite the fact that Coloureds constitute the same percentage of the South African population as whites (8.9%). Indians are only 2.5 per cent, but between them the two 'black' minorities are more than one in ten of the South African population. There are several reasons for this disparity of interest and coverage. Indians and Coloureds lack the enormous economic, social and cultural leverage that whites still possess thanks to their previous dominance. They also lack the burden of responsibility for the past which is the other legacy of that dominance, and which makes whites the focus of questions of guilt and atonement. Thirdly, they lack the extensive transnational linkages of whites into global business and media, which make them such a continuing object of fascination.

In the case of Indians, lack of numbers counts too. Two and a half per cent is a very small proportion and – as with the other minorities – it is concentrated: in six out of the nine provinces, Indians make up less than 1 per cent of the population and in none of them do they reach even 10 per cent (7.4% in KwaZulu-Natal is the largest provincial percentage of Indians). In much of the country Indians are not even a minority, they are virtually invisible. The position of Coloureds is rather different: they have greater numbers and greater concentration, which makes them of greater political interest and significance. Coloureds make up 48.8 per cent of the Western Cape's population and 40.3 per cent in the Northern Cape.[5] This is a largely poor, working-class community which in local concentrations has some notably unfavourable socio-economic indicators. These include rates of foetal alcohol syndrome that are among the worst in the world[6] and an incarceration rate (as reported by South African Institute of Race Relations (SAIRR) in 2007) which at 651 per 100,000 was almost double that of Africans (IOL News 25 November 2008).

The concentration of Coloureds in the Western Cape makes it the only province in which there is not a demographic African majority and where African nationalism (overt or implied) is not a reliable vote winner. This has enabled the DA to put together a coalition of Coloureds and whites (15.7% of the provincial population) to win elections for the Cape Town Metro and the Western Cape provincial assembly. Although it now runs on its record of delivery in local and provincial government, the DA was able originally to put together this winning coalition at least partly by playing on Coloured disaffection with affirmative action and BEE, and (controversially) using slogans such as 'Stop ANC racism' (Schulz-Herzenberg 2007: 138). Whether this should be controversial or not is a moot point however, since given Manyi's views on the employment situations of both Coloureds and Indians (discussed on pp. 297–8), it can hardly be said that the DA invented Coloured disaffection or that there were no grounds for concern on the part of Coloureds as to the ANC's official attitude to them. Coloured disaffection with the ANC and Africanism generally is also stoked by occasional bouts of racial stereotyping of Coloureds by high-profile Africans, based on the kind of popular stereotypes of Coloureds regarding alcohol, drugs and crime which are encouraged by the health and social indicators noted earlier. One such instance occurred in 2005 when Roderick 'Blackman' Ngoro, head of communications for (and allegedly lover of) the then ANC mayor of Cape Town, posted a racially defamatory editorial about Coloureds on his blog, saying that they were 'culturally inferior to Africans' and that they would all die 'a drunken death' if they do not undergo 'ideological transformation' (Jolobe 2007: 93). In the eyes of Coloureds who were subject to this racial defamation, insult may have been added to injury by the fact that Ngoro (who died in 2010) was not South African-born but Zimbabwean. Indians too are subject from time to time to such outbursts from outspoken Africans, who, like Ngoro, may not represent official ANC attitudes and policies, but who are well-enough connected to those who do, to sow doubt as to the ANC's commitment to non-racialism in minority minds.

This scepticism about non-racialism extends to minority members in the ANC's own ranks. The ANC-aligned Ahmed Kathrada Foundation carried out a study of the practice of non-racialism in ANC branches in the Johannesburg area, prompted by concerns that minorities were being sidelined. Branches in Coloured, Indian and white areas sent a clear message in the findings: 'it was clear almost across the board that members feel that there are significant problems with race relations within the ANC at all levels' (Ahmed Kathrada Foundation 2013: 13). The most deeply felt grievances were expressed in a working-class Coloured area.

It would be naïve however to portray the black minorities, especially Coloureds, exclusively as passive victims, first of white racism and then of African nationalism's hierarchy of disadvantage and redress. The UDF period in the liberation struggle laid a somewhat romantic mist over what were sometimes, and still to some extent remain, ugly racial attitudes on the part of some Coloureds. Writing of the shock engendered by the majority of Coloured votes cast for the NP in South Africa's first democratic election, a historian of Coloured identity recalls: 'Many people on the progressive Left whose wishful thinking had blinded them to the extent of Coloured racial chauvinism were shocked and shamed into more realistic appraisals of sentiment within the Coloured community generally' (Adhikari 2005:

174). The same account refers to a resurgence of 'Coloured identity' fuelled by: 'Fear of African majority rule, perceptions that Coloureds were being marginalized, a desire to counter pervasive negative stereotyping of Coloured people' (ibid. 176). However, this identity is essentially defensive, expressing the weakness, marginality and vulnerability which arise from being perpetually in an intermediate position in whatever racial hierarchy holds sway at any given time. Following this the conclusion is somewhat tentative: 'The overall sense one has regarding Coloured identity in the new South Africa is one of fragmentation, uncertainty and confusion.' Such positions as there are on 'Colouredness' have thus far 'failed to have much of a popular impact because they lack resonance with the Coloured masses and are driven by small groups of intellectuals and community activists with limited influence' (ibid. 186). This could be a polite (and reluctant) way of saying that a Coloured identity does not in fact exist in any coherent and meaningful way at all, except in the expression of electoral choice for the DA, a party that rejects identity politics, but provides a congenial home for minorities.

## Exit, voice and nation-building: Whites since 1994

The issue of emigration is central to any discussion and understanding of whites and nation-building in post-apartheid South Africa. The widely influential conceptual scheme first outlined by Albert O. Hirschman in 1970, which juxtaposes the choices 'exit and voice', provides a useful framework within which to pursue this issue (Hirschman 1970). Beginning in a business context and later extending the idea to politics and the state, Hirschman argued that faced with deteriorating conditions people had the choice of withdrawal or engagement. Actions reflecting the choice of withdrawal (exit) include change of supplier or resignation in the case of consumer or employee issues, and emigration in the face of political repression. Examples of engagement (voice) include complaint, negotiation or political protest. Hirschman invoked a third variable, 'loyalty' – exemplified, for instance, by patriotism, an attachment to a country that transcends a particular set of political conditions at any given time – which can affect the choice, as can the relative benefits and costs of choosing either exit or voice.

Figures seem to suggest that large numbers of whites have taken the exit option since 1994. However, the facts concerning numbers of white departures are disputed, and the dynamics and motivations for movements in and out of the country are underresearched, despite a superfluity of anecdotal evidence. As a result, the politics of white emigration are hard to read, and the significance for nation-building is by no means self-evident for what is indisputably a substantial movement of people, despite disagreement on the exact magnitude.

Official South African data hugely underestimate the extent of emigration. There is no incentive for people to declare themselves as emigrants and good reason to keep options open for return. It is very easy simply to leave the country and not return, while the official emigration procedures are irksome and not always efficiently handled. In many cases, moreover, people may simply not know how long they intend to be away. This is especially true of young people who have not yet acquired major family and career commitments. In this sense the very concept of who and what is 'an emigrant' becomes flexible and unstable. Foreign exchange regulations have been relaxed to the point where they are relatively undemanding. Limits to the amount of assets that can be transferred out of the country by citizens or permanent residents (in the form of annual travel allowance and allowances for overseas investments) have been raised to the point that only the very wealthy need declare themselves as emigrants to get their assets out and the very wealthy tend to have other options in any case. The Department of Home Affairs has ceased to collect passenger data at ports of departure. As a result of all these conditions, estimates of emigration tend to rely on data (census responses on place of birth, employment data) collected by authorities in the main points of destination for South Africans. Another approach has been to compare the statistical age pyramids for whites in South Africa from one census to the next.

On this basis, estimates of white emigration have varied substantially, although even the lowest is a significant number. In 2006, the liberal think tank, the South African Institute of Race Relations (SAIRR) arrived at a figure of 841,000 white emigrants in the decade from 1995, based on analyses of StatsSA household surveys.[7] This estimate was challenged by the claim that StatsSA in Census 2001 underestimated the number of whites as a result, among other factors, of obstruction by some whites who wanted nothing to do with requirements of a 'black government', and difficulties faced by (black) enumerators gaining access to high-security complexes (for a discussion see *Sunday Independent* 8 October 2006). According to critics, this underrecorded baseline distorted SAIRR findings. Estimates based on destination-country data tend to converge above the half-million mark. One such study arrived at a figure of more than 520,000 for the 5 main destination countries (United Kingdom, United States, Australia, New Zealand, Canada) between 1989 and 2003, with the rate escalating markedly in the second half of this period (Stern and Szalontai 2006: 125). The same study estimated that 120,000 of the emigrants were skilled (ibid. 126). A later estimate, also based on receiving country data (Politicsweb 14 August 2012), arrived at a figure of 588,388 for all OECD countries in 2010. Neither of these figures is likely to be an overestimate because there are complications of recording and enumeration. Such factors include arrivals in destination countries of South Africans who were not born in

South Africa and South Africans arriving on passports other than South African. Bearing in mind issues such as these, another estimate suggests 'a more realistic figure' for the United Kingdom alone would be in the region of 550,000 (Crawford 2009: 14). This might provide a more 'accurate' estimate of numbers, but the inclusion of these additional categories of departure could distort the meaning of emigration figures. That is, the inclusion of people whose roots in South Africa are not particularly deep might confuse the meaning of their departure from the country. It is not only the problem then of 'who is an emigrant?' but also that of 'who is South African?' that stands in the way of authoritative data on emigration.

Figures based on destination-country data do not allow estimates of emigration by race. If a figure for *white* emigration is required, then it is to census and other South African statistical data that researchers look, despite the methodological difficulties involved. Sometimes the census points in this direction, uninvited. For instance, the 2011 census appeared to record a notable absence of young, white men. One commentary noted a 'surprising' preponderance of females in the white, working-age population, in which there were about 68,000 'absent' males (Harrison 2012: 2). Dismissing data problems as an explanation, this account pointed to the shifting work patterns of whites, whose work environment has become increasingly constrained, 'partly because of employment equity', and who have become more geographically and contractually flexible: 'In the past they may have emigrated with their families, but prospects for permanent jobs in traditional destinations such as Australia, New Zealand and Britain have dimmed. And so they have taken up work elsewhere, especially in Africa and the Middle East, where their skills are in high demand' (ibid.).

Although not all expatriates are white or male, by working in booming areas, in high-risk occupations (mining, prospecting, security contracting) and for South African firms aggressively expanding in Africa, many white South African males may have become a 'a highly privileged class of migrants'. Certainly this would explain the demographic anomaly in the gender of working-age whites without recourse to blaming the census. It would also put the movement of these people into the context of a transnational labour market rather than emigration as such.

Even if there is not much doubt that large numbers of people, mostly young, many of them skilled, have left South Africa in the past two decades, questions remain as to the significance of this for nation-building. The first question is whether this is a largely 'white' phenomenon and if so, does it matter more or less? The answer to the first part is clearly affirmative. Crawford claims on the basis of the British 2001 census that the white share of the South African population in London dropped – but only from 91 per cent to 87 per cent (2009: 15). There is anecdotal evidence that significant numbers of Indians and Coloureds have emigrated and substantial numbers of African nurses work overseas. Whether this last example is mainly emigration or temporary work for purely economic motivation it is impossible to generalize with confidence. This anecdotal evidence finds its way into the literature on South African migration but it is not backed with hard numbers. However, surveys which ask whether respondents have or are considering emigration have registered noticeable numbers of affirmative responses from Coloureds, Indians and Africans. In 2000, at around the time when emigration of skilled South Africans was at its height, a survey of motives for considering emigration carried out among skilled people of all race groups found quite similar concerns, centring on safety and taxation. Significant differences included blacks being twice as confident in the future of their children as whites and twice as dissatisfied with their level of income as whites (Mattes and Richmond 2000). In 2008, the *Economist* quoted a survey by a commercial polling company whose results showed that 'thinking of emigrating' was evenly distributed across the races: 42 per cent of Coloureds, 38 per cent of Africans, 30 per cent of Indians and 41 per cent of whites (*Economist* 25 September 2008). The real differences between black and white, however, have been in whites' relative ease of access to foreign prospects. Ancestral visas to the United Kingdom and possession of actual passports, 'bridgehead' networks of family and friends, social capital and cultural fluency all favour whites' prospects, as does the possession of skills (although with the growth in numbers of black graduates in South Africa this particular comparative advantage is diminishing).

Contestation over numbers, as well as attention paid to the racial mix of emigrants, are indirect indications of the political sensitivity of emigration as an issue bearing on nation-building, a sensitivity that is not always apparent on the surface. In 1998, President Mandela said of emigrants: 'Let them go. In that process we are convinced that real South Africans are being sorted out. The real South Africans are the ones who are staying' (quoted in Crawford 2009: 13). Since then the government has tended to adopt a slightly pained, but more-in-sorrow-than-anger line, stressing South Africa's need for skills and the welcome awaiting those who would repatriate themselves and their abilities to contribute to South Africa's development. Underneath this mature attitude, however, both sides – white emigrants and black South Africans – are capable of seething with resentment which shades into overt racism. Inevitably the internet provides many examples of this, including websites claiming that 'genocide' is being practised against South African whites (citing farm murders in this instance). The successful application made in 2009 by a white South African for asylum in Canada on the grounds of racial persecution, provoked an angry reaction by the government in South Africa, including the accusation that the ruling would perpetuate racism in South Africa. Though this was an isolated occurrence, it encapsulated, albeit in exaggerated form, the sensitivities around white emigration.

In the presence of such mixed signals and against such background noise it is difficult to see white emigration in perspective. It is worth noting that whites who emigrate and are vocal about the reasons are often very unpopular among whites who stay. More importantly, it is important to bear in mind that whites now account for less than 9 per cent of the population, and to ask whether undue attention to emigration risks assigning too much importance to this minority in the context of nation-building. Indeed there is a temptation to write white emigration off as no more than the arrogance of a minority in a minority, which cannot come to terms with its loss of power, and refuses to face up to the reality of how it came to possess the skills and social capital that it feels entitled to use with absolute freedom in skewed 'competition' with those who, even if they are 'born free' and equal, have a very different legacy from the past. Quite apart from any irritation black people might feel on these grounds, there is a larger and more serious point that potentially can be made; undue focus on white discontents is a distraction from the bigger and more worrying question of how the African 80 per cent of the population can be forged into a more coherent and clearly articulated sense of nationhood than it currently constitutes.

On the other hand white emigration can be looked on as a response to a combination of general conditions (crime, corruption) which encourage skilled people of all races to consider emigration, and of particular circumstances affecting whites' prospects, especially affirmative action. Seen in this way, as a combination of state dysfunction and discrimination, emigration has to be taken more seriously as a pointer to national conditions and prospects. What is more, emigration can be seen as part of a vicious circle of effects in which skills flight deepens the conditions which encourage emigration in the first place. Not the least of the irritations experienced by the ANC and government in this context is the sporadic but persistent prominence given to 'white flight' by the Western media. Irritating or not, it is a real issue for a country seeking to maintain confidence in its attraction as an investment destination, its self-image as an inclusive, civic nation and its distance from the pathological example of Zimbabwe. Since angry denialism, tempting though it is to wounded African pride, only reinforces the chain of destructive effects, crafting a response is not easy.

One way of seeing white 'exit' in perspective is to think in classic migration-studies terms of 'push' and 'pull' factors. In the decade and a half between the uncertainties of South Africa's transition to democracy and the global financial crisis in 2008, push factors were certainly important to white South Africans. Under these however, the powerful pull of an increasingly transnational labour market also offered strong incentives to move. This was true of niche-skill markets, for example, in medical as well as legal and financial professionals, but also for people with high levels of general education and for less-skilled occupations (in the hospitality industry, for instance). As we have already noted, South Africa is easy to leave and return to, and white South Africans (Afrikaans-speaking as well as Anglophone) are linguistically and culturally well-attuned to transnational employment. The interplay of push and pull factors is always complex. In this case some, perhaps many, individuals may have preferred to present themselves as refugees of a kind, rather than mercenaries burdened with the stigma of a racially oppressive past. In such cases the line between believing oneself and deceiving oneself and others can come down to fine margins of emphasis; in any case the experience of being turned down for a job for some reason connected with affirmative action is well diffused among white men in particular.

States to which Hirschman's exit-voice scheme have been applied include the German Democratic Republic (Hirschman 1993) and Cuba (Hoffmann 2004). There are very obvious and substantial differences between these and South Africa, notably the fact that South Africa is an open democracy. Nevertheless, the framework still offers some suggestive possibilities. For instance, emigration can be seen as a stabilizing force by drawing off potential dissenters. White emigration may have functioned to some extent as a safety valve, not so much in drawing off political dissent, but by allowing affirmative action to proceed with less friction that otherwise might have happened, through removing considerable numbers of skilled people from the South African job market. This is in some respects a thoroughly backhanded and rather devious view. It would surely have been better for the skills to be made use of in South Africa. However, if the government was determined to push affirmative action forward at all costs – and there is every indication that it was – it is not easy to see how these 'white' skills could have been utilized without friction. Black lobbies close to the government as well as radicals and populists were already incensed at what they saw as the slow progress of affirmative action; so if the labour market still contained another 150–200,000 skilled white people, it is hard to see how the government could avoid antagonizing either its own supporters or a substantial number of whites. Another classic spin-off of the exit option is the creation of a diaspora which becomes a source of external pressure on the regime. Again the differences between democratic South Africa and authoritarian regimes are obvious. Nonetheless in an indirect way something of this effect can be seen in terms of the pressure on South Africa's reputation, when it appears that a large number of its own people find conditions so inhospitable that they leave.

## From emigration to transnationalism

In one sense, both the relevance of the scheme and the differences between its applicability to democratic and undemocratic regimes is captured in Hirschman's third variable, loyalty. These things are exemplified in the 'Homecoming Revolution', an organization that lobbies young South Africans in the United Kingdom on the benefits (for the country as well as for the individuals themselves) of returning to South Africa. The Homecoming

Revolution is independently run, funded by a major South African bank and supported by the South African government. Evidence of success in terms of numbers of returnees is difficult to come by. The corollary of ease of unrecorded exit is ease of unrecorded re-entry. There have been anecdotal media claims since 2008 of rising numbers of returnees in the wake of the global recession but it is probably safe to assume that these are considerably fewer than those who made the outward journey. It is also open to question whether the return is only a tactical necessity in the face of temporarily unfavourable economic conditions or a binding life choice. However, numbers are not really the point. The significance of the Homeland Revolution lies in the intention to create a transnational community of South Africans as a counter-influence to any negative effects of emigration on nation-building in South Africa. The government's support for the repatriation of skills is in itself a positive sign for nation-building, although possible conflicts of priority between redress and economic development will remain. Dealing with these conflicts may require revisiting the surreal world of government assessments of skill shortages. For instance, the National Scarce Skills List (Department of Labour 2008: 2) invokes 'absolute scarcity' of skills which is simple enough: there are no people in the labour market with the suitable skills. However, it goes on to call into being 'relative scarcity', which refers to 'the context where suitably skilled people are in fact available in the labour market but they do not exhibit other employment criteria'. 'Other criteria' include 'equity considerations', which require candidates with the requisite skills 'from specific groups'. Until a shortage is simply a shortage, there may be difficulties in persuading people who are not from 'specific groups' to permanently repatriate their skills.

To their credit, and of course in their own interests, black and white South Africans have by and large avoided the dangers of oversimplifying the significance of the exit option. White South African 'emigration' can be described in terms of three movements: those who are gone for good: those who may return as destination-country and home-country economic conditions change; those who participate in a global labour market from a South African home base, rather as, say, Scottish workers in the oil industry do. In practice, the boundaries between these categories are not hard and fast, but it is significant that probably most white South African families are exposed to one or more of these categories of movement. Some may embrace all three. What this does is reinforce already-existing tendencies to transnationalism in the experience of white South Africans. This means that with the exception of relatively small numbers of Afrikaners – especially those preoccupied with language issues and grievances – whites do not on the whole behave as a minority, which was the role many expected of them after the settlement. The role of *political* minority carries with it the onerous option of voice against a seemingly insurmountable, demographic majority. Very few whites have the appetite for this or the sense of solidarity it would require to sustain it. This does not mean that all whites are passive or shun voice completely. On the contrary small though respectable numbers are active and vocal in the parliamentary opposition, the media and civil society groups. However, the basis for their voice is largely (though not exclusively) equal, civic citizenship, not minority rights. It is not the least of post-apartheid ironies that the ANC – so reluctant to conceptualize whites and others as having agency as minorities in the transitional negotiations – now does its best to objectify whites as a minority, while politically active whites mostly refute this label.

In terms of identity, few whites think of themselves as a minority in any meaningful sense. Many see themselves as part of an extensive, ill-defined, global, and largely Anglophone culture of business, sport, entertainment and leisure. Privatized security, education and healthcare add to this sense of transnationalism by giving a quality of expatriate life to people born and bred in South Africa. This sense of a hybridized, transnational life is also reinforced by the dual passport syndrome and the number of foreign passport-holders. The UK Foreign and Commonwealth Office (FCO) calculates that approximately 250,000 British nationals live in South Africa, on the basis that it receives about 25,000 passport applications from within South Africa each year and about 30,000 British nationals enter South Africa each month.[8] A white, Afrikaans-speaking (or for that matter black) sports supporter can now feel at home in Melbourne, Auckland or London while following his or her team, in a way that would have been quite unthinkable to any predecessor even 25 years ago. In this way, identity now sits lightly on many white South Africans, who see themselves as citizens of the world as much or more as of South Africa. Some of them at least can choose to emphasize different identities according to the needs of the moment, a global virtual identity, intermittent (but sometimes intense) identification with black South African fellow citizens and (especially for Afrikaans-speakers) harmless minority cultural attachments. This is not exactly post-nationalism, but it is a kind of superficial buffet of cosmopolitanism, which could hardly be further removed from the austere and self-sacrificial nationalist visions of idealized patriots which inhabit ANC documents.

Two issues cut across and complicate this characterization. The first is that this set of identities is not exclusive: it is common in many respects to people above a certain economic level across the world of emerging markets and growing middle classes, and it is open to black South Africans who have access to expat-type life resources and assets, as well as the disposable income to travel. For many Africans who have these resources the hybrid identity contains strong African and African-American components: the African ingredient may itself be a mixture of continental elements and rural/parochial pieties. Gevisser's apt phrase to describe global-African style, 'Vegas-meets-Venda', has a particular resonance here. Nonetheless whatever the mix, identities are fluid and not contained by strict racial boundaries.

The second question, how many white South Africans this thumbnail sketch of hybrid identities applies to, is not easy to answer. For many, given the generally high level of affluence of white South Africans, it is a lived reality. Even for them there is a residual identification with African rootedness and spirituality, if nothing else to mark themselves off from their grey brethren in damp Northern Europe. For others who are less affluent or secure, it is something to be experienced sporadically at first hand, at others second-hand and to be aspired to full time. Of course there are exceptions to this agreeable, semi-detached basis for national identity. Despite all economic and social indicators – employment, income, education, health – favouring whites, there are pockets of white poverty. More important than this are pervasive anxieties and resentments that reveal how insecure the continued enjoyment of the material basis of this transnational identity might be and why so many whites have one eye on the future and the other on the exit.

These anxieties also erode the potential of more local and rooted national identification because both the anxieties and the resentments are focused on the amalgam of state, government and party, which is cultivated by the ANC and designed to be unmovable and unchangeable. This anxious condition is made up of a familiar patchwork of concerns, including high crime levels, fear of currency collapse, high taxes with low return to the taxpayer in the form of workable public services, resentment at affirmative action and BEE, corruption and poor capacity in government and threats to the rule of law. These concerns are common to more or less all whites, but they are more intense in certain niche groups, especially farmers. In the eyes of the ANC these concerns are the products of Afro-pessimism and racism. Underlying this difference and the anxieties themselves is an enormous gap in perceptions about the provenance and status of whites' conditions of life. For the ANC the all-purpose term 'white privilege' disposes of the matter economically and definitively. This is understandable, given that the connections between the history of white minority rule, white affluence and black poverty should not be too difficult to grasp. However, the blanket illegitimacy that 'white privilege' imposes on the conditions of whites' lives has a hinterland of half-articulated premises, ambiguous implications and coded threats which are destructive of trust and confidence. Anxiety and foreboding are also stirred by the echoes of Zimbabwe-style dispossession in South African populist rhetoric.

Twenty years into democracy all of this leaves whites' identities in a rather unstable state. Their status as Africans – both self-assigned and ascribed – is uncertain; the pull of a diffuse, transnational identity is strong and is increasingly underpinned by actual family networks of migratory employment and settlement which become pull factors in themselves; the balance between being wooed (as Zuma likes to woo Afrikaners as a 'genuine white tribe') and being rejected, is chronically unstable and unpredictable. Viewed from the ANC's perspective, these are self-indulgent details which pale into insignificance beside the sacrifices and compromises it feels it has made on behalf of black people generally in order to make nation-building work. Such details, the ANC feels, should not get in the way of a more wholehearted commitment by whites to South Africa. This is part of the difficulty, however. The ANC does not only want a commitment from whites (and from everyone else) to the territory and people of South Africa and to the values of the Constitution. It also wants a commitment to the ANC–government–state nexus, as well as the ANC-defined project of transformation, which can mean anything from nuanced non-racialism to crude Africanization. Whites tend to see the latter rather than the former in transformation policies. All of this greatly complicates whites' identity issues because, to the ANC the two commitments are identical and for whites they should, indeed must, be kept separate. In their eyes, the first commitment to the conventional idea of the nation state should be a non-negotiable condition of national citizenship; however, the second commitment to the ANC and its ideology, all South Africans should be free to accept or reject without reflection on their patriotism. This problem arises not only for whites of course, but for some black people too. However, it is with whites that the problem arises in its most concentrated and acute form. This is partly a matter of historic baggage, but it is also a function of the persistent taint of transnational identities that colours whites' way of life and identity choices. In this, the ANC sees whites as a bridgehead of the kind of 'Western' values which are ritually denounced in ANC documents, and in the legacy of Mbeki's rhetoric; that is, materialism, individualism, the creative destruction wreaked by capitalism and a deficit of deference not only to 'African' values, but to African leaders as well.

## White postscript: From eagles to sparrows – where do nations go when they die?

In March 2006, a young Afrikaans-speaking pop singer Louis Pepler (b. 1978) who performed under the name Bok van Blerk and the Mossies (sparrows), released a record called 'De la Rey', about the Anglo-Boer war guerrilla general of that name, Jacobus – 'Koos' – De la Rey (1847–1914). The song, accompanied by a music video, invoked many of the basic elements of Afrikaner nationalist iconography: burning farms, trenches, the guerrilla struggle against overwhelming odds with the 'khakies' (British army), children and women in concentration camps. It has a lugubrious, anthemic refrain, tailor-made for pop-festival sing-along, which calls on De la Rey to lead his people. The record was a sensation, not only in terms of sales but as a cultural talking-point. Bok van Blerk was a somewhat unlikely and unwilling icon whose interviews and marketing material strove to make plain how much at ease he was with multicultural South Africa, with democracy, the place of white people in general, and Afrikaans-speaking people in particular, though he did have some concerns about the Afrikaans language.

All of this notwithstanding, the song appeared to have made a striking, if diffuse and hard-to-read emotional connection with (mainly) young Afrikaans-speakers. The resulting shiver of controversy inevitably brought with it columnists in search of a story and academics in search of a publication. In both cases there was a perceived need both to talk the subject up, yet keep it in its place:

> it was a muted affirmation of white Afrikaner identity and helped reassert the imagined boundaries of white Afrikanerdom while speaking the legitimate language of history and cultural heritage. (Van der Vaal and Robins 2011: 763)

It also provoked a reaction from the Department of Arts and Culture which, despite being a classic piece of ANC commissar-speak, managed to end on a tolerant note:

> As the Ministry of Arts and Culture, we want to state it categorically that the Minister, Dr Z Pallo Jordan, together with countless unsung heroes, spent his entire adult life and much of his adolescence and youth fighting for the right of freedom of expression. . . . Whatever the intentions of the composer, be they to mobilise White Afrikaans-speakers, or 'the Boers' as the singer calls them, to oppose the democratic government, provided that opposition is within the terms of the Constitution, we as the Ministry see no problem with it. (Department of Arts and Culture 6 February 2007)[9]

What no-one seems to have asked was, 'Has it come to this?' One of the great state- and nation-building projects of the late twentieth century, whose armed forces just over 20 years ago possessed nuclear weapons and ranged freely in an arc of destruction over Southern Africa, whose arrogance and cruelty imposed real pain and life-blighting conditions of existence on millions, had shrunk to controversy over an ephemeral piece of pop music marketing.

It is not easy to assess whether or not this is a valid judgement. In the first place it is very difficult to know, not so much who Afrikaners are, but who they might be: that is, what the size of a potential group which has continuity with past forms of Afrikaner identity is. In the old South Africa it used to be conventionally reckoned that there were three white Afrikaners for every two white English speakers. If that held good today there would be just on 3 million potential 'Afrikaners' in the old sense of the term, that is based on racial classification and a sense of ethnic and linguistic kinship. An outer limit would be the number of Afrikaans first language speakers which is close to 9 million and about 13.5 per cent of the population. However, these figures include the majority of the 4.6 million (8.9%) of the population who are classified as Coloured. While many of them may have a strong attachment to the language and at least some of the culture which goes under the rubric of 'Afrikaner', including religion and conservative social values, they have plenty of historical reasons to reject Afrikaner heritage and affiliation. All that can be said with confidence about Afrikaans-speakers is that there are between 7 and 8 million people who share a first language, concerns about the hegemonic potential of African nationalism and for many of them, the conservative social attitudes that go with religious affiliation. However, what exactly it means to 'share' a language is in itself a matter of debate. The opportunities for sharp diversity of expression within the same language was being demonstrated as early as the 1980s when Coloured activists and white dissidents used 'Alternative' Afrikaans language and culture as a weapon of anti-apartheid struggle. This linguistic commonality, such as it is, is not the basis for any kind of shared and organized identity politics even under non-racial and democratic conditions (except perhaps for specialized issues of language status). Indeed the very openness of South Africa's formal commitment to diversity (for as long as it survives in practice) removes the pressure to coalesce along these lines. A very much smaller number than the outer limit of Afrikaans-speakers, that is at the most about 3 million people, might feel identity concerns which show selective continuity with past Afrikaner identities but without any explicit association with racial identity.

The identity concerns of this small number of people continue to attract attention, but even the most focused and comprehensive treatment (Davies 2009) seems tentative and non-committal – certainly by comparison with the certainties of the past. Davies notes that Afrikaners have vast material and cultural capital and that a pervasive sense of being an Afrikaner exists. However, she also points to the complexity, changing social composition and internal stratification of the 'Afrikaner population'. On this basis she concludes that 'it is not possible to suggest the presence of any broad-based communal dialogue or programmatic axis that would give impetus to the Afrikaans community as a whole' (ibid. 136) and, '[d]espite the presence of a pervasive sense of Afrikanerness or "being Afrikaans", the meanings and significance attached to this subjective groupness or self-understanding are now so varied that it is moot whether an Afrikaner grouping exists in any formal sense' (ibid. 8).

These judgements seem conclusive enough. Moreover the regular slippage from 'Afrikaner' to 'Afrikaans' is a clue to the uncertainty of the subject, perhaps even to the possibility that it is not there at all. Perhaps we should leave it at that. Yet it is a tribute to the extraordinary durability of interest in this small and by now extremely hard-to-define people that another of Davies' conclusions is: 'There are certainly hints that a postmodern Afrikaans identity might yet emerge' (ibid. 137). This would 'forgo hegemonical content . . . align resources to appropriate subnational, national and supranational levels' and 'forge alliances in common pursuit of economic, social and political interests' (ibid.).

## Once a people, always a people?

Given the nature of controversies in the academic social sciences, what the trajectory of Afrikaner nationalism 'proves' will remain moot. Those who view nations as finite in their life span, instrumental in their purposes and invented in their provenance will point to the mixture of success and failure that ushered Afrikaner nationalism out of history as an aspirant to political self-determination, as strengthening the case for their view of nationalism. It was a success in transforming Afrikaners into people who for the most part are well equipped with the material resources as well as social and cultural capital not only for survival but to flourish, in a globalized world and transnational labour market as well as their own back yard. It was a failure in being unable to impose its preferred form of political self-determination on others. If the nation was a failure in proving unable to control in perpetuity the state it inherited and then further developed, then the successor state which former Afrikaner nationalists participated in negotiating has continued up to now to provide a safe environment in which the nation's now-demobilized people can prosper. This is a broad judgement with which some of the following may differ: people sidelined by affirmative action, farmers, victims of crime and emigrants. However, it holds for most of the people who continue to think of themselves as Afrikaners, but who do not need to convert this consciousness of identity into political mobilization in order to prosper.

Those who view nations as enduring, who believe that once people constitute themselves as a people they will always be a people, who think there is a destiny to nations beyond the fulfilment of material goals, and that nations exist before they are invented, will find the Afrikaner nation a difficult case to accommodate. Arguably it always was, given the vast disjuncture between its mobilizing pretensions and its lack of a territorial base. One way of coping would be to label Afrikaners a nation without a state, but 'they' (whoever *they* are) are only a nation in a very loose sense, and since they were one in a very literal sense not so long ago, this approach would have more than a suggestion of special pleading and conceptual stretching. Another, more romantic approach is to seize on the 'De la Rey' phenomenon and believe that the nation endures but is sleeping or underground: if the hour comes when intolerable provocation makes it necessary, the nation will reform and a leader will appear. Such a view is as difficult for the objective observer to disprove as it is to him/her to believe. The same is true of the 'hints of postmodernist Afrikaner identity' whose maturity is awaited by some. In this view, identity needs endure, though the possibilities that are available to express it and uses to which it may be put are subject to endless shuffling and mutation. Whether or not such a post-modernist identity will be visible to anyone but the scholars who trade in the concept, and whether or not Afrikaners will be conscious of possessing it, it is in any case unlikely to be in the form of anything we would normally call a nation, or to have much in the way of continuity with the Afrikaner nationalism of the past and certainly unlikely to be the medium of political agency through self-determination.

# Conclusion: A minimum nation and an identity of convenience

In the years since 1994, South Africans have, considering their unpromising beginning, developed quite a serviceable sense of nationhood. The choice of the adjective 'serviceable' is meant to convey a sense of the instrumentality and the limitations of this state of national consciousness while at the same time giving it due credit. In terms of attachment to territory, of self-definition as South Africans rather than as racial, ethnic or linguistic alternatives and of seeing themselves in a host of banal ways as a distinct unit in global politics, sport, business ('national champions') and culture, South Africans do constitute a nation. They are constantly reminded of this, in ways similar to those pointed out by Michael Billig in *Banal Nationalism* (1995: 6), not only by statements of politicians and government but by the broadcast and print media, advertising campaigns and non-partisan, patriotic marketing organizations such as 'Proudly South African' and 'Homecoming Revolution'. The former tries to improve South Africa's global image and the morale of South Africans themselves in the face of what is often negative global publicity. The latter, as we have seen, tries to facilitate the return of skilled South Africans from overseas. At times South Africans are exposed simultaneously to a disorienting mixture of Afro-pessimism and Afro-boosterism: in fact individual South Africans are quite capable of moving with lightning speed to express themselves in one of these registers, then the other.

Much of the evidence for this is impressionistic and anecdotal. Where it is empirical, as in responses to survey questions about self-definition it can be somewhat unstable over time and according to the methodology and context of the study. In any case the subjective meaning of being 'South African' probably differs quite a lot across the population and its racial subdivisions. Despite this, much can be said for the state of national consciousness in post-apartheid South Africa. Secure borders and an absence of either separatism or irredentism help to give a stable platform for primary national identity as South African. The country externally projects the strong image of a global citizen in good standing, who participates strongly in continental peacekeeping and conflict resolution. It is true that South Africa has lost considerable standing and its soft power has been eroded in Western eyes, mainly thanks to Mbeki's beliefs about and policies on HIV/AIDS, as well as the equivocations of his 'quiet diplomacy' policy towards the long-running Zimbabwe crisis. However, it is debatable how much this has meant for South Africans' sense of national *amour propre*. For many of them, especially in and around the governing party, it has probably enhanced rather than diminished their country's standing. For the first decade or so of the post-apartheid era Western governments and commentators badly misread the foreign policy of the new South African government and underestimated its fear of being seen as a Western surrogate.[1] In any case, in the eyes of the ANC and its supporters whatever has been lost in the eyes of the West has been compensated many times over by acceptance into the BRICS grouping, where adding weight to a changing global balance of power in favour of emerging countries counts for much more than regime change for tyrants in the regional neighbourhood.

Despite these achievements there is nothing to be complacent about: there are substantial obstacles to further nation-building and it remains an open question whether the prospects for the official version of the civic, constitutional nation are improving or deteriorating. As we have seen, socio-economic divisions remain substantial despite progress on fronts such as reducing the level of absolute poverty, the growth of a black middle class and the changing demographic profile of the work force, especially in the public service. However, unemployment remains a scourge, an affront to the prospects of nation-building and the principal contributor to the division of the population into insiders and outsiders. Another area in which progress has been patchy has been the development of horizontal attachments and affiliations between and among citizens, especially across racial lines. Paradoxically, perhaps the largely segmented lives led by South Africans may help to alleviate the persistent racial antagonisms which remain so much part of South African life, but which are expressed less in face-to-face encounters, more in angry exchanges at one remove in politics, media and (especially) in internet forums. At the same time segmented lives help ensure the persistence of racial antagonism in the first place.

If horizontal attachments and affiliations are weak, then the weight of responsibility for nation-building inevitably falls on the state and the vertical relationships which it can foster with citizens. However, the South African state is weak in its reach and capacities, especially relative to the extensive ambitions the ANC assigns to it. Embarrassing shortcomings in health, education, local government and the criminal justice system, along with patronage, corruption, political favouritism and other inadequacies of governance, all gravely undermine state-sponsored efforts at nation-building. The indications of social fragmentation – crime, corruption, public disorder – that undermine the cohesiveness expected of a nation of citizens are both symptoms and causes of this ongoing state weakness.

Nation-building is also compromised by the chronic incoherence of discourse that flows from the ANC and the wider Alliance. Marxist rhetoric mingles with the language of growth prescriptions for winning nations in emerging markets: cosmopolitan human rights discourse and liberal constitutionalism jostle with frank demands for soviet-style political monopolism; the language of diversity and inclusiveness competes with populist African cultural chauvinism. With their well-developed post-apartheid talent for making the best of a bad job, South Africans pass off this political Babel to puzzled foreigners as 'our vibrant and noisy democracy in action'. However, this rationalization is wearing thin and a permanent condition of cognitive dissonance within the government as well as in the ruling party and the ANC Alliance is not an auspicious basis for patiently inculcating a shared national identity across the whole population.

In the end it is not easy to see in perspective the achievements of and constraints on nation-building in post-apartheid South Africa. This is partly because the terms in which we can ask, 'what is a nation *for*?' can vary a lot. To some people of course, this misses the point: to them a nation is a natural form of association – perhaps the highest form of human association – so that to ask what it is for is at best of secondary importance and at worst completely irrelevant. Plainly none of this is true for post-apartheid South Africa and the South African nation requires purposive justification. It can be argued that South Africa's official version of the nation and nation-building provides at least a minimum national identity, placing South Africa and South Africans in the world and setting out a secular and inclusive framework of values which are available to anyone to identify with, irrespective of background.

## Beyond the minimum nation

The political elites that called the nation into being in order to settle on a form of democracy that would be widely enough acceptable to bring an end to overt and destructive conflict, set a demanding exemplar of national citizenship. This ideal nation was to be composed of active, rights-bearing citizens who were conscious of the duties as well as the privileges of living under a supreme law that was respectful of their persons, their diverse natures and their hopes of material well-being and social justice. It was the values of the settlement, enshrined in the Constitution that embodied the nation and trumped all other kinships and affinities, whatever they were based on. In what amounted to an unavoidable piece of sleight of hand, this nation was treated as if it already existed, but yet still had to be brought into being. Much confusion and some conflict have resulted from this regrettable if forgivable piece of trickery, especially after Mbeki took it upon himself to banish the ambiguity with more concern for urgency, emphasis and possibly his own psychological gratification, than finesse or political good sense. The duality between being and becoming a nation that Mbeki brutally exposed has nonetheless been restored to official discourse on nation-building. The NDP as the latest expression of official nation-building confirms this, while smoothing over with sentiments of poetic aspiration the raw edges which Mbeki picked at.

Full realization of this conception of the nation as the embodiment of moral citizenship and the vehicle of social justice will be difficult. This is partly because it is so demanding. The calls for moral regeneration, the fears of social disintegration and the calls for reciprocal spiritual growth through the acknowledgement by whites of responsibility for the past and forgiveness for it on the part of blacks, are testimony to how high the bar is set for national citizenship. This is especially so since there is rarely even rudimentary guidance on how moral regeneration and spiritual reconciliation might take place. Realization may also be difficult because there is a substantial disconnect between official versions of nation-building and what might be termed their shadow counterparts. This might suggest that the civic nation is, for all but a small hard core of convinced constitutionalists (who nonetheless span both political and racial divides), an identity of convenience rather than conviction, constructed in order to accommodate difficult political realities which at least for the present time still prevail.

Among these sources of dissonance is a shadow value system which is often at odds with constitutional values. As we have seen there is more than one source for this. One is pervasive, highly conservative religious views. Another is an eclectic collection of beliefs, structures and practices to which the words 'African', 'traditional' and 'customary' are often attached in a reasonable enough attempt to capture an undeniable phenomenon, but by using labels which risk being oversimplified and sometimes misleading. Again as we have seen, those who subscribe to these values do not consciously set out to supplant the values of official nation-building. However, the stubborn coexistence of incompatible belief systems sets up all kinds of clashes, including *muthi* murders, witch and vigilante killings and corrective rape, all of which are difficult to treat as 'ordinary' crimes, as well as more legitimate, but still dissonant claims to moral authority from traditional leaders.

A second source of dissonance is ethnicity. Among the strongest prescriptions of official nation-building is the denial of validity to ethno-nationalism – the 'bad nationalism' which the NDP warns against. However, there is a shadow political market-place in the ANC which flourishes in a context of de facto one-partyism and patronage. Here, ideology is weak, fluid and incoherent and legacy attachments – exile, prisoner, UDF, military – grow weaker as time, generational turnover, social mobility and distance from the years of struggle take their toll. As all these markers of faction are eroded, there is a strong perception – within the ANC itself as well as from external critics – that ethnicity may be replacing them. Once again, there is no reasonable prospect that ethno-national identities will seriously rival primary identification with being South African, or serve as vehicles for self-conscious kinship advancement, far less threaten separatism or ethnic conflict. However, if they become the currency of self-promotion in the shadow political market-place of factionalism, power-broking and patronage, they will erode prospects of full realization of civic national citizenship. Some observers believe that this process is already far advanced, though formal evidence is hard to come by.

A third rival to the civic nation is a shadow political project which is at odds with the ideals of political pluralism and the separation of powers. It is of course something of a misnomer to call this a 'shadow' project, since the ANC makes it plain what is happening, at least to anyone with the appetite and stamina to read its ideological documents. This project is aimed at the fusion of state and party and the insertion of the ANC as the 'leading force' in society into all significant centres of power and influence. The principal medium for this is 'cadre deployment' by which ANC personnel, members or sympathizers are assigned to leading positions in all state bodies including administration, law, broadcasting and security. The principle extends to aspirations to apply it in the private sector and civil society, although the ANC and the government's reach is less certain in these areas. In both public and private sector, affirmative action and BEE are helpful to smooth cadre deployment.

The ANC claims two main justifications for this strategy: first, a revolutionary transformation of the magnitude and extent required by South Africa cannot be carried out by a neutral state and public service and must be driven at all levels by the ideologically committed; secondly, since this revolutionary transformation must take place in all sectors of society, it requires direction from the ANC as the leading force at every site for transformation. These justifications are based in turn on deeper beliefs: no other political force can be trusted with the national tasks which the ANC alone can define and carry out; political pluralism can be tolerated for strategic reasons so long as it does not threaten actual transfer of political power since by definition any party which competes with the ANC is reactionary and subversive and will at the first opportunity derail transformation. The essential credo which binds all of this together concerns the nature of the ANC itself. In its own self-estimation it is not merely a political party which holds governing power at the pleasure of the electorate to which it is accountable, but it is also the embodiment of a national will for self-realization and the vehicle of the transformation that will bring it to fruition. By confusing patriotism and civic virtue with political allegiance, the ANC sets out a rather different conception of the nation from that which many South Africans thought they were subscribing to in their new democracy and in what the rest of the world thought the 'most progressive constitution in the world' represented. The confrontation between these conceptions of the nation – both of which the ANC stoutly defends at the same time – has required an extraordinary exercise in the management of cognitive dissonance, not only by the ANC but by the generality of South Africans, save those liberal critics who regularly point out the incompatibilities between these conceptions of the nation. This task of management has been greatly assisted by more than 60 per cent of the popular vote gained by the ANC in each of the four general elections between 1994 and 2009. These victories have helped to drown out and belittle critics and to justify (to itself) the ANC's self-image as the embodiment of the national will, inspiring it to wider applications of its fusion project.[2] While critics claim that the ANC is using the platform of constitutional democracy to create a one-party state, the ANC likes to give the opposite impression – that political monopoly is the only viable means to the end of a true national constitutional democracy.

## The shadow nation

Important as the shadow value systems and the ANC's parallel political project of institutional fusion are, it is the existence of a shadow nation that poses the most significant alternative to the full realization of the civic nation as conceived by the constitutional settlement. Continuing uncertainty over the status of African nationalism and of the putative African nation hangs over the prospects of the civic nation. For many, especially those African insiders who have done best out of transformation, African nationalism was richly rewarded in the settlement. However even they, along with anyone whose claim to be 'African' is in any doubt, are nervously aware that the civic nation may indeed be an identity of convenience and that the real African nation has been marginalized to brood, unfulfilled, along with the constituency of the previously disadvantaged and still-excluded outsiders in the wings.

There is a case for saying that any anxieties along these lines are false, destructive and possibly even maliciously inspired. Of course, African identity is an inescapable and essential part of being South African: how could it be otherwise? But it is not 'bad' nationalism of cultural exclusiveness and political domination but part of the 'good' nationalism of diversity and multiple identities, fully compatible with a wider civic nationalism. In short an African identity is one of the identities available to a free people: African-South African is no more and no less significant than, say, Irish-American. If white South Africans can supplement their South African identity with others (as Afrikaans-speakers, for instance), not to mention having another passport up their sleeve, then no-one should quibble at African identity.

There are some problems with this reasonable view (which probably corresponds fairly closely with the official government line). In the first place, true African identity is available without question or qualification to 79 per cent of the population (a percentage that is set to rise): this is a figure which puts it in quite a different category to any of the 'hyphen' identities that spring to mind in South Africa or anywhere else. Indeed it represents a formidable inertial and possibly hegemonic force. This would not matter if it were an identity available to 100 per cent of the population – the African nation and the civic nation would then simply be co-terminus – but this is something on which there is chronic uncertainty. In fact, African nationalists in South Africa have never been able to give a coherent, consistent, uncontested and hence credible answer to the question, 'Who is an African?'

This is not entirely unprecedented. At various times over the past century and a half 'Afrikaner' has had different shades of meaning, expanding or contracting more according to calculations of the advantages of increasing headcount versus the disadvantages of diluting ethnic or racial stock, than to any matter of deep principle concerning kinship or culture. Be that as it may, the question 'Who is an African?' looms over nation-building in South Africa today. It shows itself from time to time in sad little skirmishes in the press, usually started by a white person of Afrikaans heritage claiming that he or she is as African as the next person and/or claiming kinship with Black Africans. This is followed by Black African gatekeepers denying these consolations to the individual concerned. Despite their generally solipsistic quality, these exchanges are the tip of a large iceberg of clashes. These clashes run deep because the issue of who is or is not an African is intimately connected to questions of authenticity, indigeneity, moral standing and, through affirmative action and BEE, access to resources. For a Black African, being African is an inalienable birthright: for whites (as well as Coloureds and Indians) it is a label that can be granted or withheld by self-appointed African gatekeepers according to good behaviour, political calculation (including the needs of nation-building) self-interest, or principles of ethno-national or racial definition. An underlying principle seems to be that 'African' is an honorary status that can be ascribed to a member of one or other of the racial minorities as a reward or an incentive but it cannot be claimed by the aspirant him or herself. To do so is to be guilty of 'appropriation', an increasingly common post-apartheid addition to whites' already extensive charge sheet.

All of this is also important according to whether being African is just another one of multiple identities or it denotes membership of the *real* nation, which gives the South African nation indigenous roots and moral content: the real nation whose interests, purposes and self-realization the constitutional nation is there to serve. Something like this latter conception seemed to lie behind Mbeki's somewhat obfuscated and elusive thoughts on nationhood. At this stage there is not much doubt that an African nation exists at least in a figurative sense, imperfectly concealed behind such neologisms as 'previously disadvantaged'. There are at least two reasons beyond those already-adduced why African identity is more than merely one among multiple identities. The first is that to fail to claim at least figurative (or perhaps virtual) nationhood for Africans is to retrospectively validate apartheid ideology, one of whose key tenets was that Africans did not and never could constitute a nation. The second is that to ascribe at least figurative nationhood to African-South Africans is the most direct and economical way to acknowledge the extent of the exclusions and deprivations visited on all African-South Africans by colonialism and apartheid and to justify race as the medium for redressing them. The question is will this shadow nation ever become a literal nation?

The answer will depend on how current developments in South African politics will play out, notably in the future of the ANC. Since 1994 the ANC has functioned as a grand coalition, able to exploit African nationalism but also to hold in check any demands for a clearer and more assertive racial, ethnic or cultural articulation of Africanism. For instance, the 'Africanism' ascribed to Mbeki by white critics was in fact 'Africanism-lite', a fact well known to real Africanists. Until recently, then, the ANC has been able to follow a dual track in which it insists that measured expression of African nationalism is compatible with (indeed in some versions an essential component of) South African civic nationalism. In doing so it has been mindful of the need to indigenize and find local roots for the Constitution. Key resources in empowering it to follow this dual track have been the moral authority of the struggle against apartheid and the massive electoral victories it has won since 1994.

However, the discipline and organizational coherence which have also been essential to the dual conception of nation-building have been slipping away, and the authority with which the ANC could simply prescribe the mutual harmony of African and civic nationalism has been greatly diluted. At the twentieth anniversary of South Africa's democracy and in its fifth democratic general election, the ANC faces invigorated challenge both from those who feel the fundamentals of civic nationalism are under threat and those who believe that a more assertive and populist African nationalism should be allowed expression. The results of the 2014 general election will offer guidance as to whether or not the ANC's historic compromise between civic and African nationalism is secure for at least the immediate future.

For the moment, however, a minimum nation and an identity of convenience are not to be sneered at. If given that choice on the brink of negotiations in 1990, as a 20-year marker of progress, most South Africans would have readily settled for it. Most of them, pragmatically conscious of their situation, settle for it today.

# NOTES

## Introduction

1 The ANC was unbanned in 1990, the first democratic election was held on 27 April 1994 and the Constitution was not finalized until 1996. However, the crucial agreements which embodied the improvised nation and which made the Constitution and the election possible were in place by the end of 1993.
2 The NDP follows what is the common practice of official South Africa by using the word 'nationalism' exclusively in negative contexts. The positive side of nationalism is rendered as 'nation-building' or 'social cohesion' or 'solidarity' or 'patriotism'.
3 The NPC strikes a folksy note by labelling the South African nation a *potjie* (Afrikaans: literal translation 'little pot') in explicit contrast to the melting pot (NPC June 2011: 14). *Potjie* is a dish in which different meat and vegetable ingredients are cooked together but not stirred, and so keep their individual flavours.

## Chapter 1

1 Noting this range in the Gini, the NPC's Diagnostic Report takes a figure of 0.67 in 2005 as a benchmark.
2 These are 2002 figures: more up-to-date figures broken down racially are less readily available than figures for the whole population.
3 An example of this is official tourist marketing for KwaZulu-Natal: arrivals at Durban airport are greeted by billboards announcing 'Welcome to the Kingdom'.

## Chapter 4

1 The subtitle of John Carlin's 'Playing the Enemy' is, 'Nelson Mandela and the Game That Made a Nation'.
2 The film's title *Invictus* (2009) is taken from a darkly melodramatic (and much parodied) Victorian poem of that name whose motifs, of a head that is 'bloody

but unbowed' and, especially 'I am the master of my fate, I am the captain of my soul' are used in the film to capture Mandela's indomitable spirit.

3  The verdict was delivered in Powell's biography of the Victorian politician Joseph Chamberlain.

4  Given his taste for the English classics, Mbeki was probably borrowing Benjamin Disraeli's (1845) characterization of an England divided into rich and poor nations, 'between whom there is no intercourse of sympathy'.

5  The transcripts of the special hearings are deposited on the Department of Justice (DoJ) website.

6  The name referred to words of (the late) Albert Luthuli who said in 1963, 'The task is not yet finished. South Africa is not yet a home for all her sons and daughters' (Matthews 2010: 7). After Mandela, his fellow Nobel Peace Prize winner Luthuli is probably the ANC leader most widely acceptable outside the ANC itself.

7  For the text see Matthews 2010.

8  Shortly after becoming the first ANC and first black finance minister in 1996, Trevor Manuel sharply expressed his frustration with foreign exchange fluctuations: 'I insist on the right to govern. . . . I insist on the right not to be stampeded into a panic decision by some amorphous entity . . . called the market.' Although Manuel went on to become a model of macroeconomic rectitude in the eyes of the same markets, the distrust of something it cannot control runs deep in the ANC.

9  In the immediate post-apartheid years the most common term for self-enrichment through politics was 'getting on board the gravy train'.

# Chapter 5

1  Zuma's patronage of the MRM was part of his vice-presidential responsibilities until Mbeki relieved him of the post in June 2005.

2  The NDP has only one reference to *ubuntu* in nearly 500 pages, which makes it remarkable, if not unique among government documents.

3  The NDP uses the terms 'social compact' and 'social contract' interchangeably.

4  The Constitution was finalized between 1994 and 1996 by which time the ANC had won the first election and was the dominant party in a power-sharing government. Similarly, some of the legislation of the government's early years – notably the laws governing a new labour-market regime – is conventionally included in a broader and looser understanding of the founding settlement. Nevertheless the symbolic weight of the pre-1994 settlement overshadows subsequent developments.

5  By mid-2013 this scenario was already unfolding, particularly over trade union resistance to the NDP's fairly mild call for reforms to the labour-market regime.

# Chapter 6

1  In South Africa the terms non-governmental, non-profit and voluntary are used interchangeably.

2  Core circulation (copies sold) is much smaller than the AMPS figures which are based on surveys of what people claim to have read. AMPS readership figures can be compared with the Audit Bureau of Circulation (ABC) data on circulation. For instance, ABC has the core circulation of the biggest-selling daily, the tabloid *Daily Sun* at 381,270 (second quarter 2011) and AMPS has its readership at 5.7 million (average for the year to June 2012). This is a multiplication factor of 14.8. By contrast, calculating on the same sources, the multiplying factor for the daily broadsheet *Business Day* is only 1.98.

3  Although the SABC is a public broadcaster, 80 per cent of its funding comes from advertising and only 20 per cent from licence fees. Hence some SABC radio stations are classified as 'commercial'.

4  This judgement of the European Court of Justice ruled that citizens of countries (such as South Africa) that have association agreements with the EU, if they have a valid work permit, must be treated on the same basis as a national of an EU country. Hence, in sport, they must not be subject to 'foreign player quotas' or similar restrictions.

5  Author observation.

6  This is true not only of South Africa of course but of many other sporting nations: Scotland's rugby-playing 'tartan kiwis' and New Zealand's Pacific islanders are cases in point.

7  England, by hosting the Rugby World Cup in 2015 will also have that distinction. There is a case for saying that England can in fact already make the claim but the Rugby World Cup in 1991 was shared by all the UK countries, as well as Ireland and France.

8  According to StatsSA this was because 'consumers of census data' regarded it as superfluous.

9  Also labelled at times as 'instituted', 'indigenous' or 'initiated'. AICs, however labelled, are churches founded in Africa by Africans and not by missionaries or settlers. They are generally regarded as representing the integration of Christianity and African traditional life, though this understanding is a broad popular generalization which is subject to much theological and sociological debate.

10  It is likely that much of the apparent rise in numbers of people identifying with Christianity can be attributed to changed methodology. The 2001 census differed from the 1996 by the use of 'imputation', usually from other household information to attribute 'unavailable, incorrect and inconsistent values'. Probably due to this innovation, the category 'refused/other unspecified' shrank from 9.4 per cent in 1996 to 1.4 per cent in 2001. The category 'other Christian' grew from 5.4 per cent to 9.5 per cent and 'no religion' from 11.7 per cent to 15.1 per cent (StatsSA 2004: 24).

11  The Survey is produced by the statutory research body the Human Sciences Research Council (HSRC).
12  In the study 'elite' was defined as: 'people who fill top positions in the largest and most resource-rich political, governmental, economic, professional, communications and cultural institutions in society' (Kotzé and Steenekamp 2009).
13  Parliament, the police, armed forces, the courts and the civil service.
14  Coloureds and Indians are more likely to split their votes between the ANC and parties perceived as 'white', but they account for only about 10 per cent of voters (Ferree 2010: 5).
15  Since 1994 the percentage of GDP in tax revenue has been in the range 24.5 to 28.1. In 2013 it is 23.8 per cent.
16  Wage statistics are contested and controversial over issues such as whether bonus and overtime payments have been adequately calculated in. However, there is widespread agreement that wages are low.
17  The 2013 budget proposes that the means test on the old-age pensions be phased out by 2016 and the grant, which will remain non-contributory, be made universal.
18  'Umuthi' is the isiZulu word for tree. *Muthi* is applied in African languages across Southern Africa as far north as Lake Tanganyika to all forms of medicine used by traditional healers, whether herbal, mineral or animal. *Muthi* has been taken up by Afrikaans and South African English not only as a literal equivalent for the African language usage but with a wide figurative (and often humorous) application to any concoction or legitimate drug.
19  This is a particularly wounding insult whose origins go back as far as the 1940s. 'Toy telephones' were the various bogus forms of representation devised by white minority and apartheid governments for African political aspirations. They had neither legitimacy nor effective powers and the label was coined by African nationalists to express the contempt and derision with which they were regarded.
20  Presumably he was speaking extempore since the reported words do not appear in the official version of the speech (Presidency 2012).

# Chapter 7

1  The government has been known to cherry pick crime figures from other countries – for instance, muggings and thefts from motor vehicles in the cities of developed countries – to 'prove' that South Africans experience less crime.
2  The minister had been invited to comment on the high-profile case in which the athlete Oscar Pistorious had been accused of the murder of his girlfriend. The ethnic tag 'Afrikaner' and the religious label 'Calvinist' which she used were in any case debatable in the case of Pistorious.

3 He was released in 2012 on medical parole. This is supposed only to be granted for the terminally ill. Several instances in which parole has been granted on these grounds in recent years have given rise to suspicions that it is being abused for politically connected felons, a category into which Selebi probably falls.
4 The Bill was passed by the National Assembly in April 2013 in a form that allayed some, though not all, of the concerns about the threat to anti-corruption investigations.
5 In 2013 left wing and populist alternatives to the SACP were founded to contest the 2014 general election.
6 The most common explanation for the derivation is that the word mimics the supposedly bird-like twittering of someone speaking in an unfamiliar African language.
7 'Let us build together'.
8 The Financial and Fiscal Commission is an independent statutory body mandated by the Constitution to advise and make recommendations on financial and fiscal matters to legislative and executive institutions of state.
9 Strictly speaking 'Soweto' (an acronym for 'South Western Townships') is a concept rather than an administratively defined entity. It is an agglomeration of several historic townships; estimates of its population vary from 1 to close to 2 million people and from 30 to 50 per cent of Johannesburg's population depending on how boundaries are conceived. However, Eskom refers to 'Soweto' as an entity in matters of consumer debt.
10 As noted above, the SABC is in fact funded on a mixed model with advertising providing considerably more revenue than licence fees.

# Chapter 8

1 One egregious example involved a (white) Cape Town artist's depiction of Zuma in the pose of Lenin at the Finland Station and with his genitals exposed. The title, 'Spear of the Nation' appropriated the name (in translation) of the ANC's military wing Umkhonto We Sizwe. This juvenile provocation predictably provoked a short-lived furore with strong racial overtones.
2 As the controversy unfolded it emerged that Manyi had also made remarks on-record that were identical in spirit to his views on Coloureds, about Indians in KwaZulu-Natal where they are demographically concentrated.
3 By June, Nedlac had dismissed the Manyi amendments, the Minister of Labour had disowned them and the process of amending the employment equity act went on without them.
4 Ahmed Kathrada was a close colleague of Mandela before and during their shared time in prison. His foundation has a particular focus on non-racialism in the ANC.
5 The Northern Cape is the biggest province geographically (30.5% of South Africa's surface area) but its population is only just over 1 million.

6  Research on Foetal Alcohol syndrome is conducted on a regional, not a racial basis: Western Cape has the highest incidence in the world and it is clear from the published research that the heaviest concentrations are in Coloured communities.
7  An indication of the instability of the debate is that this figure was frequently inflated to 'nearly a million' or 'a million' in press reports (e.g. Fin24 24 September 2006). In fact SAIRR stated that 841,000 was a best estimate in a range that went from 'not less than half a million' to not more than a million', a nuance missing from press reports (Cronjé 2012).
8  Author correspondence with FCO.
9  In fairness to the Department, the reaction came not on its own initiative but was solicited by an Afrikaans-language magazine.

# Conclusion

1  A classic instance was when George Bush publicly referred to Thabo Mbeki as 'My point man on Zimbabwe'.
2  These have included the setting up of the ANC's own company, called Chancellor House, to help finance the organization by acting as a broker in 'joint ventures' for state infrastructure contracts, especially those involving foreign companies. Its most lucrative (and hence notorious and much-troubled) deal has been for a joint venture with Hitachi in equipping the state's massive electrical infrastructure programme, from which the party receives a large rake-off.

# BIBLIOGRAPHY

Adam, H., 'Getting together', *London Review of Books*, Vol. 12 (11), 14 June 1990, 10.
—, *Modernizing Racial Domination*, University of California Press, Berkeley, 1971.
—, 'With or Without the ANC', *London Review of Books*, Vol. 13 (11), 13 June 1991, 7–8.
Adam, H., Moodley, K. and Slabbert, F. van Zyl, *Comrades in Business*, Tafelberg, Cape Town, 1997.
Adhikari, M., *Not White Enough, Not Black Enough: Racial Identity in the South African Coloured Community*, Ohio University Press, Athens, 2005.
African National Congress, *ANC: People's Movement and Agent of Change, National General Council Discussion Document*, 2000 (www.anc.org.za).
—, *Apartheid South Africa: Colonialism of a Special Type*, 24 March 1987 (www.anc.org.za).
—, *Constitutional Principles for a United South Africa*, 1991 (www.anc.org.za).
—, *The National Question, Discussion Document*, June 2005 (www.anc.org.za).
—, *The Nature of the South African Ruling Class, Discussion Document for the Second National Consultative Conference*, 1985 (www.anc.org.za).
—, *The RDP of the Soul, Discussion Document*, 30 March 2007 (www.anc.org.za).
—, *State, Property Relations and Social Transformation*, 1998.
African National Congress Youth League (ANCYL), *Manifesto*, 1944 (www.anc.org.za).
Afrobarometer, *Public Agenda and Evaluation of Government, Summary of Results for South Africa*, March 2012.
Ahmed Kathrada Foundation, *The ANC: Still a Home for All?* Ahmed Kathrada Foundation, Johannesburg, 2013.
Akenson, D., *God's People: Covenant and Land in South Africa, Israel and Ulster*, Cornell University Press, London, 1992.
Alegi, P., *Laduma!: Soccer, Politics and Society in South Africa*, University of KwaZulu-Natal Press, Scottsville, 2004.
Alexander, N., 'Language Denied Means Citizens Ignored', *Mail & Guardian*, 3 February 2012.
Alexander, N. and Bloch, C., *Feeling at Home with Literacy in the Mother Tongue, Keynote Presentation at the International Board on Books for Young People (Basel) World Congress*, Cape Town, 2004.
Allwright, P., *The Real State of the Nation*, 2013 (www.corruptionwatch.org).
Ally, Y., *Witch Hunts in Modern South Africa*, South African Medical Research Council, Cape Town 2009.

Anderson, A., *African Reformation, African Initiated Christianity in the 20th Century*, Africa World Press, Trenton, NJ, 2001.
Anderson, B., *Imagined Communities*, Verso, London, 1983.
Ashforth, A., *Witchcraft, Violence and Democracy in South Africa*, University of Chicago Press, Chicago, 2005.
Askvik, S. and Bak, N., *Trust in Public Institutions in South Africa*, Ashgate, Farnham, 2005.
Atkinson, D., 'Taking to the Streets: Has Developmental Local Government Failed in South Africa?' in S. Buhlungu, J. Daniel, R. Southall and J. Lutchman (eds), *State of the Nation: South Africa 2007*, HSRC Press, Cape Town, 2007.
Atwell, D. (ed.), *Doubling the Point*, Harvard University Press, Cambridge, MA, 1992.
Bekker, T., 'The Re-emergence of Ubuntu: A Critical Analysis', *SA Public Law*, Vol. 21 (2), 2006, 333–44.
Berger, M., 'After the Third World? History, Destiny and the Fate of the Third World', *Third World Quarterly*, Vol. 25 (1), 2004, 9–39.
Billig, M., *Banal Nationalism*, Sage, London, 1995.
Boehmer, E., *Nelson Mandela: A Very Short Introduction*, Sterling Publishing, New York, 2010.
Bompani, B., 'African Independent Churches in Post-apartheid South Africa', *Journal of Southern African Studies*, Vol. 34 (4), 2008, 665–77.
Branford, J., *A Dictionary of South African English*, Oxford University Press, Oxford, 1980.
Bratton, M., Mattes, R. and Gyimah-Boadi, E., *Public Opinion, Democracy, and Market Reform in Africa*, Cambridge University Press, Cambridge, 2005.
Buhlungu, S., Daniel, J., Southall, R. and Lutchman, J. (eds), *State of the Nation: South Africa 2007*, HSRC Press, Cape Town, 2007.
Bundy, C., 'A Rich and Tangled Skein: Strategy and Ideology in Anti-apartheid Struggles', in *Beyond Racism: Embracing an Interdependent Future*, Southern Education Foundation, Atlanta, GA, 2000 (www.beyondracism.org).
Burger, J., *Farm Attacks and Farm Murders Remain a Concern*, Institute for Security Studies, Pretoria, 2012.
Butler, A., *Contemporary South Africa*, Palgrave Macmillan, Basingstoke, 2004.
Butler, J., Elphick, R. and Welsh, D. (eds), *Democratic Liberalism in South Africa, Its History and Prospect*, Wesleyan University Press, Middletown, CT, 1987.
Cachalia, F., 'Revisiting the National Question and Identity', *Politikon*, Vol. 39 (1), 2012, 53–69.
Calhoun, C., *Nations Matter*, Routledge, London, 2007.
Calland, R., *Anatomy of South Africa, Who Holds the Power?* Zebra Press, Cape Town, 2006.
Cameron, E., 'The Constitution Is Still Our Best Practical Hope', *Politicsweb*, 1 July 2013 (www.politicsweb.co.za).
Carlin, J., *Playing the Enemy: Nelson Mandela and the Game That Made a Nation*, Penguin, New York, 2008.
Carton, B., 'Why Is the "100% Zulu Boy" So Popular?' *Concerned African Scholars Bulletin*, 84, Winter 2010, 34–8.
Centre for Development and Enterprise (CDE), *Graduate Unemployment*, Johannesburg, 2013.

—, *Healthcare in South Africa: What Role for the Private Sector?* 2011.
—, *Poverty and Inequality: Facts, Trends and Hard Choices*, 2010.
—, *Skills, Growth and Borders: Managing Migration is South Africa's National Interest*, 2010.
Chipkin, I., *Do South Africans Exist? Nationalism, Democracy and the Identity of 'the People'*, Wits University Press, Johannesburg, 2007.
Civitas, *Comparisons of Crime in OECD Countries* (www.civitas.org.uk).
Coetzee, J. M., 'Four Notes on Rugby, 1978', in Atwell (ed.), 1992.
Constitution of the Republic of South Africa, *Act 108 of 1996*.
Constitutional Court, *S vs Makwanyane and M. Mchunu*, Johannesburg, 1995.
Contralesa, *The Formation of Contralesa*, 2012 (www.contralesa.org.za).
Coovadia, H., Jewkes, R., Barron, P., Sanders, D. and McIntyre, D., 'The Health and Health System of South Africa', *The Lancet*, Vol. 374 (9692), 5 September 2009, 817–34.
Council for Medical Schemes, *Annual Report*, Pretoria, 2013.
Council for the Advancement of the South African Constitution, *CASAC Proposes a New Independent Agency to Investigate Acts of Corruption*, Cape Town, 16 March 2011.
Crawford, R., 'The Magical Million: How Many South Africans Live in London?' in *Around the Globe*, Monash Institute for the Study of Global Movements, Melbourne, 2009, pp. 12–18.
Cronin, J., 'A Luta Discontinua? The TRC Final Report and the Nation Building Project', unpublished seminar paper, 1999.
Cronjé, F., 'White Emigration: A Reply from the SAIRR', *Politicsweb*, 14 August 2012 (www.politicsweb.co.za)
Davenport, R., *South Africa: A Modern History*, Macmillan, Johannesburg, 1987.
Davies, R., *Afrikaners in the New South Africa*, I.B. Tauris, London, 2009.
Davis, G., 'The Electoral Temptation of Race in South Africa', *Transformation*, 53, 2003.
De Gruchy, J., *The Church Struggle in South Africa*, Fortress Press, Minneapolis, 2005.
Degenaar, J., *The Myth of a South African Nation*, Institute for Democracy in South Africa (IDASA), Cape Town, 1991.
De Klerk, F. W., *Submission to the Truth and Reconciliation Commission by F. W. de Klerk*, Department of Justice, Pretoria, 1997 (www.doj.gov.za/trc).
Department of Arts and Culture, *Ministry of Arts & Culture on Bok van Blerks's Supposed Afrikaans 'Struggle Song', De la Rey and Its Coded Message to Fermenting Revolutionary Sentiments*, 6 February 2007.
Department of Cooperative Governance and Traditional Affairs (Cogta), *Annual Report, 2011–12*, Pretoria, 2012.
—, *State of Local Government Overview Report*, Pretoria, 2009.
Department of Justice, *Truth and Reconciliation Commission Special Hearings Transcripts* (www.justice.gov.za/Trc/special).
Department of Labour, *National Scarce Skills List*, Pretoria, 2008.
Department of Rural Development and Land Reform (DRDLR), *A Policy Framework for Land Acquisition and Land Valuation in a Land Reform Context*, Green Paper, Pretoria, September 2011.
Department of Trade and Industry, *Broad Based Black Empowerment Act 53 of 2003*, Pretoria, 2003.

Department of Traditional Affairs, *Annual Performance Plan, 2011–12*, Pretoria, 2011.
Desai, A. (ed.), *The Race to Transform: Sport in Post-apartheid South Africa*, HSRC Press, Cape Town, 2010.
Desai, A. and Vahed, G., 'Beyond the Nation: Colour and Class in South African Cricket', in Desai (ed.), 2010, pp. 80–104.
De Silvio, L., 'Correcting Corrective Rape', *Georgetown Law Journal*, Vol. 99, 2010–11.
Doumanis, N., *Inventing the Nation: Italy*, Arnold, London, 2001.
Du Preez, J., *The Language of Our Choice: Concerns about the 2011 SA Language Bill*, Centre for Constitutional Rights, Cape Town, 2011.
*The Economist*, 'Hold Your Nose', 3 June 2010.
—, 'White Flight from South Africa: Between Staying and Going', 25 September 2008.
Edigheji, O. (ed.), *Rethinking South Africa's Development Path*, Centre for Policy Studies, Johannesburg, 2007.
Eskom, *Integrated Report*, Sandton, 2011 (www.financialresults.co.za).
Everatt, D., *Nationalism, Class and Non-racialism in the 1950s and Beyond: The Search for Convergence*, 2009a (conference paper available at www.sahistory.org).
—, *The Origins of Non-racialism: White Opposition to Apartheid in the 1950s*, Wits University Press, Johannesburg, 2009b.
Ferree, K., *Framing the Race in South Africa: The Political Origins of Racial Census Elections*, Cambridge University Press, Cambridge, 2010.
Fin24, *Million Whites Leave SA*, 24 September 2006 (www.Fin24.com).
Financial and Fiscal Commission, *Non-payment Is Crippling Service Delivery in South African Municipalities*, Policy Brief 5, Johannesburg, 2011.
*Financial Mail*, 'Economic Cost of Road Deaths', 21 January 2013.
—, 'Eskom's 3.2 bn Problem', 11 December 2012.
—, 'Taxpayers: How Many Are There Again?' 11 March 2013.
—, 'Working but Still Poor', 4 October 2012.
Frederikse, J., *The Unbreakable Thread*, Zed Books, London, 1990.
Furley, O., *Conflict in Africa*, Tauris Academic Studies, London, 1995.
*The Guardian*, 'South African Reports of Police Brutality Tripled in the Last Decade', 22 August 2013.
Gevisser, M., *Thabo Mbeki: The Dream Deferred*, Jonathan Ball, Johannesburg, 2007.
Giliomee, H., *The Afrikaners: Biography of a People*, C. Hurst, London, 2003.
—, 'Apartheid, Verligtigheid and Liberalism', in Butler, Elphick and Welsh (eds), 1987.
—, 'The Beginnings of Afrikaner Ethnic Consciousness 1850–1915', in Vail (ed.), 1991, pp. 21–54.
Giliomee, H. and Schlemmer L., *From Apartheid to Nation-building*, Oxford University Press, Cape Town, 1989.
Giliomee, H. and Simkins, C., *The Awkward Embrace: One Party Domination in Industrialised Societies*, Tafelberg, Cape Town 1999.
Glaser, D., *Politics and Society in South Africa*, Sage, London, 2001.
Goleman, D., *Emotional Intelligence*, Bantam, New York, 1995.
—, *Working with Emotional Intelligence*, Bloomsbury, London, 1998.

Goodin, R. E. and Petit, P., *Contemporary Political Philosophy*, Blackwell, Oxford, 1997.
Greenstein, R., *South Africa in Comparative Perspective*, Palgrave Macmillan, Basingstoke, 1998.
Grundlingh, A. M., 'From Redemption to Recidivism: Rugby and Change during the 1995 World Cup and Aftermath', *Sporting Traditions*, Vol. 14, 1998, 67–86.
Gumede, W. M., *Thabo Mbeki and the Battle for the Soul of the ANC*, Zebra Press, Cape Town, 2005.
Gunner, L., 'Jacob Zuma, the Social Body and the Unruly Power of Song', *African Affairs*, Vol. 108 (430), 2009, 27–48.
Habermass, 'The Public Sphere', in Goodin and Pettit (eds), 1997.
Habib, A., 'Public Opinion and the Prospects for Democratic Consolidation in South Africa 1999–2002', in *Public Attitudes in Contemporary South Africa*, HSRC Press, Cape Town, 2002, pp. 1–11.
Hadland, A., Louw, E., Sesanti, S. and Wasserman, H. (eds), *Power, Politics and Identity in South African Media*, HSRC Press, Cape Town, 2008.
Halisi, C. R. D., *Black Political Thought in the Making of South Africa*, Indiana University Press, Bloomington, 1999.
Harrison, D., *An Overview of Health and Healthcare in South Africa 1994–2010*, Henry J. Kaiser Family Foundation, Pretoria, 2010.
Harrison, P., 'Census 2011: Blame Migrant White Males, Not the Stats', *Mail & Guardian*, 14 December 2012.
Heugh, K., 'Multilingual Voices', *Agenda* (46), 2000, 21–33.
Hirsch, A., *Season of Hope: Economic Reform under Mandela and Mbeki*, University of KwaZulu-Natal Press, Scottsville, 2005.
Hirschman, A. O., *Exit, Voice, and Loyalty: Responses to Decline in Firms, Organizations, and States*, Harvard University Press, Cambridge, MA, 1970.
—, 'Exit, Voice, and the Fate of the German Democratic Republic: An Essay in Conceptual History', *World Politics*, Vol. 45 (2), January 1993, 173–202.
Hoffman, B., *Exit, Voice and the Lessons from the Cuban Case*, Institute for Iberoamerican Studies, Hamburg, 2004.
Holston, J., *Insurgent Citizenship: Disjunctions of Democracy and Modernity in Brazil*, Princeton University Press, Princeton, NJ, 2009.
Horowitz, D., *A Democratic South Africa: Constitutional Engineering in a Divided Society*, University of California Press, Berkeley, 1991.
Houlihan, B., 'Sport, National Identity and Public Policy', *Nations and Nationalism*, Vol. 3 (1), 1997, 113–37.
Human Sciences Research Council (HSRC), *Impact of the 2010 World Cup on Social Cohesion, Nation Building and Reconciliation*, HSRC, Pretoria, 2011.
—, *In the Court of Public Opinion: Attitudes Towards the Criminal Courts*, HSRC Review (www.hsrc.ac.za).
Hund, J. (ed.), *Witchcraft Violence and the Law in South Africa*, Protea Book House, Hatfield, 2003.
Huschka, D. and Mau, S., *Aspects of Quality of Life: Social Anomie in South Africa*, Social Science Research Centre, Berlin, 2005.
Independent Claims Directorate, *Annual Report 2011–12*, Pretoria, 2012.
Institute for Justice and Reconciliation (IJR), *SA Reconciliation Barometer 2010, Survey Report*, Cape Town, 2010.

—, *SA Reconciliation Barometer 2012, Survey Report*, Cape Town, 2012.
International Centre for Prison Studies, *Highest to Lowest* (www.prisonstudies.org).
IOL News, 'No Change in Road User Behaviour', 17 January 2012.
—, 'Prisons Race Shock', 25 November 2008.
—, 'Trevor Manuel's Open Letter to Jimmy Manyi', 2 March 2011.
—, 'Unlicensed Drivers Overrun Cape Roads', 13 October 2011.
James, W., 'The Meaning of Race in Modern South Africa', *Focus* (67), November 2012, 29–34.
Jeffrey, A., *Rainbow Index*, South African Institute of Race Relations, Johannesburg, 2012.
Jennings, I., *The Approach to Self-government*, Cambridge University Press, Cambridge, 1956.
Johnson, R. W. and Welsh, D. (eds), *Ironic Victory*, Oxford University Press, Cape Town, 1998.
Johnson, R. W. and Schlemmer, L. (eds), *Launching Democracy in South Africa: The First Open Election, April 1994*, Yale University Press, New Haven and London, 1996.
Johnson, S., *Strange Days Indeed: Tales from the Old and Nearly New South Africa*, Transworld Publishers, London and Johannesburg, 1993.
Johnston, A. M., 'The African National Congress, the Print Media and the Development of Mediated Politics in South Africa', *Critical Arts*, Vol. 19 (1–2), 2005.
—, 'Conflict in South Africa', in Furley (ed.), 1995, 46–71.
Jolobe, Z., 'Things Fall Apart, Can the Centre Hold? The State of Coalition Politics in the Cape Metropolitan Council', in Buhlungu, Daniel, Southall and Lutchman (eds), 2007, pp. 78–94.
Judt, T., *Postwar: A History of Europe since 1945*, Penguin Press, New York, 2005.
Kiberd, D., *Inventing Ireland*, Vintage, London, 1996.
Kotzé, H. and Steenekamp, C., *Values and Democracy in South Africa*, Konrad Adaneuer Stiftung, Johannesburg, 2009.
Krog, A., *Country of My Skull*, Random House, Johannesburg, 1998.
Labour Research Service, *Collective Bargaining Indicators*, 13 March 2013 (www.cosatu.org.za).
Lambert-Mogiliansky, A., 'Strategic Analysis of Petty Corruption: Entrepreneurs and Bureaucrats, *Journal of Development Economics*, Vol. 83 (2007), 351–67.
Lancaster, L., *The Problem with South African Criminal Justice Performance Indicators*, Institute for Security Studies, Pretoria, 2012.
Leclerc-Madlala, S., 'On the Virgin Cleansing Myth: Gendered Bodies, AIDS and Ethnomedicine', *African Journal of AIDS Research*, Vol. 1, 2002, 87–95.
Legassick, M., *Armed Struggle and Democracy: The Case of South Africa*, Nordic Africa Institute, Uppsala, 2002.
Leibbrandt, M., Woolard, I., Finn, A. and Argent, J., *Trends in South African Income Distribution and Poverty since the Fall of Apartheid*, OECD Social, Employment and Migration Working Papers, No. 101, 2010.
Lijphart, A., *Democracy in Plural Societies*, Yale University Press, New Haven and London, 1977.

Lodge, T., 'The African National Congress: Kabwe and after', *International Affairs Bulletin*, Vol. 10 (2), 1986, 4–13.
—, *Nelson Mandela: A Critical Life*, Oxford University Press, Oxford, 2006.
—, *Nelson Mandela, Assessing the Icon, Open Democracy* (www.opendemocracy.net), 17 July 2009.
—, *Politics in South Africa: From Mandela to Mbeki*, David Philip, Cape Town, 2002.
—, 'State of Exile: The African National Congress of South Africa 1976–87', *Third World Quarterly*, Vol. 9 (1), 1987, 1–27.
McKinley, D., '"Transformation" from Above: The Upside-down State of South African Soccer', in Desai (ed.), 2010, pp. 80–104.
*Mail & Guardian*, 'Manyi under Fire for Coloured Remarks', 24 February 2011.
—, 'Older Men Blamed for High HIV Rates among Schoolgirls', 14 March 2013.
—, 'Pravin's Social Contract', 29 October 2010.
—, 'Print Media Transformation "Too Slow"', 30 July 2009.
—, 'Smoke and Mirrors in the Wild East', 22 October 2010.
Mamdani, M., 'Reconciliation without Justice', *South African Review of Books* (46), November–December 1996, 3–5.
Mandela, N., *Address by President Nelson Mandela Opening the Morals Summit Called by the National Religious Leaders' Forum 22 October 1998*, Speeches by Nelson Mandela 1998, African National Congress (www.anc.org.za).
—, *Address by President Nelson Mandela to Parliament: National Assembly*, Cape Town, 5 February 1999 (sahistory.org.za).
—, *Long Walk to Freedom*, Macdonald Purnell, Randburg, 1994.
Mangaliso, M., 'Building Competitive Advantage from Ubuntu', *Academy of Management Executive*, Vol. 15 (3), 2001, 23–33.
Mangcu, X., 'The State of Race Relations in Post-apartheid South Africa', in John Daniel, Adam Habib and Roger Southall (eds), *State of the Nation: South Africa 2003–2004*, HSRC Press, Cape Town, 2005, pp. 105–17.
Marais, H., *South Africa Pushed to the Limit: The Political Economy of Change*, Zed Books, London, 2011.
Marchetti-Mercer, M. C., 'Family Murder in Post-apartheid South Africa', *Health SA Gesondheid*, Vol. 8 (2), 2003.
Marks, S., *The Tradition of Non-racism in South Africa*, University of the Witwatersrand, History Workshop Papers, Johannesburg, 1994.
Marx, A., *Lessons of Struggle: South African Internal Opposition 1960–1990*, Oxford University Press, New York, 1992.
Marx, K. and Engels, F., *The Communist Manifesto: A Modern Edition*, Verso Books, London, 2012.
Mattes, R., 'Do Diverse Social Identities Inhibit Nationhood and Democracy?', in Palmberg (ed.), 1999.
Mattes, R. and Glenn, I., *Political Communication in Post-apartheid South Africa*, Centre for Social Science Research, University of Cape Town, Cape Town, 2011.
Mattes, R. and Richmond, W., 'The Brain Drain: What Do Skilled South Africans Think?' in *Losing Our Minds: Skills Migration and the South African Brain Drain*, Southern African Migration Project, Cape Town, 2000, pp. 9–35.

Matthews, S., 'Differing Interpretations of Reconciliation in South Africa: A Discussion of the Home for All Campaign', *Transformation* (Durban) (74), 2010, 1–22.

Maylam, P., *South Africa's Racial Past: The History and Historiography of Racism, Segregation and Apartheid*, Ashgate, Aldershot, 2001.

Mbeki, T., *4th Annual Nelson Mandela Lecture by President Thabo Mbeki*, University of Witwatersrand, Johannesburg, 29 July 2006.

—, *Keynote Address to the Growth and Development Summit, Johannesburg, 7 June, 2003*, The Presidency, 2003.

—, *Statement by Deputy-President Thabo Mbeki at the Opening of the Debate in the National Assembly on Reconciliation and Nation-building*, Cape Town, 29 May 1998.

Meredith, M., *Mandela*, Simon and Shuster, London, 2010.

Miller, D., *On Nationality*, Oxford University Press, Oxford, 1995.

Mokgoro, Y., 'Ubuntu and the Law in South Africa', *Potchefstroom Electronic Law Journal*, University of North West, Potchefstroom, 1998.

Moseneke, D., *Striking a Balance between the Will of the People and the Supremacy of the Constitution*, Claude Leon Public Lecture, 10 October 2011, Legal Resources Centre, Cape Town (www.lrc.org.za).

Narunsky-Laden, S., 'Identity in Post-apartheid South Africa', in Hadland, Louw, Sesanti and Wasserman (eds), 2008, pp. 124–50.

National Labour and Economic Development Institute (NALEDI), *Findings of the COSATU Workers' Survey*, Johannesburg, 2012 (www.cosatu.org.za).

National Planning Commission (NPC), *Diagnostic Report*, Pretoria, June 2011.

—, *National Development Plan (NDP)*, Pretoria, November 2011.

National Treasury, *Budget Review 2012*, Chapter 6, 'Social Security and National Health Insurance', Pretoria, 2012a.

—, *Budget Review 2013*, Chapter 6, 'Social Security and the Social Wage', Pretoria, 2013.

—, *Local Government Revenue and Expenditure for the Period 1 July 2012–30 September 2012*, Pretoria, 5 December 2012b.

—, *Medium Term Budget Policy Statement*, Pretoria, 2011.

Nattrass, N. and Seekings, J., *Class, Race and Inequality in South Africa*, Yale University Press, New Haven and London, 2005.

Ndebele, N., *South African Literature and Culture: The Rediscovery of the Ordinary*, Manchester University Press, Manchester, 1994.

Newham, G., *How to Stop Police Brutality and the Killing of Police Officers in South Africa*, Institute for Security Studies, Pretoria, 2011.

News 24, 'Fraud Shock for Illegal Drivers', 15 May 2005.

Niehaus, I., 'Witchcraft in the New South Africa', in Hund (ed.), 2003.

O'Malley, P., *The O'Malley Archives* (www.nelsonmandela.org).

Palmberg, M. (ed.), *National Identity and Democracy in Africa*, Nordic Africa Institute, Uppsala, 1990.

Parliamentary Monitoring Group, *Justice and Constitutional Development Portfolio Committee, SIU Annual Report*, 11 October 2011.

—, *Minister on Moral Regeneration Movement*, Department of Arts and Culture Portfolio Committee, 16 March 2010.

—, *Minister on PANSALB Developments*, Department of Arts and Culture Portfolio Committee, 6 June 2012.

—, *Monitor*, January–February 2013.
—, *South African Rugby Union on Transformation*, Department of Sport Portfolio Committee, 19 February 2013.
—, *Traditional Courts Bill: Department Responds to Public Hearings*, Department of Cooperative Governance and Traditional Affairs Portfolio Committee, 24 October 2012.
—, *Traditional Courts Bill, Public Hearings, Day 3, National Council of Provinces*, 20 September 2012.
Petrus, T. S., 'An Anthropological Study of Witchcraft-related Crime in the Eastern Cape', unpublished doctoral dissertation, Nelson Mandela Metropolitan University, Port Elizabeth, 2009.
Pillay, U., Roberts, B. and Rule, S. (eds), *South African Social Attitudes*, HSRC Press, Pretoria, 2006.
Piper, L., 'The Zuma Watershed: From Post-apartheid to Post-colonial Politics in South Africa', *Representation*, Vol. 45 (2), 2009, 101–7.
Politicsweb, 'How Many South Africans Have Left the Country?' 14 August 2012 (www.politicsweb.co.za).
Powell, E., *Joseph Chamberlain*, Thames and Hudson, London, 1977.
The Presidency, *Annual Address by President Jacob Zuma to the National House of Traditional Leaders*, Cape Town, 1 November 2012.
—, *Clarifying the Second Economy Concept*, 2006.
—, *A Nation in the Making*, 2006.
—, *Social Cohesion and Social Justice in South Africa*, 2004.
—, *Towards a Fifteen-year Review*, 2008.
—, *Towards a Ten-Year Review*, 2003.
Rauch, J., *Linking Crime and Morality: Reviewing the Moral Regeneration Movement*, Institute for Security Studies, Pretoria, 2005.
Roberts, B., Kivilu, M. W. and Davids, Y. D. (eds), *South African Social Attitudes 2nd Report*, HSRC Press, Pretoria, 2010.
Rosenberg, J. and Chen, M., *Expanding Democracy: Voter Registration around the World*, Brennan Centre for Democracy, New York University, New York, 2009.
Roux, N., *Migration and Urbanization*, Department of Social Development, Pretoria, March 2009.
Rule, S. and Mncwango, B., 'Christianity in South Africa: Theory and Practice', in Roberts, Kivilu and Davids (eds), 2010, pp. 185–97.
—, 'Rights or Wrongs: An Exploration of Moral Values', in Pillay, Roberts and Rule (eds), 2006, pp. 252–76.
Sachs, A., *Protecting Human Rights in a New South Africa*, Oxford University Press, Cape Town, 1990.
SAPA (South African Press Association), *Churches Confess to Failures under Apartheid*, 17 November 1997 (available in Department of Justice TRC collection, www.justice.gov.za).
Schulz-Herzenberg, C., *Elections and Accountability in South Africa*, Institute for Security Studies, Pretoria 2009.
—, 'South African Voters 1994–2006', in Buhlungu, Daniel, Southall and Lutchman (eds), 2007, pp. 114–45.
Seekings, J., *The UDF*, New Africa Books, Cape Town, 2000.
Segal, L. and Cort, S., *One Law One Nation*, Jacana, Johannesburg, 2012.

Sithole, P., 'Fifteen Year Review on Traditional Leadership', unpublished paper for the Presidency, HSRC Pretoria, 2008.
Slabbert, F. van Zyl., 'Sham Reform and Conflict Regulation in a Divided Society', *Journal of Asian and African Studies*, Vol. 18, 1983, 34–48.
South African Broadcasting Corporation, *Annual Report*, Johannesburg, 2012.
South African Communist Party, *The Path to Power*, 1989 (www.sacp.org.za).
—, *The Road to South African Freedom*, 1962 (www.sacp.org.za).
South African History Online, *Post-election Violence* (www.sahistory.org.za).
South African Human Rights Commission, *Faultlines: Inquiry into Racism in the Media*, Johannesburg, August 2000.
South African Institute of Race Relations, *Annual Survey 1992–3*, Johannesburg, 1994.
—, *Annual Survey 2013*, Johannesburg, 2013.
South African Police Service, *Crime Statistics, 2011*, Pretoria, 2011 (www.saps.gov.za).
—, *Crime Statistics, 2012*, Pretoria, 2012 (www.saps.gov.za).
—, *Crime Statistics, 2013*, Pretoria, 2013 (www.saps.gov.za).
Southall, R. and Daniel, J. (eds), *Zunami! The 2009 South African Elections*, Jacana Media (Pty) Ltd, Johannesburg, 2009.
Southern African Migration Project, *The Perfect Storm: The Realities of Xenophobia in Contemporary South Africa*, Institute for Democracy in South Africa (IDASA), 2008.
Sparks, A., *Tomorrow Is Another Country: The Inside Story of South Africa's Negotiated Revolution*, Struik, Johannesburg, 1994.
Statistics South Africa (StatsSA), *Census 2001, Census in Brief*, Pretoria, 2003.
—, *Census 2011, Census in Brief*, Pretoria, 2012a.
—, *Mid-year Population Estimates 2010*, Pretoria, 2010.
—, *Migration and Urbanisation in South Africa*, Pretoria, 2006.
—, *National Victims of Crime Survey*, Pretoria, 2012b.
—, *Quarterly Labour Force Survey, Third Quarter 2012*, Pretoria, 2012c.
Stern, M. and Szalontai, G., 'Immigration Policy in South Africa: Does It Make Economic Sense?' *Development Southern Africa*, Vol. 23 (1), 2006, 123–45.
*Sunday Independent*, 'The Census Shrunk the White Population', 8 October 2006.
Suttner, R., 'Revisiting the National Democratic Revolution: The "National Question"', unpublished seminar paper, April 2011a.
—, 'The UDF Period and Its Meaning for Contemporary South Africa', *Journal of Southern African Studies*, Vol. 30 (3), 2004, 691–702.
—, *Understanding Non-racialism as an Emancipatory Concept in South Africa*, Codesria, 13th General Assembly, 2011b.
Turok, B., 'The ANC and Race', *New Agenda*, 30, Second Quarter 2008, p. 5.
Vahed, G., Padayachee, V. and Desai, A., 'Between Black and White: A Case Study of the KwaZulu-Natal Cricket Union', in Desai (ed.), 2010, pp. 222–58.
Vail, L. (ed.), *The Creation of Tribalism in Southern Africa*, University of California Press, Berkeley, 1991.
Van der Berg, S., 'The Demographic and Spatial Distribution of Poverty', in CDE, 2010.
Van der Waal, C. S. and Robins, S., '"De la Rey" and the Revival of "Boer Heritage": Nostalgia in the Post-apartheid Afrikaner Culture Industry', *Journal of Southern African Studies*, Vol. 37 (4), December 2011, 763–79.

Van der Westhuizen, C., *White Power and the Rise and Fall of the National Party*, Zebra Press, Cape Town, 2008.
Van Eeden, J., *The Demand for Healthcare and Health Insurance in South Africa*, Research Note 8, Econex, Stellenbosch, February 2009.
Van Onselen, C., 'A Childhood on the Edge of History', *London Review of Books*, Vol. 20 (3), 5 February 1998.
Van Schaik, *Groot Woorde-Boek: Afrikaans-Engels*, 12e, Pretoria, 1981.
Vavi, Z., *Address to SACTWU National Congress*, 23 September 2010 (www.cosatu.org.za).
—, 'Graft Hampers Service Delivery', *Sunday World*, 11 December 2011.
Villa-Vicenzio, C., 'The RDP of the Soul', in Edigheji (ed.), 2007, pp. 150–3.
Vincent, L., 'Moral Panic and the Politics of Populism', *Representation*, Vol. 45 (2), 2009, 213–22.
—, 'New Magic for New Times: Muti Murder in Postcolonial South Africa', in Kaushik Boses (ed.), *Health and Nutritional Problems of Indigenous Populations*, Studies of Tribes and Tribals, Special Issue, Vol. 2, 2008, 43–53.
Von Holdt, K, Langa, M., Molapo, S., Mogapi, N., Ngubeni, K., Dlamini, J. and Kirsten, A., *The Smoke That Calls: Insurgent Citizenship, Collective Violence and the Struggle for a Place in the New South Africa*, Centre for the Study of Violence and Reconciliation, Johannesburg, 2011.
Waldmeir, P., *Anatomy of a Miracle: The End of Apartheid and the Birth of the New South Africa*, Penguin Books, London, 1997.
Walshe, P., *The Rise of African Nationalism in South Africa*, Ad Donker, Johannesburg, 1987.
Wasserman, H., *Tabloid Journalism in South Africa: True Story!* Indiana University Press, Bloomington, 2010.
Williams, J. M., *Chieftaincy, the State and Democracy: Political Legitimacy in Post-apartheid South Africa*, University of Indiana Press, Bloomington, 2010.
Wilson, R., *The Politics of the Truth and Reconciliation Commission in South Africa*, Cambridge University Press, Cambridge, 2001.
Xingwana, L., *Speech at the Launch of the Multilingualism Campaign*, Freedom Park, Pretoria, 20 February 2010, SA Government Online (www.gov.za/speeches)

# INDEX

Adam, H. 54, 106, 120, 179
  *Modernizing Racial Domination* 53
Adhikari, M. 304–5
African Christian Democratic Party (ACDP) 239
African Independent Churches (AICs) 234–7, 329n. 9
Africanism 43, 73, 75–6, 79–81, 87–9, 91–2, 100, 132, 170, 174, 181, 195, 290–2, 304, 326
  *see also* African nationalism
African National Congress (ANC) 2–3, 6–7, 9, 13, 16, 22, 57, 59, 62–4, 68, 70, 89, 94–7, 169, 173, 196–7, 200–1, 213, 228, 266, 275, 313–14, 323–4, 326, 327n. 1, 328n. 4
  African nationalism ambiguities and 71–6
  Africanism and 92–3
  'better life for all' slogan of 259
  Chancellor House 332n. 2
  civil society activism and 210–11
  Colonialism of a Special Type (CST) and 77–81
  Constitutional Principles for a Democratic South Africa 300
  discussion document of 188
  elections and 246, 247
  election victory in 1994 and aftermath 139–40
  evolution of 75
  hostility of to the media 219
  language and ethnicity and 38–46
  Mandela and 148–52
  moral citizens making and 184–9
  nation improvisation and 119, 120, 123–33
  nation-building and 99–117, 259–60
  *The Nature of the South African Ruling Class* 104
  non-racialism of 82–5, 91, 297–302, 304, 314, 331n. 4
  planning principle of 190–7
  pragmatic relationship with religion 235
  public sphere and 218–19
  racialism and rugby and 141–5, 147
  reconciliation and 157, 160–8
  reservations about Constitutional Court 242–4
  service delivery protests and 277–8
  using soft powers, as diplomatic leverage 129
  Strategy and Tactics document at the Morogoro Consultative Conference 77
  taxation and 250
  traditional leaders and 255
  tradition and shared citizenship and 252–3
  transformation and 175–80
  Youth League (ANCYL) 44, 75–6, 242, 293
African nationalism 2–6, 10–12, 19, 42, 63–4, 69, 78, 81–9, 91, 93–5, 99–103, 106, 111, 118, 119, 293–4, 302
  ambiguities of 71–7
  decay of 170
  non-racialism and 169–70, 173–4
  *see also* Africanism; nation-building
Africanness 46, 86, 120, 130, 132, 195, 238, 303
Afriforum 210
'Afrikanerdom' 59, 121, 142, 315
Afrikaner nationalism 2–3, 97, 99–100, 106, 118, 119, 142, 146, 232, 234, 314–16
  Colonialism of a Special Type (CST) 74, 77–81

demise of 223
growth, maturity, and decay of 51–64
legacies of 69–71
non-racialism and 81–8
PAC and Black Consciousness Movement 88–93
toxic legacy of 5
Whites and 314–17
Zulu factor and 93–6
Afrikaner Volksfront (AV) 64, 70, 108, 109
Afrikaner Weerstandsbeweging (AWB) 58, 62, 64, 101, 107–10
Afrobarometer 242, 273
age distribution, between black and white population 24
Ahmed Kathrada Foundation 300, 304, 331n. 4
Akenson, D. 53
Alegi, P. 220, 224
Alexander, N. 34–5, 38
Allwright, P. 275
Ally, Y. 257
Anderson, A. 235, 236
Anderson, B. 212
anti-racist racism 301
apartheid, *see individual entries*
Ashforth, A. 258–9
Askvik, S. 283, 284
Asmal, K. 125, 139
Association for the Advancement of Black Accountants (AABA) 208
Association of Miners and Construction Union (AMCU) 280
Atkinson, D. 276
Audit Bureau of Circulation (ABC) 329n. 2

Bak, N. 283, 284
banal nationalism 215
Bekker, T. 172
Berger, M. 180
Biko, S. 91, 92
Billig, M. 215
   *Banal Nationalism* 319
Bill of Rights 18, 99, 103, 148, 172, 175, 198, 209, 253, 255, 257

Black Business Council (BBC) 208
Black Consciousness Movement (BCM) 73, 89–92, 94, 186
Black Economic Empowerment (BEE) 31, 44, 154, 175, 177, 179, 197, 208, 217, 247, 301, 302, 304, 313, 323, 325
Black Lawyers' Association (BLA) 208
Black Management Forum (BMF) 132, 208, 263
Black People's Convention (BPC) 92
Black republicanism 132–3
Bloch, C. 35
Boehmer, E. 261
Bompani, B. 236
Botha, P. W. 58, 61, 236
Branfort, J. 232
Bratton, M. 242
Broad-based Black Economic Empowerment (BBBEE) Act 175
Bundy, C. 82
Burger, J. 271
Burton, M. 162
Bush, G. 332n. 1
Business Against Crime (BAC) 276
*Business Day* 329n. 2
Business Unity South Africa (BUSA) 209
Buthelezi, M. 5, 6, 41, 42, 57, 63, 64, 70, 93–6, 101, 106, 108, 109, 112–17, 128, 151, 160, 235, 252–3
Buthelezi Commission 96
Butler, A. 19, 43

Cachalia, F. 301
Calhoun, C. 130, 131
Cameron, E. 8
Carlin J. 145, 146, 148, 327n. 1
Carton, B. 294, 295
Centre for Development and Enterprise (CDE) 25, 26, 281
Chamberlain, J. 328n. 3
Chaskalson, A. 139, 172
Chen, M. 245
Chipkin, I. 6, 11, 181
Christianity 329n. 10
   forms and legacies of 234–7

citizenship, shared
　constitution and 240-4
　polity and 240
　public services and 249-50
　taxation and 250-1
　tradition and, in democratic South Africa 252-3
　voting and 244-9
City Press 214
civic nation, see civic nationalism
civic nationalism 2-3, 8-9, 11, 47, 101, 106-7, 111, 169-70, 191, 193, 195, 207-8, 240, 243-6, 249, 272, 279, 289-91, 294, 297, 309, 322-6
civil disobedience affecting nation-building 282-5
civil society 4, 38, 107, 131, 133, 157, 185, 192, 197, 243, 274-5, 278, 312, 323
　and associational life 206-11
Civitas 268
Coetzee, J. M. 142
cognitive dissonance 239
collective political will 291
colonialism 2, 39-42, 56-7, 68, 73, 84-5, 95-6, 100, 115, 132, 142, 173, 184, 191, 212, 221, 223, 255, 281, 291, 326
　of a Special Type (CST) 74, 77-81, 103, 104, 126
Commission on Traditional Leadership, Disputes and Claims 254
Communal Land Rights Act (2004) 256
Concerned South Africans Group (COSAG) 108, 109, 113
Congress of South African Trade Unions (Cosatu) 73-4, 190, 197, 200, 242, 247, 280, 298, 299
Congress of the People (COPE) 43
Conservative Party (CP) 58, 62, 64, 101, 107, 108
constitutional court and *ubuntu* 170-2
constitutionalized apartheid 59
constitutional patriotism 7
Contralesa (Congress of Traditional Leaders of South Africa) 115, 170, 252-3, 259, 296

Convention for a Democratic South Africa (CODESA) 253
　Declaration of Intent 101, 110, 124, 125
Coovadia, H. 26
corruption affecting nation-building 273-6
Corruption Watch 274-5
Cort, S. 241
Council for the Advancement of the South African Constitution (CASAC) 274-5
Crawford, R. 307, 308
Cricket South Africa (CSA) 222
crime affecting nation-building 266-73, 275-6
Cronin, J. 158
Cronjé, F. 332n. 7

d'Oliveira, B. 142
Daily Sun 214, 215, 329n. 2
Damon, M. 145
Davenport, R. 235
Davies, R. 11, 316
Davis, G. 248
Degenaar, J. 6
De Gruchy, J. 235, 237
De Klerk, F. W. 2, 59-64, 69, 70, 106, 107, 109, 125, 137, 144
Democratic Alliance (DA) 247, 248, 277-8, 298, 303-5
Democratic Party 139, 180
　'Fight Back' slogan of 156
demography 17-24
denationalization, of Afrikaner politics 61-3
Department of Arts and Culture (DAC) 37, 187, 315
Department of Cooperative Governance and Traditional Affairs (COGTA) 253-5
Department of Justice Special Hearings Transcripts 159
Department of Labour 297, 298, 311
Department of Rural Development and Land Reform (DRDLR)
　Green Paper on land reform 290-1
Department of Trade and Industry 175

Department of Women, Children and People with Disabilities (DWCPD) 257
Desai, A. 222, 225
De Silvio, L. 269
deviance and trust affecting nation-building 286
Disraeli, B. 328n. 4
diversity 85
  division and 47
  language 33–6
  significance of 15, 17
  *see also individual entries*
divided society 16–17, 56
Doumanis, N. 134
Driver Licence Testing Centres (DLTCs) 285
Du Preez, J. 37
Dutch Reformed Church in Africa (DRCA) 234–6
Dutch Reformed Mission Church (DRMC) 235, 236

*Economist* 308
education 26–8
emigration and transnationalism, and nation-building 310–14
Engels, F.
  *Communist Manifesto* 65
English hegemony 34–5
Eskom 284, 331n. 9
ethnic census 246
European Court of Justice 329n. 4
Everatt, D. 83–4
Extension of University Education Act (1959) 90

family murders 271
Fanon, F. 91
farm murders 271
federalism 110–11
Ferree, K. 246, 248, 330n. 14
Financial and Fiscal Commission (FFC) 283, 284, 331n. 8
*Financial Mail* 251, 284, 285
Framework Response to Economic Crisis 199
Frederikse, J. 82, 84
Freedom Charter (1955) 72, 76, 78, 83, 85, 104, 118, 210

Freedom Front (FF) 110, 126
Freeman, M. 145
FRELIMO 92

Gevisser, M. 93, 94, 121, 122, 148, 153, 272, 312
Giliomee, H. 10, 19–20, 51, 54, 59, 97, 148, 246–7
Gini measure 25
Glaser, D. 40, 42
Glenn, I. 217
Goleman, D. 140–1
good nationalism 7–8
Gorbachev, M. 60, 63, 114
Gordhan, P. 250
Greenstein, R. 5
Growth, Employment and Redistribution (GEAR) programme 169, 179, 200
Growth and Development Summit 199
Gumede, W. M. 185
Gunner, L. 294

Habermas 217–18
Habib, A. 248
Halisi, C. R. D. 132–3
Hani, C. 141
Harare Declaration (1989) 99, 103, 110, 119, 124, 126, 129, 169
Harrison, D. 30–1
Harrison, P. 307
health inequality 25–6
healthcare financing, public 30
Herenigde ('Reunited') Nasionale Party 52
Heugh, K. 36
Hirsch, A. 180, 250
Hirschman, A. O. 305, 310
Hoffmann, B. 310
Hofmeyr, W. 274
Holston, J. 278
'Homecoming Revolution' 310–11, 319
Home for All campaign 162–5, 168, 185
  'Declaration of Commitment by White South Africans' 163
Horowitz, D. 246
Horton 330n. 15
Houlihan, B. 220
Human Rights Commission (HRC) 166

Human Sciences Research Council (HSRC) 191, 228, 230, 238, 248, 272, 330n. 11
Huschka, D. 265

imperialism 1, 12, 51, 68, 72, 77, 95, 100, 104, 131, 142, 173, 185
  British 51–2, 54, 55, 67, 189, 230, 232
improvised nation (1990–6)
  ambiguities of 118–27
  future and 127–34
  nation and settlement 99–117
income and poverty 29–30
Independent Claims Directorate (ICD) 270
Independent Electoral Commission (IEC) 245
Indian Premier League (IPL) 222
inequality 4, 11, 17, 24–5, 44, 60, 129, 130, 173, 191, 199, 206, 221, 228, 249, 265, 268, 278, 282, 284, 300
  health 25–6
  income 29–30
  material 152–4, 169, 175, 181, 183, 227
  racial 16, 31–2, 236, 302
  reduction in 9–10, 179
  two nations theory and 154–6
  *see also* nation-building
information order, unequal and segmented 212–17
Inkatha Freedom Party (IFP) 41, 42, 95, 96, 101, 102, 106, 107, 111–14, 116, 123–7, 129, 147, 160, 170, 186, 252
Institute for Justice and Reconciliation (IJR) 29, 162, 241
insurgent citizenship 278
IOL News 285, 298, 303

James, W. 18
Jeffrey, A. 285
Jobs Summit 199
Johannesburg Stock Exchange (JSE) 177
Johnson, R. W. 101, 107, 126, 128, 180, 247
Johnson, S. 127
Johnston, A. M. 122, 213

Jolobe, Z. 304
Jordan, Z. P. 315
Judt, T. 249

Kabwe Consultative Conference (1985) 77, 83
Kant, I. 184
Khomphela, B. 221
Kiberd 131
Kolpak ruling 225
Kotzé, H. 241, 242, 330n. 12
Krog, A. 11
KwaZulu-Natal Cricket Union 222
KwaZulu-Natal Indaba 96
KwaZulu Territorial Authority 93

Labour Research Service 280
Lambert-Mogiliansky, A. 274
Lancaster, L. 267
land tenure and administration of justice 256–7
language
  diversity 33–6
  ethnicity and 38–46
  policy, in nation-building 36–8
Leclerc-Madlala, S. 269
Legassick, M. 105
Leibbrandt, M. 32
Lembede, A. 91, 152
liberal individualism 80
Liberal Party 83
Lijphart, A. 58
Lodge, T. 75, 81, 105–6, 149–51
Luthuli, A. 328n. 6

Madonsela, T. 274
Maharaj, M. 125–6, 128, 139
*Mail & Guardian* 216, 250, 269, 275, 298
Majola, G. 222
majority rule principle 79
Malema, J. 44, 91
Mamdani, M. 158
Mandela, N. 2, 63, 72, 74, 103, 106, 109, 120, 121, 123, 125, 129, 137, 139, 143–6, 153–4, 167, 169, 184, 202, 220, 233, 260–1, 293, 308
  appraisal of 181–2
  making sense of 147–52

to moral summit of religious
    leaders 266
presidential career of 140–1
Mangaliso, M. 171
Mangcu, X. 299
Mangope, L. 109
Mantashe, G. 243, 244, 299, 301
Manuel, T. 190, 298, 299, 328n. 8
Manyi, J. 297–9, 301, 304, 331n. 2
Marais, H. 174
Marchetti-Mercer, M. C. 271
Marikana tragedy 280
Marks, S. 82
Marx, A. 86, 88
Marx, K.
  Communist Manifesto 65
*Masakhane* campaign 283
Mattes, R. 42–3, 217, 308
Matthews, S. 163, 328nn. 6–7
Mau, S. 265
Maylam, P. 272
Mbeki, T. 4, 26, 43, 45, 46, 69, 93, 108, 109, 121, 320, 322, 325–6, 328nn. 1, 4, 332n. 1
  Africanist dilemmas of 168–70
  appraisal of 181–2
  making sense of 152–4
  on nation-building 137, 139, 140, 147, 152, 154–6, 167, 266, 272, 290–4, 299, 314
  on reconciliation and social cohesion 18–92, 161, 164–6, 198–202
  shared life concept and 209, 232, 233, 247
  synthesis of Africanism 173–81
McKinley, D. 227, 230
media consumption and public sphere 211–12
Media Development and Diversity Agency (MDDA) 216–17
Medical Research Council 269
Meredith, M. 151
Meyer, R. 109, 120–1, 130
Miller, D. 130
Minister of Transport 285
Ministry of Safety and Security 277
Mlambo-Ngcuka, P. 179
Mncwango, B. 237–8

Mokgoro, Y. 172
moral citizens 183–9
Moral Regeneration Movement (MRM) 186–7, 266
moral repugnance 72
Moseneke, D. 243, 244–5
Motsoaledi, A. 269
Mtawarira, T. 222
Mugabe, R. 93
Multi Party Negotiation Process (MPNP) 124
multiracialism 83–5, 87, 133, 142, 152, 165, 214, 231, 294
*muthi* 258, 262, 263, 269, 296, 330n. 18

Narunsky-Laden, S. 216
national citizenship and deviance, *see* nation building
National Democratic Revolution (NDR) 74, 78, 219
National Economic and Labour Council 198–9
National Executive Committee (NEC) 83
National House of Traditional Leaders 254
nationalism, in post-apartheid South Africa 1–3
  problem of 4–10
  study of 10–12
National Labour and Economic Development Institute (NALEDI) 280
national liberation movement (NLM) 178
National Party (NP) 2, 58, 59, 64, 70, 76, 96, 101–3, 106, 107, 109, 110, 113, 117, 120, 123–5, 127, 128, 139, 157, 246, 304
National Planning Commission (NPC) 21, 24, 26, 29–30, 31, 327n. 3
  Diagnostic Report 27, 29
  National Development Plan (NDP) and 7, 189–98, 202, 206, 207, 256, 289–91, 297, 302, 322, 327n. 2, 328nn. 2–3, 5
National Scarce Skills List 311
National Stokvel Association 206

National Treasury 250, 251, 283, 330n. 15
National Union of Mineworkers (NUM) 41, 280
National Union of South African Students (NUSAS) 91
nation-building 137, 185, 195, 202, 205, 212, 230, 238, 249, 265, 289, 321
   Africanism and 290–2
   African National Congress (ANC) and 99–117, 290, 292–7
   and non-racialism today 297–302
   civic nationalism and 240
   civil disobedience affecting 282–5
   coloured and Indians in new South Africa and 302–5
   communication and commercial technology of 216
   corruption affecting 273–6
   crime affecting 266–73, 275–6
   deviance and trust affecting 286
   emigration and transnationalism and 310–14
   exit, voice and 305–10
   freedom of expression in context of 218
   inequality and 30, 154–6
   language policy in 36–8
   public disorder affecting 276
   secular 258
   service delivery protests affecting 276–9
   sports as essential to 220
   strikes and violence affecting 279–81
   tradition and 259–62
   Whites and Afrikaner nationalism and 314–17
   xenophobia affecting 281–2
   Zuma and 292–7
   *see also* African nationalism; *individual entries*
'A Nation in the Making' 192, 194–5
Nattrass, N. 156
Ndebele, N. 224
Nedlac 199, 200, 331n. 3
Newham, G. 270
New Person' 188, 192

NGK (Nederduitse Gereformeeerde Kerk) 234, 235, 236
Ngonyama, S. 179
Ngoro, R. 304
Niehaus, C. 162, 258
non-group group 59, 118
non-payment, for municipal services 283–4
non-racialism 3, 10, 17, 42, 74, 76–8, 92, 97, 99–100, 103–6, 132–3, 147, 151–3, 181, 193, 208–9, 222, 247, 293
   and African nationalism 169–70, 173–4
   of ANC 82–5, 91, 297–302, 304, 314, 331n. 4

O'Malley Archive 125, 126, 128

Pan Africanist Congress (PAC) 73, 76, 78–9, 88–9, 91, 94
Pan South African Language Board (PanSALB) 33, 36, 37
parity of esteem', for official languages 36
Parliamentary Monitoring Group 37, 187, 255, 257, 269, 274
Parliamentary Portfolio Committee on Arts and Culture 37
partial and selective compact 198–200
partition and apartheid 56–7
People's Contract for Growth and Development' 199, 200
Pepler, L. 314
Petrus, T. S. 258
petty apartheid 57
Pienaar, F. 145, 147
Pietersen, K. 225
Piper, L. 293
Pistorious, O. 330n. 2
Pityana, S. 274
political agency, denial of 164
Politicsweb 306
poverty 9–10, 29–32, 46, 111, 129, 130, 156, 173, 199, 229, 252, 274, 282–4, 313
Powell, E. 148, 328n. 3
Premier Soccer League (PSL) 226

Presidency 156, 191–3, 195, 242, 254, 256, 330n. 20
Promotion of National Unity and Reconciliation Act (1995) 157
Protection of State Information bill 275
public disorder affecting nation-building 276
public sphere 206, 208, 209, 213
  contentious 217–20
  media consumption and 211–12

quasi-federal structure 44

racial populism 79–80
Rainbow Nation 5, 12, 105, 137, 153, 168–9, 181
Ramaphosa, C. 108–9, 120, 121, 139, 190, 295
rape 272
  varieties of 269
*Rapport* 232, 233
Rauch, J. 187
reconciliation *see* Truth and Reconciliation Commission (TRC)
Reconstruction and Development Programme (RDP) 169, 187, 188, 190
redistribution 8, 16, 25, 30–2, 102, 105, 130, 133, 155, 169, 178, 194, 198, 234, 250, 252, 259, 292
religion 233
  affiliation 234
  Christianity and 234–7
  values and 237–40
Richmond, W. 308
Rivonia trial (1964) 72
Road Traffic Management Corporation 285
Robins, S. 315
Rosenberg, J. 245
rugby
  capitalizing on 143–5
  South Africans and 141–2
  world cup (RBC) 141
Rule, S. 237–8

SABMiller 216
Sachs, A. 110–11
SAPA (South African Press Association) 236
Savimbi, J. 41
Schlemmer, L. 54, 59, 101, 107, 126–7
Schulz-Herzenberg, C. 245, 246, 304
Seekings, J. 86, 156
Segal, L. 241
Selebi, J. 273, 331n. 3
self-determination 5, 39, 42, 52, 55–60, 62, 70, 72, 76, 80, 85, 95, 102, 104, 108–10, 117–18, 126–8, 317–18
Seme, P. ka 73, 111
service delivery protests affecting nation-building 276–9
'Shamateurism' 223
Simkins, C. 246–7
Sisulu, M. 82–3
Sithole, P. 256
Slabbert, F. van Zyl 58, 148
Smith, C. 272
Sobukwe, R. 93, 94
social cohesion 4, 15, 24, 182, 183, 188, 191, 193, 205, 228, 230, 237, 249, 286, 289, 291
  obstacles to 265
  technocracy limits and 201–2
  *see also* nation-building; solidarity
social compact 197
social contract and taxation 250
social partnership 200–1
social trust 284
Solidarity (trade union) 210, 251, 298, 299, 301
South African Audience Research Foundation (SAARF) 214
  All Media Products Survey (AMPS) 213, 214, 329n. 2
South African Broadcasting Corporation (SABC) 157, 213, 214–15, 285, 329n. 3, 331n. 10
South African Communist Party (SACP) 73–4, 77–80, 83, 87, 104–6, 114, 138, 178, 200, 235, 242, 278, 299, 331n. 5

*The Road to South African Freedom* 77
South African Defence Force (SADF) 110
South African Institute of Race Relations (SAIRR) 303, 306, 332n. 7
　Annual Survey of Race Relations 21
South African Languages Bill (2002) 37
South African Medical Association (SAMA) 208
South Africanness 120
South African Police Service (SAPS) 267–70, 277
South African Revenue Service (SARS) 250, 251
South African Rugby Union (SARU) 226
South African Social Attitudes Survey (SASAS) 228–9, 237, 238, 272, 273
South African Students Organization (SASO) 91
Southern African Migration Project (SAMP) 281
*Sowetan* 214, 243
Soweto (South Western Townships) 258, 284, 331n. 9
　uprising 55, 67, 81, 89, 92
Sparks, A. 121
Special Investigating Unit (SIU) 274, 285
sport and shared life 232–3
　identity, legacies of 220–1
　professionalization and identity and 223–5
　relaxing in diversity and 225–7
　talent for hosting and 228–9
　today 229–32
　transformation and representation and 221–2
StatsSA 18, 20, 29, 46, 214, 254, 329nn. 8, 10
　household surveys 306
　Quarterly Labour Force Survey (QLFS) 28
　Summary Code List for religion 237
　Victims of Crime Survey 273

Steenekamp, C. 241, 242, 330n. 12
Stern, M. 306
*stokvels* 206
strikes and violence affecting nation-building 279–81
*Sunday Independent* 306
Suttner, R. 84, 87, 112
Szalontai, G. 306

Tambo, O. 93, 121, 125
*The Times* 261
Third Worldism 180
'Towards a Fifteen Year Review' 192, 193
traditional authorities 253–5
　governmental policy on 255
　local government and 255–6
　today 253–5
Traditional Courts Bill 257, 259, 261
transformation 43, 54, 58, 61, 155, 158, 208, 213, 223, 225–6, 231, 233, 243, 250, 262, 266, 297, 299, 301, 304, 314, 324
　concept of 175–80
　economic 154, 175
　representation, in sports context and 221–2
　revolutionary 70, 323
　spiritual understanding and 188
Transitional Executive Council (TEC) 109, 110, 117
Transparency International (TI) 273, 274
Treatment Action Committee (TAC) 207
tribalism 6, 43, 53, 85, 93, 112, 114, 115, 118, 170, 229, 295
　demon of 42, 73, 80, 93–6, 106
　ethnicity and 39–40, 80
Truth and Reconciliation Commission (TRC) 157–66, 172, 176, 189, 235, 291
Turok, B. 299–300
Tutu, D. 95, 157, 159–60, 235
two nations theory 154–6, 173

*ubuntu* 160–1, 263, 291
　constitutional court and 170–3

UK Foreign and Commonwealth Office (FCO) 312, 332n. 8
*ukungena* 257
*ukuthwala* 257
unemployment 28–9
United Democratic Front (UDF) 86, 95, 96, 112, 114, 207, 252, 304
Uniting Reformed Church in Southern Africa (URCSA) 236
University Christian Movement (UCM) 92
urbanization 5, 21–3, 34–5, 43, 51, 112, 146, 254
Use of Official Languages Bill (2012) 37, 38

Vahed, G. 222
Vail, L. 39
Van der Berg, S. 25, 30
Van der Vaal, C. S. 315
Van der Westhuizen, C. 10
Van Eeden, J. 26
van Onselen, C. 12
Van Schaik 232
Vavi, Z. 275
Verwoerd, H. F. 298
Viljoen, C. 70, 108–10, 117, 126
Villa-Vicencio, C. 189
Vincent, L. 261, 294
*volkstaat* 108
von Holdt, K. 278–9

Vorster, J. 142
voting age population (VAP) 245

Waldmeir, P. 121, 145
Walshe, P. 73, 76
Wasserman, H. 215
Welsh, D. 180
White Paper on Traditional Leadership and Governance 255
whites, since 1994 305–10
Whites and Afrikaner nationalism 314–17
Williams, C. 145
Williams, J. 253–4
Wilson, R. 161–2
witchcraft 257–9
World Association of Newspapers and News Publishers (WAN-IFRA) World Press Trends Report 213
World Bank 330n. 15

xenophobia affecting nation-building 281–2
Xingwana, L. 33, 271

Zion Christian Church (ZCC) 236, 237
Zulu factor and ethnic politics 93–7
Zuma, J. 44, 46, 187, 190, 219, 242, 254, 261, 266, 271, 313, 328n. 1, 331n. 1
  nation-building and 292–7